A COMPANION TO GREEK AND ROMAN HISTORIOGRAPHY

VOLUME I

BLACKWELL COMPANIONS TO THE ANCIENT WORLD

This series provides sophisticated and authoritative overviews of periods of ancient history, genres of classical literature, and the most important themes in ancient culture. Each volume comprises between twenty-five and forty concise essays written by individual scholars within their area of specialization. The essays are written in a clear, provocative, and lively manner, designed for an international audience of scholars, students, and general readers.

A COMPANION TO GREEK AND ROMAN HISTORIOGRAPHY

VOLUME I

Edited by

John Marincola

Blackwell
Publishing

BLACKWELL PUBLISHING
350 Main Street, Malden, MA 02148-5020, USA
9600 Garsington Road, Oxford OX4 2DQ, UK
550 Swanston Street, Carlton, Victoria 3053, Australia

First published 2007 by Blackwell Publishing Ltd

4   2009

Library of Congress Cataloging-in-Publication Data

A companion to Greek and Roman historiography / edited by John Marincola.
     p. cm. – (Blackwell companions to the ancient world)
     Includes bibliographical references and index.
     ISBN 978-1-4051-0216-2 (hardcover : alk. paper) 1. Greece–Historiography. 2. Rome–Historiography.
I. Marincola, John.

   DE8.C65 2007
   938.0072–dc22

                                            2006032839

A catalogue record for this title is available from the British Library.

Set in 10/12.5pt Galliard
by SPi Publisher Services, Pondicherry, India
Printed and bound in Singapore
by COS Printers Pte Ltd

For further information on
Blackwell Publishing, visit our website:
www.blackwellpublishing.com

To the memory of

Eduard Schwartz
(1858–1940)

Felix Jacoby
(1876–1959)

Arnaldo Momigliano
(1908–1987)

...quia in altum subvehimur et extollimur magnitudine gigantea

Contents

Volume II

PART III Readings   **313**

Contributors

Rhiannon Ash is a Senior Lecturer at University College London. She has published various books and articles on Roman historiography, especially Tacitus, including *Ordering Anarchy: Armies and Leaders in Tacitus' Histories* (1999) and *Tacitus* (2006). She is currently completing a commentary on Tacitus *Histories* Book 2 for the Cambridge Greek and Latin Classics series.

Thomas M. Banchich is Professor of Classics and History at Canisius College in Buffalo, New York. Besides his publications on late antiquity, he has contributed commentaries on the *Pinax of Cebes* and Book I of Aristotle's *Nicomachean Ethics* to the Bryn Mawr Commentaries series. He is currently working on a translation of and commentary on Books XII.15–XIII.19 of John Zonaras' *Epitome of Histories*.

E. J. Baynham is Senior Lecturer in Classics at the University of Newcastle, Australia. Her primary interests are in Greek history, Greek and Roman historiography, and Greek and Roman art. Amongst her publications are *Alexander the Great: The Unique History of Quintus Curtius* (1999) and (with A. B. Bosworth) *Alexander the Great in Fact and Fiction* (2000).

Hans Beck is John MacNaughton Professor of Classics at McGill University in Montreal. He taught previously at the University of Cologne and held a Heisenberg Fellowship at Frankfurt University. In 2001–2 he was a Junior Fellow of the Center for Hellenic Studies in Washington, DC. He has published widely on the Roman republic, including a two-volume edition of the early Roman historians, co-authored with Uwe Walter, and a book on the republican nobility, *Karriere und Hierarchie. Die römische Aristokratie und die Anfänge des cursus honorum* (2005).

A. B. Bosworth is Professor of Classics and Ancient History at the University of Western Australia. He has published extensively on the period of Alexander the Great and the Diadochoi, and his study, *Conquest and Empire*, has been translated into five languages. A Chinese translation is in progress. At present he is completing the third (and final) volume of his commentary on Arrian's *History of Alexander*, to be published by Oxford University Press.

Benedetto Bravo is Emeritus Professor of Ancient History at the University of Warsaw. Born in 1931 in Italy, he studied Classics and Ancient History in Pisa, then spent a number of *Wanderjahre* until he married a Polish girl and settled in Warsaw. He has done work on the history of classical studies, the society and culture of archaic Greece, the inter-state relationships called *sylai*, Greek inscriptions of the Northern Black Sea, ancient historians and scholars.

Gregory S. Bucher is currently an Associate Professor of Classical and Near Eastern Studies at Creighton University. He has been a Fellow of the American Academy in Rome, the American School of Classical Studies, Athens, and the Center for Hellenic Studies. He has written articles on early Roman historiography, on Appian of Alexandria, and the intersection of the ancient world and film. He is currently at work on entries for the *Brill's New Jacoby* project and is preparing a monograph on Appian.

Craige B. Champion is Associate Professor of Ancient History and Classics in the Maxwell School of Citizenship and Public Affairs and Chairman of the History Department at Syracuse University. His research interests include Hellenistic and Roman republican history and historiography, citizenship and empire in ancient Greece and Rome, and collective identity formations in classical antiquity. He has written *Cultural Politics in Polybius's Histories* (2004), as well as numerous articles on classical history and historiography, and has edited *Roman Imperialism: Readings and Sources*

(2004). His current research focuses on comparative historical analysis of imperial citizenship in classical Athens and republican Rome.

Honora Howell Chapman is Associate Professor of Classics and Humanities and Coordinator of Classics at California State University, Fresno. She is currently helping to prepare volumes containing Books 2 and 3 of Josephus' *Judaean War* for the Brill translation and commentary series of all the works of Josephus.

Brian Croke is Executive Director of the Catholic Education Commission, Sydney, as well as Adjunct Professor of History at Macquarie University and an Honorary Associate at the University of Sydney. He is the author of several articles and books on late antique history and historiography including *History and Historians in Late Antiquity*, with A. M. Emmett (1983), *Studies in John Malalas*, with E. Jeffreys and R. Scott (1990), *Christian Chronicles and Byzantine History* (1992), *The Chronicle of Marcellinus: Translation and Commentary* (1995), and *Count Marcellinus* (2001).

Catherine Darbo-Peschanski is Chargé de Conférences at the École des Hautes Études en Sciences Sociales and Directeur adjoint of the Centre Louis Gernet, CNRS, Paris. She is the author of *Le discours du particulier. Essai sur l'enquête hérodotéenne* (1987) and editor of *Constructions du temps dans le monde grec ancien* (2000) and *La citation dans l'Antiquité* (2005).

Emma Dench is Professor of the Classics and Professor of History at Harvard University. She is the author of *From Barbarians to New Men: Greek, Roman and Modern Perceptions of Peoples from the Central Apennines* (1995) and

Romulus' Asylum: Roman Identities from the Age of Alexander to the Age of Hadrian (2005).

Carolyn Dewald teaches ancient history and classics at Bard College. Author of numerous articles on Herodotus and Greek historiography, her recent publications include *Thucydides' War Narrative: A Structural Study* (2006), the Introduction and Notes to the Oxford World's Classics translation of Herodotus (1998), and (with J. Marincola) *The Cambridge Companion to Herodotus* (2006). She is currently preparing a commentary on Herodotus I for the Cambridge Greek and Latin Classics series.

John Dillery is Associate Professor of Classics at the University of Virginia. He has written *Xenophon and the History of his Times* (1995) and revised and provided a new text, notes, and introduction to the Loeb edition of Xenophon's *Anabasis* (2001). He is currently working on a monograph on non-Greeks writing national histories in the Greek language in the Hellenistic period, as well as a translation of Xenophon's *Hellenica* and Agesilaus.

Johannes Engels is Professor of Ancient History at the Institut für Altertumskunde at the University of Cologne (Germany). He has taught ancient history at several German universities and has held a Feodor-Lynen-Fellowship of the Humboldt-Foundation at the KU Leuven (Belgium). He has published monographs and articles on Greek and Roman oratory and its *Nachleben*, ancient geography and historiography, Greek and Roman sumptuary regulations, and Greek biographers. He is currently preparing a translation and commentary on Lycurgus' *Against Leocrates*. Future projects include translations and commentaries of fragmentary texts of several ancient Greek historians and biographers.

Andrew Feldherr is Associate Professor of Classics at Princeton University. His research concentrates on Latin literature in several genres with a special emphasis on historiography (*Spectacle and Society in Livy's History*, 1998) and epic. He is currently completing a monograph on the *Metamorphoses* entitled *Playing Gods: The Politics of Fiction in Ovid's Metamorphoses* as well as editing the *Cambridge Companion to the Roman Historians*.

Gary Forsythe is Associate Professor of History at Texas Tech University. He has taught at Swarthmore College, Bryn Mawr College, the University of Pennsylvania, and the University of Chicago. His main interests are in ancient historiography and religion, Roman law, and Latin epigraphy. He has been a member of the Institute for Advanced Study, and is the author of *The Historian L. Calpurnius Piso Frugi and the Roman Annalistic Tradition* (1994), *Livy and Early Rome: A Study in Historical Method and Judgment* (1999), and, most recently, *A Critical History of Early Rome: From Prehistory to the First Punic War* (2005).

Alain M. Gowing is Professor of Classics at the University of Washington in Seattle, where he has been on the faculty since 1988 after receiving his PhD from Bryn Mawr College. His chief interests lie in the area of Roman historiography and literature, especially of the imperial period. His most recent book is *Empire and Memory: The Representation of the Roman Republic in Imperial Culture* (2006).

Vivienne Gray (MA Auckland, PhD Cambridge) is Professor of Classics and Ancient History at the University of

Auckland, New Zealand. Her major interest is Xenophon, with a secondary interest in Herodotus. She has written *The Character of Xenophon's Hellenica* (1989) and *The Framing of Socrates* (1998). Her *Xenophon on Government* (Cambridge Greek and Latin Classics) is due out in 2007 and she has been recently commissioned to edit *Oxford Readings in Xenophon*.

Peter Green is Dougherty Centennial Professor of Classics Emeritus in the University of Texas at Austin and Adjunct Professor and Editor of *Syllecta Classica* in the University of Iowa. He has published widely on all areas of classical antiquity. His most recent books are *The Poems of Catullus* (2005) and *Diodorus Siculus: Books 11–12.37.1: Greek History, 480–431 BC: The Alternative Version* (2006).

Phillip Harding is Emeritus Professor of Classics at the University of British Columbia, Vancouver. His publications include *From the End of the Peloponnesian War to the Battle of Ipsus* (1985), *Androtion and the Atthis* (1994), and *Didymos: On Demosthenes* (2006). His book *The Chronicles of Attika: The Fragments of the Atthidographers* has just been published.

Martin Hose is Professor of Greek Literature at Ludwig-Maximilians Universität in Munich. His special interests are in Greek tragedy, historiography, and the literature of late antiquity. Chief editor of *Gnomon* since 2000, his publications include *Studien zum Chor bei Euripides* (1990/1991); *Erneuerung der Vergangenheit* (1994); *Drama und Gesellschaft* (1995); and *Aristoteles: Die historischen Fragmente* (2002).

Mary Jaeger is Associate Professor of Classics at the University of Oregon.

She is the author of *Livy's Written Rome* (1997) as well as articles on Livy, Cicero, Vergil, and Horace.

Elizabeth Keitel is Associate Professor and Graduate Program Director at the University of Massachusetts at Amherst. She is the author of many articles on Roman historiography and on Tacitus.

Gavin Kelly held Research Fellowships at Peterhouse, Cambridge, and the University of Manchester before taking up his current appointment as Lecturer in Latin Literature at Edinburgh University in 2005. He has published several articles on Ammianus, and his book, *The Allusive Historian Ammianus Marcellinus*, will be published by Cambridge in 2007.

Christina Shuttleworth Kraus taught at New York University, University College London, and Oxford University before moving to Yale, where she is currently Professor and Chair of Classics. She is the author of *Livy: Ab Urbe Condita 6* (1994) and (with A. J. Woodman) *Latin Historians* (1997), and has edited *The Limits of Historiography* (1999) and (with R. K. Gibson) *The Classical Commentary* (2002). She has research interests in ancient narrative (especially historiography and tragedy), Latin prose style, and the theory and practice of commentaries.

Donald Lateiner teaches language, literature, and history at Ohio Wesleyan University. He is the author of books about the method of Herodotus and non-verbal behaviors in Homer. His current research concerns non-verbal behaviors in Greek and Latin prose, both the historians and the novelists. His annotated edition of Thucydides' *Histories* appeared in 2006.

Matthew Leigh is a Fellow of St. Anne's College, Oxford, and Professor of Classical Languages and Literature in the University of Oxford. He is the author of *Lucan: Spectacle and Engagement* (1997) and *Comedy and the Rise of Rome* (2004).

Dominique Lenfant is Maître de Conférences in Greek History at the University of Strasbourg (France). Her main research fields are Greek historiography of the Persian empire and methods in studying fragmentary historians. She is the author of *Ctésias de Cnide. La Perse. L'Inde. Autres fragments* (2004) and is completing a book on the *Persica* fragments of Dinon and Heracleides of Cumae. She has edited a collective book on Greek and Latin sources on the Achaemenid empire (forthcoming).

D. S. Levene is Professor of Classics at New York University. He has published a variety of works on Latin historiography and rhetoric, including *Religion in Livy* (1993), and articles on Cicero, Sallust, Livy, and Tacitus. His current projects include a book on Livy on the Hannibalic War and an edition with commentary of Livy's Fragments and *Periochae*.

John Marincola is Leon Golden Professor of Classics at Florida State University. His main interests are in Greek and Roman historiography and rhetoric. His publications include *Authority and Tradition in Ancient Historiography* (1997), *Greek Historians* (2002), and (with M. A. Flower) *Herodotus: Histories Book IX* (2003). He is currently working on a book on Hellenistic historiography.

John Matthews taught for many years at Oxford and is now John M. Schiff Professor of Classics and History at Yale. He has written widely on Roman history and historiography, including *Western Aristocracies and Imperial Court, AD 364–425* (1975), *The Roman Empire of Ammianus* (1989), and *Laying Down the Law; a Study of the Theodosian Code* (2000).

J. R. Morgan is Professor of Classics at the University of Wales, Swansea. He has written extensively on the ancient novel, particularly the Greek romance. His commentary on Longus' *Daphnis and Chloe* was published in 2004. Current projects include books on Longus and Heliodorus.

Roberto Nicolai is Professor of Greek Literature at the University of Rome "La Sapienza." He is the author of many contributions on Greek and Latin epic poetry and rhetorical, historical, and geographical literature, including *La storiografia nell'educazione antica* (1993) and *Studi su Isocrate. La comunicazione letteraria nel IV sec. a.C. e i nuovi generi della prosa* (2004). He is secretary of the editorial board of *Seminari Romani di Cultura Greca*, and a member of the editorial board of the Corpus dei Papiri Storici Greci.

Ellen O'Gorman is Senior Lecturer in Classics at the University of Bristol. She is the author of *Irony and Misreading in the Annals of Tacitus* (2000) and of numerous articles on Roman historiography, on Latin literature, and on theories of history. She is currently completing a book on Fantasies of Carthage in Roman literature.

Christopher Pelling is Regius Professor of Greek at Oxford University and Student of Christ Church, Oxford. He has written extensively on Greek and Roman historiography and biography, especially on Herodotus, Thucydides, Tacitus, and Plutarch. His latest books are *Literary*

Texts and the Greek Historian (2000) and *Plutarch and History* (2002). His current projects include a commentary on Plutarch's *Caesar* and a study of historical explanation in Herodotus, Thucydides, and Polybius.

L. V. Pitcher has been a Lecturer in Classics at Durham University since 2004. He has published articles on Greek epigram and Plutarch's *Moralia*, but his main research interests are in Greek and Roman historiography.

Leone Porciani has taught Greek and Roman History in the University of Pavia at Cremona since 2001. He was appointed Associate Professor of Greek History in November 2005. He is the author of *La forma proemiale. Storiografia e pubblico nel mondo antico* (1997) and of *Prime forme della storiografia greca* (2001), and is one of the editors of the *Lexicon historiographicum Graecum et Latinum* (2004–).

P. J. Rhodes was until recently Professor and is now Honorary Professor of Ancient History at Durham. His main academic interests are in Greek politics and political institutions, and in the sources both literary and non-literary for ancient history. His books include *The Athenian Boule* (1972), *A Commentary on the Aristotelian Athenaion Politeia* (1981), editions of Books 2–4 of Thucydides' history (1988, 1994, 1998), *The Decrees of the Greek States* (1997, with D. M. Lewis), *Greek Historical Inscriptions, 404–323 BC* (2003, with Robin Osborne), and *A History of the Classical Greek World, 478–323 BC* (2005).

Andrew M. Riggsby is Associate Professor of Classics at the University of Texas at Austin, and the author of *Crime and Community in Ciceronian Rome* (1999) and *Caesar in Gaul and Rome: War in Words* (2006). He works on the cultural history of republican Roman political institutions and on the cognitive history of the Roman world.

David Rohrbacher is Associate Professor of Classics at New College of Florida. He is the author of *The Historians of Late Antiquity* (2002) as well as several articles on late Latin historiography.

Tim Rood is Fellow and Tutor in Classics at St. Hugh's College, Oxford. He is the author of *Thucydides: Narrative and Explanation* (1998) and *The Sea! The Sea! The Shout of the Ten Thousand in the Modern Imagination* (2004), as well as a number of articles on Greek historiography.

Richard Rutherford is Tutor in Greek and Latin Literature at Christ Church, Oxford. Among his previous publications are *The Meditations of Marcus Aurelius: A Study* (1989), *The Art of Plato* (1995), and *Classical Literature: A Concise History* (2004).

Suzanne Saïd is Professor of Classics at Columbia University. Her interests include Greek tragedy and comedy, the Greek novel, and the role of myth. She has written widely on Greek literature, including *La faute tragique* (1978), *Approches de la mythologie grecque* (1993), and, with Monique Trédé and Alain Le Boulluec, *Histoire de la littérature grecque* (1997; English translation, 1999).

Guido Schepens is Professor Ordinarius for Ancient History at the K. U. Leuven, where he teaches courses on the History of Ancient Historiography and the translation and interpretation of Greek historiographical texts. His research activities concern the development and the theory of historical writing in antiquity. He coordinates the continuation project of Jacoby's *FGrHist* Part IV (Biography and Antiquarian Literature), of which three volumes have been published to date.

Clemence Schultze is Lecturer in the Department of Classics and Ancient History at the University of Durham. Her interests include Roman republican history, Greek and Roman clothing, ancient historiography, and the reception of antiquity in later literature and art. She has written papers on Dionysius of Halicarnassus (sections of whose work she is currently translating and annotating), on the elder Pliny, and on the influence of Greek myth on the Victorian novelist Charlotte M. Yonge.

Philip Stadter is Professor Emeritus of Classics at the University of North Carolina at Chapel Hill. He has written or edited books on Thucydides, Arrian, and the library of San Marco in Florence. He has had for many years a special interest in Plutarch, concerning whom he has published numerous articles and several books, including a *Commentary to Plutarch's Pericles* (1989) and *Sage and Emperor: Plutarch, Greek Intellectuals, and Roman Power in the Time of Trajan (98–117 AD)* (2002).

Gregory E. Sterling is Professor of New Testament and Christian Origins in the Department of Theology and the Executive Associate Dean for the College of Arts and Letters at the University of Notre Dame. He is the author or editor of five books, including *Historiography and Self-Definition: Josephos, Luke-Acts, and Apologetic Historiography* (1992; repr. 2006). He has published more than thirty-five articles and chapters. He serves as the co-editor of *The Studia Philonica Annual* and editor of two major monograph series.

Christopher Tuplin is Professor of Ancient History at the University of Liverpool. His publications include *The Failings of Empire* (1993), *Achaemenid Studies* (1996), *Science and Mathematics in Ancient Greek Culture* (ed. with T. E. Rihll, 2002), *Pontus and the Outside World* (ed., 2004), *Xenophon and his World* (ed., 2004), and numerous shorter studies, mostly on the history or historiography of Achaemenid Persia and classical Greece.

Pietro Vannicelli is Associate Professor of Greek History at the University of Urbino. He is the author of *Erodoto e la storia dell'alto e medio arcaismo (Sparta-Tessaglia-Cirene)* (1993) as well as several articles on Greek history and historiography. His current project is a commentary on Herodotus Book 7.

Riccardo Vattuone is Professor of Greek History and Greek Historiography at the University of Bologna. He is the author of *Logoi e storia in Tucidide* (1978), *Sapienza d'Occidente: Il pensiero storico di Timeo di Tauromenio* (1991), and *Il mostro e il sapiente. Studi sull'erotica greca* (2004). He has edited *Storici greci d'Occidente* (2003) and is working now on a historical commentary on Diodorus.

Frank W. Walbank was Rathbone Professor of Ancient History and Classical Archaeology at the University of Liverpool from 1951 to 1977, and is currently Professor Emeritus at Liverpool and an Honorary Fellow at Peterhouse, Cambridge. His many publications include *Philip V of Macedon* (1940), *The Awful Revolution* (1946, 1969), *A Historical Commentary on Polybius* (3 vols., 1957–1979), *Polybius* (1972), *The Hellenistic World* (1981), and, with N. G. L. Hammond, *A History of Macedonia: Vol. III: 336–167 BC*

(1979). He also served as the joint editor of volumes 7 and 8 of the second edition of the *Cambridge Ancient History.*

Stephanie West is an Emeritus Fellow of Hertford College, Oxford. She has written extensively on Greek literature, including Herodotus, and is currently preparing a commentary on Herodotus Book 4 for the Cambridge Greek and Latin Classics series.

T. P. Wiseman is Emeritus Professor of Classics at the University of Exeter; he was Lecturer and then Reader at the University of Leicester before going to Exeter in 1977. He has written widely on Roman history and literature, including the books *New Men in the Roman Senate 139 BC–AD 14* (1971), *Catullan Questions* (1969), *Cinna the Poet and Other Roman Essays* (1974), *Clio's Cosmetics* (1979), *Catullus and his World* (1985), *Roman Studies Literary and Historical* (1987), *Historiography and Imagination* (1994), *Remus: A Roman Myth* (1995), *Roman Drama and Roman History* (1998), and *The Myths of Rome* (2004), which won the American Philological Association's Goodwin Award of Merit for 2005. He is a Fellow of the British Academy and an honorary D.Litt. of the University of Durham.

A. J. Woodman, Basil L. Gildersleeve Professor of Classics at the University of Virginia, is author of two volumes of commentary on Velleius Paterculus (1977, 1983), *Rhetoric in Classical Historiography* (1988), *Tacitus Reviewed* (1998), and *Tacitus: The Annals* (2004); and co-author of commentaries on Tacitus' *Annals*, Books 3 (1996) and 4 (1989), and of *Latin Historians* (1997). He is co-editor of *Quality and Pleasure in Latin Poetry* (1974), *Creative Imitation and Latin Literature* (1979), *Poetry and Politics in the Age of Augustus* (1984), *Past Perspectives* (1986), *Author and Audience in Latin Literature* (1992), *Tacitus and the Tacitean Tradition* (1993), and *Traditions and Contexts in the Poetry of Horace* (2002). He is currently translating Sallust and co-authoring a commentary on Tacitus' *Agricola.*

Andrea Zambrini is Professore Associato di Storia Greca in the Dipartimento di Scienze del Mondo Antico at the Università della Tuscia in Viterbo. He has written a number of articles on Arrian and the Alexander historians, as well as the commentary on Books 5–7 of Arrian's *Anabasis* in *Arriano: L'Anabasi di Alessandro* (2004).

Preface

My goal in this collection has been to assemble a variety of approaches in the study of classical historiography. I outline in the Introduction some of the trends in such study over the last generation, and I will here only note that I have tried to present a number of viewpoints in what follows, without either imposing uniformity of approach or suggesting that any particular approach is to be desiderated over another.

Part I treats some of the larger issues involved in the study of the Greek and Roman historians, and seeks to situate classical historiography in the contexts of the societies that produced them and the generic traditions that developed over many centuries. Part II presents surveys of the major genres, while in Part III contributors examine individual episodes or themes while simultaneously trying to draw some larger conclusions about what such analyses tell us of the interests and aims of the writers involved. Part IV deals with genres that bordered on and influenced ancient historians, while Part V looks at the continuity and change that accompanied the movement to the medieval world.

I owe thanks to many people who have assisted me in this undertaking. First of all I am grateful to Al Bertrand, the commissioning editor at Blackwell, for inviting me to put this collection together, for encouraging me throughout its long gestation, and for showing great patience while awaiting the final result. Angela Cohen, Sophie Gibson, and Ben Thatcher at Blackwell all made my task immensely easier and more enjoyable. I owe thanks also to my copy editor, Brigitte Lee, who imposed order and method on a large project with impressive speed and skill. Many colleagues and friends have likewise offered support, advice, and assistance in intellectual and pragmatic ways, and I thank especially Carolyn Dewald, Christina Kraus, David Levene, Nino Luraghi, and Christopher Pelling. My home institution, Florida State University, offered me release time that allowed me to complete the volumes. For help with the bibliography I thank Tony Woodman, and for assistance in compiling the Index Locorum I am grateful to Thomas Paterniti. To Laurel Fulkerson, my actual companion who has lived too long with her rival, I owe more than I can adequately express.

I have taken the liberty of dedicating these volumes to the memory of three great scholars in ancient historiography, on whose shoulders all who work in this field stand.

J. M.

Acknowledgments

The editor and publisher gratefully acknowledge the permission granted to reproduce the copyright material in this book.

Material on pages 23, 24, 123, 124, 149–150, 151–152, 362, and 562 reprinted by permission of the publishers and the Trustees of the Loeb Classical Library from *Polybius: The Histories*, Loeb Classical Library Volumes 1, 2, 4, and 6, translated by W. R. Paton, Cambridge, Mass.: Harvard University Press © 1922, 1925, 1927, by the President and Fellows of Harvard College.

Material on pages 79, 85, and 86 reprinted by permission of the publishers and the Trustees of the Loeb Classical Library from *Diodorus of Sicily*, Loeb Classical Library Volume 2, translated by C. H. Oldfather, Cambridge, Mass.: Harvard University Press © 1935, by the President and Fellows of Harvard College.

Material on page 80 reprinted by permission of the publishers and the Trustees of the Loeb Classical Library from *Pausanias: Description of Greece*, Loeb Classical Library Volume 3, translated by W. H. S. Jones, Cambridge, Mass.: Harvard University Press © 1933, by the President and Fellows of Harvard College.

Material on page 126 reprinted by permission of the publishers and the Trustees of the Loeb Classical Library from *The Roman Antiquities of Dionysius of Halicarnassus*, Loeb Classical Library Volumes 4 and 7, translated by Earnest Cary, Cambridge, Mass.: Harvard University Press © 1943, 1950, by the President and Fellows of Harvard College.

Material on page 135 reprinted by permission of the publishers and the Trustees of the Loeb Classical Library from *The Works of Tacitus*, Loeb Classical Library Volume 3, translated by J. Jackson, Cambridge, Mass.: Harvard University Press © 1931, by the President and Fellows of Harvard College.

Material on pages 226–227 reprinted by permission of the publishers and the Trustees of the Loeb Classical Library from *Manetho*, Loeb Classical Library, translated by W. G. Waddell, Cambridge, Mass.: Harvard University Press © 1940, by the President and Fellows of Harvard College.

Material on page 328 reprinted by permission of the publishers and the Trustees of the Loeb Classical Library from *Thucydides: The Peloponnesian War*, Loeb Classical Library Volume 1, translated by C. F. Smith, Cambridge, Mass.: Harvard University Press © 1919, by the President and Fellows of Harvard College.

Material on pages 374 and 375 reprinted by permission of the publishers and the Trustees of the Loeb Classical Library from *Quintilian: The Orator's Education*, Loeb Classical Library Volume 2, translated by D. A. Russell, Cambridge, Mass.: Harvard University Press © 2001, by the President and Fellows of Harvard College.

Material on pages 401, 556, and 557 reprinted by permission of the publishers and the Trustees of the Loeb Classical Library from *The Geography of Strabo*, Loeb Classical Library Volumes 1 and 3, translated by Horace Leonard Jones, Cambridge, Mass.: Harvard University Press © 1917, 1924, by the President and Fellows of Harvard College.

Material on pages 462, 463, 465, and 466 reprinted by permission of the publishers and the Trustees of the Loeb Classical Library from *The Roman History of Cassius Dio*, Loeb Classical Library Volumes 6 and 9, translated by Earnest Cary, Cambridge, Mass.: Harvard University Press © 1917, 1927, by the President and Fellows of Harvard College.

Material on page 487 reprinted by permission of the publishers and the Trustees of the Loeb Classical Library from *The Elder Seneca: Declamations*, Loeb Classical Library Volume 2, translated by Michael Winterbottom, Cambridge, Mass.: Harvard University Press © 1974, by the President and Fellows of Harvard College.

The Loeb Classical Library® is a registered trademark of the President and Fellows of Harvard College.

Material on page 135 reprinted by permission of Penguin Books from *The Annals of Tacitus*, translated with an Introduction by Michael Grant (Penguin Classics 1956, sixth revised edition 1989). Copyright © Michael Grant Publications Ltd, 1956, 1959, 1971, 1973, 1975, 1977, 1989.

Material on page 210 reprinted by permission of Faber and Faber and Grove Atlantic NY from *Waiting for Godot: Tragicomedy in 2 Acts*, by Samuel Beckett. Copyright © 1954* by Faber and Faber. Copyright © 1954 by Grove Atlantic, NY.

Material on page 261 reprinted by permission of Oxford University Press, Inc. from *Cicero: On the Ideal Orator*, edited by J. M. May and J. Wisse. Copyright © 2001 by Oxford University Press.

Material on pages 374, 376, and 377 reprinted by permission of Aris and Phillips from *Julius Caesar: The Civil War Books I & II*. Edited with an Introduction, Translation, and Commentary by J. M. Carter. Copyright © 1991 Aris and Phillips. Aris and Phillips is an Imprint of Oxbow Books Ltd.

Material on pages 553 and 557 reprinted by permission of University of California Press from *Collected Ancient Greek Novels*, edited by B. P. Reardon. Copyright © 1989 by the Regents of the University of California.

Every effort has been made to trace copyright holders and to obtain their permission for the use of copyright material. The publisher apologizes for any errors or omissions in the above list and would be grateful if notified of any corrections that should be incorporated in future reprints or editions of this book.

Ancient Authors: Abbreviations

The fragments of the Greek historians are cited from *FGrHist*, or, if not included there, *FHG*. Fragments of the Roman historians are cited from Peter, *HRR*, except for the early Hellenophone historians who are cited from *FGrHist*. The Index Locorum contains a concordance of Peter's and Jacoby's fragments with the newer editions, *AR* and *FRH*. The fragments of Posidonius are cited according to *FGrHist*. The Index Locorum contains a concordance of these fragments with Edelstein–Kidd. The fragments of Ennius' *Annals* are cited according to Skutsch's edition. The fragments of Sallust's *Histories* are cited according to Maurenbrecher's edition. The Index Locorum contains a concordance of these fragments with McGushin's edition.

Ael.	Aelian (Claudius Aelianus), Greek writer, 165/70–230/5 CE	
	VH	*Varia Historia* (*Historical Miscellany*)
Aesch.	Aeschylus, Athenian tragedian, first half 5th c. BCE	
	Ag.	*Agamemnon*
	Cho.	*Choephori*
	Eum.	*Eumenides*
	Pers.	*Persae* (*Persians*)
	PV	*Prometheus Vinctus* (*Prometheus Bound*)
	Sept.	*Septem contra Thebas* (*Seven Against Thebes*)
	Supp.	*Supplices* (*Suppliant Women*)
Aeschin.	Aeschines, Athenian orator, 4th c. BCE	
	Ctes.	*Against Ctesiphon*
	Tim.	*Against Timarchus*
Amm. Marc.	Ammianus Marcellinus, Roman historian, 4th c. CE	

Ammon.	Ammonius, lexicographer, of indeterminate date, poss. Byzantine	
	Diff.	*De Adfinium Vocabulorum Differentia*
Andoc.	Andocides, Athenian orator, ca. 440–390 BCE	
Anth. Pal.	*Anthologia Palatina* (*Palatine Anthology*)	
Antiph.	Antiphon, Athenian orator, ca. 480–411 BCE	
App.	Appian, Greek historian, 2nd c. CE	
	BC	*Bella Civilia* (*Civil Wars*)
	Iber.	*Iberica* (*Spanish Wars*)
	Ill.	*Illyrica* (*Illyrian Wars*)
	Mac.	*Macedonica* (*Macedonian Wars*)
	Mith.	*Mithridatica* (*Mithridatic Wars*)
	Pun.	*Punica* (*Punic Wars*)
	Syr.	*Syriaca* (*Syrian Wars*)
Apul.	Apuleius, Roman novelist, 2nd c. CE	
	Met.	*Metamorphoses*
Ap. Rhod.	Apollonius Rhodius, Greek poet, 3rd c. BCE	
	Argon.	*Argonautica*
Arist.	Aristotle, Greek philosopher, 384–322 BCE	
	Ath. Pol.	*Athenaiōn Politeia* (*Constitution of the Athenians*)
	Cat.	*Categories*
	Eth. Eud.	*Eudemian Ethics*
	Eth. Nic.	*Nicomachean Ethics*
	GA	*de Generatione Animalium* (*On the Generation of Animals*)
	Hist. an.	*Historia animalium* (*History of Animals*)
	Metaph.	*Metaphysics*
	Poet.	*Poetics*
	Pol.	*Politics*
	Rhet.	*Rhetoric*
	Soph. el.	*Sophistici elenchi* (*Sophistical Refutations*)
	Top.	*Topics*
Aristid.	Aelius Aristides, Greek orator, 2nd c. CE	
	Orat.	*Orations*

Arr.   Arrian, Greek historian, ca. 86–160 CE

Anab.	*Anabasis*
Cyn.	*Cynegeticus* (*On Hunting*)
Ind.	*Indica*
Tact.	*Tactica*

Ath.   Athenaeus, Greek writer of *Deipnosophistai* (*Professors at Dinner*), 2nd c. CE

August.   Augustine, bishop of Hippo and Christian apologist, 354–430 CE

Conf.	*Confessions*
Doct. Christ.	*De Doctrina Christiana* (*On Christian Doctrine*)
Serm.	*Sermones*
Solil.	*Soliloquies*

Aurel. Vict.   Sextus Aurelius Victor, Roman politician and historian, 4th c. CE

Caes.	*De Caesaribus* (*On the Caesars*)

Auson.   Ausonius, Latin poet, 4th c. CE

Ep.	*Epistulae*
Prof.	*Professores*

Bacchyl.   Bacchylides, Greek epinician poet, 5th c. BCE

Caes.   C. Iulius Caesar, Roman politician and writer, 100–44 BCE

BC	*Bellum Civile*
BG	*Bellum Gallicum*

Callim.   Callimachus, Greek poet, 3rd c. BCE

Cassiod.   Cassiodorus, Roman writer and historian, ca. 490–585 CE

Inst.	*Institutiones*

Cato   M. Porcius Cato, Roman writer, 234–149 BCE

Orig.	*Origines*

Catull.   C. Valerius Catullus, Latin poet, 1st c. BCE

Chariton   Chariton, Greek novelist, 1st or 2nd c. CE

Chaer.	*Chaereas and Callirhoe*

Cic.   M. Tullius Cicero, Roman politician and writer, 106–43 BCE

ad Brut.	*Epistulae ad Brutum* (*Letters to M. Brutus*)
Amic.	*De amicitia* (*On Friendship*)
Arch.	*Pro Archia* (*For Archias*)

Att.	*Epistulae ad Atticum* (*Letters to Atticus*)
Brut.	*Brutus*
Cael.	*Pro Caelio* (*For Caelius*)
Cat.	*In Catilinam* (*Against Catiline*)
De Or.	*de Oratore* (*On the Orator*)
Div.	*de Divinatione* (*On Divination*)
Fam.	*Epistulae ad familiares* (*Letters to Friends*)
Fin.	*de Finibus* (*On the Ends* [*of Good and Evil*])
Leg.	*de Legibus* (*On Laws*)
Leg. man.	*de lege Manilia* (*On the Manilian Law*)
Mil.	*Pro Milone* (*For Milo*)
Nat. D.	*de Natura deorum* (*On the Nature of the Gods*)
Offic.	*de Officiis* (*On Duties*)
Orat.	*Orator ad M. Brutum*
Part. or.	*de Partitione oratoria* (*On the Classification of Rhetoric*)
Phil.	*Orationes Philippicae* (*Philippic Orations*)
Pis.	*In Pisonem* (*Against Piso*)
Prov. Cons.	*de Provinciis Consularibus* (*On the Consular Provinces*)
Q. fr.	*Epistulae ad Quintem fratrem* (*Letters to his brother Quintus*)
Rep.	*de Republica* (*On the State*)
Sen.	*de Senectute* (*On Old Age*)
Sest.	*Pro Sestio* (*For Sestius*)
Verr.	*In Verrem* (*Verrine Orations*)

Claud. Claudian, Latin poet, ca. 370–404 CE

Curt. Q. Curtius Rufus, Latin historian, prob. 1st c. CE

Dem. Demosthenes, Athenian orator, 384–322 BCE

Leg.	*De False Legatione* (*On the False Embassy*)
Olynth.	*Olynthiac Orations*

Dio Cassius Dio, Greek historian, ca. 164–after 229 CE

Dio Chrys. Dio Cocceianus (Dio Chrysostom), 1st c. CE orator and philosopher

Or.	*Orations*

Diod. Diodorus Siculus, Greek historian, 1st c. BCE

D. Hal.   Dionysius of Halicarnassus, Greek historian, 1st c. BCE

                    AR   *Antiquitates Romanae* (*Roman Antiquities*)

                    Comp.   *de Compositione Verborum* (*On the Arrangement of Words*)

                    Imit.   *de Imitatione* (*On Imitation*)

                    Isoc.   *de Isocrate* (*On Isocrates*)

                    Lys.   *de Lysia* (*On Lysias*)

                    Orat.   *de Oratoribus Veteribus* (*On the Ancient Orators*)

                    Pomp.   *Epistula ad Pompeium* (*Letter to Pompeius*)

                    Thuc.   *de Thucydide* (*On Thucydides*)

D. L.   Diogenes Laertius, biographer of the philosophers, early 3rd c. CE

Enn.   Ennius, Latin poet, 239–169 BCE

                    Ann.   *Annales*

Eratosth.   Eratosthenes, Greek geographer, ca. 285–194 BCE

Eunap.   Eunapius, Greek biographer and historian, mid-4th c.–mid-5th c. CE

Eur.   Euripides, Athenian tragedian, 5th c. BCE

                    Alc.   *Alcestis*

                    Andr.   *Andromache*

                    Bacch.   *Bacchae*

                    Cyc.   *Cyclops*

                    El.   *Electra*

                    Hec.   *Hecuba*

                    Hel.   *Helena*

                    Heracl.   *Heraclidae*

                    HF   *Heracles Furens*

                    Hipp.   *Hippolytus*

                    Hyps.   *Hypsipyle*

                    IA   *Iphigeneia at Aulis*

                    IT   *Iphigeneia among the Taurians*

                    Med.   *Medea*

                    Or.   *Orestes*

                    Phoen.   *Phoenissae* (*Phoenician Women*)

                    Rhes.   *Rhesus*

                    Supp.   *Supplices* (*Suppliant Women*)

                    Troad.   *Troades* (*Trojan Women*)

Euseb.	Eusebius, Greek bishop and historian, ca. 260–339 CE	
	Chron.	*Chronica*
	HE	*Historia Ecclesiastica*
	Vit. Const.	*Vita Constantini*
Eutr.	Eutropius, historian, 4th c. CE	
	Brev.	*Breviarium*
Fest.	Rufus (?) Festus, Roman senator and historian, 4th c. CE	
	Brev.	*Breviarium*
Fronto	Fronto, Roman orator, ca. 95–116 CE	
	Ver. Imp.	*Ad Verum Imperatorem* (*To the Emperor Verus*)
Gell.	Aulus Gellius, Roman miscellanist, 2nd c. CE	
	NA	*Noctes Atticae* (*Attic Nights*)
Gran. Lic.	Granius Licinianus, Roman historian, 2nd c. CE (?)	
Hdn.	Herodian, Greek historian, 3rd c. CE	
Hdt.	Herodotus, Greek historian, 5th c. BCE	
Heliod.	Heliodorus, novelist, 4th c. CE (?)	
	Aeth.	*Aethiopica*
Hell. Oxy.	*Hellenica Oxyrhynchia*, fragments of a Greek history found at Oxyrhynchus, Egypt; prob. 4th c. BCE	
Hes.	Hesiod, Greek poet, prob. 7th c. BCE	
	Cat.	*Catalogus mulierum* (*Catalogue of Women*)
	Op.	*Opera et dies* (*Works and Days*)
	Theog.	*Theogony*
Hippoc.	Hippocrates, Greek physician, 5th c. BCE	
	AWP	*Airs, Waters, Places*
Hirt.	Aulus Hirtius, Roman politician and military man, 1st c. BCE	
	BG	See Caes. *BG*
Hom.	Homer, Greek epic poet, prob. 7th c. BCE	
	Il.	*Iliad*
	Od.	*Odyssey*
Hor.	Horace, Latin poet, 1st c. BCE	
	Ars	*Ars Poetica*
	Carm.	*Carmina* or *Odes*
	Epist.	*Epistulae*
	Sat.	*Satirae* or *Sermones*

Hyp.   Hyperides, Athenian orator, 389–322 BCE

    Dem.   *Against Demosthenes*

Isid.   Isidore, bishop of Seville, ca. 600–636 CE

    Orig.   *Origines* (also called *Etymologiae*)

Isoc.   Isocrates, Athenian orator, 436–338 BCE

    Antid.   *Antidosis*

    Panath. *Panathenaicus*

    Paneg.   *Panegyricus*

Jer.   Jerome, Latin writer, ca. 347–420 CE

    Chron.   *Chronica*

    Vir. Ill.   *De Viris Illustribus* (*On Distinguished Men*)

    Ep.   *Epistulae*

Jord.   Jordanes, Gothic historian, 6th c. CE

    Get.   *Getica* (*Gothic History*)

    Rom.   *Romana* (*Roman History*)

Jos.   Josephus, Jewish historian, 1st c. CE

    AJ   *Antiquitates Judaicae* (*Jewish Antiquities*)

    Ap.   *Contra Apionem* (*Against Apion*)

    BJ   *Bellum Judaicum* (*Jewish War*)

    Vit.   *Vita* (*Life*)

Jul.   Julian, Roman emperor, 331–363 CE

    Epist.   *Epistulae*

    Or.   *Orationes*

Just.   Justin, epitomator of the *Philippic Histories* of Pompeius Trogus, 2nd, 3rd or 4th c. CE

Juv.   Juvenal, Latin satirist, 2nd c. CE

    Sat.   *Satires*

Lib.   Libanius, Greek orator and rhetorician, 4th c. CE

    Or.   *Orationes*

Livy   Titus Livius, Roman historian, ca. 59 BCE–17 CE

[Long.]   Pseudo-Longinus, 1st c. CE

    Subl.   *De Sublimitate* (*On the Sublime*)

Luc.   Lucan, Latin epic poet, 39–65 CE

Lucian	Lucian, Greek satirist and essayist, 2nd c. CE	
	HC	*De Historia Conscribenda* (*How to Write History*)
	Macr.	*Macrobioi* (*On Long-Lived Men*)
	Philops.	*Philopseudes* (*Lover of Lies*)
	VH	*Verae Historiae* (*True Histories*)

Lucr. — Lucretius, Latin didactic poet, 1st c. BCE

Lycurg. — Lycurgus, Athenian orator, 4th c. BCE

Lydus — John Lydus, Greek writer, 6th c. CE
    Mag. *De Magistratibus*

Macr. — Macrobius, Latin commentator and writer, 5th c. CE
    Sat. *Saturnalia*

Manil. — Marcus Manilius, Latin poet, 1st c. CE

Mart. — Martial, Latin poet, 1st c. CE

Nep. — Cornelius Nepos, Latin biographer and historian, 1st c. CE
    Att. *Atticus*
    Epam. *Epaminondas*
    Hann. *Hannibal*

Nicolaus — Greek rhetor, 5th c. CE
    Prog. *Progymnastica* (*Preliminary Exercises*)

Oros. — Orosius, Latin writer, 5th c. CE

Ov. — Ovid, Latin poet, 43 BCE–17 CE
    AA *Ars Amatoria* (*Art of Love*)
    Am. *Amores*
    Fast. *Fasti*
    Met. *Metamorphoses*
    Trist. *Tristia*

Paulinus — Paulinus of Nola, Christian priest and bishop, 4th–5th c. CE
    Ep. *Epistulae*

Paus. — Pausanias, Greek traveler, 2nd c. CE

Pers. — Aulus Persius Flaccus, Roman satirist, 1st c. CE

Petron. — Petronius, Latin novelist, 1st c. CE
    Sat. *Satyrica*

Philo — Jewish philosopher, writer, and politician, 1st c. CE

	De Pr.	*De praemiis et poenis* (*On Rewards and Punishments*)
	Hypoth.	*Hypothetica: Defense of the Jews*

Philostr.   Lucius Flavius Philostratus, Greek orator, ca. 170–ca. 247 CE

| | *Gym.* | *de Gymnastica* |

Phot.   Photius, Greek patriarch, 9th c. CE

| | *Bibl.* | *Bibliotheca* |

Pind.   Pindar, Greek epinician poet, 5th c. BCE

| | *Pyth.* | *Pythian Odes* |

Plat.   Plato, Athenian philosopher, ca. 429–347 BCE

	Gorg.	*Gorgias*
	Hipp. Mai.	*Hippias Maior*
	Leg.	*Leges* (*Laws*)
	Menex.	*Menexenus*
	Phaedr.	*Phaedrus*
	Prot.	*Protagoras*
	Rep.	*Respublica* (*Republic*)
	Symp.	*Symposium*
	Tim.	*Timaeus*

Plaut.   Plautus, Latin comic playwright, late 3rd–early 2nd c. BCE

	Amph.	*Amphitruo*
	Asin.	*Asinaria*
	Bacch.	*Bacchides*
	Most.	*Mostellaria*
	Trin.	*Trinummus*

Plin.   Pliny the Elder, Roman writer on geography and history, 23/4–79 CE

| | *NH* | *Naturalis Historia* |

Plin.   Pliny the Younger, Roman orator, ca. 61–112 CE

	Ep.	*Epistulae*
	Pan.	*Panegyricus*

Plut.   Plutarch, Greek biographer and essayist, mid-1st c.–2nd c. CE

Moralia

| | *de glor. Ath.* | *de Gloria Atheniensium* (*On the Glory of the Athenians*) |

dHM	*de Herodoti malignitate* (*On the Malice of Herodotus*)
Exil.	*de Exilio* (*On Exile*)
Fort. Rom.	*de Fortuna Romanorum* (*On the Fortune of the Romans*)

Lives

Aem.	*Aemilius Paulus*
Ages.	*Agesilaus*
Alc.	*Alcibiades*
Alex.	*Alexander*
Ant.	*Antony*
Arist.	*Aristides*
Artax.	*Artaxerxes*
Brut.	*Brutus*
Caes.	*Caesar*
Cam.	*Camillus*
Cat. Mai.	*Cato Maior* (*Cato the Elder*)
Cat. Min.	*Cato Minor* (*Cato the Younger*)
C. Gracch.	*Caius Gracchus*
Cic.	*Cicero*
Cim.	*Cimon*
Cleom.	*Cleomenes*
Crass.	*Crassus*
Dem.	*Demosthenes*
Demetr.	*Demetrius*
Eum.	*Eumenes*
FM	*Fabius Maximus*
Flam.	*Flamininus*
Galb.	*Galba*
Luc.	*Lucullus*
Lyc.	*Lycurgus*
Lys.	*Lysander*
Mar.	*Marius*
Marc.	*Marcellus*
Nic.	*Nicias*
Num.	*Numa*
Pel.	*Pelopidas*

Per.	*Pericles*
Phil.	*Philopoemen*
Phoc.	*Phocion*
Pomp.	*Pompeius*
Publ.	*Publicola*
Pyrrh.	*Pyrrhus*
Rom.	*Romulus*
Sert.	*Sertorius*
Sol.	*Solon*
Sull.	*Sulla*
Them.	*Themistocles*
Thes.	*Theseus*
Ti. Gracch.	*Tiberius Gracchus*
Tim.	*Timoleon*

Pol.   Polybius, Greek historian, ca. 200–118 BCE

Polyaen.   Polyaenus, Macedonian rhetorician and military writer, 2nd c. CE

praef.   *praefatio* (preface)

Procop.   Procopius, Greek historian, 6th c. CE

Aed.	*Aedificia* (*Buildings*)
Goth.	*De Bello Gothico*
Vand.	*De Bello Vandalico*

Prop.   Propertius, Latin poet, 1st c. BCE

Ptol.   Ptolemy, Greek geographer, 2nd c. CE

Geog.	*Geography*

Quint.   Quintilian, Roman rhetorician, 1st c. CE

Sall.   Sallust, Roman historian, ca. 86–35 BCE

Cat.	*De Catilinae Coniuratione* or *Bellum Catilinae*
Hist.	*Historiae*
Jug.	*Bellum Jugurthinum*

schol.   Scholiast or scholia

Sen.   Seneca the Elder, Roman rhetorician, mid-1st c. BCE–mid-1st c. CE

Contr.	*Controversiae*
Suas.	*Suasoriae*

Sen.   Seneca the Younger, Roman politician and philosopher, 1st c. CE

Ep.	*Epistulae*

Serv.	Servius, commentator on Vergil, prob. 4th c. CE	
Sext. Emp.	Sextus Empiricus, Greek writer, 2nd c. CE	
	Math.	*Adversus Mathematicos* (*Against the Professors*)
SHA	*Scriptores Historiae Augustae*, 4th c. CE biographies of emperors	
	Hadr.	*Hadrian*
	Quad. Tyr.	*Quadrigae Tyrranorum* (*Firmus, Saturninus, Proculus and Bonosus*)
Sil.	Silius Italicus, Latin poet, ca. 26–101 CE	
	Pun.	*Punica* (*Punic Wars*)
Soph.	Sophocles, Athenian tragedian, 5th c. BCE	
	Aj.	*Ajax*
	Ant.	*Antigone*
	El.	*Electra*
	OC	*Oedipus Coloneus*
	OT	*Oedipus Tyrannus*
	Phil.	*Philoctetes*
	Trach.	*Trachiniae* (*Women of Trachis*)
Sozom.	Sozomen, Greek historian, 5th c. CE	
	HE	*Historia Ecclesiastica*
Stat.	Statius, Latin poet, 1st c. CE	
	Silv.	*Silvae*
Str.	Strabo, Greek geographer and historian, 1st c. BCE	
	Geog.	*Geography*
Suet.	Suetonius, Latin biographer, ca. 70–130 CE	
	Aug.	*Divus Augustus*
	Calig.	*Gaius Caligula*
	Claud.	*Divus Claudius*
	DJ	*Divus Julius*
	Dom.	*Domitianus*
	Galb.	*Galba*
	Gramm.	*De Grammaticis et Rhetoribus* (*On Teachers of Grammar and Rhetoric*)
	Ner.	*Nero*
	Tib.	*Tiberius*
	Vesp.	*Vespasianus*
	Vit.	*Vitellius*

Symm.   Symmachus, Roman senator and orator, 4th c. CE

              Ep.   *Epistulae*

Tac.   Tacitus, Roman historian, ca. 56–after 118 CE

              Agr.   *Agricola*

              Ann.   *Annales*

              Dial.   *Dialogus*

              Germ.   *Germania*

              Hist.   *Historiae*

Theodoret   Theodoret, Syrian bishop and historian, ca. 393–466

              HE   *Historia Ecclesiastica*

Theoph.   Theophrastus, Greek philosopher, late 370s–early 280s BCE

              Char.   *Characters*

              HP   *History of Plants*

Thuc.   Thucydides, Athenian historian, 5th c. BCE

Tib.   Tibullus, Latin poet, 1st c. BCE

Trog.   Pompeius Trogus, Roman historian, 1st c. BCE/CE

Varro   Varro, Roman scholar and antiquarian, 116–27 BCE

              Ling.   *De Lingua Latina* (*On the Latin Language*)

Veg.   Vegetius, Latin writer, prob. mid-4th c.–mid-5th c. CE

              Mil.   *De Re Militari* (*On Military Matters*)

Vell.   Velleius Paterculus, Roman historian, 1st c. CE

Verg.   Vergil, Latin poet, 70–19 BCE

              Aen.   *Aeneid*

Vitr.   Vitruvius, Roman architect and engineer, 1st c. BCE

Xen.   Xenophon, Athenian historian and essayist, ca. 430–mid-4th c. BCE

              Ages.   *Agesilaus*

              Anab.   *Anabasis*

              Cyn.   *Cynegeticus* (*Treatise on Hunting*)

              Cyr.   *Cyropaedia* (*Education of Cyrus*)

              Hell.   *Hellenica*

              Mem.   *Memorabilia* (*Memoirs*)

              Vect.   *Vectigalia* (*Ways and Means*)

Zon.   Johannes Zonaras, Byzantine historian, 12th c. CE

Reference Works: Abbreviations

A&A	*Antike und Abendland*
A.Ant.Hung.	*Acta Antiqua Academia Scientiarum Hungaricae*
AC	*L'Antiquité Classique*
AHB	*Ancient History Bulletin*
AJAH	*American Journal of Ancient History*
AJPh	*American Journal of Philology*
ALLG	*Archiv für lateinische Lexikographie und Grammatik*
AncSoc	*Ancient Society*
AncW	*The Ancient World*
ANRW	*Aufstieg und Niedergang der römischen Welt* (Berlin, 1972–)
APF	*Archiv für Papyrusforschung und verwandte Gebiete*
AR	M. Chassignet, *L'Annalistique Romaine*, 3 vols. (Paris, 1996–2004)
ASNP	*Annali della Scuola Normale di Pisa*
BCH	*Bulletin de Correspondance Hellénique*
BICS	*Bulletin of the Institute of Classical Studies*
BMCR	*Bryn Mawr Classical Review*
CAH	*Cambridge Ancient History*
CdE	*Chronique d'Égypte: Bulletin périodique de la Fondation Égyptologique Reine Élisabeth, Bruxelles*

CHCL	*Cambridge History of Classical Literature. I. Greek Literature*, ed. P. E. Easterling and B. M. W. Knox (Cambridge, 1985); *II. Latin Literature*, ed. E. J. Kenney and W. V. Clausen (Cambridge, 1982)
CJ	*Classical Journal*
ClAnt	*Classical Antiquity*
CM	*Classica et Mediaevalia*
CPh	*Classical Philology*
CQ	*Classical Quarterly*
CR	*Classical Review*
CW	*Classical World*
DNP	H. Cancik and H. Schneider (eds.), *Der Neue Pauly*, 16 vols. in 19 parts (Stuttgart, 1996–2004). English version in progress
EMC	*Echos du monde classique/Classical News and Views*
FCH	R. Blockley, *The Fragmentary Classicizing Historians of the Later Roman Empire*, 2 vols. (Liverpool, 1981–1983)
FGE	D. L. Page (ed.), *Further Greek Epigrams. Epigrams before AD 50 from the Greek Anthology and other sources, not included in the "Hellenistic Epigrams" or "The Garland of Philip"* (Cambridge, 1981)
FGrHist	F. Jacoby et al., *Die Fragmente der griechischen Historiker* (Berlin and Leiden, 1923–1958; Leiden, 1994–). Jacoby's commentary is cited as *Komm.* followed by volume and page number
FHG	C. and F. Müller, *Fragmenta Historicorum Graecorum*, 5 vols. (Paris, 1841–1847)
FLP	E. Courtney, *The Fragmentary Latin Poets* (Oxford, 1993)
Fornara	C. W. Fornara, *Archaic Times to the Peloponnesian War*. Translated Documents of Greece and Rome, vol. 1 (Cambridge, 2nd edition, 1983). Citations refer to document number
FRH	H. Beck and U. Walter, *Die Frühen Römischen Historiker*, 2 vols. (Darmstadt, vol. 1, 2nd edition, 2005; vol. 2, 2004)
G&R	*Greece and Rome*
GGM	C. Müller, *Geographi Graeci Minores*, 2 vols. (Paris, 1855–1861)
GRBS	*Greek, Roman and Byzantine Studies*
H&T	*History and Theory*

Harding	P. Harding, *From the End of the Peloponnesian War To the Battle of Ipsus.* Translated Documents of Greece and Rome, vol. 2 (Cambridge, 1985). Citations refer to document number
HCA	A. B. Bosworth, *A Historical Commentary on Arrian's History of Alexander*, 2 vols. to date (Oxford, 1980–)
HCP	F. W. Walbank, *A Historical Commentary on Polybius*, 3 vols. (Oxford, 1957–1979)
HCT	A. W. Gomme, A. Andrewes, and K. J. Dover, *A Historical Commentary on Thucydides*, 5 vols. (Oxford, 1945–1980)
Hornblower, *CT*	S. Hornblower, *A Commentary on Thucydides* (Oxford, 1991–)
HRR	H. Peter, *Historicorum Romanorum Reliquiae*, 2 vols. (Stuttgart, 1906–1914)
HSCPh	*Harvard Studies in Classical Philology*
HTR	*Harvard Theological Review*
ICS	*Illinois Classical Studies*
IG	*Inscriptiones Graecae* (Berlin, 1873–)
ILS	H. Dessau (ed.), *Inscriptiones Latinae Selectae*, 5 vols. (Berlin, 1892–1916)
ILLRP	A. Degassi, *Inscriptiones Latinae Liberae Rei Publicae*, 2 vols. (Florence, 1957–1963)
JAS	*Journal of the Asiatic Society of Great Britain and Ireland*
JCS	*Journal of Cuneiform Studies*
JEA	*Journal of Egyptian Archaeology*
JECS	*Journal of Early Christian Studies*
JHS	*Journal of Hellenic Studies*
JRS	*Journal of Roman Studies*
JTS	*Journal of Theological Studies*
JWCI	*Journal of the Warburg and Courtauld Institute*
LCM	*Liverpool Classical Monthly*
LEC	*Les Études Classiques*
LHG&L	C. Ampolo and U. Fantasia (eds.), *Lexicon Historiographicum Graecum et Latinum* (Pisa, 2004–)
MD	*Materiali e discussioni per l'analisi dei testi classici*

Migne, *PL*	J. P. Migne, *Patrologiae cursus completus, series Latina* (Paris, 1844–1864)
ML	R. Meiggs and D. M. Lewis (eds.), *A Selection of Greek Historical Inscriptions to the End of the Fifth Century* BC (Oxford, 1969; revised with addenda, 1988)
NLH	*New Literary History*
Oakley, *CL*	S. Oakley, *A Commentary on Livy, Books VI–X.* 4 vols. (Oxford, 1997–2005)
*OCD*³	S. Hornblower and A. Spawforth (eds.), *The Oxford Classical Dictionary,* 3rd edition, revised (Oxford and New York, 2003)
PACA	*Proceedings of the African Classical Association*
P. Amh.	*Amherst Papyri* (London, 1900–1901)
PBA	*Proceedings of the British Academy*
PCPhS	*Proceedings of the Cambridge Philological Society*
PLLS	*Papers of the Liverpool/Leeds/Langford Latin Seminar*
PLRE	A. H. M. Jones, J. Martindale, and J. Morris (eds.), *Prosopography of the Later Roman Empire* (Cambridge, 1971–)
PMG	D. L. Page (ed.), *Poetae Melici Graeci* (Oxford, 1962)
POxy	*Oxyrhynchus Papyri* (London, 1898–)
PP	*Parola del Passato*
PSI	*Papiri Greci e Latini* (Florence, 1912–)
PVS	*Proceedings of the Virgilian Society*
QS	*Quaderni di Storia*
QUCC	*Quaderni Urbinati di Cultura Classica*
RAC	*Reallexicon für Antike und Christentum* (Stuttgart, 1950–)
RE	A. von Pauly, G. Wissowa, and W. Kroll (eds.), *Realencyclopädie der classischen Altertumswissenschaft,* 84 vols. (Stuttgart, 1893–1980)
REA	*Revue des Études Anciennes*
REG	*Revue des Études Grecques*
REL	*Revue des Études Latines*
Rev. Arch.	*Revue archéologique*
RFIC	*Rivista di filologia e di cultura classica*

RhM	*Rheinisches Museum für Philologie*
RL	P. J. Rhodes with D. M. Lewis, *The Decrees of the Greek States* (Oxford, 1997)
RO	P. J. Rhodes and R. Osborne, *Greek Historical Inscriptions 404–323 BC* (Oxford, 2003)
Röm. Mitt.	*Mitteilungen des deutschen archäologischen Instituts. Römische Abteilung*
RPhilos.	*Revue Philosophique de la France et de l'étranger*
RSA	*Rivista Storica dell'Antichità*
RSI	*Rivista Storica Italiana*
SCI	*Scripta Classica Israelica*
SCO	*Studi Classici e Orientali*
SEG	*Supplementum Epigraphicum Graecum* (Amsterdam, 1923–)
SemRom	*Seminari Romani di cultura greca*
SIG[3]	W. Dittenberger, *Sylloge Inscriptionum Graecarum*, 3rd edition (Leipzig, 1915–1924)
SO	*Symbolae Osloensis*
Staatsverträge	H. Bengtson and H. H Schmitt, *Die Staatsverträge des Altertums* (Munich, 1962–)
TAPhA	*Transactions of the American Philological Association*
Tod	M. N. Tod, *A Selection of Greek Historical Inscriptions*, 2 vols. (Oxford, 1946–1948)
TrGF	B. Snell et al., *Tragicorum Graecorum Fragmenta* (Berlin, 5 vols. [in 6]; Göttingen, 1986–2005)
VDI	*Vestnik drevneĭ istorii: Journal of Ancient History*
VS	H. Diels and W. Kranz, *Die Fragmente der Vorsokratiker*, 3 vols., 6th edition (Berlin-Grunewald, 1951)
WJA	*Würzburger Jahrbücher für die Altertumswissenschaft*
WS	*Wiener Studien*
YCS	*Yale Classical Studies*
ZPE	*Zeitschrift für Papyrologie und Epigraphik*

Introduction

John Marincola

It is not my intention here to give a history, however brief, of Greco-Roman historiography. Much of that information can be found in other works (see Further Reading) or will emerge in the course of this collection. Instead, I supply here a brief background to some of the issues that will arise in the contributions that follow.

1 Approaching Classical Historiography

The historical writing of the Greeks and Romans covers some 800 years, from Herodotus' *Histories* written in the mid- to late fifth century BCE to the *Res Gestae* of Ammianus Marcellinus who composed his history in the late fourth century CE. Within these two boundaries, thousands of men (and a few women) sought to create some record of the past, either of their own or earlier times, in a variety of formats. Of that vast historical literature only the tiniest portion has come down to us, and the surviving literature represents some eras well, while others are hardly represented at all. For the fifth and fourth centuries BCE, we have Herodotus, Thucydides, and Xenophon – considered by the ancients the three greatest historians – but for the Hellenistic era, the 300 years from the death of Alexander the Great to the battle of Actium (323–31 BCE), where we know the names of over 600 historians just on the Greek side, only three historians – Polybius, Diodorus, and Dionysius of Halicarnassus – survive, and even they not entirely. For the Romans, the situation is equally bleak. The entire cadre of early Roman historians, writing from the early second to the mid-first century BCE, have completely disappeared, and only a small part of Rome's three greatest historians has survived: Sallust's *Histories* are lost, as are over 100 books of Livy (including all the contemporary portions of his history), and nearly two-thirds of Tacitus' *Histories* and *Annals*. All of our evaluations of the ancient historians, therefore, are based on the tiniest percentage of what was actually written by the Greeks and Romans.

Our knowledge is supplemented in part by fragmentary evidence. This information is of several types. There are testimonia, i.e., informational remarks made by surviving writers (not just historians) about the scope, arrangement, and/or nature of lost historical works. We also have "fragments," i.e., citations (either verbatim or not) by later writers that inform us of the contents of lost works. Finally, we have summaries or outlines (known as epitomes or *periochae*) of lost works, though these are often extremely brief: a lost book of Livy, for example, might be summarized in no more than a paragraph, or a mammoth work such as Pompeius Trogus' forty-four-book universal history (five times the size of Herodotus' or Thucydides' work) is known to us only from a later epitome of some 200 pages. These testimonia, fragments, and summations must all be used with great caution for several reasons. First, writers in antiquity often quoted from memory and although they may get the general gist of a passage or remark correct, they can often be vague or confused about details, or can misremember the context of certain remarks. Second, the quoting author will often weave his citation of a lost historian into his own account in such a way that it is nearly impossible to separate the "fragment" from its new context in the author who cites it – not to mention that the quoting author may use the citation in an interpretation that was not the lost author's own. Third, authors who write summaries will naturally be highly selective, and there can be no certainty that their selection of events or incidents is representative of the lost work. Finally, and perhaps most worryingly, an author who cites or quotes a lost work will often do so in a polemical context, where he is asserting his own superiority *vis-à-vis* his predecessor, and in such cases he often misrepresents, either by omission or commission, the work of the lost author.

Such limitations must always be borne in mind when approaching the Greek and Roman historians. If even one of the major lost historiographical works from antiquity were to come to light today, it might fundamentally alter our knowledge and understanding of those authors who survive.

2   Evolving Approaches

Ancient historiography is important not only for its own sake, but also because it has furnished an enduring model, both in form and subject matter, for the western literary tradition. Anthologies of historical writing as well as handbooks on the writing of history begin not infrequently with Herodotus and Thucydides, the latter of whom is still considered by some to be the greatest historian of all time.

Even so, the modern study of ancient historical works has evolved a great deal over the last decades. Earlier scholars, basing themselves on nineteenth-century views of history and historical writing, approached the ancient historians most often with a view to determining how reliable they were, in terms of both factual accuracy and impartiality. These investigations were concerned, above all, with what sources the historians used, what methods they had employed in putting together their works, and how well they understood the concerns and demands of pragmatic political history. Many of those who studied these histories were primarily interested in using the information contained in them to reconstruct the *Realien* of ancient history, for it happens to be the case that despite the important contributions of archaeology, epigraphy, and numismatics, most of what we know about Greek and Roman history comes from the texts of ancient historians.

It seems fair to say that the last thirty years have seen a somewhat different approach in the way historical texts are analyzed and evaluated, and the old questions, while not completely disappearing, have begun to be seen as more complicated. The discipline of history itself has been undergoing a fairly thorough reevaluation, and both philosophers and practicing historians have begun to question the value and epistemic claims of traditional narrative history. There is today a greater realization that no history can be complete (since selection of what the historian considers important is essential to his presentation), nor can it be free from some (often culturally predetermined) viewpoint. The status of history has also been questioned from a different direction, namely its literary form, and scholars now emphasize the affinities of narrative history with fiction and other forms of discursive prose, calling attention to the many characteristics that both "factual" and "fictional" discourse share.

This reevaluation of history in general has naturally influenced the approach taken by scholars of the ancient world, whose inquiries now tend to look away from the traditional questions of reliability and sources, and focus instead on the examination of ancient histories as literary artefacts, as the products of individual artistry with their own structure, themes, and concerns. This new generation of studies often seeks to uncover the rhetorical workings that underlie the text, most especially the way that meaning and explanation are constructed at the level of language. General studies of individual historians tend to emphasize the "construction" that the historian engages in while narrating his version of the past rather than on the past reality that the history is supposed to represent: in other words, Thucydides' account of the Peloponnesian War is studied for what it tells us of the author's own view of the conflict, and of the preconceptions shared by him and his audience, rather than for what it tells us of the actual historical circumstances of the years 431 to 411: his text is *a* Peloponnesian War rather than *the* Peloponnesian War. Or, to take a different example, it is no longer assumed that if Livy does not write history in the way that we would, it is because he did not understand *how* to go about compiling a reliable record of the past. The belief that Livy would have been more like us, if only he had known, pays far fewer dividends than the more worthwhile approach that looks at what Livy (and, by implication, his audience) *did* consider important, and how Livy managed to construct a history of Rome that his contemporaries and later generations considered authoritative and permanent.

Predictably, more "literary" studies have been greeted with suspicion by traditional historians, since in not a few cases these newer works have called into question the very possibility of reconstructing ancient history from the ancient historians. Faced with an "overly" literary approach, traditional scholars have emphasized that ancient historians considered research an important component of their work: nearly every historian from Herodotus to Ammianus makes some claim to have practiced inquiry. These scholars have also reacted by averring the reliability of the literary record when it is tested against non-literary evidence, especially archaeology and epigraphy. Indeed, there is merit to this case, and it would be overly simplistic to assume that the writing of history is no different from the writing of any other narrative, factual or fictive. Clearly the ancients thought that history was an area with its own subject matter and method, and the very real debates in the pages of the historians over the accuracy of their predecessors and whether something happened in this or that way shows that they had some sense that their task was not simply to present a plausible narrative; they must have thought there was some underlying and preexisting reality that they were trying to recapture and represent. This *Companion* to ancient historiography, therefore, tries to represent both approaches to the Greek and Roman historians. Such a twofold approach should lead to a better appreciation of what the ancients were doing when they attempted to create a record of what had happened (or what they thought had happened). As historians are analyzed and appreciated on their own terms, we can, of course, decide that this or that historian executed his task with greater or lesser accuracy or fidelity, but it is no longer necessary to have a teleological view of history writing, in which the first chroniclers of the past are seen as well-meaning but ultimately ineffectual, soon to be replaced by practitioners with a more "scientific" (i.e., nineteenth-century) viewpoint. In fact, as studies both in classics and in history in general have shown, the use of the past is always intimately connected with the present, and often (though not always) with structures of power and authority. Moreover, a "singular" view of what constitutes history and how it should be written overlooks (or minimizes) the vast array of different approaches to the past taken by the ancient historians. In the end, ancient historians become *more* interesting for their complex construction of the past – i.e., their re-visioning of the past in light of the present – than they would be if considered mere repositories of fact.

3   Developmental Models

In both the Greek and Roman tradition, we find developmental models proposed by the ancients that sought to explain the rise and development of historiography. On the Greek side, Dionysius of Halicarnassus, in his essay *On Thucydides*, believed that the origins of Greek historical writing lay with "local" historians, writers who, whether treating Greek or non-Greek history, wrote accounts of their own particular home town or country, with the general aim of making available the traditions of the past as found in local monuments and religious and secular records. They wrote, he says, without ornament and included much of "the mythical," i.e., tall tales or marvelous stories that had been believed from ancient times. Herodotus, however, chose not to write about a particular time or place, but gathered together many events in Europe and Asia, and included in a single narrative all the important events of the Greek and non-Greek world. Thereafter, he continues, Thucydides wrote of a single war, considering the themes of the early writers too paltry and that of Herodotus too large a subject for the human mind to study. He therefore concentrated on a single war, basing his narrative on his own inquiry and autopsy, and rigorously excluding all "mythical" material (*Thuc.* 5). This developmental thesis probably goes back to Aristotle's successor, Theophrastus, who wrote a (lost) *On History* in which he may have discussed such issues. However that may be, it is clear that in Dionysius' reconstruction Herodotus is a pivotal figure, subsuming and amalgamating what came before and pointing the way towards Thucydides. Nor is this surprising given the later belief that Herodotus and Thucydides were the two foundational and best historians.

Modern scholars have generally abandoned Dionysius' schema and substituted different models, replacing it with one of their own. By far the most influential has been that of Felix Jacoby, the greatest modern scholar of Greek historiography. Before beginning his collection of the fragments of the Greek historians (*FGrHist*), he set out his understanding of the development of Greek historiography, an analysis that has in turn influenced scholars of Roman historiography.

Jacoby divided the historical writing of the Greeks into five sub-genres, arranged according to the order in which he believed they developed. He postulated as the earliest genre "mythography," which sought to bring order and/or consistency to the variety of Greek traditions and to establish a record for mythical (i.e., earliest) times. The first mythographical work was the *Genealogies* of Hecataeus of Miletus, writing in the late sixth and early fifth century BCE. This treatise tried to make sense of the conflicting genealogies of gods and heroes (and the humans who claimed descent from them), and it seems to have done so by a process of rationalization (however inconsistently applied). It is not known whether Hecataeus or any other "mythographer" commented upon the quality of the tradition or sought to elaborate a methodology for solving the problems of conflicting and/or fabulous traditions.

The second genre to develop, according to Jacoby, was ethnography, a study of lands, peoples, their customs and marvels; again it was Hecataeus who established the seeds of this genre with his *Circuit of the Earth* (*Periodos* or *Periēgēsis Ges*), a work that progressed around the coastline of the Mediterranean and described the lands and the peoples therein. Jacoby postulated that the first full-scale ethnography was Dionysius of Miletus' *Persica*, written in the early fifth century BCE and arising from the Ionians' desire to know more about Persia, the power that had conquered and ruled them. In form, ethnography is a hybrid, containing both historical accounts (which could be lengthy) and descriptive accounts of the land and its people, such accounts being based on autopsy and oral inquiry.

The third sub-genre, chronography, began with Hellanicus of Lesbos' *Priestesses of Hera at Argos*. Although chronography is usually linked to the development of local history (Jacoby's fifth sub-genre), it is formally separate. Chronography shares with local history, however, a style of dating by annual magistrates, in Hellanicus' case, the year of office of the chief priestess of Hera at Argos. Under this rubric, Hellanicus arranged the events of individual years, not only for Argos but also for all Greece. Thus despite its "local" dating system, the *Priestesses* is Panhellenic and embraces events throughout Greece.

The most important sub-genre of all for Jacoby was contemporary history (*Zeitgeschichte*), the writers of which he defined as "those authors who without local restriction narrated the general Greek history of their own time or up to their own time" (Jacoby 1909: 34). The distinguishing marks of *Zeitgeschichte* are: (1) a narrative mainly of the author's own time, irrespective of where it begins; (2) a viewpoint from the Greek side; and (3) a Panhellenic treatment, i.e., embracing events of all the Greek city-states rather than a single locale. The sub-genre is first glimpsed in Books 7–9 of Herodotus, for in Herodotus the descriptive element (the hallmark of ethnography) becomes subsumed within historical thought and within the search for historical causation. In the next generation Thucydides' work on the Peloponnesian War brings the sub-genre to full fruition. Jacoby thus saw a teleological line of development in historiography, namely Hecataeus–Herodotus–Thucydides.

After Thucydides, writers of *Zeitgeschichte* chose either to write up individual wars, or to continue the chronicling of contemporary history now focused not on a particular event but rather on a chosen segment of time, as Xenophon did in the *Hellenica* and as the many serial continuators in Greek (and later Roman) history attest. Histories centered on individuals – Theopompus' *Philippica*, histories of Alexander or of his successors – also qualify, provided that they are not limited by a local focus. Thus contemporary history, itself a sub-genre, could have sub-categories of its own: war monographs, perpetual or continuous histories, and individual-centered histories.

The final sub-genre for Jacoby was horography or local history. Unlike Dionysius, who saw this as the earliest form of historical writing amongst the Greeks, Jacoby believed that local history was the last sub-genre to develop, and that it developed largely in response to Herodotus' work. Horography had a fixed annalistic structure, concentrated on an individual city-state, and included not only political and military events but also religious, cultic, and "cultural" material.

These five sub-genres, then, form Jacoby's view of the development of Greek historiography. As for Dionysius, so for Jacoby, Herodotus was the crucial figure, for Jacoby argued that the disparate material in Herodotus' *Histories* contains the traces of his "development" from a geographer (Book 2) to ethnographer (Books 2 and 4, especially) to composer of war monograph (Books 7–9), and thus a historian. Jacoby in so doing located the development of an entire genre and an entire people's historical consciousness in Herodotus' own transformation. In the next generation, Thucydides took what he had learned from Herodotus and brought history to its full perfection, writing a work that was outstanding for the equilibrium it maintained between historical methodology and historical imagination.

Recently, however, doubts have been expressed about this model, though these can only be summarized here. First, Jacoby's view is teleological: early writers are primitive, leading on to Herodotus, and finally Thucydides, who is represented as the pinnacle of Greek historiography. The "peak" of historical writing is thus put extremely early, and later historiography is seen largely as a decline from the greatness of Thucydides (Jacoby had little sympathy with Hellenistic and later Greek historiography). Second, Jacoby's view of the development of Greek historiography relies largely on the development of a single individual, Herodotus, and only with Herodotus' own development does Greek historiography come into being. Amongst other problems, such an individualization of historiography's development limits the ability to see that historians were not the only ones engaged in the preservation, understanding, and establishment of the tradition of the past. Finally, Jacoby's categories do not always map clearly onto ancient terminology, especially in the areas of ethnography and *Zeitgeschichte* (both of which lack ancient equivalents). This suggests that he may be imposing modern categories on ancient practices. And the view pays very little attention to the innovativeness of the classical historiographical tradition. For all that, Jacoby's approach is hardly without merit, and clearly is right about some very important aspects of Greek historiography. In some of the chapters below, authors will continue the discussion of the ways in which such approaches help or hinder our understanding of the ancient historians.

Roman historiography, while not subject to the same type of developmental model, has nevertheless been influenced by Jacoby's schema for Greek writers. We should mention, however, that the development of Roman historiography is particularly problematic, because all of its early practitioners are lost. In addition, there are some unusual features of early Roman historiography. To begin with, the first historian, Q. Fabius Pictor, wrote his history of Rome in Greek, as did his immediate followers. Only with Cato the Elder's *Origines* almost a century later was Roman historiography in Latin born. Second, Roman historiography developed comparatively late: Fabius wrote in the mid-third century BCE, by which time Roman history was more than four centuries old. (By contrast, Herodotus' work was only a generation or so after most of the events it records.) Third, although the Romans maintained an annual priestly record which could on some level be considered historical, it is uncertain what relationship, if any, this chronicle has to the development and characteristic forms of Roman historiography.

That priestly chronicle looms large in the developmental model proposed for Roman historiography by Cicero (perhaps, like Dionysius, basing himself on Theophrastus). In Cicero's account (as in Dionysius'), the early historians lack ornamentation in their writing, just like the priestly annals, and are concerned only to record traditions: Cicero even goes so far as to compare the early Latin historians with the Greek "local" historians (*De Or.* 2.53). The major difference in Cicero's model is that no Herodotus, much less a Thucydides, has yet appeared amongst the Romans, and Cicero is at pains to delineate the qualities (mainly stylistic) that are necessary for such a one to arise. Yet there is very good evidence to show that Cicero's characterization of the early Roman historians is nearly wholly false.

Nevertheless, his comparison with the Greek "local" historians may lie behind the beliefs of some scholars that the early Roman historians were simply that, and thus followed the conventions of local history (that is where Jacoby places Pictor and his Hellenophone followers). As a "local" historian, Pictor might very well have used the kinds of materials (including religious lore) that his earlier Greek counterparts did, but that is not what the description of his work suggests: Dionysius tells us (*AR* 1.6.2) that Pictor treated the foundation of Rome fully, then briefly touched on

events between the foundation and the beginning of the First Punic War (264 BCE), then wrote a full account of events following up to his own times. Even without this information, it is not at all clear either that all local historians wrote in a certain way or that Pictor would have felt himself bound to follow each and every convention that may have existed. Again, generic presuppositions may be misleading.

Some scholars have tried to differentiate Roman historians by distinguishing between "historians" proper and "annalists." The former are seen as "serious" writers of political and military events, who emphasized contemporary history, either, like the Greek writers of *Hellenica*, in a *perpetua historia*, a continuous history (Sisenna, Sallust in the *Histories*, Asinius Pollio), or in *bella*, accounts of individual wars (Sempronius Asellio on the Second Punic War, Sallust's *Catiline* and *Jugurtha*). Annalists, on the other hand, treated Roman history from its origins in a strict year-by-year manner dictated by the priestly chronicles (the *Annales Maximi*), and gave, it seems, far more generous treatment to the events that the earliest Roman writers had treated briefly, i.e., the four and a half centuries from around 700 BCE to the First Punic War. The annalists are also presumed to have included much material designated as antiquarian, involving matters such as religion, cult, and culture, and, more seriously, to have filled out their histories with embellishments, fictions, and falsified traditions. Much of the discussion then centers around who should be considered a "historian" and who an "annalist." Nonetheless, it remains questionable whether this approach too has any validity. First, such a distinction cannot be found in the ancient authors, where "scriptor annalium" or the like serve as a designation for all writers of history. Second, the Latin word *annales* means both history (in the aggregate and objective sense) and a particular history (the literary representation of events). Third, citations of Roman historians refer indiscriminately to *annales* and *historia*, which suggests not only that the writers themselves did not assign any such title as *Annales* to their works, but also that there cannot have been a recognized sub-genre of *annales*.

*

In sum, then, the variety of classical historiography cannot be easily reduced to formulas and linear progressions (or regressions, for that matter). The writing of history is always dependent on contemporary concerns, and the many historians of antiquity who created their accounts of the past were responding in some measure to the needs of their own times. Both Greece and Rome were traditional societies that looked to the past for understanding but also for inspiration and guidance, and our best hope for understanding what ancient historians were up to is to keep before ourselves constantly the many factors that went into the creation, appreciation, and (ultimately) survival of the works of the Greek and Roman historians.

FURTHER READING

For surveys and general treatments of Greek and Roman historiography see Strasburger 1966, Mazzarino 1965–1966, Usher 1969, Fornara 1983, Grant 1995, Marincola 1997, Pani 2001, Duff 2003, and (for late antiquity) Rohrbacher 2002 and Marasco 2003b. Overviews of Greek historiography can be found in Bury 1909 (still worth reading), von Fritz 1967, Brown 1973, Meister 1990, Lendle 1992, Hornblower 1994b, and Luce 1997. For surveys of Roman historiography see Laistner 1947, La Penna 1978, Kraus and Woodman 1997, Flach 1998, and Mehl 2001 (an English translation is forthcoming). Walter 2004, though not a survey, has much of importance on historical culture in Rome.

On the origins and development of Greek and Roman historiography see the fundamental article of Jacoby 1909. Different approaches to the issue can be found in Châtelet 1962, Mazzarino 1966: I.23–121, Starr 1968, Gozzoli 1970–1971 and Porciani 2001a; see also below, Chs. 2 and 3. Jacoby's developmental schema has been discussed by Fowler 1996, Humphreys 1997, Schepens 1997, and Marincola 1999. The developmental model for Roman historiography has been well treated in Eigler et al. 2003: 1–38 (with many references); see also below, Chs. 5 and 21.

For cautions and important methodological approaches to dealing with fragments see Brunt 1980 and Schepens 1997. Finally, there is much of value about ancient historians and ancient historiography scattered throughout the collected papers of Ronald Syme, Arnaldo Momigliano, and Frank Walbank.

PART I

Contents

CHAPTER ONE

The Place of History in the Ancient World

Roberto Nicolai

1 Preliminary Considerations

According to a generally accepted opinion, the discovery of history in the western world is owed to the Greeks. One must admit, however, that history did not enjoy a privileged position within Greek culture; rather, its role was marginal whether we compare the study of history with other intellectual activities or try to examine its presence in education and in school (see Momigliano 1983; Nicolai 1992; below, §4). To begin, we must clear up several ambiguities. First, our concept of history – by which I mean the concept of history developed between the eighteenth and nineteenth centuries as a consequence of the integration of narrative history and the study of antiquity (Momigliano 1950) – is profoundly different from that of the Greeks and the Romans: both have a diegetic aspect, since history, both for us and the ancients, is a narrative of facts. The means, however, by which a story is conveyed and the aims of the historians are different. At least up until Herodotus there is no interest in chronology, either absolute or relative (see Finley 1975: 15, 17–18; for archaic Greece one can speak rather of an extreme interest in genealogical sequences), and it took centuries before chronological systems were established for general use; by contrast, modern historiography, the child of a culture obsessed with the measurement of time, cannot avoid placing facts into a chronological grid. Second, the account of an ancient historian tends to absorb – and therefore to make disappear, in varying degrees in various epochs – every trace of documentation used by the author, while the modern historian by contrast searches to bring forth the facts from the documents. (For the use of documents see Biraschi et al. 2003; below, Ch. 4; the

Translated by Ginevra Adamoli and Kyle M. Hall.

modern idolatry of the document, however, has also rightly been questioned: see, most recently, Canfora 2003: 9). The rhetoric of the document is directly opposed to the rhetoric of ancient historians, which derives from epic poetry and constructs the character (*ēthos*) of the historian as the omniscient, or at least competent and authoritative, narrator (Marincola 1997). Third, the goal of an ancient historical account is never purely scientific and cognitive, but is always linked to creating paradigms, predominantly politico-militaristic or ethical ones (for the different goals that historians proposed for themselves from time to time see Finley 1975: 23). All of historiography's paradigms had a paideutic end and in some sense a political end: to form a governing class, offering it analytical instruments and behavioral models (as in Thucydides); to put forward great personalities, positive or negative, as *exempla*, so as to fix the parameters of moral evaluation (as with Theopompus, Tacitus, and the biographical tradition); or to construct memory and collective identity (as in local historiography and *ktiseis* [foundation narratives]). (For historiography's contribution to the construction of Greek identity see Cartledge 1997b.)

But ancient historiography is not a homogeneous whole, with a limited internal evolution. Under this label we in fact assemble authors and works that are extremely different (cf. the panorama of Latin historiography in Cizek 1985), sharing only the minimal common denominator of being a narration of events (Canfora 2003: 14). A further distinction must be made between history, understood as the whole of past events, and historiography, understood as a literary genre charged with the narration of events. Using this outline, one can say that the past (also including in this term the mythic past, brought in through the poetic tradition) has its own important place in Greek and Roman cultures, while the narration of the past, and above all the investigation into the past, occupy a much more modest place.

2   The Place of History and the Place of Historiography

Moses Finley (1975: 14) emphatically ruled out the possibility that epic poetry, whatever else it was, could be considered history. Greeks of any epoch would have expressed their perplexity at this statement or at least would have called for a debate. No Greek in fact ever held such an opinion. On the contrary, Thucydides, in the so-called "Archaeology" (1.2–19), sought to demonstrate the superiority of his argument and of his account with respect to the *Iliad*, and moreover, he compared the degree of reliability of Homer's testimony with the much more accurate investigations that he himself had conducted on a history even more ancient than Homer's (1.10, 1.21: see Nicolai 2001b). The fact that Thucydides dedicates one of the more demanding sections of his work to this confrontation with Homer and to the demonstration of the superior paradigmaticism of the Peloponnesian War *vis-à-vis* the Trojan War demonstrates that for Thucydides the most important touchstone in the Greek intellectual sphere was in fact Homer. And if it is true that in the light of modern historiography (and also several tendencies in ancient historiography) epic cannot be defined as history, it is just as true that for centuries epic represented the only reliable record of the past that the Greeks had at their disposal, and that even after the invention of historiography, when one wanted to take a look at more ancient history, one could not do more than go back to epic poetry (Nicolai 2003a).

I believe that it is not sufficient to search Homeric epic for historical information or for the elements that came to be considered characteristic of historical narration. Rather, it is appropriate to try to take another look at epic poetry, in order to see what a Greek found there in terms of an awareness of his own past and the construction of his own identity. A narration of past events that forms the identity of a people, whether at a collective level or at the level of a single city or single clan (*genē*), and that constitutes for that people the principle paradigmatic reference, cannot be ignored by those who seek to delineate the proper place of history and of historiography in the Greek and Roman world.

The first and most important indication of the strength of epic in Greek culture is the link that it created between the identity of the Greeks and "glorious deeds" (*klea andrōn*: *Il.* 9.189, 524; *Od.* 8.73) worthy of being saved from oblivion with song. In the *Iliad* Achilles, the hero *par excellence*, sings to Patroclus the glorious deeds of men (9.189), to show that Homeric heroes also had a past to sing and from which to take models. The paradigmatic value of *klea andrōn* is then continued by Phoenix (9.524), where he introduces an exemplary event. In the absence of political unity and also of a strong and unifying religion (such as, e.g., the monotheism of the Jews), the Greeks identified themselves in epic song, or, to be more precise, in their past, from which poetry had selected and transmitted the most memorable events. The Greeks also recognized that the poets had identified and in some ways founded their religion (Hdt. 2.53.2–3). That the Homeric poems are the book of Greek culture entails (and not as a secondary consequence) the utilization of a human past as a model and foundation of the present. The *Iliad* is not a sacred book like the Bible, and it does not recount the acts of a single hero, such as Gilgamesh, who searches for divine immortality, but recounts instead human events, with the gods as helpers or opponents.

For the public, epic recalled events distant in time: the bards knowingly archaized their works, both in language and in content, creating that inextricable mixture of past and present characteristic of every epic. One must strongly emphasize that this archaization, besides being a necessity of the genre and strengthening the exemplary force of an event, is a sign of the basic understanding of chronological distance from the events narrated. Furthermore, the stratified composition through the centuries introduced anachronisms and other blendings. To give a single example, the place names of the "Catalogue of Ships" (*Il.* 2.484–779, with Visser 1997, who provides an ample bibliography) are the result of the desire for amplification, accumulating names upon names, and assigning them formulaic epithets that dignify even lesser-known localities; and, in the desire to antiquate, choosing names of cities that contained a veiled memory, or in some cases inventing one for the occasion. The resulting picture is not a description of Greece in the Mycenaean age or the archaic age, but rather an indecipherable mixture upon which whole generations of ancient and modern philology have been based. Nonetheless, for the Greeks the presence or absence of a city in the Catalogue was a cause for pride or shame, and in certain cases the verses of the Catalogue were used to solve political and territorial controversies. Epic, in short, was an irreplaceable document, a type of historical archive, to be consulted and at times to be interpolated or falsified, but always to be interpreted (for the exegesis of epic poetry as a part of genealogy and historiography see Nicolai 2003a). One of the main supports for epic poetry was genealogy, which identified characters connected to each other through means of the simple patronymic and stabilized a series of relations with the heroes of preceding generations. The creation of genealogical epics by Hesiod at both the divine (*Theogony*) and human (*Catalogue of Women*) level indicates that the public had a specific interest in this kind of material.

It was precisely the immense awareness required by catalogue poetry that drove the poet who composed the prologue to the "Catalogue of Ships" (*Il.* 2.484–493) to confront the limited knowledge founded on *kleos* (reputation) with that of the omniscient Muses, who are present and aware. The Muse, daughter of Mnemosyne (Memory), is able to compensate for the limitations of the poet, who becomes the latest ring of collective memory. Thanks to the Muse (*Od.* 8.488–491), Demodocus can sing the sufferings of the Achaeans and the capture of Troy, events at which he had not been present, with such precision as to provoke the admiration and the tears of Odysseus, who was a protagonist of the story (*Od.* 8.521–531). Epic, therefore, is a product of the memory of a people, and at the same time an encyclopedia and cultural book of that people (Rossi 1978, esp. 87–92). Historiography, heir of epic poetry, will retain this goal of preserving memory (cf. Herodotus' preface) and also the goal of suggesting itself as a repertoire of dynamics and behaviors, in other words of paradigms (especially, with Thucydides, politico-military paradigms: see his famous formulation, 1.22.4).

The paradigmatic and educative aim on the one hand removes ancient historiography from its modern counterpart with its claim to be a science, while on the other hand links history to other genres that had among their goals the construction of a collective identity and the telling of paradigmatic events: I am referring particularly to tragedy, but also to oratory, both epideictic, as it can be seen in the funeral oration (see, above all, Loraux 1981), and deliberative. In the funeral oration Athens' past occupies a central position, but one searches in vain here for a serious reconstruction of the city's history; on the contrary, the history of this genre seems to reflect the precept of Tisias and Gorgias (*ap.* Plat. *Phaedr.* 267b1), picked up by Isocrates: "to go through ancient events in a new way and to speak in an old-fashioned manner of recent events" (*Paneg.* 8, with Marincola 1997: 276–277; Nicolai 2004: 75–76, 129–131). The clear intent is to render the recent past paradigmatically by placing it on the same level as that mythic past which time, distance, and the works of the poets (including tragedy) had made exemplary.

The importance of paradigms derived from past history continued, in different literary genres and various forms, the goals and in certain ways the criteria that presided over the narrative choices of epic song. But alongside the exemplary history of the tragedians and orators, other genres developed that had as their subject past events: genealogies, which continued and interpreted the epos and had the aim of consolidating and organizing the memories of aristocratic clans (*genē*); various forms of local historiography, either strictly local or regional; antiquarianism, necessary to create and reinforce identity and the sense of belonging to a community; and works on the customs of foreign peoples, which exhibited and explained the "other." All of these genres constituted a type of galaxy (rather difficult for us to decipher because of the loss of so many works) that was linked to other galaxies, such as the various genres of geographic literature which also gave space to genealogical, historical, and ethnographic concerns. None of these early genres that handled historical material possessed the paradigmatic force of epic or the capacity to involve a Panhellenic public. Therefore, it was not Hecataeus, indissolubly linked to epic and limited to genealogical material, who created a new literary genre directed towards the conservation of the historical memory of the Greeks (see Nicolai 1997): rather, it was Herodotus and Thucydides who confronted epic poetry and tried to substitute new models for those offered by Homer; both men responded to the needs of an age that sought more extended and reliable knowledge (Herodotus especially), to be utilized in particular for the formation of a governing class (Thucydides especially). Historiography is one of the products of this period that is often known as an age of sophists, and there is no doubt that Herodotus and Thucydides were strongly influenced by sophistic ideas; it is possible that they even considered themselves sophists. Certainly the methods by which Herodotus published his work were not very different from the recitations of Lysias or Protagoras that we know from Plato's dialogues (Thomas 1993; Thomas 2000, esp. 258, 284). The historians shared with the sophists the goal of transmitting useful knowledge into political life, enough so that historiography was classified by Aristotle as a part of politics (*Rhet.* 1360a).

3 Historiography as a Literary Genre rather than a Science

It is commonly accepted that history was not included in the disciplines that moved towards exact knowledge, truth in the philosophical sense of the term, and that the results of historical research were part of *doxa* (opinion). This arrangement of history as foreign to philosophy was consolidated specifically in the great systematic philosophies of the fourth century and the Hellenistic age. The Greek and Roman philosophers did not dedicate themselves to historiography and did not elaborate historiographical theories (Finley 1975: 12). The sole exception is Posidonius, who also wrote history, but I would be very cautious before attributing to him (and by extension to Stoicism) a complete philosophy of history that incorporates the study of the past into a philosophical system (Pani 2001: 66 speaks of Posidonius' systematic conception of history, but cf. Nicolai 2003b: 689–691). It was only with Christianity that history became a part of a vision of the world and the destiny of man: on the one hand, the faith founds itself on the historical veracity of the coming of Christ, of his death and resurrection, while, on the other hand, history had for the first time a goal and an end, the second and definitive coming of Christ for the final judgment (from the enormous bibliography, Press 1982: 61–119 is useful for a terminological start). After Christianity imposed a theological conception onto history, many metaphysical and political philosophies elected history as their foundation and, as a consequence, many diverse philosophies of history were elaborated. But this perspective is completely foreign to Greco-Roman antiquity, just as the idea of history as a science is foreign. A view of history as a science is wrong in its assumptions because the historical event is not only in itself subject to doubt but above all not repeatable, according to the required principle of modern science, and it cannot be anachronistically projected onto classical antiquity in the search for a scientific method in historians such as Thucydides and Polybius: both in a way satisfy the standards of modern historiography for very different reasons. The only system which historiography was always part of was the literary system, and not only because historiography was labeled as literature. Herodotus and Thucydides, as we have been suggesting, were the first historians to confront epic and to introduce epic narrative techniques into their works (the most outstanding being the speeches given to various characters; below, Ch. 9).

If we investigate the history of historiography as the history of a literary genre we find at the outset the problem of deciding what should be included and what excluded. Traditionally, modern histories of historiography concentrate on the great authors and on the two main lines, one inaugurated by Herodotus, the other by Thucydides (Strasburger 1975; Momigliano 1990: 29–53). All the rest are either relegated to forerunners (as in the overvaluation of Hecataeus' alleged rationalism) or placed in the indistinct limbo of minor historiography (including, to hint at only a few kinds, local and regional historiography, antiquarianism, monography, and biography). This outlook is wrong in two aspects: what has survived is due to the tastes of the public in several crucial ages and to the fortuitous chances of destruction; the number of authors and works belonging to so-called minor historiography is an indication of their success with the public, in many cases limited in terms of time and place, but an indication nonetheless of a more complex and varied reality (Gabba 1981; Schepens forthcoming). And what is the border separating historiography from genealogy, from *ktiseis*, from antiquarian *periēgēseis* and even from the narrations to which we give the modern name of novels, such as the works under the names of Dictys of Crete and Dares of Phrygia from the Trojan saga, or those on the fortunes of Alexander the Great? One cannot deny that these narratives have some historiographic characteristics (Canfora 2003: 15; on the boundary between historiography and novel see Treu 1984; below, Ch. 56). The typical answer is that the difference lies in method, but this seems an ambiguous response leaving wide swaths of uncertainty. Another possible response could come from examining the expectations and reactions of the public, trying to understand what was considered authentic and authoritative narration, but in this case too the results are not secure. Let us only consider the fact that for ancient history the poets were considered repositories of tradition, and this is true not only for Homer and the archaic poets but also for relatively recent poets: Strabo cites Callimachus and Euphorion, putting them on the same level as Homer and Aeschylus; the scholiasts compare Lycophron with Homer on the number of ships sent to Troy. Citation of poets in controversial cases had the validity of testimony rendered at a trial, and the poets were often cited as a source of international law. In this case as well, the key lies in detecting what ancient conceptions of historical truth were, and how much these overlap with modern conceptions. If modern historiography tends to be more or less aware of an absolute truth (which can be the foundation of philosophical thought) or a scientific truth (which is independent of any subjectivity), the truth of ancient historians generally rested upon the impartiality and honesty of the historian, viz. on subjective and relative values (Woodman 1988: 83, 197ff.; cf. Vercruysse 1984 on the importance of the subjective aspect in historiography and on the care in confronting truth and lies). Next to the truth of the authoritative historian exists another recognized truth, the paradigmatic truth of traditional narrations and history used by orators (for the exemplary value of traditions handed down by poets see Cic. *Leg.* 1.3–4, with Nicolai 2001a). But if these are the main ancient conceptions of the true historian, it is evident that neither the criterion of method nor that of public reaction to the authority of the narrations can be used with any hope of success. The only possibility is to leave open the borders of the historiographical genre, distinguishing from time to time the goals of individual authors and judging their works not in terms of a canon, either Thucydidean or modern as it may be, but in the context that produced them and that they served.

4   The Study of the Past: Historiography in the Ancient School-System

In the ancient school-system, history was not an autonomous discipline (Momigliano 1987a: 161–162), but consciousness of the past did enter into various subjects and at different moments in the curriculum. The reading of historians could be required of students either at the stage of grammatical (primary) or rhetorical (secondary) instruction. In contrast to modern schools, in which history is a construct around which the contents of many disciplines (literature, art, philosophy) come to be included, in ancient schools a normative (synchronic) scheme prevailed over a historical-evolutionary (diachronic) one. The main foundation of teaching was imitation, and paradigms were the fundamental didactic tool; in the case of grammar and rhetoric, they were the works of the great authors: Homer and the tragedians in the first rank, but also Thucydides, Plato, Isocrates, and Demosthenes for the Greeks; Vergil, Sallust, Terence, and Cicero at Rome. These paradigmatic texts were both formal models and vehicles for ethical content, and they were rich in paradigms taken from past history. These paradigms in turn worked to integrate and reinforce ethical judgment and norms, gaining a depth that they did not possess by themselves.

In rhetorical theory one finds articulated norms for the use of the historical *exemplum* in oratory, and one encounters various *exempla* taken from historiography, in particular through description (*ekphrasis*). Attempts to classify historiography within oratorical genres that have their place in the epideictic or deliberative genres are not lacking. Ancient rhetoric, as has been argued, tended to encompass all the literary genres and to draw models and *exempla* from all genres, both poetry and prose. Historiography also came to be taken as a stylistic model for orators, whether because of the presence of direct speeches or because it was a narrative and descriptive genre (Nicolai 1992: 61–83). The imitation of Thucydides on the part of orators was the object of a lively debate in the first century BCE that involved both Greek and Roman rhetors. The constant presence of examples taken from historiography in rhetorical treatises is a confirmation of the firm position of historiography in the literary system next to traditional poetic genres (primarily epic and tragedy, but also lyric, elegy, iambus, and comedy) and prose (oratory and philosophy). The existence also of a canon of Greek historians, which arose and developed to indicate excellent authors worthy of imitation, is another confirmation of the place of the genre.

Grammar as a skill (*technē*) was born much later than rhetoric and shaped its own space; in defining itself, it often overlapped with the field of rhetoric. This could happen because of the non-institutionalized character of ancient schools and the absence of rigid walls between the disciplines. One of the institutionalized tasks of grammar was the "narration of histories" (*historiōn apodosis, historiarum enarratio*), or rather the explanation of the contents of the narrative in texts chosen for commentary. In the case of poetic texts, the grammarians above all concerned themselves with clarifying the references to mythical material but in several cases also had to confront recent history, as, for example, in historical tragedies (such as Aeschylus' *Persians*) and, in much greater measure, comedies. The scholia to tragedy show scant concern with the identification of true or presumed allusions to contemporary facts and characters (a staple, of course, of modern scholarship). The only case of identification of a contemporary character, even in dubious form, that was adumbrated in a tragic role was that of the demagogue in Euripides' *Orestes*, which, according to the scholiasts, alluded to Cleophon (schol. Eur. *Or.* 903, 904). In other cases one cannot speak of allusion or allegory, but rather of analogical reference: for example, when the scholiasts on the *Andromache* point out that Euripides is reviling the Spartans because of the ongoing war, it is the Spartan Menelaus, present on stage, who refers to the unreliability of the Spartans (schol. Eur. *Andr.* 445). Thus tragedy worked on the analogical plane of exemplarity, not the allegorical one of allusion. But the grammarians also occupied themselves with explaining the prose texts of historians, orators, and philosophers. By the second century BCE, Aristarchus composed a "commentary" (*hupomnēma*) on Herodotus (*P. Amh.* II.12) and the oldest nucleus of the scholia to Thucydides was written (Luschnat 1954–1955). In commenting on historians the grammarians did not concern themselves with method, and only rarely criticized historical choices. They worked to complete and make understandable the narrative content, not necessarily to evaluate their reliability. In grammatical theory there existed a classification of the historical part (*historikon meros*) of grammar, that derived from the rhetorical theory of *diēgēsis*, but this classification placed on the same level – that of "true narratives" – the events of gods, heroes, and illustrious men, narratives of places and times, and narratives concerning deeds (Asclepiades of Myrlea *ap.* Sext. Emp. *Math.* 1.252–253; see Rispoli 1988; Nicolai 1992: 195–197). In the view of grammarians, therefore, historiography was not an exclusive location of truth that had to be reconstructed with a rigorous method of investigation, but rather was a genre that, like epic poetry and tragedy, did not indulge in the seductions of what was incredible or impossible by nature, as did genealogies (which were classified under "false narratives"), and did not invent plausible events attributable to fantastic characters, as did comedy and mime.

It might seem unnecessary to be reminded that the Greek and Roman historians came from the schools of grammarians and rhetors: the formation of the historian was the same as that of the orator and there was no specific preparation for the writing of history. A recent work on *progymnasmata* (the preliminary exercises practiced in the schools) has surmised that the presentation of facts by historians was influenced by the practice of creating narration (*diēgēma*), description (*ekphrasis*), panegyric (*enkō-mion*), and so on (Gibson 2004; cf. esp. 124–125, where he underlines that "Modes of discourse . . . are modes of thought"). That such an influence existed is very likely, but this does not necessarily lead to a vision of ancient historiography as integrally submissive to the demands and techniques of rhetoric and almost indistinguishable from the fictitious oratory of declamation on historical themes. To recognize the presence of models and narrative techniques that derive from rhetoric is instead valuable when analyzing the works of historians and distinguishing various levels of elaboration (see, e.g., Comber 1997 on Tacitus). It requires, in short, overcoming a dichotomy: on the one side are scholars of rhetoric and literature, who emphasize the distortions of history inspired by the rhetorical texture of narration, and who can conclude by even considering ancient historiography as a genre of invented narrative (see, e.g., Wiseman 1979; Woodman 1988; of this tendency I welcome only a few positions: the idea of truth as impartiality; and the need for submitting historiograph-ical texts to an attentive rhetorical and literary analysis); on the other side are militant historians, who defend the reliability and accuracy of their ancient predecessors (see, in different ways, Pritchett 1993; Porciani 1997; Bosworth 2003; Rhodes 1994 is one of the most balanced defenses). It must be realized that both are correct: ancient historians use the forms taken from the schools of rhetoric, but their works should not be considered unreliable testimonies because of this. The Greeks and Romans were very clear about the difference between an oration and a historical work. A famous passage of Cicero's *Brutus* (42: "since indeed it is conceded to orators to lie in history, so that they might say something more pointedly") shows Atticus giving a lesson to Cicero himself, pointing out the difference not so much between oratory and historiography as between the orator who can lie even when writing a historical work (Cleitarchus, Stratocles, Cicero himself, who prefers the "dramatic" version of Coriolanus' death) and the historian (Thucydides, Atticus) who holds to the facts (see Nicolai 1992: 86–87). It is precisely belonging to the literary system that guarantees that ancient historians had, in different forms and measures according to the genres and epochs, an awareness of the role of historiography and the duties of the historian.

Cicero, in his totalizing conception of rhetoric, declares that history is not treated in specific sections within rhetorical treatises (*De Or.* 2.64; cf. 2.62; Nicolai 1992: 95–96). He brings forward, however, a conception of rhetoric that is not technical, intending not so much to fill the gap as to demonstrate that the orator must master every situation and all the literary genres. The only link between the teachings of rhetoric and historical method can be found in the type of oratory that seems farthest from historiography: judicial oratory. In fact the testing of instruments of proof and the evaluation of clues and testimonies practiced in the courts certainly influenced many ancient historians, beginning with Thucydides (Butti de Lima 1996; Porciani 1997: 143ff., esp. 144 n. 173; Ginzburg 2000). The analogy between the historian and the orator who supplies his own partial (in both senses of the word) reconstruction of the facts contains in itself an obvious danger: just as the orator needs to convince the judge that his reconstruction, and only his, is the truth, so the historian must present himself as a convincing and authoritative narrator, being able to put into the background those facts that do not fit into his reconstruction. This danger is not exclusive, however, to rhetorically dominated cultures, such as Greece and Rome, but is also very strong in our own culture dominated by science and technology; the rhetoric of words is often replaced by rhetorics that are less glaring but more insidious: those of documents, statistics, and numbers.

If we ask ourselves which works of history entered into the teaching of grammarians and orators, we have to respond with a preliminary question: why did grammarians and orators look to historiography? An elementary necessity was that of providing models for literary language: Herodotus responded to this need for Ionic Greek, Thucydides and Xenophon for Attic, and the great Latin historians Sallust and Livy for Latin. A second necessity, specific to the grammarians, was that of the *historiarum enarratio*: to explain Aristophanes it was necessary to turn to Thucydides and Athenian local historians, and the same occurred with orators whose historical references were integrated and clarified through historiography. A third necessity was to have available a repertoire of *exempla* to introduce in support of appropriate arguments. If a complete reading of historical works that were always growing larger (from Polybius' 40 books to Livy's 142) required too much time, one could turn to the didactic poems, such as the four-book *Chronica* of Apollodorus of Athens (2nd c. BCE). In the first century BCE, brief usage manuals appeared for the schools of rhetoric. Cicero (*Orat.* 120) praises his friend Atticus "who has gathered together in one book the memory of seven hundred years, with the dates preserved and noted, and passing over nothing of importance." Similar summaries were made by Ateius Philologus for Sallust (Suet. *Gramm.* 10), by Cornelius Nepos and Varro, not to mention epitomes made of Polybius, Sallust, and Livy (Plut. *Brut.* 4.8; Stat. *Silv.* 4.7.53–56; Mart. 14.190). Even more directly used were collections of *exempla*, such as that of Valerius Maximus, who says in his preface that he has collected memorable facts and sayings "so that those wishing to gather examples may be spared a lengthy search." One can hypothesize that didactic poems and brief manuals were the only systematic narrations of history that regularly entered into ancient schools from the second century BCE. In fact, it is difficult to think that students of rhetoric read a complete "historical cycle" (on this concept see Canfora 1971) or even a universal history, such as that of Ephorus, or an ample *Historical Library* such as that by Diodorus in 40 books. Obviously the first and the third needs (models of style and a repertoire of *exempla*) concerned either teachers or students, the second (historians as sources for *historiarum enarratio*) dealt with grammarians only, who transmitted to their students the results of their research.

The historians, therefore, entered into ancient schools primarily as models of style; students were not introduced to local historians nor, thanks to the Atticism of the first century BCE, to the Hellenistic historians. (Local history was transmitted in appropriate recitations, *akroaseis*, such as those of the grammarian Ti. Claudius Anteros, mentioned in an inscription of 127 CE from Labraunda in Caria: Crampa 1972: 134–137.) A unique situation resulted: the narration of Greek history stops, generally, around the fourth century BCE (Herodotus, Thucydides, Xenophon, Ephorus, and Theopompus, to whom at times Anaximenes and Callisthenes were added); Timaeus and Polybius appear occasionally in the canon of historians (the first in Cic. *De Or.* 2.58, the second in the Byzantine canons). The Roman student could know his country's history through Sallust and Livy, and later through Tacitus. Polybius was a historian who was very popular, especially in Rome, but his simple and poor style doomed him (D. Hal. *Comp.* 4, II.20–21 U-R), and soon epitomes and then collections of *excerpta* appeared. A knowledge of all of Livy was precluded due above all to the size of his work: direct readings were limited to a few books; for the rest, one used epitomes not very different from the summaries (*periochae*) of his work that have come down to us.

5   Historiography's Audience

The use of historical works in grammatical and rhetorical schools allows us to pinpoint the main recipients of historical works among the social classes that had access to instruction. However, this apparently obvious formulation must be integrated and made more precise. First, the *logoi* of Herodotus were meant for public readings, in which a fairly heterogeneous public that was not necessarily very cultured could participate. The practice of public readings of historians continues for the whole of antiquity (Chaniotis 1988: 365–382) and is attested for the Middle Ages as well. Historical works were never school books in the modern sense: as we have seen, they could be utilized in different phases of instruction and for distinct tasks, but, with few exceptions (I refer to the didactic poems and synthetic manuals mentioned above, p. 22), were not conceived as a help for teaching. Those who had received the regular grammatical and rhetorical instruction could read historiography, but the reasons that impelled them to do so were very different. Polybius offers a possible picture of the potential public of historiography, based on their tastes and experiences (9.1.2–5, Paton tr., with modifications):

> I am not unaware that my work, owing to the uniformity of its composition, has a certain severity and will suit the taste and gain the approval of only one class of reader. For nearly all other writers, or at least most of them, by dealing with every branch of history, attract many kinds of people to the perusal of their works. The genealogical side appeals to those who are fond of a story, and the account of colonies (*apoikiai*), the foundations of cities (*ktiseis*) and their ties of kinship (*suggeneiai*), such as we find, for instance, in Ephorus, attracts the curious and lovers of recondite material, but accounts of the doings (*praxeis*) of nations, cities, and rulers attracts the political man (*politikos*). As I have confined my

attention strictly to these last matters and as my whole work treats of nothing else, it is, as I say, adapted only to one sort of audience, and reading it will have no attraction for the majority of people.

Polybius explains and updates Thucydides' general formulation (1.22.4: "in the hearing, the lack of a mythic element will perhaps seem less pleasurable") about the lack of success that he foresaw with regard to the public, and briefly delineates the sociology of the readers of history: the reader eager for stories is attracted by genealogies, the curious one by *apoikiai*, *ktiseis*, and *suggeneiai*, the one who deals with politics by *praxeis*. The reader defined as *politikos* is the one who wants to participate in public life or at least wants to understand the mechanics of it. His passion is not just a simple passion for fascinating reading or the curiosity of local history; rather, it is the matter of a reader who searches for utility, who does not look too much for elegance of style, who asks the historian to contribute to his formation as a citizen – all in all, a man of power. The portrait delineated by Polybius corresponds more to his ideal reader, to the public to whom the author wishes to address himself, than to a specific public. Interesting nonetheless is the schematic distinction between historians who deal with various topics in order to win over readers, and the almost completely isolated historian who concentrates on *praxeis*. We find ourselves before a customary binary opposition between pleasure (*delectatio*) and utility (*utilitas*), part of the programmatic remarks of Thucydides and one of the constants not only of historiographical theory, but also of ancient literature more generally. Polybius recognizes his relative isolation, but far from lamenting it, he embraces it: his aspiration is to emulate Thucydides, the great model whom he only once mentions in the surviving books.

Like many other Greek historians, Polybius was an exile, a man who held important positions, but when he writes his work, he is far distant from active political life. That many historians were concerned with the experience of exile was already noticed by Plutarch (*Exil.* 14, 605C), although over time the conditions under which historians worked changed (cf. Porciani 1997: viii: "After Thucydides the historians appear very integrated in the political and cultural texture of Greece"; cf. also Porciani 2001b: 25, 33–35). The Roman historians, although with few exceptions (Cato, Tacitus) part of the governing class, did not occupy political offices of the first rank (for the republican age see La Penna 1978: 43–104). Some dedicated themselves to historiography after abandoning active politics (Sallust, Asinius Pollio). Distance favors critical analysis, and, in some cases, one could think that historiography was felt as a sort of continuation of politics by other means (so Syme 1958b; Porciani 1997: viii): the political man who failed in action ennobles himself by becoming an educator of the ruling class and creating for himself an authoritative role. The principate radicalized the historian's position: some took sides with the emperors, falling at times into encomium (Velleius Paterculus), while others opposed them in the name of republican ideals (Titus Labienus, Cremutius Cordus), and the greatest historian of this period, Tacitus, tried to get to the roots of the empire by taking an increasingly pessimistic position. The censorship exercised by the government towards these authors is a new aspect of the ancient link between historiography and politics.

The position taken by historians in their confrontation with the power of the empire introduces another key theme, that of their relation to political power. The habitual attitude of the ancient historian was of keeping a certain distance from the events he narrated, and this contributed to the construction of his character as impartial and authoritative. However, there were many different positions: some historians (like Callisthenes and Ptolemy, the first historians of Alexander, who accompanied him in his enterprise) were involved personally in the events they narrated; others dedicated themselves to the genre of *commentarii*, supplying a partial version of the story focused on the author/protagonist; still others, like the historians of the opposition in the Imperial Age, exalted the ancient tyrannicides, such as Brutus and Cassius, and the martyrs who fell in defense of republican freedom. With these historians, unfortunately lost, history becomes in some way a testimony that keeps memory alive and shapes conscience. The term *memoria*, in fact, recurs with insistence in the prologue of Tacitus' *Agricola*. The surviving historian (3.2: "we are the survivors not only of others but also of ourselves") denounces the effects of Domitian's oppression, of which only the memory survives (2.3: "we would have lost memory itself together with our voice, if it had been as much in our power to forget as to be silent"), and concludes (3.3):

> Yet it will not be an unpleasant task to compose, even in an uncouth and rough style, the memory of our past slavery and a testimony of our present blessings. In the meantime this book, dedicated to the honor of my father-in-law Agricola, will be praised or perhaps excused as a profession of piety.

The role of historiography acquires a profound ethical dimension that is not limited to traditional moral judgment, but in difficult times takes for itself the task of preserving and transmitting memory. The historian is witness of the *virtus* of Agricola and it is his own *pietas* that is the most intimate justification for the work he has undertaken. One can see that same appeal to the function of history as testimony in the authors of the Gospels and Acts of the Apostles, who, at just about the same time, founded a religious doctrine based on the memory of events and of Jesus' teaching that moved beyond history towards transcendence.

FURTHER READING

The problem of locating historical knowledge and the historiographic genre in Greek and Roman culture is studied, sometimes superficially, in the main histories of ancient historiography. Generally in these investigations, the link between historiography and contemporary society gains more attention in the Roman world than in the Greek one: a noticeable example is Mazzarino 1965–1966: II.59–117. A synthesis is proposed in Porciani 2001b, which is attentive, above all, to the controversial relationship between history and rhetoric, a relationship that conditions the evaluation of the entire phenomenon of ancient historiography. Porciani follows and deepens the line traced by Momigliano 1975d, 1983, 1985, and in many of the studies collected in his *Contributi*. Finley 1965 is fundamental for the entire theme of myth and history. Marincola 1997 examines the critical question of the construction of authority for the historian. For the problem of the genres of historiography, their contents and their conventions, see Gabba 1981 and Marincola 1999. For the position of history in rhetorical and grammatical theory and the school use of historiography see Nicolai 1992. For methods of publication and the interaction between the historian and the public see Porciani 1997 and Thomas 2000, together with the classic study of Momigliano 1978. For the relation between historians and political powers in both republican and imperial Rome see La Penna 1978: 43–104 and Syme 1958a and 1958b. Chaniotis 1988 collects and expertly annotates the epigraphic documentation on the social position of the historian and his activities.

CHAPTER TWO

The Origin of Greek Historiography

Catherine Darbo-Peschanski

1   Terms of the Problem

Talking about the origin of Greek historiography is not easy; both "origin" and "historiography" are words leading to a dangerous path. So before one starts using these terms one needs to move cautiously and to evaluate the difficulties as well as the dead ends one might encounter.

In the study of the history of ideas and knowledge, Foucault (1994: 683–687) has shown that the notion of origin traditionally gives history the task to "awaken forgotten elements, to clear up what is hidden, and to erase – or secure again – barriers." If this is the case, it is linked on one hand to the subject, which in the course of time elaborates significations that it transcribes in discourse, and, on the other hand, to the implicit meaning of such discourse. In doing so, the significations are not always open or even yet conscious. It is then the responsibility of the historian, from a present analytical perspective, to demonstrate in the ideas of the past the divisions that are expressed in three metaphors: evolutionary, biological, and dynamic, distinguishing (respectively) what regresses as opposed to what adapts, what lives from the inert, and movement from immobility.

As for the notion of historiography, it is a threefold one. First, it means historical consciousness. One can say then with Veyne (1971: 99) that human beings have always had such a consciousness because they have always known that "humanity was evolving and its collective life was dependent upon its actions and passions"; but one also knows that this conscience is dependent on a particular history. This history concerns the forms of historicity, i.e., the ways (which are historically and culturally

Translated by Virginie Lorang-Woodward and Carolyn Dewald.

variable) of conceiving of development and its dynamic (Darbo-Peschanski 2000, 2001), or the emphasis on the relationships, themselves variable, between past, present, and future (Sahlins 1985: 9–19), as well as on the extension and the importance given to each of these segments of time (Koselleck 1989, esp. 119–131; Hartog 2003: 22–27, 33–39). Second, it is a form of knowledge: historical knowledge. Finally, as its name suggests, "historiography" goes back to a genre of written discourse, a literary genre.

Many questions, then, need to be answered. Is historiography merely the giving of form to historical research, a discourse transcribing its significations and its methods? If so, the only thing left to do would be to create its history and, as has been said before about the traditional history of ideas, to locate its delays, its ruptures, its advances, its enduring aspects and survivals.

One will notice, for example, an epistemological gap between historical research based on direct experience (or the report of direct experience), primarily visual, and research based on traces, relying on documentation (see Pomian 1984: 20ff.; Ginzburg 1989: 139–180; Ricoeur 1983–1985: III.171–183). The ancients, and the Greeks in particular, could not have *known*, could not have *been able to* have access to the second stage. They could not have given thought to establishing a hierarchy of sources, primary versus secondary.

If the accepted criteria involve the secular demand for truth, then in Greece itself the break is situated with Hecataeus of Miletus, according to Jacoby (1926). The fragment from the *Genealogies* in which Hecataeus "laughs" at the multitude of tales among the Greeks (*FGrHist* 1 F 1a) would be, in effect, the birth of historical reason, simultaneously a critical point of view and a quest for truth, or the way in which criticism serves truth.

Greek history, even as imperfect as it is, would then be the conclusion of a progressive conquest, built on displacements and adaptations, of progress and decadence. It would be the daughter of "Ionian *science*" (so one might translate *historiē*: see Thomas 2000: 270), which was characterized by the attention given to phenomena and by the wish to explain rationally the movement of nature which generates the phenomena. Hence the so-called ethnographic or geographic dimensions that one can see not only in Anaximander but also in Hecataeus or Herodotus. In this perspective the forms of its birth can be varied: either one observes that from Hecataeus onward, inquiry dedicated to observable phenomena in the present could henceforth be applied to past events, and one decides that in this way history was born; or one sees within the work of Herodotus a fundamental change, which joins an attention to morals, customs, and geography to a historical framework (cf. Drews 1973: 45–93). But if this is the case, two other positions have to be considered. In the first, history, in Herodotus' work, would be the result of the encounter of epic with Ionian *historiē*, the one, through the Trojan War, giving form to the major "historical" intrigue of the conflict between the Greek west and Asiatic east, the other applying itself to the search for rational explanations of natural phenomena (Pohlenz 1937: 190–196; Schwartz 1928; Schadewaldt 1934; cf. Jacoby 1913a: 352–360). The second position would see history arising in spite of this confluence (e.g., Fornara 1983: 17ff.). The differences, however, matter little: in every case history is born from a displacement of the object of *historia*, which will have led to a methodological adaptation.

The essential adaptation will have concerned the use of *autopsy* or personal visual experience, which is implicit in the very etymology of the word *historiē/a*, directly derived from the noun *histōr*, itself derived from the root **wid* meaning "see" and which also gives the verb *oida*, "I know." Just as *histōr* means "the one who knows because he has seen" (Benvéniste 1948: 29, 32, 35, 51), so *historiē* would be, or would prepare one for, a knowledge founded more specifically on visual observation (see, e.g., Müller 1926; Nenci 1955). Although essential in studies of the physical world, autopsy could not have been practiced as fully or directly when it was a matter of knowing the course of events and, moreover, past events (Schepens 1980: 44–45; cf. Zangara forthcoming). All that was left for history was to perfect itself. With Thucydides, Greek historiography would have reached its apex, at least within the limits of its methodology (Jacoby 1926: 87). For certain people, including Ranke himself, history, to all intents and purposes, already existed, at least as long as rhetorical games did not get in the way of its vigor and its capacities for progress (Schwartz 1928; cf. Humphreys 1997: 208).

In considering the origin of Greek historiography, a recent trend in scholarship has deliberately inverted the way in which the relationship between, indeed the assimilation of, writing and historical knowledge operates. Discourse is no longer considered as the simple translation of the epistemological evolution of the Greek subject, but is viewed rather as the very locus of its appearance; discourse no longer reflects the mode of historical knowledge but is the very instrument of its emergence (e.g., Lateiner 1989: 6). This is more a shift, however, than a radical change, because it is still necessary to designate the origin (in the present case, the text) starting from an idea of historical knowledge that has been necessarily imported. The hard part is showing *how* writing helped it to emerge and recognizing it in its first stirrings or sounds, because it creates the possibility of later historical productions where this idea will be developed and asserted (though not without obstacles and delays).

Herodotus' text, ancient, expansive, and complex as it is, which presents itself moreover as a "display of *historiē*" (*praef.*), lends itself perfectly to the kind of reading which, using all the resources of narratology, explores both its most prominent and its most subtle thematic and formal structures. A large and profitable body of analytical work has also revealed the mechanisms by which the narrator sets himself into the text and creates, under various forms, a presence and even an "authorial" authority.

But the idea of historical knowledge on which this work depends is a weakened form of something valid for us because of centuries of thinking about history. Indeed, through scattered remarks rather than in characteristic theoretical developments, it associates references to the development of a method of scientific approach that took place within, for instance, the framework of positivist history or the work of the Annales School on temporal rhythms and the objects that determine each among them. One also finds the traces of the semantics of relationships between micro- and macroanalysis or of the need to take into account the "temporal reconfiguration" that the narrative effects (Ricoeur 1983–1985), the subtleties of its explanatory logic, and the relationships that truth and fiction maintain within it.

Thus history would be born, in the Herodotean narrative, from the establishment of a *narrative schema* (the series of conquests leading to the establishment and expansion of the Persian empire) *that integrates and coordinates* the most diverse accounts up to Book 5, and then becomes the theme for the books that follow. It would also be born from the fact that the story conforms to *rules of factual verification* and that it analyzes the *causes* in order to deliver a *rational and non-fictional account (apodexis) of the movements of history.* Narrative reconfiguration, a method guaranteeing conformity to the facts, rationality, design of truth – such are the components of the concept that one seeks to recognize in Herodotus' work. It can also be seen as the interpenetration between history as rhetoric and history as human science, through the study of the "double voice" of the Herodotean narrator: one voice relating the accounts while the other critiques them. Indeed, the voice of the narrator appears in many cases as an implicit extension of that of the critic, as well as simultaneously encoding in the text "the sense of dialogism that is essential to the invention of history as a human science" (Dewald 2002: 286). History is thus defined as historiography, that is to say, inextricably linked to a story of multipolar origin that develops while explaining background details and causal relationships.

But historiography can also be seen as *the place* where implicit or explicit notions of historicity are inscribed. It has been shown (Meier 1987) that the Greeks did not possess our present-day concept of history. Suppose, for example, that two ideal types of history (*Geschichte*) can be isolated: a history of actions and events in which a limited number of subjects interact with one another in a contingent manner, in the frame of limited sequences of events (battles, diplomatic missions, etc.); and a history of processes in which everything is moved according to forces independent of individual actions and without any possible comparison with particular events: "a radical change of all the conditions of life" and "a force with a movement over which the individual person has very little control." For the Greeks, only individual phenomena would have occurred, which were not then integrated into a comprehensive process. As for Herodotus, he would differentiate himself somewhat since, while maintaining a multisubjective and contingent approach to history, he would organize it according to relatively long sequences that covered several generations.

Thus, one folds back history and historicity onto historiography as if they overlapped exactly. The reactions to this type of overlapping are of two orders: dissociation and enlarging/broadening. The first consists in temporarily emancipating historicity from the two other terms, history and historiography. If all that matters is to narrate the past and to interest oneself in the development of this or that individual or society, one can then go back further than Herodotus, leaving behind texts traditionally called historiographical, and take as witness other older texts. Any account of what occurs and has occurred will do, whatever its form, whatever its genre: whence works devoted to historiography that start with Homer (e.g., Marincola 2001), or studies that stress the historical dimension of elegiac poetry (e.g., Boedeker 1995, 1996). The result is to considerably extend the dimensions of the field of historiography. One gives historical consciousness its largest sense if one refuses to stick exclusively to the canons of positivist method in order to integrate what later epistemological research has introduced: objects other than those of political events, because drawn according to slower temporal rhythms. These include the explanatory resources and logic of the narrative; acknowledging the heuristic value of fiction; study of the mechanisms of the tradition, of transmission and of memory. If we proceed in this way, Herodotus has his place after the other texts where the Greeks spoke about their past.

The second reaction consists in refusing a premature amputation of the discipline and putting forward the cognitive activity that is *historiē*, rather than talking right away about history or historiography. In particular, it is a question of returning Herodotus to the intellectual field which is his in the second half of the fifth century: a field in which medicine, philosophy of nature, and rhetoric are in consonance, exchanging their topics, structures of reasoning, argumentative modes, and agonistic characteristics. The problem is that this setting in context does not manage to take into account what specifically in Herodotean *historia* concerns human actions in the past, other than by making of it a survival (Thomas 2000: 285), because *historia* has now too radically, and perhaps anachronistically, been assimilated to science.

Consequently, how does one try once again to move our *aporiai* away from the questions of origins? Initially, no doubt, by speaking Greek, since one is dealing with Greece: that is to say, *historia*, a word one will not be too quick to translate as "science," nor analyze from its morphological derivations in modern languages, but whose aspects will be studied in context. To speak Greek and study Greek concepts in their contextual relations with others makes it possible, in effect, to place oneself in Greek culture and its actual history.

In the second place, one must be careful not to confuse historicity, historical consciousness, and historiography. The question to be asked is, how, in the unity of the cognitive steps that qualify as *historia*, did the type of written composition called *historia* which specialized in the account of human actions in time develop, and within the framework of which forms of historicity? This means, as has been previously said, that one does not believe it is possible to assign a place and a moment of birth to the Greek conscience of development (historicity); rather, one believes that its successive forms can be analyzed. Here one seeks what the Greeks teach us about the birth of a literary genre (*historia*), a birth which must be correlated with a mode of knowledge that is characteristically Greek (*historia*).

2 *Historiographos, Historia*

The Greeks begin rather late to speak of *historia* as a genre of written composition. The title "*historia*," or "*historia peri phuseōs*," given to many works dated from the end of the sixth or the beginning of the fifth century, occurs in fact only in later testimonia that refer to them, beginning in the fourth century at the earliest. The term *historiographos* (writer of *historia*) seems to appear later still, certainly by the third century BCE, within the framework of the phenomenon of professionalization of the Hellenistic age (Polybius presumes the currency of the word: 2.62.3, 8.11.2, etc.). When, at the end of the sixth century, Heraclitus attacks Pythagoras, *historiē* is still a cognitive operation, condemnable in fact because of a diversity which prevents it from reaching authentic knowledge (*VS* 22 B 129):

> Pythagoras, son of Mnesarchus, practised *historiē* beyond all other men and, having made a selection (*eklexamenos*) of these written compositions (*tas suggraphas*), claimed for his own a wisdom (*epoiēsato heautou sophiēn*), which was multiple learning (*polumathiēn*), and an art/science of bad quality (*kakotechniēn*).

If it is a question of written compositions here, *historia* is not one. Indeed, it indicates very clearly a *form of choice* in a preliminary written material or in inquiries that are not defined. It is a question of *discriminating* among the various and the multiple, in order to turn them into knowledge of the same type: a *polymathy.*

Herodotus also speaks of *historia* merely to designate a form of research, and presents his work as an *apodexis* or a *logos* (e.g., 1.5), without other qualification and without attributing to himself the specific title of editor. However, whereas up to this point *historia* floats in a nebula without contours and is practiced without inscribing itself into a discursive genre, Thucydides takes a different position in the matter, one that makes possible the appearance of *historia* as a literary genre. Indeed, on the one hand he gives his activity the name of "examination" (*zētēsis*), a term which is moreover very vague and general, but one that has the virtue of setting at a distance the specifically cognitive practice of *historia*. On the other hand, he also characterizes it as a particular form of writing; he "composes by writing" (*suggraphein, suggraphē*). Research, however, is not the first step in the establishment of the facts, which the composition then puts into its final form. Indeed, in Thucydides the reality of events is not worked out. It is not grasped because of the cutting one performs on it, or because of the innumerable and indeed infinite emplotments by which one travels through it; rather, it exists objectively in a given form and it offers this form for understanding (positivist history shares this conviction). Consequently indeed, such "material" has only to be collected; everything centers on the question of the quality of one's dispositions for reception, and research consists of the use of these dispositions. At the heart of these is precision (*akribiē*: Thuc. 1.22.2), which guides the uncompromising choice of traditions (Thuc. 1.20.1: one must "torture" the traditions, because it is reprehensible to accept them as they are [*abasanistōs dechesthai*]) and which supports constant effort (Thuc. 1.22.3: *epiponōs*).

Thus, as Loraux (1980) has demonstrated, the work of Thucydides offers itself up as reality itself without any interpretive distance: "Thucydides has composed the Peloponnesian War by writing": this is not to say that Thucydides composed a book entitled *The Peloponnesian War*, but rather that he operates on the war itself. This is so because, in every case, he knows how to recognize the kernel of reality beneath the shell of words, beneath the charges which the belligerents exchange, the truest of causes, as well as their concerns and their passions (1.9.1–5). When it is a question of oral discourse, he knows how to restore the foundation (*gnōmē*) of truth beneath the fabric of other words (Woodman 1988: 1–40). How? Thucydides does not say, not because he does not wish to say and hides a method that would bring him closer to positivist historians (Vercruysse 1990: 17), but because there is nothing to say about it. His research is more of an ethical method than a cognitive one.

This in turn makes it possible, moreover, to rely on what the mass of one's predecessors wrote, no matter what the quality of what they said. Thucydides considers that the period preceding the Peloponnesian War had been told by others (Homer, Herodotus, Hellanicus) and that one can find within them the substrata of reality. However, in the objective course of time that the events, in themselves objective, reveal, previous historians have left large sections unnarrated. It is, therefore, these gaps that must be filled. In effect, Thucydides says (1.97.2; the translation tries to exploit the spatio-temporal representation of time):

> If I have written the preceding and if I have made this digression, it is because all of my predecessors have left this *space* (*chōrion*) aside and have gathered together in writing either Greek affairs *before* the Persian wars or the Persian wars themselves (*ē ta pro tōn mēdikōn Hellēnika xunetithesan ē auta ta mēdika*). The one of them who wrote a composition on Attica evoked it rapidly and *without temporal precision* (*tois chronois ouk akribōs*).

Thus Thucydides provides the "Archaeology" – which stretches just to the point of the Persian Wars – and the great analepsis of the *Pentecontaetia*, which treats from the end of the Persian Wars to the beginning of the Peloponnesian War. The objectivity of the facts and of their spatio-temporal coordinates renders the types of accounts that treat them indifferent, so that one can, even by scorning their principles of composition and their aims, link one's own account to them.

Two consequences result from this. First of all, Thucydides initiates the mechanism of the continuity of accounts, which is only the setting in words of the temporal continuity of the events. There is no question of claiming here that one is dealing with a survival of the continuations of epic. As Aristotle (*Poet.* 1455b15–16, 1456a10–16) later emphasizes, when the epics follow one another, they are laid on the substrate of a traditional account (*logos*), for example, the Trojan War, and from it they cut out shards of narrative intrigue on which to compose a song, for example, the return of the heroes of the war or those of their descendants. In the form of continuation that Thucydides inaugurates, it is time (*chronos*), which centuries of study of physical nature and mathematical work had taught men at the end of the fifth century BCE to consider as continuous, that is used as substrate.

Xenophon in turn links his story to that of Thucydides in the manner of "after which" (*meta de tauta*) and, at the end of *Hellenica*, invites another man to do the same (7.5.27):

> As far as I am concerned, my work will stop here; another man will perhaps concern himself with what follows (*ta meta de tauta*).

Photius (*Bibl.* 121a23–36) says that Isocrates had entrusted to Ephorus the treatment of the periods "previous to" those narrated by Thucydides, and to Theopompus those that came "after," according to the idea that it is necessary to have a chronology uniting all the Greeks that goes back to the "Return of the Heracleidae." Moreover, Demophilus, who happened also to be the son of Ephorus (i.e., one personally "inscribed" in a genealogical time that redoubles one temporal sequence with another), begins his work where his father completed his (Diod. 16.14.3). Posidonius and Strabo link their work to Polybius' by extending his narrative, with some variation, over other periods. In addition, it is enough to modify or change the topic of chronology so that other sequels become possible, in a neutral or polemical manner. Nor does anything stand in the way of the same temporal segment giving rise to several accounts. Callisthenes chooses to tell the stories of Greece while using the same caesura – the Peace of Antalcidas – that Polybius uses to tell the destiny of Rome (Diod. 14.117.8). "Partial" narratives, which deal with only one part of the world for a time, can also be integrated into a "universal" narrative, that is, one that takes into account all the populated parts of the world (or almost all of it). Polybius thus continues several predecessors: Timaeus for Sicilian affairs and Aratus of Sicyon for some Greek affairs. Finally, certain works attempt to retrace all that has occurred since the most distant times (*archaia*: things which are close to the *archē*, or beginning; or *palaia*, very old things), up to the moment of the writer's composition. Their own continuity allows them to embrace that of the time of human events. One could continue to multiply examples (see Marincola 1997: 289–292 for a chart of continuators). But for whatever solution is adopted – continuing an account, treating the course of events in their entirety, or supplementing the gaps between other accounts – it is a question of creating a coherent temporal framework.

Consequently, heterogeneous practices find themselves joined together in the same discursive unit, so that the *historia* of Herodotus and the *suggraphē* of Thucydides quickly become interchangeable. The *suggraphē* that *historia* initially seems to have subsumed under its name (Arist. *Poet.* 9, 1451b1–7) becomes its synonym, and, in a complete reversal, comes to indicate the genre of which *historia* is then the species: that of the "written composition," in this case, in prose as opposed to poetry. Dionysius of Halicarnassus (e.g., *AR* 1.4.3; *Thuc.* 19.2) employs on occasion the expression "to write histories" (*graphein historias*) to designate the activity of the *suggrapheus*, while Ammonius, a lexicographer of the first or second century CE, and author of a treatise on the differences of synonymous expressions, sees in *historia* a form of *suggraphein*. While trying to distinguish *historiographos* from *suggrapheus*, he specifies in effect that the latter indicates the one who gathers by writing (*sug-graphomenos*) what has occurred in the past, while the former does the same for events of the present (*Diff.* 250).

The phenomenon of narrative continuation, based on the idea of continuity of time and on that of the objectivity of facts, thus made it possible to constitute a genre which, *a posteriori*, has absorbed in itself the Herodotean exposition of *historia*, from which Thucydides, however, had taken great care to be dissociated. *Historia* as a genre is a matter of retroactive assimilation. It follows that the unit thus composed rests neither on a commonality of method nor on the same philosophy of history. But the ontological status which is lent to the facts and the claim of truth that renews again and again each of the narratives like that of Thucydides have given them an air of resemblance to positivist history. This positivist history never ceases plumbing those depths using its method, and has continuously been disappointed never to find it there.

Two questions then remain on hold. The first concerns the *historia* of Herodotus. If it is a mode of knowledge and became a form of written composition only by the retroactive effect of the narrative sequence carried out by Thucydides' *syggraphē*, what is this mode of knowledge and what does it share with all the other *historiai*? The second question asks why Thucydides breaks with the mode of knowledge that is *historia*, while preserving only the link (in his view completely exterior) of chronology with his predecessor's work.

3 "Historical" Understanding

Historia indicates a cognitive step whose first details show that its unity did not lie in an exclusive relationship with what had occurred and the time which can be "reconfigured" in a narrative – in other words, in an exclusive relationship with something like history. One can even say, going back to Heraclitus on Pythagoras, together with what Herodotus asserts, that *historia* was neither originally nor exclusively attached to history.

If one wants to take account of the full extension of its uses, it appears then that its unity is found in the structure of the cognitive operation in which it is inscribed, a double structure that one could define as that of a *judged judgment* ("judgment" being understood in either its epistemic or legal sense). *Historia* is a first judgment (or group of judgments) made about the phenomena by a first authority. It will itself be the object of a new judgment, this time a decisive one, emanating from a second authority. It thus constitutes an operation necessary but not autonomous, which leads to a ruling on what is just or real, and sometimes on both when reality is justice, as in Herodotus (see Darbo-Peschanski 1998).

Let us look at three examples. First, the *historia* of which Heraclitus speaks in connection with Pythagoras (above, p. 32). Pythagoras attains, according to Heraclitus, a knowledge only of the various and the multiple (*polymathy*) rather than a single knowledge of a different nature (a *sophiē*). For Heraclitus, knowledge/wisdom (*to sophon*) consists in effect of "knowing that a thought (*gnōmē*) governs all through all" (*VS* 22 B 41). In his criticism of Pythagoras, he thus gives *historia* the form of a judgment related to the data of experience, which must be subjected in its turn to reason, because only the order of the *logos* coincides with knowledge. Because one has a knowledge that is only individual ("knowledge specific to itself") and which cannot master diversity and plurality, it becomes itself plural and false ("multiple learning/art of bad quality").

Second, there is the *historia peri phuseōs* that Plato attributes to Anaxagoras. Here again one sees in yet another way the double structure of a judged judgment, although Plato, by refusing to take into account a knowledge rooted in the phenomena, polemically attributes to it the claim of being in itself a knowledge of causes sufficient to stop wisdom. As with all "wisdom" (*sophia*) of this type, it is supposed, he says, "to know the causes of each thing, under the terms of which each one comes to existence, under the terms of which it perishes, under the terms of which it exists" (*Phaedo* 98b5–e1). Anaxagoras, however, gives a single causal principle to each thing: Mind (*Nous*). But as soon as it is a question of knowing the causes of the order of things in detail, he makes nothing more of Mind and interposes between it and reality a quantity of other causes. One would thus confuse what is really a cause with that without which a cause cannot be a cause (*Phaedo* 99b3–4).

Anaxagoras' physics indeed establishes a hiatus, but also a form of continuity, between the fundamental reality of the world governed by Mind and what we can perceive of it. Mind (*Nous*) has set in motion a material mixture made of germs or seeds (*spermata*) unlimited in number and smallness (*VS* 59 B 1, 4), inducing separations and recombinations from which bodies come. In this, *Nous* is an efficient cause of what exists. But the seeds are not atoms, the ultimate degree of smallness, from the composition of which bodies are made. Infinitude of smallness in matter prohibits it. So there is a real gap between the reality of the matter moved by Mind and what actually appears to us, but it is a matter only of that which increases the limitations of the capacities of the senses to know the infinite smallness of the mixtures that are the seeds and the number of things differentiated. Because of their weakness, Anaxagoras denies to the senses the role of judges of truth (*VS* 59 B 21), but can affirm that "the phenomena are the sight for invisible entities" (*opsis tōn adēlōn ta phainomena, VS* 59 B 21a). It will then be necessary to apply oneself to the study of the phenomena and to *judge* their causes, which is what Plato gives both as task and as limit to the *historia peri phuseōs* of Anaxagoras.

Plato, however, for his part, stops Anaxagoras' step towards *historia* and, by doing so, isolates it from a cognitive movement in which it does not have full autonomy, although it still constitutes a necessary part. By radically separating the cause that is *Nous* from the swarm of other causes and by posing a radical incompatibility between the two systems of explanation, he refuses to take into account the continuity that Anaxagoras establishes between perceptible reality and imperceptible reality, and perhaps between the knowledge of *Nous* and that of some "of the things possessing Mind in themselves" (*VS* 59 B 11). If one maintains with Plato that Anaxagoras was really engaged in a *historia peri phuseōs*, it is nevertheless necessary to restore to it the character of which it was deprived by the Platonic problematic, and which does not seem to contradict in any way our hypothetical definition. We are dealing with research into the causes of perceptible reality, thus with an ensemble of judgments that deal with the data of sensory experience, but which do not suffice in and of themselves and must be related to the *supreme cause* that is *Nous*, and by a more subtle mode of knowledge, in the same category as that of *Nous* itself, which loses its affinity with phenomena in order to effect their imperceptible foundations.

Finally, there is Herodotus. For him, the phenomenal objects of *historia* are "those things that have come into existence by the acts of men" (*ta genomena ex anthrōpōn, praef.*), the grand deeds that the Greeks and barbarians have made manifest and thus are given for observation (*apodechthenta*) – that is, the entire material that time threatens to eradicate by eroding the perception that one can have of it (*exitēla, aklea*), everything that one observes or hears through the narrative. His *historia* does not refute the hypothesis of definition advanced above. This hypothesis marks in effect its connection to the judiciary activity of the *histōr*, well attested in *Iliad* 18, most notably in the description of the famous scene represented on Achilles' shield. The *histōr*, solicited by both parties, is embodied in the ancient judges who render their sentence at the end of the scene and, like them, would also be the object of a judgment on the question of knowing who has pronounced the straightest judgment. He has knowledge of the totality of the cause, yet he too cannot escape the procedure of judged judgment that remits the definitive sentence, itself superior to that of the judges, perhaps the sentence of the people assembled around them. In Herodotean *historia*, where, as has been said, all reality is a matter for justice, the investigator gathers diverse accounts of the same event and, either tacitly by writing them in his text or explicitly by giving his own opinion (*doxa*) on events in relation to other opinions, judges them in the first instance. However, in the second and last instances, it is to the reader/auditor, invited repeatedly in programmatic declarations throughout the entire work to choose on the basis of his own convictions, that the right to give the final judgment belongs.

4   The Thucydidean Rupture

In order to respond to the second of the two questions posed above, i.e., the reason for Thucydides' rupture with the mode of knowledge that is Herodotean *historia*, it is necessary to introduce a change in the form of historicity. For Thucydides, in fact, the order of development ceases to correspond to the balance of the offenses against justice, and the reparations that reestablish it. Admittedly, the protagonists of the Peloponnesian War continue to exchange accusations in order to justify their actions, but "what is just" is henceforth an object of discourse without end, redefined and inverted into its opposite, while the reality of events depends on other issues altogether.

For example, there is the fear of the expansion of Athenian power that preoccupies the Peloponnesians (Thuc. 1.23.6). There is no need to resort to a form of aspiring judicial consciousness as in the work of his predecessor. Instead, from now on, human nature (*anthrōpeia phusis*), always identical to itself (3.82, 84), is the principle that animates the course of events and suggests by its very permanence situations which, despite their novelty, will be no less analogous.

The rejection of Herodotean *historia*, rendered inoperable since events are no longer driven by justice, is coupled with the type of *logos* associated with *historia*. The author of the *Peloponnesian War* is indeed wary of uncontrolled chattering coming from the depths of the ages and from different groups. One must "put it to the torture" (*basanizein*) in order to extract from it a degree of truth. (Athenian justice could make slaves testify under torture: if the words were not forced, they did not have any truth-value.) One cannot invite it, as in *historia*, to speak itself in the abundance of its sources of enunciation in the hope of judging it, while confusing what it is with what one decides to admit into the record as such. The plural *logos* of

Herodotus will be nothing more than subsidiary material, while the essence of the historian's work is provided by the real experience (or at least the claim of it) of the author of *The Peloponnesian War*. *Logos* thus identifies itself with political reason, the privilege of certain leaders and of the author. It is then due to this "logical" dimension that the work can, in Thucydides' view, be utilized "analogically," in order to understand comparable situations to come and become thus a "treasure for all time" (1.22.4).

One can, therefore, think of the origin of Greek historiography as the confluence of a mode of knowledge proper to the Greeks (*historia*), a modification of the form of historicity, and a form of its continuation, in which the continuity of the narratives is presumed to reflect, in a supposedly objective manner, the course of events.

FURTHER READING

For a global approach to Greek historiography see Hornblower 1994a; Marincola 1997, 2001; and Shrimpton 1997. On the question of historical methodology see Loraux 1980, and for the question of historicity and the Greeks see Hartog 1998 and Darbo-Peschanski 2001. Finally, on Herodotus and/or the beginnings of history in Greece, see Boedeker 1987 and Bakker et al. 2002.

CHAPTER THREE

History and *Historia*: Inquiry in the Greek Historians

Guido Schepens

1 Introduction: The Long-Lasting "Greek" Tradition of Historical Research

In the twilight of antiquity the fourth-century CE Roman historian Ammianus stated that he wrote his work as a former soldier and in the Greek fashion – *ut miles quondam et Graecus* (31.16.9). With this *sphragis* the author set himself consciously in the tradition of Greek predecessors like Thucydides and Polybius, who appealed to their own observation and interrogation of eyewitnesses as conferring authority on their accounts of contemporary history. Applying a similar method for narrating the events of his own lifetime, Ammianus had written: "Using every effort to investigate the truth, I have set out, in the order of their occurrence, events which my age allowed me to see myself or to know by thorough questioning of those who took part in them" (15.1.1; cf. Barnes 1998: 66; Matthews 1989: 454–464). The passage is a strikingly "classic" formulation of the method of personal inquiry in history: it envisages *veritas* as the result of a process of research and evaluation (*scrutari*) through autopsy or the careful interrogation of participants in the events. Ammianus' affinity with this research tradition is likewise displayed in his geographical and ethnographical accounts and in other digressions on a wide variety of topics, in which he claims, in true Herodotean fashion, autopsy of the phenomena described (e.g., 14.4.6; 17.4.6; 22.8.1; 23.6.36). What it means for Ammianus to belong to the Greek tradition is intimated in one of these excursions. Introducing the Augustan historian Timagenes as an authority on the ethnography of Gaul, he identifies him as "a *Greek*, in diligence and in language" (15.9.2). The order of the words *et diligentia Graecus et lingua* is significant: "it is his expertise in research that stamps Timagenes as a Greek even more than the language in which he wrote" (Barnes 1998: 66).

At the time of Ammianus' writing, some 900 years had passed since the intellectual revolution of Ionian *historiē* had given rise to the tradition of inquiry he seems to refer to in particular. Actually, with its literary pedigree in the epic poets' appeal to the Muse, the truth-claim based on "autopsy" was a few centuries older still. The poets call on the Muses as goddesses "who are present and know all things"; mortals, by contrast, "have heard only the rumor of it, and know nothing" (Hom. *Il.* 2.484–493; cf. Accame 1964). In the *Odyssey* (8.487–491) Demodocus is praised for narrating the sufferings and toils of the Achaeans with a degree of clarity "as if you were present yourself, or heard it from one who was." While his narrative is still Muse-inspired, the qualification "as if" is a remarkable anticipation of the "emanci-pated" method of the later historians (Hartog 1998: 131–133). More telling examples from the *Odyssey* could be cited which privilege the information obtained from seeing over and against hearsay (see Marincola 1997: 63–64). But "history" came into existence as a self-conscious break with epic literature as soon as an author – assuming the persona of "inquirer" – took responsibility himself for giving an account of human affairs in the past. Herodotus' preface is, as far as we can tell, the first instance of the use of *historiē* in this sense of the word.

The word *historia* (*historiē* in Herodotus' Ionian dialect) derives from the Greek transitive verb *historein*, which primarily means "to learn by inquiry," i.e., active learning. Much has been written on the origin of the Greek historians' spirit of inquiry in Ionian culture. Herodotus' background and education leave no doubt that he was in many different ways influenced by the outburst of intellectual activity in the cities of Asia Minor, from Thales onwards. But given the many connotations attached to the concept of *historiē* – starting from epic tradition, through its use by the pre-Socratics, where it includes critical investigation of all "nature" (*physis*), to the teachings of contemporary medical schools (Lateiner 1986; cf. Thomas 2000) – there is a growing awareness that it may be counterproductive to try to identify the author of the *Histories* as an adherent of any particular school of thought. Herodotus' various research practices make it *a priori* unlikely (*pace* Sauge 1992) that the word put on prominent display in the opening line of his work would not (or not yet) have the broad, generic meaning of "research" or "inquiry." Attempts to connect his *historiē* with a particular field of investigation (either geographical, ethnographical, or historical: Drews 1973) or to scale down its polyphonic largess (Lateiner 1989: 56) to one privileged central meaning – be it seeing, questioning, judging, or hearing – fail to convince. *All* these modes of inquiry are involved in Herodotus' active quest for data (see Hdt. 2.99.1; cf. Müller 1926; Bakker 2002: 15–19, with reservations with regard to "seeing"). With its various layers of meaning, *historiē* functions in Herod-otus' work as a *mot carrefour*, indicating an intellectual activity rather than a particular field in which it would operate (Hartog 2001a: 27–28; Lachenaud 2004: 12–19). It is appropriate, then, to stress the open character of the notion and the rich potential for further development that seems to be inherent in Herodotus' under-standing of the concept of *historiē*. At a time when "history" writing is beginning to find its feet in the intellectual ferment of fifth-century Ionia and Athens, this sounds very promising, even when we have to acknowledge that Herodotus' work, which was deemed a *historical* account only in retrospect, may predate any formal awareness of "history" as a genre (cf. Boedeker 2000).

But to quote Momigliano (1990: 59), "Thucydides saw to it that Herodotus should not prevail." Indeed, the former's impressive account of the Peloponnesian War, written entirely on the basis of visual evidence, is widely regarded by scholars as the perfect, emblematic realization of the Greek idea of historical inquiry. Jacoby (1926: 95) felt that historiography reached its *telos* in Thucydides. Today this view, although stripped of its problematic evolutionary and teleological presuppositions, is still very much alive: it runs like a guiding thread through a recent collection of essays (Hartog 2005). The root meaning of *historiē* (*wid-, *weid-, *woid-, "see" or "know" for having seen) would seem to have crystallized in the work of Thucydides. And the influence exerted by him on all subsequent Greek historians would have been the decisive factor in narrowing down the idea of "proper" history writing to a narrative of events more or less contemporary with the writer (*Zeitgeschichte*, in Jacoby's definition). Such, at least, is the main thrust of Momigliano's seminal articles (1990: 29–79) where he explains how in consequence of the "fact" that Thucydides was "chosen as model historian," history became a narration of political and military events, with preference given to the events which the writer had witnessed. "All the classic historians," argues Momigliano, "conformed to this pattern," pointing out that Polybius accepted "all the fundamentals of Thucydides' method" (Momigliano 1990: 59, 47). In this view there is one distinct line of thought from the invocation of the "omnivision" and "omniscience" of the Muses through Thucydides and the entire tradition of ancient and western historiography up to Gibbon: "the history of western historiography can be written in counterpoint of a history of the eye and of vision" (Hartog 2005: 33).

One of the problems we will address in this chapter is the issue of the value and representativeness of Polybius' views. In close connection with this, we will also have to see whether or not the evidence that can still be gleaned from the fragmentary remains of post-Thucydidean historiography tends to support the static and monolithic view of its (non-)development that has been outlined above. In addition to the fundamental ideological and methodological critical observations Humphreys (1997) has made about the failure of modern scholars to devote appropriate attention to the proper dynamics of post-Thucydidean Greek historiography, we may ask the following simple question: Should not the very fact that Thucydides avoided – deliberately, it would seem – using the word *historiē* in itself be enough to inspire second thoughts? (Cf. Shrimpton 2003, although I do agree with all of his observations.)

Etymological speculation that would restrict *historia* to contemporary history written on the basis of eyewitness accounts appears only late in antiquity, notably in Servius' tentative but problematic definition opposing *historia* and *annales* (Dietz 1995: 84–95; equally misleading is Isidore's definition of *historia, Orig.* 1.41.1–2). Herodotus, for one, is not afraid of using the phrase *akoē historeōn* (2.29.1). Equally controversial is the possible linguistic support (Floyd 1990) for the otherwise interesting view that would model Herodotus' intellectual activity as a *historian* on the task of the *histōr* or *istōr*. According to the evidence of the Homeric poems, archaic poetry, and inscriptions, the *histōr* acts as "arbitrator," weighing up the conflicting claims of contending parties (cf. Connor 1993). To pass judgment is, definitely, an important aspect of most Greek historians' conception of their task. But to argue with Darbo-Peschanski that Herodotus, Thucydides, and Polybius made it their prime business to "judge the past" and act as "adjudicators" rather than try to investigate and accurately report events, problematizes the truth-claims of these historians to an extent that is hardly reconcilable with their emphatically professed aims (Darbo-Peschanski 1998, 2003; above, p. 35; on Herodotus anchoring his work in the "realm of opinion," see Darbo-Peschanski 1987: 164–188). The fact that they "judge" need not preclude their trying to report events and their causes as accurately as they can. Herodotus' most famous judgment – the Salamis statement of 7.139 – draws its particular strength from his conviction, and actual demonstration, that his opinion (*gnōmē*) conforms to true fact. In this sense he has transcended the model of the *histōr* that he ultimately found confining (cf. Connor 1993: 15). In Polybius' view (1.14), a reader can derive profit only from a truthful account. The aim of the historian, he says, is to "record the truth ... and to instruct and persuade serious students by means of the truth of the words and the actions" (2.56.11–12; cf. 38.4.8).

2 Herodotus and Thucydides: Contending Founders of the Tradition of Inquiry in Greek Historiography

To assess Herodotus' idea of research in history, one needs to set the author "in context" by tracing the origin of the concept of *historiē* back to science, philosophy, or social institutions. At the same time, though, it is equally crucial to allow for the possibility that he was not merely on the receiving end but was himself a participant in the intellectual debate (Thomas 2000; Bakker 2002: 15; Raaflaub 2002a). When Herodotus defined his mode of inquiry in terms of using one's eyes and ears, he was most certainly not the first to rely, for research purposes, on the principle that the eyes are more trustworthy witnesses than the ears. Thales and Heraclitus, for instance, seem to have done so before him (cf. Marincola 1997: 65). But, as I intend to argue, it was by the methodically conscious application of this principle to a new field of inquiry – research about human affairs in the past – that Herodotus established the authority of an enterprise that was entirely his own. To that end, Herodotus need not have paid special regard, as is sometimes suggested (see esp. Nenci 1955), to the epistemological theories of the pre-Socratic philosophers concerned with sorting out questions about the relative value of sensorial perceptions or with arguing the need of subordinating the information of the senses to the *nous*. Nor would it seem that Herodotus, merely by employing such a method, wanted to make his position clear in the debate opposing wisdom and *historiē/polymathiē* (above, p. 32; a different issue is the relevance of this theme for patterns of thought in Herodotus: Węcowski 2004). His purpose of putting on record the deeds of men in the predominantly oral culture of the fifth century BCE may rather have been in line with the popular Greek manner of making distinctions between more reliable and less reliable information, depending, as the Homeric characters knew already, on the degree of closeness of that information to the facts reported (cf. Schepens 1980: 1–31). At the beginning of the *Histories* Herodotus reminds his readers of this common-sense truth. Candaules wants Gyges to believe that his wife is the most beautiful woman in the world. He keeps praising her appearance in Gyges' presence, but feels uncertain whether he has succeeded in convincing him. What preoccupies him is not a question about sense perception – whether optical sensation is sharper than aural – but the fact that he thinks that Gyges does not believe him when he *tells* him about his wife's looks (*ou...peithesthai moi legonti*). He then enjoins Gyges, quoting the popular saying that "people trust their ears less than their eyes," to find a way to see his wife naked (Hdt. 1.8). The passage is mostly commented upon for the disastrous consequences this perverse invitation entails for Candaules' life and reign. For our purposes it is enough that this scene illustrates the credibility gap that apparently exists between a *logos* told by someone else and the certainty of seeing for oneself. According to this interpretation, the eyes and the ears appear, in the oral culture of the fifth century BCE, as terms of a paradigm expressing the important distinction between direct and indirect information. Still today it is a characteristic feature of the parasitic discipline of history that its terminology, even for key concepts of method, is largely made up of common words, which may then be used in a less familiar, more technical sense (Ritter 1982: xv–xix).

Herodotus' actual research practices bear out the importance attached to the distinction between direct and indirect sources of information. Throughout his account, especially in Books 1–4, the author takes care (sometimes with scrupulous precision: see 2.148.6) to indicate whether he has acquired his knowledge by *opsis* or *akoē*. Sometimes the distinction appears in the terms of a crude opposition between the two "polar" terms, but more often his procedures leave room for several means and corresponding gradations in directness (full discussion of the relevant evidence in Verdin 1971; Schepens 1980: 33–93). The natives (*epichōrioi*) are in a category of their own as direct informants in a spatial sense of the word. Herodotus' inquiry (*historiē*, in the general sense as used in the *Preface*) involves *opsis* (seeing), *historiē* (in the narrow sense of the word, the questioning of informants), *akoē* (hearing), and *gnōmē* (indicating that the whole process of collecting data through seeing and hearing demands "judgment"). On the basis of such a method Herodotus claims to have given, up to 2.99, his geographical and ethnographical description of Egypt. From that point onwards in his *logos*, he is going to relate Egyptian accounts *according to what he heard*, but supplementing them with what he himself saw. *Opsis* of monuments, material remains, artefacts is a further remarkable aspect of Herodotus' method as a researcher. These visual objects perform the double role of reminders or prompts which trigger stories, and, more often, of verifications which demonstrate the truth or untruth of the tales (Hedrick 1995: 60–65). The adoption of this principle of source criticism whereby sight is the verification of hearing is quite prominent in Book 2, but is attested elsewhere as well: the dedications in Delphi, for instance, confirm the stories told in the Lydian *logos* about Croesus (1.50–51, 92). The story of Arion's adventure ends with the reference to the "bronze statuette dedicated by Arion, of a man riding a dolphin" (1.24). In the latter case, Periander's inquiry mirrors Herodotus' in its use of material proof (Gray 2001). Such use of *opsis* illustrates that it was seen by Herodotus as a superior mode of inquiry. But this appraisal does not prevent him from being aware that seeing can lead to real knowledge only if it is attended by intelligence (*synesis*, 2.5). Also with respect to oral inquiry, Herodotus likes to stress his immediate contact with his informants. Where this is not possible, the intermediate stages of transmission are indicated.

An analysis of the extensive vocabulary used by Herodotus to discuss his relationship with sources – perceptively categorized by Hartog (2001a: 395–459) as four different enunciation marks – cannot detain us here. But a few general points must be made. First, when one looks at the way in which major distinctions are made between the available means for obtaining information, there seem to be no grounds for holding the view that Herodotus would generally subsume the questioning of informants (*historiē*, in the narrow sense, as mentioned in 2.99) under *akoē* (Hartog 2001a: 407–411). In the key passage 2.99, Herodotus, using the connecting particles *te…kai*, links *opsis*, *historiē*, and *gnōmē* together as his first- and second-degree means of *direct* inquiry and sets them off, as a whole, against his rendering of the Egyptian accounts based on hearsay. Quite clearly this arrangement does not obey a logic of sense perception – which would, of course, consider the questioning of witnesses as a form of hearing. As an (oral) historian Herodotus appears to follow a logic of his own and values the distinction between direct and indirect forms of information.

A further point, which the peculiar language of 2.99 suggests, is the author's typical approach to "sources." In the tradition of Greek historiography, apparently founded by Herodotus, historical method and sources are conceptualized and described in terms of a paradigm *sui generis* that is quite different from modern categorizations (cf. Schepens 1975a). Whereas current handbooks of historical method define evidence as the objective, material medium between the historian and past reality and tend to formally exclude as subjective means the various capabilities and activities of the researcher, Greek theory – as far as it can be reconstructed from the most representative pronouncements of the historians – appears to focus precisely on those "subjective means." It is a characteristic feature of Herodotus' statement on method that the terms "my own sight, judgment, and inquiry" constitute the subject of the periphrastic and emphatic verbal form *legousa estin*, a particularity of the Greek sentence that is usually lost in translations (cf. Schepens 1975a: 261 n. 15). A close (if odd-sounding) rendering would be: "Thus far it is my own sight and judgment and inquiry that say this." Still, it is crucial to realise that Herodotus – and other Greek historians in his wake – think of *opsis*, *historiē*, and *akoē* as *active* faculties deployed by the historian in his inquiry. The objective materials – sources in the modern sense of the word – that Herodotus has access to through these means are both many and varied: in addition to the monuments and artefacts mentioned above, *opsis* brought him into contact with inscriptions, manners, and customs of foreign people, natural phenomena, geographical features, climate, fauna, and flora. Through *historiē* he was able to obtain information from all sorts of more or less qualified informants, whereas *akoē* introduced him to the written – the ancients did their reading aloud – as well as to the mainly oral traditions (cf. Johnson 2000). The criticism often leveled at Herodotus and other Greek historians for not drawing clear, or clear enough, distinctions between the specific categories of historical evidence appears somewhat irrelevant because it is formulated from a modern, anachronistic point of view. In the Greek paradigm, discussion of the sources is inextricably linked with a discussion of the *ways* in which the historian establishes contact with the reality to be examined. The question is: "How close were you to the thing itself?" (Shrimpton 1997: 119–120). In a sense, it is true to conclude with Wilamowitz (1908) and Hartog (1998: 124; 2000; 2005: 46) that if the Greeks were inventors of anything, they invented the historian rather than history. But in view of their particular approach to historical research and sources, to divorce history from the historian is hardly conducive to a proper understanding of what the Greeks achieved in this field of intellectual activity. It is *a fortiori* premature to draw from such a separation the far-reaching conclusion that in Greek antiquity reflection on history as such did not exist (Hartog 2005: 20) or that the Greeks, including even Polybius, lacked any notion of sources or source-criticism (Wilamowitz 1908: 15).

To return to Herodotus, it has rightly been observed that the most distinctive thing about him is his constant talk about sources and how to assess them. As to method, this distinguishes him more than anything else from his contemporaries and predecessors (Fowler 1996: esp. 62, 76–77). No doubt, the main reason for under-taking extended travels was for Herodotus to get in touch with as many sources as possible and to verify information by cross-checking (Murray 2001; Evans 1991: 89–146; Schepens 2006a). Even where information is sketchy, he wishes to learn what can be known on the basis of the available evidence. Thus his curiosity about the nature of Heracles led him to sail to Tyre and Thasos (2.44, cf. 2.102), "as though there were nothing remarkable in making such a lengthy journey for the sake of researching a single point" (Romm 1998: 51–52). The whole passage is "peppered with his most scientific vocabulary of proof and evidence" (Harrison 2003b: 239). It is to Herodotus' credit that he succeeded in interlinking the traditions of different communities about the Persian Wars into one story. It is significant that the majority of those places where Herodotus speaks *in propria persona* refer to his role as an inquirer, inspecting sites or monuments, interviewing witnesses or locals, evaluating stories (De Jong 2004). I take these self-presentations, as a matter of principle, at face value, *pace* Fehling (Schepens 2006a: 84–87 for a brief discussion, with bibliography).

There were, of course, limits to what Herodotus' active pursuit of data could achieve. But again, it is revealing of his "empiricist" cast of mind that these limitations are reflected in the often-repeated acknowledgment that he can report only on what he has been able to reach in his inquiries. For Herodotus it is essential that his account rests on evidence. In the opening phrase he defines his work as *historiēs apodexis*, intimating that his *historiē* is aimed at producing an account that is "apodeictic" in the sense that it does not "invent." The task of the historian, as he understands it, is to bring, if not "proof," at least evidence for what is asserted. Given the demonstrative character of his account, Herodotus makes the claim that his data provide real information about the world and the past (see, e.g., 2.4). But, at the same time, "he remains aware, and wants us to be aware too, of the fact that as data they are only as good as the quality of the sources allows" (Dewald 1998: xxix). Herodotus' respect for the fundamental value of information is likewise expressed in his self-imposed first duty to report stories as they are told: *legein ta legomena*. Failure to appreciate this important principle as an essential part of the historiographical legacy left by Herodotus has misled scholars into charging historians such as Curtius Rufus or Dio Cassius with a lack of seriousness as researchers, with credulity, and so forth (Bosworth 2003 and Lachenaud 2003 rightly plead for a more equitable approach).

As mentioned above, Herodotus' preface is the first recorded instance of the word *historiē*. The loss of so many works of Herodotus' predecessors makes it nearly impossible for us to judge how many of these writers might have schooled him, and to what extent, in the technique of *historiē* (Fowler 1996: 69). A prominent role is mostly claimed for Hecataeus (Bertelli 2001), the *pater semper incertus* of Greek historiography (Nicolai 1997; above, p. 17). He is the only *logopoios* actually named by Herodotus. The subjective and arbitrary element in his rationalistic criticisms of myths and legends precludes our defining his *Genealogies* as a work resting on *historiē*. But the *Periēgēsis* presents a different case. The "much-traveling man" (*anēr polyplanēs*, *FGrHist* 1 T 12a) Hecataeus greatly impressed his contemporaries with the amount of geographical and ethnographical detail that he was able to locate on Anaximander's map of the world. The vast problem of Herodotus' indebtedness to him cannot be discussed here, but the following general observation should be made. The agreement on the basic fact that both Hecataeus and Herodotus may have undertaken travels for the purpose of *historiē* should not blind one to the difference in method between the rather "constructivist" approach of the former and the latter's outspoken "empiricist" approach to evidence (Müller 1981: 299–318; Romm 1998: 89–91, 134–139). In line with what has been said above about Herodotus' attitude to sources, the Halicarnassian surely marks an advance in empirical and historical argument (Lateiner 1989: 93–94). I tend to agree with Thomas' highly apposite remark (2000: 173 n. 19; more detailed discussion in Schepens 1980: 84–90): "Studies of Hecataeus which credit him with many of the attributes of Herodotus' techniques of *historiē* . . . seem to be taking for granted what they need to prove."

After Hecataeus, Charon and Xanthus merit special attention – a fact that Jacoby's influential but over-schematic theory of the origins of Greek historiography tends to obscure. With regard to Xanthus, we have Ephorus' valuable testimony (cf. Kingsley 1995) that he provided Herodotus with a "starting point," "sources" or "resources" (*FGrHist* 70 F 180). What we know about Xanthus' methods of drawing inferences from all sorts of tangible evidence (geography, fossils, linguistic materials) and bringing them to bear on the data of tradition indicates a similarity to the procedures employed by Herodotus himself (von Fritz 1967: II.348–377). If Herodotus did not borrow directly from Xanthus, both authors must at least have shared a similar intellectual background (Mehl 2004). For the rest we can only speculate on Herodotus' debt to this predecessor – author of a history of Lydia down to the fall of Sardis – in making Croesus the oldest *historically* ascertained starting point for exploring the *aitiē* of the war that opposed the Greeks and the Barbarians (Hdt. 1.5).

In conclusion: as far as we can judge by Herodotus' own use of the concept of *historiē* – the noun as well as the verb – he seems to lay claim to a distinct research activity that was typical of the way *he* conducted his inquiries. Ancient authors who thought of themselves as continuing the activity of Herodotus agreed with his emphasis on research, without necessarily agreeing in all particulars about his ways and methods. Later accounts written in line with the *peculiar* interests and objectives of Herodotus gradually became known as "historical" narratives, as works of history. By conferring upon him the title "pater historiae," ancient tradition acknowledged that Herodotus' concept and practice of *historiē* had opened up a new field of intellectual activity.

Nevertheless, disagreement over Herodotus' approach was swiftly voiced by his immediate successor, Thucydides. He seems to have consciously avoided using the term *historiē* for characterizing the account he *wrote* of the war that the Peloponnesians and the Athenians fought against one another. Still, there is a growing awareness among critics that he and later historians only developed the fundamentals of the historical method already implicit and sometimes explicit in the *Histories* (Lateiner 1989: 56, with ref. to Verdin 1977). Like Herodotus, Thucydides accepted oral tradition and visual testimony as the primary sources for history writing. But compared to his predecessor – who narrated a war he had not witnessed and told stories and described customs of people whose language he could not understand – Thucydides applied much stricter critical standards. He confined himself to relating events he was able to observe from beginning to end during his lifetime (5.26.5; cf. Fornara 1993), excluding from his project as "ancient" (*palaia*) events that occurred before the Peloponnesian War (1.1.3). It seems clear that Thucydides' tacit but manifest disclaimer with regard to *historiē* has everything to do with his conviction that Herodotus "heard" too much and "saw" too little. He respects Herodotus more than any other "logographer" (see Tsakmakis 1995 and 1996 on Thucydides' avoidance of open polemic with Herodotus), but still puts him in the company of writers of *logoi*, who seek to please the ear rather than to speak the truth (1.21.2). Thucydides' "examination" (*zētēsis*) steps up the rigor of inquiry.

There is a further quite obvious contrast between the two authors: whereas Herodotus presents himself as a researcher in action, Thucydides is content with serving up the result of his painstaking inquiry. His chapter on method informs the reader that his account is based on his personal observation *and* interrogation of witnesses directly involved in the events (1.22.2). So, quite consciously, he puts first- and second-degree visual evidence at the center of his historical method. Yet nowhere does the historian of the Peloponnesian War suggest that autopsy would be superior to inquiry (cf. Marincola 1997: 67–69): both methods are presented as equally important and closely interlocked. A close study of the text does not warrant the conclusion that he learnt some events through personal observation, while others – where he was not present – were narrated on the basis of eyewitness accounts. The idea that Thucydides would be making an "objective" distinction between things seen by himself and those he heard about from others runs counter to the idea that Thucydides, in accordance with the particular Greek approach to the information problem, merely singles out the two *ways* in which he acquired his knowledge of the events (cf. Schepens 1975a; 1980: 113–146). It follows logically from such an interpretation that the critical testing of the information on its conformity, as far as possible, with external reality is aimed at his autopsy as well as at his interrogation of eyewitnesses (for this "objective" meaning of *akribeia*, see Schepens 1980: 133–148; Fantasia 2004: 46–49). Bias and the faulty memories of witnesses made it hard to discover the truth (1.22.3).

In the "Archaeology," the references to material objects still observable likewise point to the careful use of *opsis* as part of the author's method of drawing inferences from *tekmēria* and of subjecting tradition to verification. Autopsy of monuments can be a misleading guide to political realities (1.10.1–3; cf. Marincola 1997: 67–68).

Thucydides alludes once more to his inquiry in the "second preface," where he notes his banishment from Athens not to apologize for his failure as a general at Amphipolis, but to draw attention to the wider opportunities that his twenty-year exile afforded "for being present with both parties, and more especially with the Peloponnesians" (5.26.5; Schepens 1980: 168–187). It is characteristic of the seriousness with which he conducted his research that Thucydides raised what must have been a dramatic event in his personal life to the elevated plane of historiographical discourse. He presents his exile, strictly from a methodological view, as offering an advantageous situation and providing him with the "leisure to observe affairs more closely."

The foregoing demonstrates that Thucydides played a large part in perfecting and sanctioning the method of direct inquiry as the most reliable one for writing history (Hornblower 1994a: 24). In a sense Thucydides attempted to base the "science" of history on observation in a manner similar to Hippocratic medicine (see Thuc. 2.47–54) and natural science (Anaxagoras). It is not a mere accident that in the narrative he stresses the importance of autopsy only once, notably in his description of the plague at Athens, with which he himself was afflicted and which he witnessed others suffering (2.48).

3   Continuity and Discontinuity

Greek historiography in the fourth century BCE begins with a series of *Hellenica* continuing Thucydides' incomplete account of the Peloponnesian War. By this very act the respective authors – Cratippus (whom I consider to be the author of the *Hellenica Oxyrhynchia*), Xenophon, and Theopompus – acknowledged their predecessor as an important and, in a sense, also as a "referential" historian. Yet there is a "nearly complete silence about Thucydides in what remains to us of ancient writers before the age of Cicero and Dionysius of Halicarnassus (by which time he was established as *the* great historian)" (Gomme, *HCT* III.523, with addendum, p. 733; see also Hornblower 1995, for some important qualifications of Gomme's view). In effect, as I have explained elsewhere (Schepens 2007), none of Thucydides' continuators went so far in their admiration that they refrained from finding fault with one or the other aspect of his representation of history and/or his method of inquiry.

Ephorus, for one, made Thucydides his prime source for his account of the Peloponnesian War, but not without supplementing him in his usual manner and criticizing him for his failure to spell out the extent to which Pericles could be held personally responsible for bringing about the war. Thus, right from the beginning of the fourth century, and throughout the Hellenistic period, the question of how history should or could most adequately be written and researched continued to be debated in a lively way among its many practitioners. Historians habitually discussed both in their Prefaces and occasionally in the course of their narratives the principles and subject matter of history. Quite often they did so in a truly polemical spirit (cf. D. Hal. *AR* 1.1 on Anaximenes and Theopompus; cf. Duris, *FGrHist* 76 F 1; for Polybius' many criticisms see Schepens and Bollansée 2005). Even if such methodological statements largely served the self-promotion of the historians as writers with better knowledge and superior methodology, these texts did provide opportunities to step back from their researches and offer some reflection on the nature of the genre. In the Preface to his *Philippica*, Theopompus called upon the writer of history to approach his task with seriousness and "professionalism," especially with regard to assembling his materials. Pointing out that he was sufficiently rich to be independent and to afford the huge expenses required for visiting all important places in Greece, he proudly asserted (*FGrHist* 115 F 26) that he "personally observed many things and interviewed for the sake of history many great men of the time – military as well as political leaders, and philosophers. For he did not, like some, consider the writing of history a part-time occupation, but an activity taking the highest priority of all."

It was in the context of such debates that the hierarchy which Herodotus and, above all, Thucydides had established regarding the use of *opsis* and *akoē* in historical research was restated, questioned, and eventually also challenged. This state of affairs, which can only be very incompletely sketched here, makes it impossible to agree with the often repeated idea that the Thucydidean model in particular set the pattern for *all* subsequent Greek historiography. To be sure, there were many authors whose contemporary or near contemporary political and military histories were written more or less according to Thucydides' manner. But his history of the Peloponnesian War was by no means representative of the range and variety of historical writing in the fourth century BCE and the Hellenistic period. Many understood their task as history writers and researchers rather after the example of Herodotus (Murray 1972; Clarke 2003), continued in the track of the "logographers," or were encouraged by the success of Hippias of Elis, whose lectures on all things ancient (*archaiologia*) had had such a strong appeal to the Spartan public (*FGrHist* 6 T 3). It is significant for the development of history in this period that, by the middle of the second century BCE, Polybius finds himself, as a writer of contemporary political and military history, in a position where he feels the need to justify the choice of his narrow and austere subject (9.1.2): "Most other writers, if not everyone, can appeal to a wide and diverse public by including all the various modes of historical writing in their works." The implications of Polybius' statement are rarely realized and have yet to be properly drawn. His "description des lieux" obviously raises major questions with regard to the label "mainstream" history that is so readily attached to the writings of contemporary political and military history. The label obscures more than it reveals. I shall come back to this at the conclusion.

I would like to single out for brief discussion, *pars pro toto*, the fragmentary historians Ephorus and Timaeus. Inevitably we will also have to deal with Polybius since he opposes his own views to those of Timaeus, whom we get to know only through the often distortive lens of the former's criticism.

At the threshold of the Hellenistic period, Ephorus was the first historian to attempt universal history. The large scope of his work brought with it a rethinking of the *opsis–akoē* hierarchy. His methodology was still grounded on the main principle laid down by Herodotus and Thucydides according to which direct sources were more reliable than indirect (later) ones; but, with a shift away from the research on the contemporary or nearly contemporary history towards the investigation of the more distant past, he significantly modified the main tenets of "inquiry." In his argument against Timaeus, Polybius drew on Ephorus' authority to support his view that autopsy was a superior method of inquiry: he noted (12.27.7 = *FGrHist* 70 F 110) that Ephorus had acknowledged that being personally present at all events would be the best source of information. But the more relevant point is that Ephorus made this statement in a contrary-to-fact condition, his intention being foremost to stress the limited range for applying such a method (Schepens 1970). This implies that Ephorus made this statement in a context (most probably his general Preface) in which he advocated the necessity and the legitimacy of *his* historical method as compared to that of his prominent predecessors. As it is, Ephorus' ideas on this matter prove to be in line with Isocrates' defense of *akoē* against the superior claims of *opsis* (*Panath.* 149–150; cf. Marincola 1997: 276–279). Ephorus' *Histories* are, indeed, a prime example of a historical work which puts written sources and the critical exploitation of all sorts of "documentary" evidence at the center stage of historical method. The details of his actual method cannot be discussed here (see Schepens 1977a, 2003), but for our present purposes it is vital to note that Ephorus supported his historiographical praxis with conscious, critical reflexion on the possibilities and limits of historical inquiry. Echoes of his methodological defense of the use of written records can be found in Diodorus (1.9; cf. 4.1.3–4). And his method for judging the trustworthiness of historical traditions (*FGrHist* 70 F 9) earned him the admiration of Niebuhr, one of the founders of modern historical method (Schepens 1977b). Delineating history as a genre against rhetoric, Ephorus stated that "the mere collection of the materials required for writing a history was a more serious task than the complete course of study of the art of declamatory speaking" (F 111). Apart from the relevance of the fact that Ephorus, very much in the same spirit as his fellow "rhetorical" historian Theopompus, considered "inquiry" – sources and source-criticism – to be the key discriminating factor between history and oratory (on the uselessness of the term "rhetorical history," see Marincola 2001: 111–112), the comparison of the two disciplines makes it likely that Ephorus may, indeed, have been the first in the history of Greek historiography to address history as a genre and to use the term *Historiai* for the first time in the sense of "historical work" (cf. Porciani 1997: 83–84).

Ephorus' stance on the difference between rhetoric and history was, according to Polybius (12.28.8–28a.3), later repeated by Timaeus (*FGrHist* 566 F 7). And although Polybius admired the former and despised the latter, their agreement on this particular topic was certainly not the only point of affinity between these historians. As already suggested, some evidence can still be gleaned from Polybius' Book 12, which suggests that Ephorus' idea about the greater importance of written sources compared to autopsy and oral inquiry was further developed by Timaeus into a theory which openly challenged the traditional hierarchy. Before looking at some of these passages, it is imperative to say a word or two on Polybius' own position in this debate. His *Histories* (and especially Book 12 devoted entirely to criticism of Timaeus) constitute our fullest extant source on the subject of "inquiry" in Greek history. Polybius' declarations on his own method and frequent polemics against other historians have been the object of much scholarly attention (see, e.g., Pédech 1961, 1964; Sacks 1981; Schepens 1990; Musti 2003; Schepens and Bollansée 2005): they are sufficiently familiar and need not be rehearsed here, except for a few points which help explain why Polybius' criticism of Timaeus' "bookish" attitude is so fundamental to him and why this accusation in particular aims at his predecessor's *full* disqualification as a historian. Indeed, when Polybius has some occasional positive comment on Timaeus' competence as a researcher, such "acknowledgments" are but a platform for launching charges. This can be seen, for instance, where Timaeus' great industry and talent as a meticulous researcher of the king lists at Sparta, the archons at Athens, the priestesses of Hera at Argos, the victors at Olympia, and inscriptions found "at the back of buildings and lists of *proxeni* on the doorjambs of temples" (12.11.2) is recalled only to accuse Timaeus of having committed deliberate falsehood in his controversy with Aristotle over the origins of the Epizephyrian Locrians (12.5–16, esp. 11.5 and 12a.6–7; cf. Walbank 2005). By the way, how could Timaeus possibly have conducted his "autoptic" inquiries of these documents if, as Polybius contends elsewhere, he remained "sitting" all the time in Athens (12.25d.1), doing his research "reclining on a couch" in the library (12.27.4–5)?

Polybius' contemptuous remarks about Timaeus' reliance on written sources are undoubtedly the most salient – and to readers habituated to the practices of historians today also the most astounding – feature of his strictures. More than any other Greek historian on record, Polybius championed the method of direct inquiry. He prided himself not only on having been an eyewitness of the greater number of the events covered in the final section of his *Histories*, but also on having taken an active part in some of them and on having directed the course of others (3.4.13). As a consequence, Polybius gradually shifted his position from an external narrator in the earlier parts of this work to the internal narrator of the more recent events (36.12.2–4). In his work, the historiographical topic of autopsy and cross-questioning witnesses is further enriched. Expounding the need and usefulness of topographical knowledge for the study of history, Polybius elaborates a theory of travel (especially at 3.57–59; cf. Zecchini 1991; Schepens 2006a). Following the lead of "predecessors" (whom I have tentatively identified as writers of mimetic history), he also emphasizes that the qualities of vivid and expressive representation of the historical narrative, deemed essential to its usefulness for the reader, can only be ensured by authors who have experienced the (kind of) events they narrate or describe (12.25h.5; cf. Schepens 1975b): historians without *autopatheia* (12.25h.4) fall short of the indispensable requirements of history.

Polybius' grounds for putting travel, autopsy, and political and military activity before library research were thus many and varied. In his attempts at systematic presentation of those key elements of historical method, *akoē* invariably ranks last. Polybius' bipartite and tripartite classifications do not perfectly overlap (Walbank 1972: 71–74). The details of this question need not detain us here (see Schepens 1974, 1975a), but one thing should be noted: an important reason for variation within these classifications can be linked to the double aim with which Polybius discusses these matters. Depending on their place and function within his polemical argument, his rankings are either focused on the question of the "sources" – the "technical" means for gathering information (12.27) – or on the closely related but quite different issue of the fundamental qualifications of the historian that can respectively be derived from travel and actual participation in the events and from reading books (12.25e). To fault Timaeus for failing to collect the major part of his information by means of *opsis* and interrogation of eyewitnesses was not the strongest possible argument to disqualify a historian whose work was, after all, mainly concerned with past history. Ultimately, for Polybius, the worst offense perpetrated by the Sicilian historian was that he preferred the easier way of inquiry through *akoē* (in his case the "reading" of books in the library), while simultaneously depriving himself of the proper training and experience (*empeiria*) that can only be acquired through travel and personal participation in the events.

Particularly relevant in this connection is the well-known passage opening Polybius' discussion of Timaeus' "life" (*bios*, 12.25d.1). Using Timaeus' remark that he had settled down (*apokathistēmi*) in Athens for a period of nearly fifty years, Polybius maliciously interprets this as an admission by Timaeus that he simply remained seated in town, never leaving the city during that long period. Polybius even intimates (12.28.6) that Timaeus, spending all his life in exile "at one single place," deliberately denied himself the personal experience that can be gained by travel or observation. As Walbank rightly observed, it does not ring true that Timaeus ever made *such* a statement. Like Thucydides, he may rather have portrayed his exile as some sort of advantage (Marincola 1997: 71), stressing, in conformity with the spirit of the age, the unrivaled opportunities which the Hellenistic libraries afforded for new types of historical research. Indeed, as one can read in this very passage, Timaeus claimed that in Athens, with plenty of books available to him, he was in possession of the most important resources (*megistas aphormas*) for the writing of history. The idea that books provided the greatest "starting point" for undertaking historical research points to a real paradigm shift. Although significant changes had already taken place within the paradigm before this, the argument that a historian was better off with plenty of books at his disposal than with being an eyewitness was something new. It claimed the superiority of *akoē* over *opsis*.

Another clue to the prime attention given to books by Timaeus – disparagingly called "bookish disposition" (*bibliakē hexis*) by Polybius – is his assertion that the expense and difficulties that he had incurred in gathering the books and information for writing his work were so great as to provoke disbelief in his readers (12.28a.3). In Polybius' eyes, Timaeus "usurped" a topic that before this was exclusively linked with the tradition of traveling, autopsy, and personal inquiry on the spot (cf. Theopompus 115 T 20 and, for the germ of it, Thuc. 1.22.2–3). Thus working on the basis of written sources became integrated into the motif of the historian's labors.

A further relevant aspect stressed by Polybius thoughout Book 12 is Timaeus' habit of harshly criticizing other historians. Polybius attributes this to Timaeus' quarrelsome character (12.25.6), points to "his great severity and audacity in accusing others" (12.24.5), and concludes that, if Timaeus enjoys a widespread reputation, this is due to the impression he makes as a critic rather than to the qualities of his own account. One of the most original aspects of Timaeus' critical method is obscured by these accusations (cf. Pédech 1961: 117–118). Rewriting the history of Sicily and the Greek West, Timaeus systematically subjected all extant accounts to critical scrutiny, taking full advantage of the new types of history writing based on so-called "antiquarian" research, for which the Peripatetics had provided the intellectual foundation. Polybius had no affinity at all with this. Generally, he shows a great lack of understanding and know-how when it comes to dealing properly and critically with sources on non-contemporary history (see, e.g., Pol. 6.45; cf. Schepens 2003: 353–356). In Polybius' view, historians who study the past cannot but compare the errors of their predecessors (12.27.5). He seems to have missed the point that something could be achieved in this field too.

The evolution of historiography we have tried to outline here is, of course, indicative of a larger cultural change: the passage from a predominantly oral to a predominantly written culture. The library centers of the Hellenistic world established a wholly new attitude to written evidence and gave an unprecedented impetus to document-oriented scholarly investigations. Through the introduction of a new method of research, and the concomitant general broadening of its subject matter, the Lyceum played a crucial part in the development of Greek historiography in the Hellenistic period. A decisive moment was the export of the Peripatetic *modus operandi* to what soon became the cultural and intellectual center of the Mediterranean, the *Museion* of Alexandria. There the library (another idea borrowed from the Lyceum) quickly became the heart of activity, holding by the mid-third century BCE a copy of nearly every Greek literary work composed up to that point in time. From that moment on the written word superseded oral communication as the most authoritative source of information (see Pretagostini 2000: 6). This resulted in a new, document-oriented form of investigation based on the reading, analysis, and excerpting of written sources (Jacob 1996b).

Looking back to Polybius through the eyes of Strabo (2.5.11), who held the view that *akoē* should not be deprived of its proper relevance because, for the purposes of science, it could accomplish a lot more than "seeing," I tend to agree with Laffranque (1968: 263–272) who termed Polybius' disparaging criticism of the "bookish" Timaeus "reactionary," out of tone with the metamorphosis undergone by Greek historiography in the Hellenistic period. The issue, of course, is not that Polybius is not entitled to have and defend his own views on "history" and "inquiry," nor that he has no right to point out the weaknesses in the methods of others, but rather that he looked at Timaeus' work through the unjustifiably narrow partition of the methodological principles underlying contemporary political and military history. And even so, he exalted the value and the importance of personal inquiry beyond realistic standards: he himself owed a lot more to written sources than his declarations on method would have us believe.

4   Final Thoughts

At the end of this investigation "history" and "inquiry" still stand out as terms in need of definition. It has not been our intention to give simple answers to difficult questions. All we can hope for is that the present, tentative survey, imperfect and imbalanced as it may be, at least provides a few parameters for following the course of an ongoing debate within Greek historiography, and stimulates reflection and further research, especially with regard to the important developments that took place after Thucydides. There is a growing awareness now among scholars that so-called *histoire événementielle* is over-represented in our surviving historians and that especially in the Hellenistic period the historiographical genre saw a huge increase in the number of authors writing history and a great diversification in terms of their themes. It is surely one of the major challenges of present and future research in classical studies to address the question of the composite nature of history.

Since, according to Strasburger's estimate (1977), hardly 2 percent of Greek historical writing has come down to us directly, it is clear that the idea of "history and inquiry" in Greek antiquity can only be adequately studied (of course within the limits imposed by our documentation) if scholars are prepared to engage seriously and systematically with the fragmentary remains. Such a study should include the all-important sector of local historians (below, p. 180) and furthermore ought not to sideline the many practitioners of what has come to be designated quite disparagingly "antiquarian history" (cf. Schepens 2006b, for a critical reassessment of the separation of "antiquarian" literature from "history"; below, p. 515). The greater part of the numerous fragments pertaining to the huge variety of sub-genres lumped together under this collective term is still to be edited and commented upon within the framework of the ongoing project *FGrHist Continued* (Schepens 1997, 1998).

It seems to me that no definitive canon or master narrative exists and that any attempt to construct either must be resisted. To quote a phrase (cf. Bercovitch 1995), we can only write "federated histories" of the many branches and genres which together embody the idea of history writing in Greek culture.

FURTHER READING

The questions of beginnings and genre are treated in two excellent articles: Marincola 1999 and Pelling 1999a. Pleading the case for seriously engaging with the study of the fragmentary remains of post-Thucydidean historiography, Humphreys 1997 challenges the traditional and still widespread "Whig" interpretation of Greek historiography based on a limited number of selected "canonical" historians, which sees the development of the genre in terms of progress until Thucydides and, from then onwards, in terms of decadence or return to Thucydidean standards. As to beginnings of Greek historiography, the Whig interpretation rests on what Thomas (2000: 24) has called the "linear development fallacy." In a similar vein, Desideri 1996 offers pertinent, more general criticism of Jacoby's and, above all, Momigliano's excessively "presentist," static, and monolithic views of Greek historiography.

Both Murray 1972 and Gabba 1981 provide stimulating and insightful introductions into how the pluriform and open Greek concept of *historiē* responded in the Hellenistic period to the new challenges connected with the widening of the geopolitical horizon and the creation of the Hellenistic monarchies. At the same time they show how historiography catered to the new tastes of the reading public.

The many and wide gaps in the textual tradition from antiquity until today make it virtually impossible for us to think of local history, and of city histories in particular, as a type of history writing that might have been as vitally important to the competitive world of the individual poleis as *Hellenica* or universal histories were to the Greek world at large. Since space precluded treatment of this major branch of the Greek historical literature here, I take the liberty of referring to Schepens 2001a (and cf. below, p. 180).

CHAPTER FOUR

Documents and the Greek Historians

P. J. Rhodes

For the purposes of this chapter I take a document to be "something written, inscribed, engraved, etc., which provides information or serves as a record, *esp.* an official paper" (*New Shorter Oxford English Dictionary*, I.719b, definition 3). It may be displayed in public or kept in storage somewhere; it may be generated by an official body at any level from a council of allies to an Athenian deme, or by an unofficial body such as an Athenian *hetaireia*, or by an individual (e.g., that person's will), but it is a text which serves as a record – and, I further assume here, intentionally so: I thus distinguish documents from other texts, whether (for instance) the writings of historians or (for instance) the poems of men such as Tyrtaeus and Solon, which might be considered documents in an extended use of the term.

It is uncontroversial that the earliest Greek historians relied primarily on oral sources, on talking to people who either were themselves participants in or witnesses of the events in question or else claimed to repeat what they had heard (whether directly or ultimately) from people who were participants or witnesses. Herodotus repeatedly refers to what identified or unidentified people say (after his prefatory sentence he moves on immediately in 1.1.1 to "Learned men among the Persians say..."); he distinguishes between reports of witnesses and hearsay (3.115.2; 4.16.1); he remarks that he is obliged to report what he hears but not necessarily to believe it (3.123.1; 4.195.2; 7.152.3). Thucydides in connection with his speeches refers to those which he heard himself and those which were reported to him by others, and in connection with his narrative of events says that beyond his own experience he did not rely uncritically on chance informants but investigated what he was told as precisely as possible (1.22.1–3). Quite apart from the consideration that in the fifth century oral testimony may have been judged more valuable than written evidence (West 1985: 304–305; cf. Thomas 1989: 89–93), they could not do otherwise, since there would be no documentary evidence of much that they wanted: Greek states in the classical period might record, and even publish, decrees of their assemblies, but as far as we know they did not record who said what in the debate, as the cities of Egypt were to do later (e.g., the Loeb *Select Papyri* II, nos. 240, 241, cf. RL, pp. 461–469); documents might record who commanded an expedition, with what forces and what funding, but they would not record what happened on the campaign. But already in Herodotus we find references to inscriptions, and also passages which, though no source is specified, are likely to derive ultimately from documents; and from Herodotus onwards it is possible to trace a growing awareness among Greek historians of how documentary evidence can be exploited.

Herodotus' use of inscriptions has been discussed by West (1985) and Osborne (2002: 510–513). There are nineteen occasions when he explicitly mentions an inscription, in four cases an inscription which still survives, but by the standards of modern academic historians his use of them is unimpressive: there are some cases where he claims to have seen the text (inscriptions in "Cadmean letters" at Thebes from the legendary past, 5.59–61; the inscription on Cheops' pyramid, which an Egyptian translated for him, 2.125.6), but more often he does not, and sometimes he cannot have done so (the alleged inscriptions from the tomb of the legendary Nitocris at Babylon, 1.187; the alleged messages left by Themistocles when the Greeks abandoned Artemisium, calling on the Ionians to defect from Xerxes, 8.22).

One of his texts which still survives is the Serpent Column (ML 27), and since it was at Delphi it is likely that he saw it: he correctly notes that the Tenians were added to the original names (8.82.1, cf. coil 7); but at that point and later (9.81.1) he seriously misdescribes the monument, and as Plutarch was to complain later (*dHM* 870D), he fails to draw any conclusion about the contribution of the Corinthians to the Greek victory from their being named third in the list (coil 2). He is aware that inscriptions can be forgeries, and has learned from his Delphic informants that what was inscribed as a Spartan dedication in fact came from Croesus (1.51.3–4); but he accepts as "Cadmean letters," supporting a story about the development of the Greek script from the Phoenician, hexameter inscriptions at Thebes (5.59–61), whereas Josephus was later to insist that the Greek alphabet was much later than the Trojan War (*Ap.* 1.10–12). His first Thermopylae epigram (7.228.1) is shown by its text to be not, as he claims, an epitaph for the Greeks who died there but a commemoration of the Peloponnesians who fought there (cf. below, Ch. 26). In the Near East, the "*stelai* of Sesostris" which he claims to have seen in Palestine (2.106.1) are most commonly identified with the *stelai* of Ramses II at the mouth of the Nahr el-Kelb (on which see Pritchard 1969: 255–256), and are in any case most unlikely to have shown female *aidoia* (private parts); the "reliefs of Sesostris" (with an alternative identification rejected), on two different roads in Ionia (2.106.2–5), are identified with the reliefs of a Hittite war god, on opposite sides of the road through the Karabel Pass, which cannot be either of his roads, and the inscription does not run, as he says, from shoulder to shoulder (for a photograph see MacQueen 1986: 24, ill. 14; for an account of how Herodotus and his informants could have come to believe what they did believe about these monuments see Dalley 2003: 174–177). Commonly, it seems, a reference to an inscription (whether or not he also saw it) has come to Herodotus with a story, as something mentioned by his informant to support the story, and if he had been more critical he might have realized that in fact the inscription does not always support the story.

It is likely enough that there were documents, whether inscribed or not, relevant to many points in his narrative where he does not mention a document: the names of the three hundred Spartans who died at Thermopylae (7.224.1) were inscribed at Sparta (Paus. 3.14.1); after Athens' victory over Chalcis ca. 506, for which he cites the Athenian dedication on the acropolis (5.77.4; cf. ML 15), the treaty and the sending of cleruchs to Chalcis (5.77.2) will surely have generated documents, of which texts might have survived even if they were not inscribed for public display. The accounts of Darius' provinces and their tributes (3.89.1–97.1), of the royal road from Sardis to Susa (5.52–53), and of the national contingents in Xerxes' army in 480 (7.61–99) are likely to have a documentary origin, and it is becoming increasingly credible that there were Greeks in Persian service from whom Herodotus could have obtained such information (cf. Lewis in Burn 1984: 597–598). But we should not credit Herodotus with a more serious use of documents where he does not mention them than where he does: most of what he recorded came from oral informants; in some cases there will have been relevant documents, of which his informants or their informants may have been aware, but they will not necessarily have given Herodotus references which he then failed to pass on to his readers. There was not yet any sense that documents provide an important basis for reliable history.

Gomme in the Introduction to his *Historical Commentary on Thucydides* had a section on "sources other than Thucydides," in which he discussed "official documents" and "unofficial documents," including in the second all contemporary literature (*HCT* I.30–39), but he did not there discuss Thucydides' own use of documents. (Smarczyk 2006 was published while this book was in the press.) In 1.22, as we saw above (p. 56), Thucydides refers only to his own experience and witnesses; but he mentions a great many public decisions which will have generated documents, both decrees of single states and other organizations (such as the Peloponnesian League) and treaties between states. Notoriously, in two parts of his history but not elsewhere he directly quotes documents (4.117–5.81, Book 8). 5.47 quotes an alliance made by Athens with Argos and other Peloponnesian states of which the copy published in Athens survives (Tod 72 = *IG* I^3 83): there are several verbal differences, but there are often verbal differences between inscribed copies of the same text, and, for all that we know to the contrary, Thucydides may have reproduced entirely accurately the text which he saw. However, there are many other places where it is plausible to think that he could have quoted if he had chosen to do so. 4.16.1–2 gives a detailed version in indirect speech of the truce at Pylos in 425, and 3.114.3 summarizes the hundred-year treaty made in the northwest in 426; we seem to be close to the language of a document in, for instance, 2.24.1 on Athens' setting aside of a 1,000-talent reserve in 431 and 5.28.1 on an Argive decision in 421. Thucydides surely could if he had wished have found and quoted, for instance, the Thirty Years' Peace of 446/5 (1.115.1) or the treaty of Gela of 424 (4.65.1–2), but we cannot tell whether his investigations did include consultation of those texts. As for the quantified survey of Athens' resources in a speech of Pericles summarized in indirect speech in 2.13, we can only wonder whether Thucydides remembered the details from Pericles' speech or did some research in the documents to help him construct his summary of the speech; but both there and in 1.96.2 Thucydides gives surprisingly high figures for the tribute of the Delian League, and it may be that these are derived from optimistic assessment lists (cf. Rhodes 1985: 8).

There are places where we may think that documents would have improved his account but it is not surprising that documents were not used. In 5.68 he tries to calculate the size of the Spartan army at Mantinea in 418 (and, many scholars think, makes a mistake: see Andrewes *ad loc.* in *HCT* IV.110–117, believing in an error, but starting from the material of Gomme, who did not), and complains that "the numbers of the Spartans were unknown, because of the secrecy of their régime" (5.68.2). In 8.65–70.1 and 8.97 he has accounts of the institution at Athens in 411 of the régime of the Four Hundred and the intermediate régime which followed it which owe nothing to documents – but, of course, he was in exile at the time, and he might have revised these accounts after his return if he had lived longer. We shall see below that on the Four Hundred the author of the *Ath. Pol.* (below, p. 62) did have access to an account based on documents, which he tried to combine with Thucydides' account, but on the intermediate régime he did not.

For the passages which quote documents, Gomme was most interested in questions about when and how Thucydides obtained the texts (e.g., *HCT* III.606–607, 680–682); Andrewes asked why texts are quoted in some parts of the history only, and thought it more likely that they represent provisional work, which would have been replaced by summaries, than a deliberate change in method (*HCT* V.374–375, 383); Hornblower, with whom I agree, favors a deliberate change in method, "an extreme case of Thucydides' desire to get small things right, and to emphasize that he had done so" (Hornblower, *CT* II.113–119, quoting 117, cf. 356–360). Connor, who reads his way through Thucydides on the assumption that the text which we have is exactly the text which Thucydides intended, sees the quoted documents as marking the stages in a complex diplomatic narrative, and as pointing the contrast between professed intentions and actual consequences (Connor 1984: 144–147, cf. 217–219, 254 app. 4; cf. the approach of Rood 1998).

Otherwise Thucydides quotes texts in connection with earlier history. "Inscriptions are more appropriate evidence for the past than for the present, where personal inquiry and research offer superior guidance"; for instance, what Thucydides could discover by oral inquiry about Athens' treatment of Mytilene in 427 (3.25–50) was more important than what he could have learned from the text inscribed as Tod 63 = *IG* I³ 66 (Hornblower 1994a: 89–91, quoting 90–91). On the boastful couplet of Pausanias, originally inscribed on but subsequently deleted from the Serpent Column (1.132.2–3), we are not yet far from Herodotus: Thucydides cannot have seen the offending text; it will have come to him with the hostile story about Pausanias which was told in Sparta when Pausanias was dead and unable to reply. Herodotean again is his quotation of the epitaph of Hippias' daughter Archedice, married to Aeantides of Lampsacus (6.59.3). However, we see Thucydides using inscriptions to argue a case, as Herodotus did not, in the polemical part of his account of the Peisistratid tyranny. That Peisistratus the younger held the archonship under the tyranny is supported by appeal not to the inscribed archon list, though that existed when Thucydides was writing (ML 6 = *IG* I^3 1031 ~ Fornara 23), but to two dedications, one still surviving, whose lettering he surprisingly describes as faint (ML 11 = *IG* I^3 948 ~ Fornara 37), the other already obliterated in his own time (6.54.6–7). He then goes on to argue that Hippias must have been the eldest son of Peisistratus the tyrant on the grounds that he was the only one to whom offspring were attributed on the *stēlē* set up after the fall of the tyranny – not a cogent argument, since the other sons were certainly born early enough to have fathered children (cf. Davies 1971: 446–450) – and that he was named there next after Peisistratus (6.55.1–2). Thucydides' purpose is to demonstrate that Hippias must have been the reigning tyrant in 514, but in insisting that there must have been one reigning tyrant he perhaps mistook the nature of tyranny.

Like documents in the strict sense, texts of other kinds can be used not simply to support the story but as the basis for an argument. He says we can calculate from Homer (in spite of poets' tendency to exaggerate) how many Greeks took part in the Trojan War – but if he had done the calculation he would have found that it did not support the point which he was trying to make (1.10.3–5, using the catalogue of ships in *Iliad* 2); he quotes the Homeric *Hymn to Apollo* to prove that there was an ancient Ionian festival on Delos, which included a musical competition (3.104.3–6). His treatment of oracles "is certainly sparing" (Hornblower 1994a: 81–83, quoting 81), but we see his rationalism at work when, in response to the plague which hit Athens in 430, old men remembered an oracle about a Dorian war accompanied by a *loimos* (plague) or a *limos* (famine), and he remarks that in the circumstances the *loimos* version was judged correct, but if a later Dorian war were accompanied by a famine the *limos* version would then be preferred (2.54.2–3).

Thucydides was still working primarily by oral inquiry, as Herodotus did, but at least for treaties he came to see the importance of the actual text of a document, we may suspect some use of documents beyond the passages in which they are directly quoted, and to establish points about the past he was prepared to argue from inscriptions and other texts as Herodotus was not.

Xenophon has disappointed scholars who see him as failing to live up to standards set by Thucydides, though his *Hellenica* is one of the histories which deliberately begin where Thucydides ends. This has led to a problem over how he should be categorized, with some regarding him as a writer not of history but of something else, for instance a didactic work; but it is better to recognize that Thucydides' was not the only way of writing history (as today learned tomes published by university presses are not the only way of writing history), and that Xenophon was writing history in his own way (a didactic work, Grayson 1975; his own kind of history, Rhodes 1994: 167). He tells his story without ever giving any indication of his sources or laying any claim to reliability, and Krentz in his recent editions says, "Most likely Xenophon relied exclusively on his eyes and ears" (Krentz 1989: 6, repeated in Krentz 1995: 5).

Of course, in his case as in others there will have been documents relevant to much that he reports. There are some places where he seems to report accurately information which the documents will have contained: the peace between Athens and Sparta at the end of the Peloponnesian War (2.2.20), but omitting the clause which states that Athens is to withdraw from all the cities but retain its own territory, and perhaps conflating with the peace treaty, though correctly formulating, what was in fact a separate treaty by which Athens became a subordinate ally of Sparta (conflation of peace treaty and alliance, de Ste. Croix 1972: 343 n. 2); Plut. *Lys.* 14.8 quotes in Doric a text slightly earlier than the final peace treaty); the terms of the King's Peace which Tiribazus read out to the Greeks in 386 (5.1.30–1); the peace of summer 371, before Leuctra (6.3.18–19, in indirect speech but with credible detail); the peace of autumn 371, after Leuctra (6.5.2, quoting the oath in direct speech) – and in each of these cases, whether or not he has perfectly reproduced the document, his account seems at any rate to be closer to it than the corresponding account of Diodorus. The list of the Thirty at Athens (2.3.2), probably an interpolation rather than a part of Xenophon's own text, is perhaps a list of three men from each tribe, named in the official tribal order (see Whitehead 1980: 208–213; Rhodes 1981: 435), and tribal order suggests a documentary source. On the other hand, what Xenophon says of the other common peace treaties, actually ratified or merely attempted, is cast in more of a narrative form and does not look as if it is equally close to a document. I do not wish to suggest that Xenophon did after all engage in research in the archives: it does appear that, however he set about finding his material, for some treaties what he obtained was or was close to the official text, but the fact that this is true only for some treaties indicates that he did not set great store by reproducing the official text.

In the surviving fragments of the *Hellenica Oxyrhynchia* there is nothing which strongly suggests a documentary source, but there is little for which a documentary source would be appropriate. The material to which documents would have been most relevant is the account of the Boeotian constitution (19.2–4 Chambers): however, the style is narrative rather than documentary, nothing is said which could not have been discovered easily by talking to Boeotians, and this is preceded in 19.1 and followed in 20 by an account of political division in Boeotia which will certainly not have had a documentary basis (Bruce 1967: 8 suggests, "His summary of the Boeotian Constitution could perhaps have been obtained from some documentary source").

The *Hellenica Oxyrhynchia* was used for the period it covered (411–386?) by Ephorus, and Ephorus was used for the fifth century and as much of the fourth as he covered by Diodorus. We have already noticed that for some treaties Xenophon gives an account which seems close to the original document but Diodorus' version is less close; and Diodorus' version looks no more likely to be close to the document when Xenophon's is non-documentary too. Likewise there is nothing to suggest consultation of documents behind Diodorus' account of fifth-century treaties which are mentioned by Thucydides. However, a documentary basis is possible for the first peace treaty between Dionysius I of Syracuse and the Carthaginians, in 405 (Diod. 13.114.1); on the foundation of the Second Athenian League Diodorus' account is narrative in form, but it contains details on the order in which Athens acquired allies and on the promises which Athens made to the allies which are borne out by Athenian inscriptions (esp. *IG* II^2 34, 41, 43 = RO 20, Tod 121, RO 22 ~ Harding 31, 34, 35). Most strikingly, 12.4.5 gives the most detailed account which we have of the terms of the Peace of Callias allegedly made between Athens and Persia in the mid-fifth century: those who believe in the treaty and those (including myself) who do not can agree that Diodorus' terms are likely to derive ultimately from a document, but disagree as to whether that was an authentic survival from the fifth century or a fourth-century reconstruction of what was then believed to have been agreed in the fifth (cf. below). It is possible that Ephorus had documentary material which has been rendered invisible by Diodorus' use of him, but on the basis of Diodorus we can credit him with the use of documents only for the Peace of Callias (very probably) and for the Second Athenian League (possibly). The Sicilian treaty of 405 probably came to Diodorus ultimately from Dionysius' backer Philistus, through either Ephorus or Timaeus (on Diodorus' sources for Sicilian history in this period see Lewis 1994: 121–123).

But the Peace of Callias leads us to a more careful use of documents which we can see developing in the fourth century, for it was probably this treaty that Theopompus claimed (*FGrHist* 115 F 154, cf. F 155) was a fabrication, being inscribed not in the local alphabet which the Athenians used to the end of the fifth century but in the Ionian alphabet which they formally adopted in 403/2. Both those who accept the treaty and those who reject it can believe that what Theopompus saw and denounced as a fabrication was a text inscribed in the fourth century.

The Aristotelian *Athenaiōn Politeia* (*Athenian Constitution*), I have argued, was based for its historical part, to the end of ch. 41, not on original research but on earlier written accounts (though these will have included pamphlets as well as works of history), but for its descriptive part, 42–69, on direct consultation of the laws of Athens and on personal observation (Rhodes 1981: 15–30, 33–35, and notes on particular passages). The second part, then, shows the author's own awareness of the importance of documents for certain kinds of inquiry. In the first part, if I am right, there is a documentary basis where his own sources consulted the documents, and there are some sections where it is evident that that occurred. As a source on Solon and the situation which he faced I have argued for a work used both by this author and by Plutarch (cf. Rhodes 1981: 118), a work based not only on Solon's poems (from which *Ath. Pol.* and Plutarch give overlapping but not wholly the same quotations) but also on Solon's laws: in particular, *Ath. Pol.* 8.3 quotes phrases from "the laws of Solon which they no longer use." It is not clear whether it is from this joint source that Plutarch (*Sol.* 19.4, 23.4, 24.2) obtained his numbered references to the 8th law on the 13th *axon*, the 16th *axon*, and the 1st *axon*.

For the institution of the Four Hundred in 411 *Ath. Pol.* combined the narrative of Thucydides with another source (above, p. 59), and that other source made use of documents: the decree of Pythodorus and the amendment of Clitophon on the appointment of the thirty *suggrapheis* (29.2–3; but the unparalleled mention of Melobius' speech introducing the motion is probably not due to a document: cf. Rhodes 1981: 366–367, 370); the "future" and "immediate" constitutions, which were perhaps formally promulgated when the Four Hundred entered office (30–31: cf. Rhodes 1981: 386–389). Frustratingly, on the intermediate régime which followed that of the Four Hundred, *Ath. Pol.* was able to add to Thucydides' account only archons' names and months (Thuc. 8.97; *Ath. Pol.* 33). *Ath. Pol.*'s narrative of 404–403 relies on a tendentious source, which apparently distorted the chronology to minimize the responsibility of Theramenes for the misdeeds of the Thirty, but documents seem to lie behind the naming of Dracontides as proposer of the decree under which the Thirty were appointed and of Pythodorus as archon of 404/3 (34.3–35.1), and the reference to the laws which paved the way for the elimination of Theramenes (37.1); a proviso in a law of Solon which the Thirty annulled is quoted (35.2); and, most importantly, there is a detailed though apparently abbreviated account of the terms of reconciliation in 403 (39) (cf. Rhodes 1981: 420, 462–464). Unfortunately, the "constitution of Draco" (4), which seems to have been inserted by a reviser, is not an authentic early document but a concoction of the late fifth or early fourth century (cf. Rhodes 1981: 84–87).

Otherwise, the non-Herodotean material on Cleisthenes (21.1–22.2) includes some passages which certainly do not suggest a document, and nothing which seriously does apart from the archontic dates for the enactment of the reform (21.1: Cleisthenes' opponent Isagoras, presumably not in fact still present in Athens) and for its completion (the council's oath and the ten generals, 22.2) (cf. Rhodes 1981: 240–241; Rhodes 1983: 57–58). Other passages with dates likely to come from documents deal with the ostracisms and other events of the 480s (22.3–8), the three dated laws of the 450s (26.2–4 – but not the undated introduction of jury pay, 27.3–5), and perhaps the dated institution of the Delian League as a full offensive and defensive alliance, its permanence marked by the dropping of lumps of metal into the sea (23.5) (cf. Rhodes 1981: 266–267, 285; Rhodes 1983: 55). 22.3–8 and 26.2–4 most probably come from an *Atthis*, one of the histories of Athens written between the fifth century and the third, and (since there is reason to think 22.3 on ostracism is derived from him) specifically from that of Androtion, the most recent when *Ath. Pol.* was written.

Outside the *Ath. Pol.*, there are other pointers to the use of documents by Androtion in his naming all the generals of 441/0 (*FGrHist* 324 F 38), and perhaps in his naming of the three Spartan envoys who negotiated an otherwise unattested exchange of prisoners between Sparta and Athens in 408/7 (F 44). There are also signs of the use of documents by Philochorus, the other Atthidographer to give a serious account of Athens' history from the late sixth century onwards: he perhaps included a catalogue of Cleisthenes' demes, and explained their names (*FGrHist* 328 FF 25–29, 205–206); he gave an account of the procedure of ostracism, not used after 415 (F 30); he reported the check on the citizens' registers in 445/4 in response to a gift of corn from Egypt (F 119), a law of 410/09 requiring members of the council to sit in the seat assigned to them (F 140), the organization in 378/7 of men liable for the property tax, *eisphora*, in groups known as *summoriai* (F 41). Notes on officials under the régime of Demetrius of Phalerum, from 318/7 to 308/7 (FF 63–65), may point to a document-based account of that constitution, but this was a period which he himself lived through (on the Atthidographers see Rhodes 1990: esp. 76–81; and below, Ch. 14).

To return to Aristotle's school, in many fields he was interested in collecting particular instances as a basis for generalizations. The school probably compiled 158 *Constitutions* in all (D.L. 5.27: on the different numbers in different catalogues of Aristotle's works see Rhodes 1981: 1–2), and the Athenian was not the only constitution whose student incorporated documentary material: it is generally thought that the text of Sparta's Great Rhetra and (some would say, wrongly distinguished from it) its amendment in Plut. *Lyc.* 6 was derived from the *Lakedaimonion Politeia*, since "Aristotle" is cited for the elucidation of part of it (e.g. Talbert 1988: 4–5). Among other works attributed to Aristotle are four books of *Laws* (D.L. 5.26). His pupil and successor Theophrastus is credited with twenty-four books of *Laws* and ten books of an *Epitome of Laws* (D.L. 5.44): the *Laws* seems to have been a collection and discussion of laws from many states, arranged under subject headings (see Szegedy-Maszak 1981, particularly his F 21). However, Isocrates disparaged the collecting of laws which had found favor in various places as something which anybody could do (Isoc. *Antid.* 83).

By the late fourth century it had come to be seen that documents were an invaluable source of certain kinds of information: in particular, constitutional arrangements within states and larger organizations, constitutional changes and other formal decisions of these bodies, lists of officials (the works of Hellanicus of Lesbos included one on the priestesses of Hera at Argos: *FGrHist* 4 FF 74–84), and treaties of peace or alliance between states. It was not only historians who realized this: the *suggrapheis* who ushered in the régime of the Four Hundred at Athens in 411 were instructed "in addition, to search out also the traditional laws which Cleisthenes enacted when he established the democracy, in order to listen to these also and deliberate best" (*Ath. Pol.* 29.3: cf. above, p. 62). In the fourth century various fifth-century Athenian documents were either discovered or reconstructed and were cited by the orators, including the Peace of Callias with Persia, to be contrasted with the shameful King's Peace of 386 (e.g., Isoc. *Paneg.* 117–121: cf. above, pp. 61–62), and the Decree of Themistocles and other texts purporting to date from the Persian Wars, to encourage a patriotic resistance to Macedon in the 340s (e.g., Dem. *Leg.* 303, mentioning Aeschines' reading out of that decree and other texts in 348) (see particularly Habicht 1961, believing as I do that these texts were fourth-century reconstructions rather than authentic fifth-century texts).

In dealing with later writers I shall have to be highly selective. At the beginning of the third century the Macedonian Craterus made a collection of decrees, running to eight or more books (*FGrHist* 342: Book 8 cited in FF 5–8): the collection included the Peace of Callias (F 13: cf. below, p. 65), but our few fragments do not mention the Decree of Themistocles. It seems that Craterus did not compile a bare anthology of texts but included other material with references to historians. Plutarch (*Arist.* 26 = F 12) says that he reported a conviction of Aristides for taking bribes, but provided no lawsuit or decree to support this, "although he was accustomed to write such things quite well and to cite those who investigate/report (*historein*)." Polemon of Ilium, in the early second century, included in his works accounts of the various Greek states, with particular attention to buildings and monuments (*FHG* III.108–148): he was such an enthusiast for collecting and citing inscriptions that he was referred to as a *stēlokopas*, a glutton for *stēlai* (Ath. 6.234 d).

Polybius, in the second century, saw himself as returning from the rhetorical and sensational kinds of history which had become fashionable to the kind of history written by Thucydides (Walbank 1972: 40–43). This included the questioning of witnesses (12.4c.3–5) and the writing of speeches which purported to reflect what had actually been said (2.56.10, 36.1.6–7). He criticizes the Sicilian Timaeus for his copious citation of inscriptions (12.10.9–11.3), and probably did not himself have much access to or make much use of documents (Walbank 1972: 82–84). But he did, rather self-consciously, survey the inscribed treaties between Rome and Carthage (3.21.9–26.7: see Walbank, *HCP* I.338), and use an inscription giving Hannibal's detailed arrangements in Spain and his crossing of the Alps, in 218 (3.33.5–18, 56.2–4) and an admiral's dispatch preserved in the *prytaneion* in Rhodes (16.15.8) – on which Walbank (*HCP* II.520) comments that this "may but need not necessarily imply that he had seen it himself." There appears to be a contradiction between the interpretation which he attributes to Flamininus of the treaty of 212/1 between Rome and the Aetolians (18.38.8–9) and the inscribed text of the treaty, of which fragments survive (*IG* IX.² i 241 = *Staatsverträge* 536): many scholars have judged Flamininus and/or Polybius dishonest, but Walbank thinks that if we had the complete text it might resolve the contradiction (Walbank, *HCP* II.599–601; 1972: 43 n. 59).

Josephus not merely refers to decisions which must have been documented (e.g., *AJ* 12.119–128, at least in part from Nicolaus of Damascus) but also in Books 12–14 and 16 quotes a large number of documents. They are quoted for a purpose, to demonstrate the favorable treatment of the Jews by the Hellenistic rulers and the Romans (14.186–188; 16.174–178); he insists that while other documents are harder to track down the Roman documents can easily be found on the capitol (14.187–188). At times their authenticity has been doubted, but it is now generally accepted that although there may have been some tampering in places they are essentially authentic (e.g., Rajak 1984: esp. 109). We noticed above (p. 57) in connection with Herodotus' "Cadmean letters" Josephus' insistence that the Greeks did not learn the art of writing until long after the Trojan War; even Homer did not write down his poems; one reason why so much in Greek history is controversial is that not even the Athenians produced written documents until the laws of Draco, "a man who lived only a short time before the tyranny of Peisistratus" (*Ap.* 1.10–23).

Plutarch for his *Lives* used a wide range of sources, and the variety of source material with which they provided him. He consulted Craterus' collection of decrees on controversial matters. Most people said that Aristides died either on public business abroad or respected in Athens; Craterus said he was convicted of bribery and left Athens because he could not pay the fine; but he cited no document and no other source mentions it (cf. above, p. 64). The Athenian victories at the Eurymedon so lowered the morale of the Persian King that he agreed to the Peace of Callias: Callisthenes denied (*or* did not mention) the treaty but said the King in fact ceased troubling the Greeks (*Cim.* 13.4 = *FGrHist* 124 F 16: on the meaning of Plutarch's *ou phēsi* here see Bosworth 1990), but Craterus included a copy of the treaty as something which happened (*Cim.* 13.4–5 = *FGrHist* 342 F 13). In Plutarch's essay *On the Malice of Herodotus* the argument is not uniformly of high quality, but he knows how to argue from inscriptions. To demonstrate that the Greeks did not withdraw defeated from Artemisium he cites the victory epigram set up in the temple there (867D–F); to confirm that the Naxians fought on the Greek side in 480 he cites an epigram celebrating Democritus (868F–869C: Democritus is mentioned as committing the Naxians to the Greek cause at Hdt. 8.46.3); against one of Herodotus' most palpably unfair chapters, suggesting that the Corinthians tried to flee from Salamis but ending with the admission that this was an unsupported Athenian allegation (8.94), he cites the epitaph which the Athenians allowed the Corinthians to set up on Salamis and other inscriptions (870B–871C: the epitaph is ML 84 ∼ Fornara 21); he responds with another inscription and with the Serpent Column to Herodotus' allegation (9.85.3) that cities which did not fight in the battle of Plataea created fake graves there subsequently (872B–873E). So I end this chapter with inscriptions used intelligently as a basis for argument.

CHAPTER FIVE

The Prehistory of Roman Historiography

T. P. Wiseman

1

The Greeks come before the Romans, in this book as in all accounts of the ancient world. That priority is not a historical datum – on the contrary, the city-states of Athens and Rome came into being at much the same time – but in the discussion of ancient literature it is inevitable. Uniquely, and astonishingly, in the sixth century BCE Greeks used the medium of alphabetic writing not just for lists or laws or epitaphs, but also to preserve the songs of epic bards and lyric poets; and so they created a literature. Neither Latins nor (so far as we know) Etruscans did that until three centuries later.

It is not that the Latins and Etruscans were backward, or peripheral. Horace's famous lines on the rude farmers of the Roman republic, wholly innocent of Greek culture until "the peace that followed the Punic Wars" (*Epist.* 2.1.156–163), are demonstrable nonsense. Of course classicists want to believe what a classic author tells them; but a few archaeological glimpses of the archaic world of Latium and south Etruria may help us to overcome that mindset.

The earliest alphabetic Greek inscription known from anywhere was scratched on a pot about 800 BCE in an Iron Age community in Latium, just 20 km east of Rome (Ridgway 1996); Euboean potters can be detected working at Veii in the eighth century BCE (Ridgway 1992: 131–137); in the mid-seventh century, Kleiklos, "famed for fame," is attested on a Corinthian vase in the Esquiline cemetery at Rome (*SEG* 31.875), and Aristonothos, "bastard noble," painted the blinding of Polyphemos on a mixing bowl made for an Etruscan magnate at Caere (Schneider 1955); other Greeks known as living and working in Etruria at that time include Larth Telikles and Rutile Hipukrates (Ridgway 1988: 664–665); in the sixth century, Ionians and Samians were frequenting the trading post of Gravisca (*SEG* 27.671, 32.940–1017), at about the same time as a bronze plaque attests the cult of the Dioscuri at Lavinium (*ILLRP* 1271a), while at Rome an Attic black-figure krater showing Hephaestus appears at the Volcanal (Coarelli 1983: 176–177) and a terracotta statue group portrays the apotheosis of Heracles in the Forum Bovarium (Cristofani 1990: 115–118).

These are just the most striking examples of an archaeological record which led its most authoritative interpreter to the following conclusion (Pallottino 1981: 44, my translation): "The effect of the refined Ionian civilization on the cities of Tyrrhenian Italy is widespread and deeply felt in the second half of the sixth century BCE. We could even say that there comes into being a genuine cultural and artistic *koinē* consisting equally of the Greek colonies and the Campanian, Latin, and Etruscan centers."

So it should be no surprise that Hesiod (*Theog.* 1011–1016) – or a sixth-century pseudo-Hesiod (West 1966: 435–436) – makes Latinos, eponym of the Latins and ruler of "the famed Etruscans," a son of Circe and Odysseus. Circe's island was just off the coast of Latium, directly across the water from the north coast of Sicily, where in the early sixth century lived the greatest poet of the Greek West, Stesichorus of Himera. Though he wrote in lyric meters, Stesichorus' grandeur and ambitious heroic narratives put him in almost the same category as Homer himself (Quint. 10.1.62). A late source, not necessarily untrustworthy (Horsfall 1979), says that Stesichorus related Aeneas' voyage to the west, and recent discoveries have revealed much of his *Geryoneis* (Page 1973), the narrative of Heracles' tenth labor which ultimately lies behind the Roman story of Hercules' meeting with Evander.

Pallantion, Evander's Arcadian home, was mentioned in the *Geryoneis*, and one of the versions of the poet's own life (*Suda* s.v. "Stesichoros") says that he was born in Pallantion but went into exile – just like Evander. If that reflects the characteristic biographical method of borrowing episodes from an author's works as if they were evidence for his life (Harvey 2004: 298–300), perhaps we might even infer that the Roman story goes back to Stesichorus himself. Of course we do not know enough to *assert* that, but it is not inconceivable. Rome and early Greek poetry did not exist in separate worlds.

The same is true of early Greek prose. Those Ionian dedications at Gravisca were set up by people not unlike the pioneer *logopoios* Hecataeus of Miletus, whose "circuit of the earth" naturally included western Italy – not only the predictable islands (Elba, Capri, etc.) but also inland centers like Nola and Capua in Campania, the latter of which he derived from "Capys the Trojan" (*FGrHist* 1 FF 59–63). Rome would not have been beyond his scope. The early fifth century may be when Promathion of Samos wrote his *Italica*, which contained the earliest version of the Romulus legend (Wiseman 1995: 57–61); and the unknown author of the "Cymaean chronicle" (Alföldi 1965: 56–72), which probably dealt with the descendants of Demaratus of Corinth who ruled in Rome (Zevi 1995), may also belong to that period. Towards the end of the fifth century Hellanicus of Lesbos reported a view of Rome's origin – founded by Aeneas "with Odysseus" (*FGrHist* 4 F 84) – which looks like a combination of two separate traditions existing already. Hellanicus also seems to have known some Latin, since his account of Heracles' return with the cattle of Geryon includes a derivation of "Italia" from *uitulus* (*FGrHist* 4 F 111).

He may have regarded Latin as a Greek dialect (Gabba 2000: 159–165). Certainly in the fourth century BCE Heracleides of Pontus (F 102 Wehrli) called Rome "a Hellenic *polis*," and Aristotle (F 609 Rose) believed it had been founded by Achaians blown off course by storms in the return from Troy. Theophrastus (*HP* 5.8.3) knew the Roman colony at Kirkaion, where the inhabitants pointed out the tomb of Elpenor, and his circumstantial report of a Roman attempt to found a city in Corsica (5.8.1–2) shows that he was well informed. At this point we have visual evidence again, with the engraved bronze mirrors and *cistae* which attest the thorough familiarity of Latin and Roman craftsmen with Greek artistic traditions; the inscribed names on some of the scenes depicted provide vivid evidence of their creative exploitation of the stories of Greek mythology (Wiseman 2004: 87–118).

In the third century BCE, Eratosthenes of Cyrene found it natural to include Romulus, son of Ascanius and grandson of Aeneas, in his chronological researches (*FGrHist* 241 F 45), and it is not at all paradoxical that his contemporary Callimachus used the story of "Gaius the Roman" to illustrate the virtues of *Panhellas* (*Aitia* 4.106).

2

It is clear, then, that as far back as our information extends – more than half a millennium before Horace imagined the dawn of Hellenic consciousness in his Roman peasants – Rome and her Latin and Etruscan neighbors were an integral part of the Greek world. What effect did that have on the Romans' perception of themselves?

Whether or not the expulsion of the Tarquins was inspired by that of the Peisistratids, the Romans must have been aware of the parallel. The early republican cult of Liber may well have been influenced by the Athenian Dionysus Eleuthereus; much more certain is the influence of the "Solonian" law-code on the Twelve Tables, visible even in the fragments that survive (Crawford 1996: 560–561). Moreover, there are structural elements in the "history" of the early republic, as we have it in Livy and Dionysius, which strongly suggest the influence of Athenian events: the attack of Porsenna to restore Tarquin parallels that of the Spartans to restore Hippias, the exile of Collatinus parallels the ostracism of Hipparchus, the exile of Coriolanus parallels the ostracism of Themistocles, and so on (Mastrocinque 1988: 32–35). The cults of the Spartan Dioscuri in the Forum and of Arcadian Pan at the Lupercal, and the "chapels of the Argives" listed in a liturgical document quoted by Varro (*Ling.* 5.45–54), show that Athens was not the only influence, but by the end of the fourth century her imperial democracy may well have seemed a particularly appropriate paradigm for the Roman republic's domination of central Italy. It was at the time of the Samnite Wars that the statue of Alcibiades, "the bravest of the Greeks," was erected in the Comitium (Plin. *NH* 34.26).

That choice implies familiarity with recent historiography – Thucydides, Xenophon, Ephorus of Cyme. And there is reason to suppose that some Romans also read the "Atthidographers," whose narratives of the long history of their city's political development conspicuously prefigured the later historiography of Rome. A particularly revealing parallel is the description in Cleidemus (*FGrHist* 323 F 18) of Theseus' battle with the Amazons in what was in historical times the middle of Athens: the topographical details are used as "evidence" in just the same way as the Lacus Curtius and the Iuppiter Stator temple in the story of Romulus' battle with the Sabines in what was in historical times the middle of Rome.

Cleidemus was probably an *exegetēs* (*FGrHist* 323 F 14), using his cultic expertise to create the material for his history. In Rome the *annales* of the *pontifices*, considered by Cicero (*De Or.* 2.51–53) to be fundamental for the development of Roman historiography, may have begun in 300 BCE with the creation of the reformed college of *pontifices*, now with plebeian parity of membership (Livy 10.9.2). It is usually thought that the *annales* began much earlier than that (Cornell 1995: 13–15); but the main evidence for that position has been shown to be textually unreliable (Humm 2000: 106–109, on Cic. *Rep.* 1.25), and in any case it may be thought unlikely that the unreformed patrician college had been interested in making its knowledge public.

A similar point may be made about another potential source of historical information, the list of annual magistrates. Such lists certainly existed after the power-sharing compromise of 367 BCE, which required the election of one plebeian and one patrician consul each year; however, magistrate lists reaching right back to the expulsion of the Tarquins were available to the historians of the first century BCE, and to whoever created the sequence of consuls and triumphs inscribed on Augustus' triumphal arch, and it is usually thought that they are broadly reliable (Cornell 1995: 218–221). But if the reform of 367 marked the final achievement of a *polis* constitution which required formal record keeping, it may well be doubted whether the patrician magistrates of the previous 140 years felt the need for such an archive. We know that some later historians, faced with an absence of authentic record for the years before the Gallic sack of the city in 387, were driven to the conclusion that the Gauls had burned the city, and all the records had perished in the fire (*FGrHist* 840 F 3). In fact, as the archaeological evidence shows, there was no fire. The suspicion must be that what passed for the "early republican" magistrate list in Livy's time was the result of antiquarian scholarship of the same kind as that of the Atthidographers who reconstructed the earliest Athenian archon list.

It happens to be recorded (Plin. *NH* 33.119–120) that in 304 BCE the aedile Cn. Flavius set up a shrine of Concordia to mark the reconciliation of the "orders," and that in the inscription he dated it to 204 years after the dedication of the Capitoline temple. That may imply that the only way of counting the years before 367 BCE was by the nails that were annually driven into the wall of the temple of Iuppiter Optimus Maximus on the Capitol (Livy 7.3.5). That great monument to the power and ambition of the archaic tyranny, conceived on the lines of the cult of Zeus at Olympia, still dominated the Romans' memory of their own past (Purcell 2003: 26–33).

Cleidemus was writing in the mid-fourth century BCE. Whether or not his work in particular was influential in Rome, it now seems clear that it was in the generation after that – the pivotal period at the turn of the fourth and third centuries – that the main outlines of "Roman history" were formed (Gabba 2000: 16–19).

3

How that came about is a question fraught with methodological difficulty. What can we know about the communal memory of a pre-literary society, when our evidence comes from much later literary texts whose authors (remember Horace!) had little or no understanding of it? Any hypothesis can only be tentative – but even so, there are hints in our literary sources that may help us to imagine some aspects of the Rome of 300 BCE.

The most famous such item, first exploited by the Dutch scholar Perizonius in 1685 (Momigliano 1957), is Cicero's reference to a passage in the elder Cato's *Origines* (F 118) about a custom – obsolete in Cato's own time – of guests at banquets singing songs to the music of the pipe "in praise of famous men." Modern scholarship is divided on the value of this evidence, which on the one hand is certainly consistent with what we know of the archaic *symposion* (Zorzetti 1990), but on the other might be just Cato's exploitation of Greek antiquarian scholarship about the archaic past (Horsfall 1994: 70–73). My own view is that it may well have been a genuine memory from the pre-literary world, offering an insight into how the past was remembered in one stratum of Roman society. One might imagine that banquets where the friends and relatives of an Appius Claudius or a Quintus Fabius were gathered were not unlike those implied by the poetry of the early Greek elegists, with the values of an aristocratic elite being rehearsed and reinforced by the example of admired ancestors (Wiseman 1994: 30–32).

Aristocrats also had more public ways of making sure the deeds of their ancestors were remembered. Cicero (*Brut.* 62) refers to the survival of early funeral orations, Livy (8.40.2) to the inscriptions attached to ancestral portraits, and the earliest Scipionic epitaphs (*ILLRP* 309–310) give us an idea of the sort of information that might be transmitted. The fact that both Cicero and Livy thought it was unreliable need not concern us: what matters is the creation of communal memory through the pride of noble families.

Was that all there was? One influential modern view holds that the creation of the Roman historical tradition was solely the work of the elite, as if the Roman ruling class were identical with the republic (Timpe 1988: 283–285). But since the Latin for "Roman history" is *res* (*gestae*) *populi Romani*, literally "the deeds of the Roman people" (Sall. *Cat.* 4.2; Livy *praef.* 1), that can hardly be true. The deeds of noble leaders do indeed feature prominently in the later historical tradition, but they do not monopolize it. Where should we look for the communal memory of the People as a whole?

It may be helpful to apply to the citizens of Rome something that Pausanias wrote in the second century CE about the Athenians, who believed that their democracy was set up by Theseus. As Pausanias rather snobbishly comments (1.3.3), "there are many false beliefs current among the mass of mankind, since they are ignorant of historical science and consider trustworthy whatever they have heard from childhood in choruses and tragedies." The "choruses" he refers to were part of everyday experience, hymns in honor of the gods at the sacrifices and rituals that were familiar to every adult and child in the *polis* (Buxton 1994: 21–26); and since Plato says much the same thing about "stories repeated in prayers at sacrifices" (*Leg.* 887d), I think we are entitled to use Pausanias here as evidence for more than just his own time and place.

There are three passages in Dionysius' history of early Rome where the author alludes to hymns still sung in Rome in his own time. At 1.31.2 he refers to Faunus, king of the Aborigines, "a man of prudence as well as energy, whom the Romans in their sacrifices and songs honor as one of the gods of their country"; at 1.79.11 he comments that the young Romulus and Remus were looked on as offspring of the gods, "and as such they are still celebrated by the Romans in the hymns of their country"; and at 8.62.3 he says of Marcius Coriolanus "though nearly five hundred years have already elapsed since his death down to the present time, his memory has not become extinct, but he is still sung and hymned by all as a pious and just man." A possible context for the first of these may be the sacrifice to Faunus at the Tiber Island on February 13; for the second, either the Lupercalia two days later, scene of the suckling of the twins, or the Parilia, anniversary of the foundation of the city, on April 21; and for the third, the sacrifice to Fortuna Muliebris at the fourth milestone of the Via Latina on July 6 (8.55.3–5 gives the date and the reason). It is not necessary to suppose that the hymns Dionysius knew in the late first century BCE were themselves archaic compositions; the mere fact that such hymns were sung at Roman sacrifices is enough to attest one more traditional source of communal memory.

Tragedies, according to Pausanias, were the other main source of the ordinary Athenian's historical knowledge. Here too there is a Roman analogy, in Plautus' casual remark (*Amph.* 41–44) that gods in tragedies regularly reminded the audience of the good things they have done for Rome. That suggests plays on Roman historical themes, no doubt the *fabulae praetextae* discussed by historians of Roman drama from Varro onwards (Kragelund et al. 2002). Since the earliest *praetexta* our sources refer to is Naevius' *Clastidium*, on the single combat of the consul Marcellus with a Gallic king in 222 BCE, modern scholars have usually inferred that the genre was an invention of Naevius himself – and no doubt that is true as far as *literary* drama is concerned. The question is, was there drama before there was literature?

One revealing piece of evidence is Varro's citation of a play on a quasi-historical subject not by the author's name, or even the title, but by the context of its performance (*Ling.* 6.18): "the People were taught the reason for this by the *togata praetexta* presented at the Games of Apollo." What matters here is the assumption that performances at the theater games "teach the People." The particular play Varro refers to can hardly predate 212 BCE, when the *ludi Apollinares* were inaugurated, but the principle may well date back to before our imagined 300 BCE horizon, since the *ludi Romani* certainly, and the *ludi plebeii, Cereales,* and *Liberales* probably, were already in existence at that time (Wiseman 2005). Moreover, it is clear from the iconography of the bronze mirrors and *cistae* mentioned above that Latins and Romans in the fourth century BCE were familiar with dramatic performance, in a

Dionysiac context which might even involve the plots of Euripidean tragedies (Wiseman 2000: 274–289).

So it may well be that when the citizens of Rome gathered at the "games" in honor of their gods – Iuppiter Optimus Maximus at the *ludi Romani* and *plebeii*, Ceres, Liber, and Libera at the others – they were taught what they needed to know about the gods, about their rights and duties, and about the history of their city, by exemplary narratives presented in dramatic form. As always, our inference can only be a provisional hypothesis. But it is at least consistent with the little we know about plays presented in the later Rome of our literary sources, which dealt with divine punishment of wrongdoers (Cic. *Pis.* 46), the power of the gods as revealed on earth (Ov. *Fast.* 4.326), the miraculous ways in which the Romans of the past overcame their enemies (Livy 5.21.9), and the rewards of victory as manifested in the triumphal celebration (Hor. *Epist.* 2.1.187–193). It is, I think, reasonable to assume that much of Rome's communal memory consisted of what the citizen body saw regularly performed before its eyes.

The very fact that later historians might suspect material in their sources of having been invented for the stage (Wiseman 1995: 131–132) is enough to confirm that dramatic performance was one of the ways in which historical knowledge could be created and perpetuated. There were of course other ways, which hardly need argument: the instruction of the young by parents and teachers, for example, or the commercial activity of professional storytellers (Plin. *Ep.* 2.20.1; Dio Chrys. 20.10). But the contexts suggested above, preserving the remembered past of the leading families or of the citizen body as a whole, may be more important for our purposes, as possible conduits for the historical tradition of the Roman People.

4

In his preface to the *Lays of Ancient Rome*, Macaulay notes with regret that the Romans – unlike Sir Walter Scott – never sought out and recorded examples of oral poetry in order to prevent them from being forgotten. But Macaulay was wrong: it seems that at least one such collection was indeed made, "a book of very ancient *carmina*, which was said to have been put together before anything written in Latin" (Macr. *Sat.* 5.20.18). Only scraps from it survive, preserved in learned authors from Varro to Macrobius, but some of them may be of interest for our subject.

Here for instance is a quasi-Homeric moment quoted by Festus (214L) from the *vetera carmina*: "But now Aurora, withdrawing from the sky, reveals her father." That must be from a narrative poem, as perhaps was this line, quoted by Varro in his *De vita populi Romani* (*ap.* Nonius 31L): "There the shepherds hold the Consualia games with hides." The reference is evidently to Consus' altar in the valley north of the Aventine; that was where the Sabine women were abducted at the Consualia on August 21 in the first year of Rome, so the "shepherds" may well be Romulus' men. Two other *carmina* were certainly narrative, entitled "Priam" (Varro *Ling.* 7.28, an invocation to the *Casmenae*) and "Neleus" (Festus 418L, 482L). Priam's scepter was one of the divine talismans of Rome (Serv. *auctus* on *Aen.* 7.188), and Neleus was one of a pair of divinely begotten twins who were exposed, rescued, and brought up in secret before freeing their mother from servitude; the parallel with Romulus and Remus extends even to the cradle (*skaphē*) which featured in the recognition scene (Arist. *Poet.* 1454b; D. Hal. *AR* 1.82–83).

The most important feature of these tantalizingly enigmatic fragments is their anonymity, which suggests that they did indeed originate in a world before authors. The transition to literature proper is marked by the *carmen belli Punici*, which is always attributed in our sources to its author Cn. Naevius. This was a poem of which the written text was preserved – but even so, it was not designed primarily for reading. Before C. Octavius Lampadio divided it into seven books, it existed as "a continuous script" (Suet. *Gramm.* 2.2), which I think means that Naevius wrote it for recitation in the traditional way: the script was his personal property, not copied until after his death.

Naevius' *carmen* is an important milestone in the development of Roman historical consciousness. No doubt bigger, better, and more comprehensive than any of its predecessors, it must have taken five or six hours to deliver. Its audience of Roman citizens – at the *ludi Romani*, perhaps – will have learned about Aeneas' flight from Troy, Jupiter's prophecy of Roman greatness, the origins of Carthage and its enmity with Rome, the foundation of Rome by Aeneas' grandson Romulus, and the course of the great Punic War in which the poet himself had fought. Ennius was right about Naevius' Saturnian meter, "in which of old the Fauns and prophets sang" (*Ann.* F 207). It was indeed a traditional form – but it was used at a high level of literary sophistication (Goldberg 1995: 73–82), and Naevius' poem deserves to be thought of as the first true history of Rome.

There was another form of literary sophistication, however, which despised the historical epic and its mass audience (Callim. *Anth. Pal.* 12.43.1–4). Those who knew the Greek historians knew Thucydides' pointed contrast (1.21.1, 22.4) between the performances of poets and *logographoi*, competing for a particular audience's favor, and his own historical research, entrusted to a written text which would be a possession for ever. The Hannibalic War was a time when men might well remember Thucydides, and his insistence that the war he narrated was the greatest and most terrible in history: no doubt that had been true two centuries earlier, but the Romans knew it was true no longer. Even so, the first *historiai* of Rome were not (or not only) Thucydidean war narratives.

Fabius Pictor and Cincius Alimentus – and Postumius Albinus too, in the next generation – were Roman senators who wrote their histories in Greek. Despite authoritative opinion to the contrary (Gruen 1992: 231), that must mean that at least they hoped for a Greek readership. Since 1974 we have known that Fabius Pictor's history began with "the coming of Herakles into Italy" (*SEG* 26.1123.3a); Plutarch tells us (*Rom.* 3.1, 8.7) that Fabius' detailed and theatrical narrative of the overthrow of Amulius by Romulus and Remus was taken from a Greek author, Diocles of Peparethos; Postumius Albinus is likely to be responsible for casting the victory of his ancestor Aulus Postumius at Lake Regillus into the "purely Homeric" narrative followed by Livy and Dionysius (Wiseman 1998: 86–87). That looks like *prima facie* evidence that these authors were writing for an international Greek-speaking audience.

Part of their motive was no doubt to present Rome in a sympathetic light. Fabius will have presented Herakles as the ancestor not only of himself but also of the great commander who defied Hannibal (Plut. *FM* 1.1). One of the few surviving items of Cincius' history (*FGrHist* 810 F 4) reassuringly presents the Roman ruling class as a strong oligarchy trusted by the People: the Senate decrees the execution of Sp. Maelius without trial, and entrusts the deed to Servilius Ahala, who takes a sword and cuts Maelius down in the Forum; the citizens are indignant, but when he shouts that he has killed a tyrant by order of the Senate, they accept the sentence without demur.

One can hardly imagine Naevius, that scourge of the nobility (Gell. 3.3.15), telling the story to the Roman People in quite those terms. And of course there were other differences too between the Saturnian bard and the Hellenizing historians. "Naevius . . . , by choosing to write a poem rather than a history, did not submit the Roman past to the process of rational elucidation in the interest of truth which is characteristic of Greek historiography" (Momigliano 1990: 91). But there is no need to privilege one style over the other. It was a combination of their methods (and their prejudices) that defined the past of a city which in their day had already seen a century and a half of military struggle and success, three centuries of creative tension between the respective interests of the many and the few, and more than half a millennium (*pace* Horace) of varied cultural evolution. It is not surprising that the resulting tradition of Roman historiography was so rich and complex.

FURTHER READING

First, six chapters from three separate volumes of *CAH*[2]: Ridgway 1988; Ogilvie and Drummond 1989; Torelli 1989; Momigliano 1989; Drummond 1989; and Rawson 1989. Tim Cornell's chapters in *CAH*[2] VII.2 are subsumed into his magisterial synthesis Cornell 1995, an essential work; much of interest will also be found in Oakley, *CL* I.21–109, and in the essays in Gruen 1990 and 1992. Two valuable studies on Roman religion are relevant to the theme: Beard et al. 1998: I.1–72, and Feeney 1998 (short but stimulating).

All those are predominantly background reading. For the central problem of how to understand non-literary culture, three recent items may be recommended, not least as examples of contrasting scholarly approaches: Horsfall 2003; Purcell 2003; and Wiseman 2004: chs. 2–7.

CHAPTER SIX

Myth and Historiography

Suzanne Saïd

1 Introduction

" 'Myth' and 'history' . . . have been perceived as virtual opposites and contradictory ways of looking at the world" (Henrichs 1999: 223). Myth was defined as irrational fiction produced by collective imagination, and history as objective truth resulting from rational inquiry. It was widely held that Greek thought evolved *Vom Mythos zum Logos*, to quote Wilhem Nestle's famous book (1940), and Thucydides was regarded as the first "scientific" historian precisely because of his claim to have excluded all mythical material from his work. But Hellenists have come to feel uneasy with various aspects of this model, as demonstrated by the title of a recent volume, *From Myth to Reason?* (Buxton 1999), now tellingly followed by a question mark. On the one hand, ancient history has been redefined by Woodman (1988: 197), echoing Cicero's conception of history as *opus oratorium maxime* (*Leg.* 1.5), primarily as a rhetorical genre to be classified (in modern terms) as literature rather than as history. On the other hand, myth has been upgraded to the status of "intentional history," which is "of fundamental significance for the way in which a society interprets and under-stands itself" (Gehrke 2001: 186). Thus the relation between these two notions has to be reconsidered. Such a reconsideration may take different forms.

(1)   History of myths has changed. Nineteenth-century mythologists looked for an origin of myths supposedly to be found in a historical event. Among contem-porary historians, some make them into a "nouvel objet d'histoire" and a privileged way of discovering "toute la pensée d'une société" (Detienne 1974: 73); others pay more attention to the conditions of their development (e.g., Brillante 1990) or to their role in the culture that defined and unified the elite of the Greco-Roman world (Cameron 2004).
(2)   New attention has been paid to the so-called "mythicizing" of the recent past, not only by early Greek elegists (Bowie 1986, 2001; Boedeker 1995, 1996),

but also by historians who introduced gods and heroes into their narrative of recent events or included mythical motives in their relation of the lives of historical characters such as Cyrus or Alexander (e.g., Flashar 1996; Gehrke 2001; Boedeker 2002).

In this chapter I have chosen to focus on the status of myth in ancient Greek historiography (in the broadest sense of the word, that is, an entity including genealogies, local history, geography, and so on) from its beginnings to the Roman empire by examining what Greek historians call myth (*muthos*), mythical (*muthōdes*, *muthikos*), and mythical time, then by looking at the way in which they deal with what we call "myth," that is, a peculiar kind of tale characterized by its location in primordial time and/or its superhuman characters, its traditional (or allegedly trad-itional) origin, and its collective significance.

2 "Myth" and *Muthos*

It is obvious that *muthos* is not coextensive with our "myth" (Calame 1999: 121–122). The most famous myth of the *Works and Days*, the myth of the ages, is introduced as a *logos* (106) and the father of history, Herodotus, nearly always uses *logos* and *legein* to introduce what we would call a "myth" (Nickau 1990: 83), making no explicit contrast between *muthos/logos/historiē* (Murray 2001: 24). Cen-turies later, Pausanias still used the same word for a typical "myth," the story of a young man transformed into a river (7.23.3), whereas Dionysius of Halicarnassus used *historia* for the story of Rhea Silvia raped by a dog (1.77). But it is also true that *muthos* had two well-defined and opposite meanings.

When there was only one authorized version of the past, guaranteed by the Muses, who are divine eyewitnesses, myth was a positive value-word. Martin (1989: 29–30) aptly demonstrated that in Homeric diction "the word *muthos*, as opposed to *epos*, implies authority and power." Following Detienne (1967), he explained its early association with poetry by the status of the archaic poets as "maîtres de vérité." This is the reason why Empedocles presents the actual exposition of his doctrine as a *muthos* (Calame 1999: 122), and also why Hecataeus, in the famous opening sen-tence of his *Genealogies*, uses a derivative of *muthos* for his own account, whereas he uses *logos* for silly tales of the Greeks (*FGrHist* 1 F 1a):

> Hecataeus of Miletus gives the following account (*mutheitai*). I write these things as they seem to me to be true. For the stories (*logoi*) of the Greeks are many and ludicrous, as they appear to me.

Yet *muthos* also acquired a negative value, at least from the fifth century: "One well-known and recurrent motif in a variety of writers from the fifth century onwards is to represent what their predecessors or contemporary rivals offer as *muthos*, whereas what they themselves provide is *logos*" (Lloyd 1990: 45). Among the historians, Herodotus would be the first to use *muthos* to dismiss a tale he does not agree with. But is he? If Herodotus in 2.23, as well as in 2.45, is launching a scathing attack against Hecataeus, without quoting him by name – a convincing suggestion made recently by Nickau (1990: 85–87) – it is tempting to interpret these two – and only – occurrences of *muthos* as an ironic echo of Hecataeus' *mutheitai*.

In fact it is in Thucydides (1.21) that we first find a word coined – maybe by Thucydides himself – on the root *muth-* with a distinctly negative content: in his programmatic remarks, *muthōdes* designates what is to be excluded from the history of the Peloponnesian War: the miraculous aspects of traditional tales that have nothing to do with "truth" – they do not admit testing – but are attractive and entertaining. The illustrations given by Dionysius in his commentary on this text – "Lamias issuing from earth . . . the offspring of mortals and gods and many other stories that seem incredible (*apistous*) and foolish (*anoēton*) for our time" (*Thuc.* 6) – all suggest that "myths" in the modern sense were Thucydides' real target here.

Muthos was also used by ancient critics in order to downgrade some historians, beginning with Herodotus who was considered a teller of myths (*muthologos*) by Aristotle (*GA* 3.75b5) and, together with Ctesias, a composer of monstrous little myths (*terastia muthidia*) by Lucian (*Philops.* 2). In the same way Hellanicus, Cadmus of Miletus, and Hecataeus were criticized for their "mythical" assertions by Diodorus (1.37.3), and Cicero finds in Herodotus as well as in Theopompus "innumerabiles fabulae" (*Leg.* 1.5).

Thus it comes as no surprise to find out that, from Polybius to Strabo, "mythical" is often associated with "bizarre" (*xenos*), "excessive" (*perittos*), "marvelous" (*thaumastos*), or "prodigious" (*teratōdes*). It is supposed to be a "lie" (*pseudos*) or a "melodramatic fiction" (*dramatikon*), since it is "beyond belief" (*apithanos* or *apistos*). It is opposed to what is "historical" (*historikos*), "true" (*alēthes*) or "similar to true" (*alēthēiai eoikos*), "likely" (*eikos*), or "believable" (*pistos, pithanos,* or *pisteuomenos*).

These uses of *muthos* and *muthōdes* in the historiography of the Hellenistic or Roman periods appear to coincide with the definitions that opposed *muthos/fabula* to *historia* and *plasma/argumentum*, and are found in the preliminary exercises (*progymnasmata*) of rhetorical handbooks (Barwick 1928; Nicolai 1992: 124–138) or scholia (Lazzarini 1984; Meijering 1987: 79–90). As opposed to *historia* which is true, and *plasma* which is "as if true," myth lacks any kind of verisimilitude (e.g., Quint. 2.4.2); it is a narrative of events which are against the laws of nature (Isid. *Orig.* 1.44.5), such as the metamorphoses of Diomedes' companions into sea birds, an illustration given by Sextus Empirus (*Math.* 1.263) and Strabo (6.3.9).

In short, when one looks at the uses of *muthōdes* and *muthikos* in Greek historiography after Thucydides, it is tempting to say that it is history that made "myth" – or better, "the mythical" – into the antonym of history.

3   Spatium Mythicum?

According to Finley (1975: 24–25), "Greek thinking divided the past into two parts, two compartments, the heroic age and the post-heroic (or the time of gods and the time of men). The first was the part fixed, defined and described by the myth-makers who worked in the centuries which are to us prehistoric in the strict sense." Actually this is true for Homer who presupposes a qualitative difference between the heroes and the men of today (his Diomedes could lift a huge stone "which no two men could carry such as men are now," *Il.* 5.303–304). The same awareness of an unbridgeable gap separating the audience from "mythical" times appears in the *Catalogue of Women* and the *Genealogies* of Acusilaus (*FGrHist* 2) which ends with the heroes.

But this gap was bridged by the "full" genealogies of Pherecydes (he gave a "full" genealogy for the Philaids from Philaias, son of Ajax, to the elder Miltiades), Hecataeus (according to Hdt. 2.143, he "connected his paternal line to a god as his sixteenth ancestor"), and Herodotus, who enumerated all the ancestors of the Spartan kings Leonidas (7.204) and Leotychidas (8.131) beginning with Hyllus son of Heracles. As a matter of fact, one must conclude that "the twofold division of mythical and historical time does not really apply to Herodotus" (Cobet 2002: 411; *contra*, Vidal-Naquet 1960). When he describes Polycrates' thalassocracy as the first of what is called the time of men, as opposed to Minos "and any other whose army may have controlled the sea before him" (3.122.2), he only distinguishes between those about whom he had reliable information and those about whom he did not. "It is this criterion of knowledge that determines the definition of a *spatium historicum* introduced by Herodotus" (von Leyden 1949–1950: 95); what he knows from first-hand information and what he does not. Thucydides' division of time relies upon the same principle when he opposes the present to "what comes before it" and to a more remote past "which cannot be known clearly because of the length of time" (1.1.3), or underlines the continuity of the Athenian way of life from the time of Cecrops to his own day (2.14.2–15.1). Diodorus' *Library*, with six books devoted to events before the Trojan War, also clearly interrelates mythical past and present "in ways which form an historical continuum" (Clarke 1999a: 255), as attested by the recurrence of the expression "down to our times." Actually, when Diodorus lists the many changes of fortune experienced by Thebes, he does not distinguish between "mythical" events (the flood in Deucalion's time, Cadmus' foundation of the city, the building of the lower city by Amphion and Zethos, etc.) and historical ones, such as Alexander's capture and destruction of the city (19.53.4–8).

Yet Diodorus is also, to my knowledge, the first among the historians "to abandon the principle of current things and admit that in mythical times conditions could have been different from our own" (Veyne 1988: 99). He prefaces his account of Heracles' labors with a criticism of some readers who (4.8.3–4):

> using their own life as a standard, pass judgment on those deeds the magnitude of which throw them open to doubt, and estimate the might of Heracles by the weakness of the men of our day, with the result that the magnitude of the deeds makes the account of them incredible.

Later on Pausanias (8.2.4) will also admit that "in mythical times conditions could have been different from his own" (Veyne 1988: 99):

For men of those days, because of their righteousness and piety, were guests of the gods, eating at the same board; the good were openly honored by the gods and the sinners were openly visited by their wrath. Nay, in those days men were changed to gods, who down to the present day have honors paid to them.

4   Myths and Historical Sub-Genres

Historiography was born out of myth: according to Strabo (1.2.8), the first "historians" (*historikoi*) were also "mythographers" (*muthographoi*). To give but one example, Pherecydes of Syros, who is known as the composer of a theogony and genealogies, was listed among the historians by Lucian (*Macr.* 23). Ancient historians – including Thucydides – could never do without myths. But their place varies according to the various sub-genres.

Local histories (a genre which enjoyed a full life extending from the early fifth century to the late Roman empire), dealing either with Greek city-states or foreign peoples and beginning with the *Persica* of Dionysius of Miletus, usually included a development on a locale's mythical origins, as did the elegiac poems of the sixth century that preceded them, such as Eumelus of Corinth's *Corinthiaca*, Mimnermus' *Smyrneis*, Panyassis' *Ionica*, or Semonides of Amorgos' *Archaeology of the Samians* (Lasserre 1976: 123–125; Bowie 2001). But the space devoted to mythical times varied greatly according to the authors, as demonstrated by a comparison of the *Atthides* that narrated the whole history of Athens from primeval times and the earliest king, Cecrops, down to the time of the authors. The first historians of the West, Antiochus of Syracuse and Philistus, also began with myth (the arrival of Daedalus under the reign of the Sican king Cocalus). The most famous of them, Timaeus of Tauromenium, who devoted five books out of thirty-eight to the most ancient times and "set out to graft the rich mythology of mainland Greece onto the West" (Walbank 1989–1990: 47), went even further back. Among the twenty books devoted by Dionysius to *Roman Antiquities*, four are devoted to the "most ancient myths" (1.8.1) and the origins of the city.

Even in histories dealing with "historical" events or characters (predominantly belonging to the near past) and written by authors who are openly critical of their use, myths appear as digressions (in the narrative) or argument (in speeches). Thucydides, who proudly pointed out the lack of mythical element in his work (1.22.4), used them not once – as claimed by the scholiast on 2.29.3 – but many times: in the "Archaeology," in digressions explaining the present by the most ancient past (2.14), or in allusions to legends associated with a given place (2.102; 4.24; 6.2.1). Ephorus blamed lovers of myths, praised truth, and chose to pass over earliest history because "it is hardly accessible to investigation" (*FGrHist* 70 F 31b). Yet he occasionally backtracks and is caught telling fabulous stories by the critical Strabo (9.3.11–12). Even Strabo's statement (9.4.18) – "I must omit most of what is really ancient and mythical (*muthōdē*)" – and his harsh criticism of those who combine myth and history and attempt to make the myths believable (1.2.35) are equally misleading and contradicted by his own text (Clarke 1999a: 246).

Those who criticize the inclusion of myths in history by their fellow historians claim that their only purpose was to please an audience delighting in the narrative of wonders (Diod. 1.69.7), since the wondrous is known to be pleasant (Arist. *Pol.* 1460a17). But Polybius has to admit that even "the most thoughtful of ancient writers were in the habit of giving their readers a rest ... by employing digressions dealing with myth" (38.6.1). Yet they were supposed to "acknowledge expressly that they were dealing with myths" (Str. 1.2.35) and leave the reader free to take the story as they like (Luc. *HC* 60).

5 Approaches to Myths

The Earliest Historians

From Hecataeus to Arrian, Greek historians approached myths in many different ways. One can roughly distinguish three periods: the first historians who flourished before the Peloponnesian War; the classical historians of the fifth and fourth centuries; and the historians who lived during the Hellenistic period and Roman empire.

According to Strabo (1.2.6), "the first historians who flourished ... before the Peloponnesian War preserved most of the qualities of poetry" (Acusilaus even claimed, like the epic poet, to owe his knowledge of genealogies to an external source, the written bronze tablets bequeathed to him by his father: *FGrHist* 2 T 1). Like the poets, they intended to "bring to common knowledge whatever records or traditions were to be found among the natives ... and to deliver these just as they received them, without adding thereto or subtracting therefrom, rejecting not even the legends which had been believed for many generations nor the sudden reversals of the action that are characteristic of the stage, and seem to men of the present time to have a large measure of silliness" (D. Hal. *Thuc.* 5). Actually, according to Josephus (*Ap.* 1.16), "Acusilaus often corrected Hesiod" and as far as we can tell from the meager fragments we have, he was right.

The Classical Era

The scientific historiography of the classical period was characterized by "critical analysis (*historiē*) and authorial self consciousness" (Gehrke 2001: 298). Beginning with Hecataeus, who writes "what seems [to him] to be true," historians selected or often constructed a probable version of the mythical past, suppressing from the tradition traits that were contrary to nature, incredible, or improbable. In short, they were the first to "describe persons and events ... of the most remote past as if they belonged to the present time" (Jacoby 1949: 133) and systematically apply what has been aptly labeled by Veyne (1988: 14) "the doctrine of current things."

It is well known that Hecataeus eliminated the miraculous elements from ancient myths to make the stories more credible: he made Geryon a king in Ambracia, substituting a place from mainland Greece for the fabulous Erythia (*FGrHist* 1 F 26), and reduced the number of Aegyptus' sons from fifty to twenty (F 19). According to Pausanias (3.25.5 = F 27), "he found a likely account (*logon eikota*) for Cerberus" by saying that it was in fact "a terrible serpent . . . called the dog of Hades because anyone bitten by it was killed immediately by the venom," one of the first instances of rationalization relying on an ambiguous metaphorical use of language. But this rationalization has its limits, for Hecataeus did not object to the talking ram of Phrixus and Helle, the bitch giving birth to a stalk (F 15), or to Zeus making Danae pregnant.

Herodotus' strategy is more complex. He often disclaims any responsibility for the mythical stories he reports and refers to various sources. Sometimes these are left undefined: "as it is said" (7.20) or "there is also a story" (4.179.1) which introduces the account of the Argonauts in Libya. When he names his sources, he usually refers to population groups, the Greeks in general or the inhabitants of some *polis*, major (e.g., 6.52, the Lacedaemonians) or minor (e.g., 4.8, "the Greeks who live on Euxine sea"), but also barbarians such as Egyptians, Persians, Phoenicians, Lydians, and Scythians. Sometimes he alludes to a collectivity of "well-informed" people, the *logioi* among the Persians or the Egyptian priests (e.g., 2.120). Explicit allusions to written sources such as "a poet" (e.g., 3.115; 6.52), "the poets" (2.56), "the epic poets" (2.120) or Homer (2.23; 2.116–117), Aeschylus (2.156), or mythical Aristeas (4.13–16) are exceptional. In his prologue, after echoing contradictory reports of Io's departure to Asia, he refuses to vouch for their truth and concludes: "I am not going to say about these matters that they occurred one way or another" (1.5.3).

A closer reading of the prologue also demonstrates that he did attempt, like Hecataeus, to rationalize myth, by dismissing all supernatural elements: Zeus is replaced by a Phoenician ship's captain (Io) or "some Greeks" (Europa). Concerning Medea's abduction, the wording is kept deliberately vague: the Argonauts become "the Greeks" and their conquest of the golden fleece becomes "the achievement of the objectives they had in coming" (1.2). As for Helen, her abduction is no longer the consequence of the judgment of the goddesses. If Paris decided to get her, it is only because he had heard what happened in the past and knew for sure that he would not have to pay for this kidnapping, since the earlier kidnappings have gone unpunished (1.3). Accordingly, in the rest of his *Histories*, Herodotus only mentions Heracles' mortal father, Amphytrion (2.43, 44, 146; 6.53) and refuses to trace the genealogy of the Spartan kings further back than Perseus, "since no name is known for him for a mortal father" (6.53). Minos, who is identified only as "the son of Europa" (1.173), becomes a powerful king who did not impose any tribute on the Carians, but used them to man his ships (1.171) and got the upper hand in a dispute against his brother Sarpedon (1.173).

Moreover, Herodotus often openly relies on his judgment (*gnōmē*) to dismiss or validate some myths. If in 2.45 he contemptuously dismisses as "silly" (*euēthes*) the story (*muthos*) of Heracles who, at the last moment when he was led to the altar to be sacrificed by the Egyptians, killed thousands of them, it is because it is not plausible: first, it demonstrates a complete ignorance of the national character (*phusis*) and the customs (*nomoi*) of the Egyptians, which Herodotus was able to observe (implying that these customs were always the same as they are now): the Egyptians who consider the sacrifice of animals unholy cannot have indulged in human sacrifices. Second, the story is psychologically unlikely, since one does not wait until the last moment to react, as did Heracles. Last comes the killer argument: it is a physical impossibility for a man to accomplish such a feat (and at this time Heracles was still a man). Conversely, Herodotus accepts the story that Helen, instead of going to Troy, spent some time in Egypt in the palace of Proteus. First, he finds believable that after being driven by a tempest to the Canobic mouth of the Nile, Paris and Helen took refuge in a sanctuary of Heracles (this agrees with what he has seen, since the sanctuary still exists and the custom that suppliants there cannot be touched has survived unchanged from its ancient origins right up to his own day). He also believes this story, even if it is belied by Homer because he quotes – out of context – some lines that demonstrate that Homer had some knowledge of this journey, but chose to discard it as "less suitable (*euprepes*) for epic" (2.116). Moreover, he trusts the priests' careful investigation and questioning of Menelaus himself. But his major reason for siding with the Egyptian version, which is suspiciously close to a rationalized version of Stesichorus' "Palinode" (only the phantom is missing!), is here also psychological verisimilitude: "If Helen had been in Ilium, she would have been returned to the Greeks with or without Alexander's [i.e., Paris'] consent. For Priam and the rest of his family would have been completely insane (*phrenoblabeis*) to choose to put themselves, their children, and their city in danger just so that Alexander could live with Helen" (2.120).

In the *Histories* myth can be used as an argument. Herodotus' Persians systematically exploit myths (Nesselrath 1995–1996: 283–288) either to shift the blame for the beginning of evils to others (Phoenicians or Greeks in the prologue) or to persuade the Argives that it would be wrong for them to wage war against the Persians who are their offspring via Perseus, father of Perses (7.150). But the Greeks also know how to use the mythical past. When the Tegeans and the Athenians argue over the command of the left wing before Plataea, they bring forward not only the recent but also the most ancient past: the Tegeans boast about the victory of their king over Hyllus (9.26), whereas the Athenians list the exploits that will be treated at greater length in the Athenian funeral oration, that is, their reception of the Heraclidae, their recovery of the bodies of the Seven, their campaign against the Amazons, and their contribution to the Trojan War (9.27). Yet the Athenians conclude in a typical Herodotean way with a dismissal of arguments from the most ancient past, given the fundamental uncertainty of human life.

Like Herodotus, Thucydides puts the heroic tales in quotation marks. However, unlike Herodotus, he never precisely identifies his sources but uses expressions such as "as we know by hearsay" (*akoē*: 1.4.1) or "it is said" (*legetai*: 2.14.5; 2.102.5; 4.24.5; 6.2.1). When he reports the story of Alcmeon in a digression devoted to the Echinades islands, he carefully frames it by "it is said" (2.102.5) and "this is the story told to us about Alcmeon" (2.102.6).

Usually he radically historicizes the myths he reports, dismissing any detail that does not agree with his own experience and giving a reinterpretation of the heroic tales strongly influenced by contemporary events. This is the reason why, in spite of the tradition that links the legendary Tereus, who married Procne the daughter of the

Athenian king Pandion, to Thrace, he relocates him in Daulis, relying on the authority of the poets – "many of them referring to the nightingale [Procne] call it 'the Daulian bird'" (2.29.3) – and even more on probability and a realistic definition of alliance: "Also it was likely (*eikos*) that Pandion, in making an alliance for his daughter, would have an eye on the possibilities of mutual aid. This would be more practicable in the case of such a short distance than in the case of the many days' journey between Athens and the Odrysae" (2.29.3). In the "Archaeology," according to the same principle, he transforms Minos into a prototype of Athenian maritime imperialism, whose power relies on the control of the sea and the "revenues," who puts down piracy in order "to ensure that the revenues might reach him more easily" (1.4); makes the story of Pelops into a demonstration of the essential role of money in the creation of a dominion (1.9.2); and explains the leadership of Agamemnon by his naval power and the fear it inspires (1.9.3–4) – all interpretations obviously influenced by Thucydides' own understanding of contemporary events and the motivations underlying them (Kallet 2001: 25–26). This becomes even clearer in his explanation of the protracted length of the Trojan War, "written on the basis of his observations about the Sicilian expedition" (Kallet 2001: 99). Such an interpretation of heroic tales is not limited to the "Archaeology," as demonstrated not only by the story of Tereus but also by the portrait of Theseus, who becomes a precursor of Pericles because of his cleverness (2.14.2), and the reinterpretation of a synoecism achieved by force and compulsion (*anankē*), as was the Athenian empire.

Like Hecataeus, Herodotus, and Thucydides, the authors of *Atthides* often attempted to "convert into the stuff of history the archaeology" (Jacoby 1949: 133). They rationalized the ancient legends by eliminating more or less thoroughly the miraculous. In contrast to Hellanicus, who kept the legendary Minotaur (*FGrHist* 4 F 14), Cleidemus (323 F 5) gets rid of him: his Theseus, after a violation of an international agreement of Minos about the use of warships, secretly built a fleet, captured the harbor by surprise and vanquished the Cretans "before the gates of the Labyrinth," killed the son of Minos, who succeeded his father to the throne, and ended the war by a treaty signed by his successor Ariadne. Both Philochorus (328 F 3) and Demon (327 F 17) transformed the monster into a general of Minos called "the bull."

When Ephorus deals with mythology in his extensive digressions, he is close to the Atthidographers, as far as we can judge from his fragments. Like them, he historicizes myths: he transforms Rhadamanthus and Minos into human legislators who "alleged" or "pretended that they brought from Zeus the laws they promulgated" (*FGrHist* 70 F 147), and makes the mythical Python shot by Apollo into a man "nicknamed the serpent" (70 F 31b).

The Post-Classical Era

As well pointed out by Gabba (1981: 53), at the end of the classical period and in the Hellenistic period "the mythical and legendary phases of Greek prehistory and protohistory with their store of divine and heroic genealogies . . . recovered a role and function in works of history." Theopompus' *Hellenica* and *Philippica* were full of countless myths according to Cicero (*Leg.* 1.5), but far from historicizing the myths by eliminating the miraculous, Theopompus acknowledged them as such. This is obviously the case for his most famous myth, the narrative of the meeting between the Phrygian king Midas and Silenus (*FGrHist* 115 F 75). This description of utopian places located beyond the Ocean combines an ethical lesson (the description of two cities, the warlike and the pious, Hyperboreans and the Meropis) with sheer fantasy, the serpent fighting against a warship (F 296).

Timaeus gave pride of place to legends in his attempt to create a distinct western Greek mythology by associating wandering heroes such as Heracles, the Argonauts, Odysseus, and other survivors from Troy with Italy and Sicily. Like the Hellenistic poets, he often supports the historicity of his narrative by resorting to the authority of ancient writers and/or by pointing out present traces of this remote past such as survivals of customs, existing cults, place names, or still extant objects. He displaced the rape of Core to the Sicilian Enna in a meadow still remarkable for its beauty (Diod. 5.3.1–3) and made Sicily (instead of Attica) into the birthplace of agriculture, "the first place where grain grew because of the fertility of the soil" (Diod. 5.2.4). As evidence he relies on the authority of Homer, who praised the fertility of the land of the Cyclops (later identified with Sicily) as well as the doctrine of present things: "even to this day, the so-called wild wheat grows in the plains of Leontini and throughout many parts of Sicily" (*FGrHist* 566 F 164).

Polybius, who is well known for his rejection of melodramatic history (Walbank 1955, 1960), explicitly leaves aside stories such as the fall of Phaethon (matter better suited for tragedy, 2.16.13–15), chooses to omit the fabulous origins of families, colonies, and cities (9.2.1), refuses to rely on the testimony of poets and mythographers (4.40.2), and harshly criticizes historians such as Timaeus who fill their narrative with "dreams, prodigies, and incredible myths, in one word, ignoble superstition and womanish love of the marvelous" (12.24.5).

Still, he sometimes reminds his readers of legends associated with place names (Clarke 1999a: 94–95), carefully placing them in inverted commas. On the Asiatic coast, the promontory called the "Cow" is the place where Io landed after her crossing of the Hellespont "as the myths say" (4.43.6). He agrees that the Homeric poems are not to be read as fictions: even if some fabulous elements have been added by the poet, on the whole the Trojan War and the wanderings of Odysseus are historical facts (34.2.9–11). Like his predecessors, he also rationalizes ancient legends: Aeolus becomes a man who gave sailing directions for the seas near the Straits of Messina and who was said to be, "because of his knowledge, 'the steward of the winds and their king'" (34.2.4). Moreover, his history demonstrates that myth was still used as argument: the inhabitants of Ilium rely on their kinship with the Romans to spare the Lycians and their request is met (22.5.3–4).

Diodorus, Strabo, and Dionysius all make lavish use of myths and share many characteristics. First, instead of criticizing the polyphony of Greek mythology, like Hecataeus, they accept it as a given (Diod. 4.44.4):

> As a general thing we find that ancient myths do not give us a simple and consistent story; consequently it should occasion no surprise if we find, when we put the ancient

accounts together, that in some details they are not in agreement with those given by every poet or historian.

They even seem to relish "the multiplicity and the diversity of the stories handed down by historians and mythographers" (Diod. 6.1.3) and the opportunity to display their erudition by reporting as many versions as possible (Diodorus explicitly says that he does not want "to leave aside anything which is recorded about Dionysus," 3.66.5). Moreover, the nature of the sources has changed: they mostly rely on written reports and the extant works of poets, mythographers, and historians, privileging antiquity (e.g., Diod. 4.8.5) and reputation (e.g., Diod. 5.2.4; D. Hal. *AR* 1.11.1).

Not only do they put various versions side by side, they also explicitly refuse to choose, and give the choice to the reader. Were there golden apples or golden sheep in the garden of the Hesperidae? "With regard to such matters, it will be every man's privilege to form such opinion in accord with his own belief" (Diod. 4.26.3). In the same way Dionysius, after giving various versions of Aeneas' flight beginning with the one he considers as "most reliable (*pistotatos*)" and following with others which he regards as "less convincing (*pithanous*)," concludes: "Let every reader judge as he thinks proper" (1.48.1). Actually this kind of juxtaposition followed by a refusal to choose is characteristic of the *Roman Antiquities*.

Like the Hellenistic poets, these authors are interested in aetiology and report how various peoples support their mythical claims by pointing out some traces left by the mythical past into the present (Diod. 3.66.2):

> The Teans advance as proof that the god was born among them the fact that, even to this day, at fixed times in their city a fountain of wine of unusually sweet fragrance flows on its own accord (*automatōs*) from the earth; and as for the peoples of the other cities, they point out in some cases a plot of land which is sacred to Dionysus, in other cases shrines and sacred precincts which have been consecrated to him from ancient times.

In the same way, the Armenians support a genealogy that traces their origin back to one of the Argonauts, the Thessalian Armenus, by saying "that the clothing of the Armenians is Thessalian ... and the style of horsemanship is Thessalian. The Iasonian monuments also bear witness to the expedition of Jason" (Str. 11.14.12). Dionysius substantiates the story of the arrival of Aeneas and the Trojans in Italy by existing festivals and sacrifices (1.49.3), and uses as "proofs" (*tekmēria*, 1.53.1) of their landing in Sicily the altar and the temple they constructed. All these "proofs" matter, since myths are still used as arguments for political claims.

Like the classical historians, they are prone to reconstruct the most ancient past along the lines of their present. Thucydides transformed his Minos into a blueprint of Athens' thalassocracy. Diodorus assimilates the campaign of Dionysus against the Titans to the "just" wars waged by Roman generals: like them, the god knew how to transform former enemies into faithful allies by his *clementia* (3.71.5): "he gathered a multitude of captives ... who suspected that they would be executed, but got them free from the charges and allowed them to make their choice either to join him in his campaign or to go scot free; they all chose to join him." In the same way, "the more truthful (*alēthesteros*)" version of the arrival of Heracles in Italy, according to

Dionysius (1.41.2), portrays the hero as a general "at the head of a great army, after he had already conquered Spain, in order to subjugate and rule the people in this region." And it has been convincingly suggested that in Strabo's *Geography* (10.4.8), the administrative divisions of Crete established by king Minos are a retrojection of the contemporary situation created by the Romans in 67 BCE (Stergiopoulos 1949).

They go on correcting and rationalizing myths using the same well-proven methods: "Tradition has recorded that the head of Ammon was shaped like that of a ram," because "as his device he had worn a helmet of that form in his campaigns" (Diod. 3.73.1–2). Dionysius, before relating the fabulous version of the conception of Romulus and Remus – their mother was made pregnant by the specter of a god (1.77.2) – reports the most believable (*pithanōtata*) one: she was raped by a human being, either one of her suitors or by her uncle Amulius in disguise (1.77.1).

In contrast with classical historians, who were only interested in constructing the historical narrative by deconstructing myths, Diodorus also attempts to explain the creation of fabulous stories. He echoes the explanation given by the Egyptians of the Greek myth of Hades (1.92.3): according to them, it was Orpheus who combined an existing custom of the Egyptians, which he had seen (*theasamenon*) and reproduced (*mimēsamenon*), and a fiction he invented (*plasamenon*). In 4.34.3 anonymous poets transformed a real fact (the diversion of a river by Heracles) into a myth (*muthopoiēsai*), the fight between the hero and the Achelous metamorphosed into a bull, since the result of Heracles' feat was the recovery of a large amount of fruitful land, metaphorically assimilated to the legendary horn of Amaltheia. The most complex instance of *muthopoiïa*, which could be very well compared to the exemplary tale of Fontenelle about the golden tooth, is to be found at 1.23.4–8. The starting point of the myth that locates the birth of Dionysus at Thebes is a real fact: Semele happened to give birth to a child who looked like Osiris/Dionysus. Relying on this appearance, Cadmus, motivated by self-interest (he wanted to avert slander from his daughter who had been raped), "attributed this birth to Zeus." At a later time, Orpheus, who was then held in high regard by the Greeks, transferred the birth of Osiris to more recent times, in order to please the descendants of Cadmus who had lavishly entertained him. The common people, deceived both by their ignorance and by Orpheus' reputation, believed it. And last but not least came "the mythographers and the poets who took over this genealogy." As a consequence, "the theaters were filled with it, and among following generations faith (*pistin*) in it grew strong and immutable."

6 Conclusion

Classical historiography, which was born out of myths and invented the "mythical" as its foil, obviously did not succeed in putting myth out of business. It even paid attention to its invention. But its criticism of fabulous stories constitutes a major contribution to our understanding of what ancient historians considered as "historical." When they attempted to tell "how things really were," they were not the

Suzanne Saïd

precursors of Ranke; they were just looking for verisimilitude. To quote the late sophist Nicolaus (*Prog.* p.12.19–22 Felten), the historical is "what is acknowledged as such by a consensus" (*homologoumenos*), as opposed to the mythical, "which is not to be given undisputed credit."

FURTHER READING

The topic of myth in historiography has been addressed by Wardman 1960 and Pierart 1983; by recent introductions to Greek mythology (Graf 1993: 121–141; Calame 2000: 146–152, 207–230), Greek historiography (Fornara 1983: 4–12; Marincola 1997: 117–127); and, last but not least, by two books, Veyne 1988 (French original 1983), which has been very influential, and Calame 2003, which is mostly devoted to the foundation narratives of Cyrene.

CHAPTER SEVEN

The Construction of Meaning in the First Three Historians

Carolyn Dewald

1 Introduction

Near the end of Book 7, Thucydides paints a wonderful scene of Athenian soldiers standing at the edge of the great harbor of Syracuse, watching the unfolding of the sea-battle in front of them that will determine whether they can escape home to Athens (7.71). Their bodies torque in agony as they watch, some of them shouting, "We are winning!," some shouting, "We are losing!," depending on what part of the battle each man is looking at.

The idea of history itself – the acknowledgment that a collective human past can be studied and is worth studying – is today in something of the same condition as those Athenian soldiers in Syracuse. On the one hand, "history," defined as the study of some part of the human past, is being generated and also energetically consumed in a variety of media. History book clubs abound, and national magazines and newspapers often purvey relatively responsible narratives about the origins of both national and international crises, some of them starting in the distant past. Intuitively, people feel that the past matters; one can even find the ancient Greeks and Romans appearing almost daily on a variety of television channels. Seen from this angle, history is thriving.

In the "we are losing!" camp, however, those who care about history see at least two kinds of massive attacks sustained, affecting both the merit and the very possibility of history, at least if it is defined as the systematic and careful study of a "real" past.

One comes from various political groups and even some thoughtful cultural historians, like Peter Novick or Robert Berkhofer. They point out that our over-informed age makes an objective and inclusive history increasingly impossible, replete as our world is with abundant documentation of varying quality, decentralized modes of rapid and far-flung communication, and a vigorous resurgence of small-group identities. Each separate interest group now wants to tell its own story, dismissing as vicious or uninformed a story that opposes or even modifies it. Western culture as a whole no longer appears to trust learned expertise or privilege the judgment of a group of people (traditionally called historians) who are more entitled to tell the story of the past, because they have at their disposal more reliable data, and more techniques and experience interpreting the data, than does the average man or woman on the street. If this trend continues, it is possible that "history" will become little more than popular mythmaking expressed in historical novels and films, generated in order to amuse, comfort, inspire, or confirm a group in its sense of itself, rather than to tell accurate but potentially uncomfortable truths about a complex past that needs to be understood on its own terms, in its very differences from the present.

A second, more sophisticated attack on the possibility of "real" history comes from the academy, especially its literature departments. It owes its intellectual origin to poststructuralists and postmodernists and entails the realization that language, as the medium we use to think about and communicate our thoughts about the past, is most intimately connected not to the articulation of non-linguistic reality but rather to a larger and pervasive, interlocking web of language itself. That web is largely shaped by ideology, or the unconscious need to see the past in terms that we already know, that is, our contemporary set of intellectual assumptions. Much of what the scholars say who cast doubt on the traditional western project of history, writing from this angle, is true; Louis Mink, Hayden White, Michel Foucault, Jacques Derrida, and Roland Barthes, to name a few of them, deserve our reluctant gratitude for forcing us to think about their arguments.

In what is often called the "linguistic turn," some professional historians also follow this line of reasoning and claim that the project of creating an accurate representation of the past, when carefully examined, is a chimerical one, nice to imagine but not attainable in practice. Historians and historiographers like Alun Munslow or Keith Jenkins point out that "the past" is a construct that does not exist except as a hypothesis. Certainly, it is not an object in front of us that can be examined objectively. As Foucault and his followers have argued, the elements from the past that we do have in front of us – the written and otherwise tangible detritus from vanished times – are things we largely understand in terms of our own ideological presuppositions. We are creatures, even prisoners, of our particular Foucauldian *epistēmē* or intellectual and social cohort. We write things that seem reasonable to us, using terms, explanations, and plot devices that matter to us, not necessarily those that would have made sense to the actors of the vanished past we claim to be investigating.

Archimedes' fulcrum often appears at this point in the argument. We cannot stand outside ourselves, to understand the Other, the human being different from ourselves. Mink's general observation (1987: 199) about history as, in the final analysis, a narrative made up of words, remains pertinent here as a provocative general summary of the problem:

> So we have a . . . dilemma about the historical narrative: as historical it claims to represent, through its form, part of the real complexity of the past, but as narrative it is a product of

imaginative construction, which cannot defend its claim to truth by any accepted procedure of argument or authentication.

Faced with such issues, it is instructive to return to the first generation of Greek historians, to look at the kinds of meaning that their histories conveyed. Why did they undertake to write as they did? How was their work really different from that, say, of Homer and his *epigoni* before them? These are not new questions, of course, but our current epistemological dilemma has given us some new ways to think about them. The observations expressed in this chapter are not the only ways into understanding the work of Herodotus, Thucydides, and Xenophon, but they seem particularly relevant to the questions raised by the role of history and history writing in our own culture.

I will argue here that if we look carefully at the work of the first western historians and the basic assumptions undergirding their histories, we can see an intellectual project emerging that is indeed literary, "a product of imaginative construction," as the poststructuralists claim, but imaginative construction of a very particular kind. In the very details of its literariness, history as shaped by its first three Greek practitioners makes good on its claim to belong to the human sciences – and even to reach a kind of truth that marks the study of history as a distinctive intellectual discipline. The analysis is a formal one, examining how the first three historical narratives are constructed. Herodotus, Thucydides, and Xenophon all privilege four ways of making meaning that together largely define the genre that their work began. I call them below: rescuing the remarkable from oblivion; recording judgment; deploying the authorial narrator's voice; and (only half tongue-in-cheek) recounting "one damn thing after another."

2   Rescuing the Remarkable from Oblivion

Herodotus begins his history by emphasizing that its purpose is to preserve the memory of past greatness (*praef.*):

> This is the display of the investigation of Herodotus, so that the things that occurred from human beings (*ta genomena ex anthrōpōn*) should not become worn away (*exitēla*) through time, and so that great and wonderful deeds (*erga megala te kai thōmasta*), some displayed by Greeks, others by barbarians not become unrenowned (*aklea*).

Herodotus' definition of great past achievements is much broader than those of Thucydides and Xenophon, partly because, as the first historian, he must not only retell whatever great and wonderful things he thinks worthy of memorialization yet in danger of being forgotten but also reveal their significance by retelling them within a larger narrative backdrop that lets their remarkableness emerge.

What he gives us, therefore, is not just the "great and wonderful deeds" or even the "things that exist from human beings," but a gigantic grid of the entire Aegean world, natural and cultural alike. His idea of what is worth memorializing is very heterogeneous. He loves firsts and bests – the first people to use gold and silver coins, the best law, the most outstanding warrior in a particular battle, etc. (e.g., 1.94; 1.194; 1.196; 7.117; 9.25). But overhanging all the individual achievements of this kind is the Panhellenic Greek achievement of 481–479, when the small and often disunited Greek force repulsed the massive attack of Xerxes and won the Persian Wars. This astonishing accomplishment fills the final three books of Herodotus' history and is the heart of what he has endeavored to memorialize.

Thucydides writes within a generation of Herodotus and ostensibly rejects Herodotus' notion of memorialization as recording the (literally) remarkable things from the past that people have told him; he emphasizes instead the usefulness of his much more focused narrative to future generations (cf. below, p. 100). But although he memorializes much less overtly and inclusively than Herodotus does, in some ways the task of recording past greatness is an even more important part of his focus as a narrator. Thucydides makes clear in his opening pages that he thinks the twenty-seven-year Peloponnesian War itself is worthy of record as the greatest war of all time, far greater than either the Trojan or Persian Wars. He occasionally notes people worthy of recognition for exceptional qualities or actions: Phrynichus, Antiphon, the 5,000 non-democratic leaders of the Athenian state after the coup of 411, even Nicias and Alcibiades (8.27; 8.48; 8.68; 8.97; 7.86; 8.86). Most strikingly of course, Pericles is framed as an almost-superhero, someone able to lead the state with extraordinary foresight, justice, and self-control (2.65). In Pericles' mouth Thucydides puts sentiments that are almost Homeric in their privileging of glory (*kleos*): the task of the citizen is to become the lover of his city, dedicating himself to its fame so that it does not slip from the role it achieved in the days of the fathers (2.43); that even if Athens loses the war, her greatness in undertaking and waging it valiantly will assure her future renown (2.64). The *way* to memorialize has changed, but the *purpose* is still there – even more ferociously for Thucydides, perhaps, than for Herodotus, since it is in effect Thucydides himself as a writer who will complete the Periclean project and fulfill its promise. Indeed, it is because Thucydides wrote up the Peloponnesian War as he did that we continue to study it today as a twenty-seven-year war that began in 431 BCE (Ste. Croix 1972: 3, 50–51). Thucydides' text stands as a tribute to Athens' grand, if ultimately unrealized, imperial ambitions.

Xenophon, seen through the lens of his two great predecessors, proves both an exception to and an instantiation of this first generalization about meaning-making in the early Greek historians. Where Herodotus and Thucydides define glory that needs memorialization (at least for Greeks) in terms of the achievement of the city-state and of individual Greek leaders within that context, Xenophon begins to articulate it in terms of personal military leadership and individual achievement, achievement he largely defines in technical, but also private, ethical terms. In the *Hellenica* he repeatedly singles out individual commanders – Hermocrates of Syracuse (1.1.27–31), the Spartans Teleutias (5.1.3, 13–24, 37–43) and especially Agesilaus (3.4.11, 21–24; 4.1.38–40; 4.3.19–21) – for their display of good military practices, fair-mindedness, and a personal integrity and thoughtfulness that are recognized by their troops and result in their being excellent leaders. Maintenance of disciplined order and decisive, intelligent alertness in the crucial moment are the qualities that define excellence in his featured commanders. Their loyalty to their cities is part of that excellence (cf. Teleutias' exhortation to remember Sparta, 5.1.16), but the city itself as a vital political entity has largely vanished from Xenophon's vision. Cawkwell (1966: 39) acutely notes Xenophon's clear approval of Spartan dismemberment in 385 of Mantinea into its composite villages. Xenophon even says that the property owners of Mantinea were pleased to see the city walls come down, since this absolved them from the need to pay attention to democratic demagogues, liberating them to return to the good old days of aristocratic military dominance of the village (5.2.7).

So in Xenophon the scope of civic achievement and individual achievement within a civic focus, memorialized in Herodotus and Thucydides, has given way to a more individualistic focus of attention typical of the fourth century (we can think of the new genre of encomiastic biography, or changes undergone in fourth-century Attic comedy, for instance, in its emphasis on the private, domestic sphere). Pericles' dictum (Thuc. 2.41, 60), that individual glory comes from belonging to a great and glorious city, no longer prevails; Xenophon expressly and uniquely singles out for praise the ethics of the small and insignificant city of Phlious, since the Phliasians remained faithful to Sparta even under extraordinary pressure – little cities need praise for excellence too, he says (7.2.1). Earlier he had approvingly quoted Theramenes' witticisms as he was about to be killed by the Thirty, adding that he knows this is not the stuff of history (*axiologa*) but thinks it worth mentioning nonetheless, since Theramenes' admirable ability to joke at the point of death revealed his good sense and wit under the ultimate pressure (2.3.56).

Sometimes Xenophon's interest in Greek engagement in Asia Minor is assessed as closer in spirit to Herodotus than to Thucydides, since the *Hellenica* returns to a more Panhellenic and internationalist scope after Thucydides' intensive focus on Athens and Athenian politics, but to emphasize this apparent similarity is to miss a crucial difference. As we have seen, Xenophon's Panhellenism is not a matter of Greek civic politics, but rather takes place on a large and relatively atomistic canvas, on which a talented individual soldier with the right kind of leadership qualities can sometimes make his mark. At least in their larger ambitions, Greek states *per se* often seem somewhat adrift; Xenophon's narrative begins with the decline of the Athenian empire, and ends with the moral and military diminishment of Sparta after Leuctra and Mantinea. While Herodotus glorifies the joint actions undertaken by Greek city-states confronting the autocracies of the expansionist east, Xenophon throughout the *Hellenica* writes of individual military commanders negotiating a world of unstable and shifting loyalties, in which the most pressing concern was often how to get the troops fed and paid. Properly read, his world points to and in part explains the coming of the Macedonians a scant generation later.

The three historians' interest in recording great and memorable deeds was deeply rooted in earlier Greek culture; sociology and geography combined to produce in the classical era a common culture, whose Panhellenic values were male, competitive, and aristocratic. War was the medium in which these values most tellingly emerged; both communities and individuals owed their status in large part to the public recognition of past military and political achievement (one's own or one's ancestors'). This interlocking and far-flung culture, connected by trade, marriage, and a common cultural patrimony (e.g., the Homeric narratives), was also sharply divided politically, into small face-to-face communities separated from each other by sea and mountainous terrain. It was earlier the epic poet's job, and then later the historian's, to acknowledge and bind into a single story the multiple competing accounts generated by the various Greek communities, to make sure many different community voices were folded in. Herodotus first had to negotiate which events would be the most important, and which actors the most prominent within those events, which leads us to our next topic.

3   Recording Judgment

Herodotus does not intend his record of great and astounding things from the past to be read as a Ripley's *Believe It Or Not*. He makes this clear by the way he begins his narrative, straight-faced, with accounts of the abductions of four clearly mythic women (1.1). Persian *logioi* (knowledgeable men) had issued an account of the causes of Greco-barbarian hostility by retelling tongue-in-cheek the tit-for-tat exchanges of Io, Europa, Medea, and Helen – exchanges that, not entirely coincidentally, make Phoenicians and Greeks the principal causes of the ancient enmity. But Herodotus himself dismisses this whole line of thinking with a shrug, moving on "to the man I know (*oida*) first committed injustices against the Greeks" (1.5). This *oida* in some ways is the real beginning of history writing, since it signifies the idea of critical judgment underlying and structuring the choice of events to be memorialized. In each of our three historians, authorial judgment is exercised both about what to include in the text in the first place and about how to evaluate the actions of the individuals involved as the narrative unrolls.

In a sense, this feature of Greek historiography was from the beginning a necessary concomitant of the Panhellenic process mentioned just above, the glorification of great achievement in a far-flung and culturally cohesive but competitive aristocratic community. In the *Iliad* a *histōr* is the judge at the finish line of a horse race (23.486), or an adjudicator among competing claims (18.501) – and part of the task of folding many different Greek communities' stories into one story was the need for the memorialist to judge, if only tacitly, among conflicting stories about great past deeds. As a memorialist, whom does one glorify, and why?

Herodotus calls his work the "display of his *historiē*," or investigation (*praef.*). He structures the *Histories* so that the process of adjudicating among competing and sometimes exaggerated variant *logoi* (accounts) of past events is a prominent part of the narrative. Throughout, he often cites two or more variant versions of events, sometimes (but not always) noting when he judges one superior to the other: Lateiner (1989: 84–90) lists 150 instances of alternative accounts. Whether or not Herodotus chooses, however, it is clear that both versions cannot be true. The structure of the narrative itself indicates that we, the readers, must see this and also in consequence become part of the investigative process.

Herodotus overtly judges not just the stories themselves but also the behavior of various people within the stories. He records or at least speculates about instances where the gods punish impiety: Croesus' son Atys died, possibly because Croesus overestimated his own happiness (1.34); Pheretime was eaten by worms, possibly for taking excessive vengeance (4.205). Sometimes irony suggests judgment that is not made explicit, as at the very end of the *Histories*, where the Athenians behave cruelly toward their Persian captives, whereas Pausanias, the Spartan victor at Plataea, has just recently refused to indulge in such behavior (9.120, 79). Herodotus also sometimes judges by deliberate exclusion, for instance, choosing not to record false Greek claims to have invented metempsychosis (2.123.3), or deliberately omitting the details of Polycrates' horrible death (3.125).

On the surface Thucydides explicitly disdains the whole process of overt authorial judgment of this sort. There are few variant versions of events, because what he records is, as he emphasizes, his own best judgment about what happened. The whole *History* performs Thucydides' continuous exercise of judgment, about what events and speeches to include, and what to say about them. The critique he makes of individual people emerges from the details of the narrative itself; in the *Methodenkap-itel* (1.20–22), and then again in the "second introduction" (5.26), he tells us just enough so that we may understand how seriously he has gone about his task: he is the final arbiter in all matters of record. When he says that he gives us the "necessary parts" (*ta deonta*, 1.22.1) of the speeches he has collected, he is tacitly assuring us that he has selected out the aspects from the hundreds of speeches given that he thought most valuable for understanding the war, aspects that allow his readers to judge the effectiveness of the various political and military decisions depicted in the narrative. Although Thucydides, unlike Herodotus, has largely shut us out of his historian's workshop, he nonetheless assures us that he has conscientiously exercised an appropriate historical judgment, both about what to include and what meaning to assign it. Until very recently, that made him seem the most trustworthy of all ancient historians, even if some of the scholars of the "we are losing!" camp now regard him as little more than a brilliantly persuasive historical novelist.

With Xenophon, we again feel that we have entered a different world. Where Herodotus grids and judges as many *logoi* about the past as allow him to tell a comprehensive story of the Persian empire and its check in Greece, and where Thucydides assures us that he has gone to every effort to collect and assess the raw materials out of which he constructs a careful *logos* of the Peloponnesian War, Xenophon's judgment takes place on a canvas simultaneously much broader and much more limited than those of his predecessors. Xenophon does not write a narrative that is conscientiously inclusive in its choice of events to report. Even if it is too harsh to call the *Hellenica* not history but "memoirs written for connoisseurs" (Cawkwell 1966: 28, 35, 45), Xenophon nevertheless often seems to be exercising little thoughtful selectivity about what to narrate and how to interpret what is narrated. We know from other histories of the period that he leaves out several crucial developments in the forty-odd years he recounts: the role of Sparta in imposing the Thirty on Athens in 403, for instance, or the establishment of the Second Athenian League, or the careers of the vitally important Thebans, Pelopidas and Epaminondas.

A current scholarly argument underway centers on whether Xenophon's egregious omissions are themselves the sign of political bias, recognizable by the cognoscenti among his readers. But even if we look only at his depictions of the historical actors that play such a large role in his narrative, Xenophon's account of his hero Agesilaus' career is suspiciously spotty and differs in its details and even its judgments from his laudatory biography of the Spartan king. Xenophon's judgments, as already mentioned, are most conspicuously military ones, seasoned with a strongly ethical overlay: Tissaphernes as an oathbreaker (3.4.6), or the disgraceful Spartan seizure of the Theban Cadmeia (5.2.26–36). Even one of his favorites, the Spartan Teleutias, is judged severely for his thoughtless anger and the disaster that it brings on for the men under his command (5.3.3–7).

Xenophon is sometimes compared to Herodotus in his privileging of the gods and their punishment of human misbehavior. But Herodotus almost always brings in the gods as part of the *logos* that he is retelling and professes authorial doubt both about their identities and their ultimate purposes – they are as mysterious as the shape of history itself as it unrolls; only afterward, as Solon says (Hdt. 1.32), can we look back and see what it was all about. Xenophon, on the other hand, leaves us in no doubt of his personal piety and belief that divinity truly controls human existence. Witness his final judgment on the frustratingly inconclusive battle of Mantinea (7.5.26–27):

> But God so ordered things that both parties put up trophies . . . both sides claimed the victory, but it cannot be said that with regard to the accession of new territory, or cities, or power either side was any better off after the battle than before it. In fact, there was even more uncertainty and confusion in Greece after the battle than there had been previously.

In this way the narrative line of the *Hellenica* ends, and the only kind of judgment Xenophon thinks he can make, in the breakdown of his mid-fourth-century world, is that things are very confusing, and that the divine has willed it that way.

Thus although all three historians exercise judgment as a vital aspect of the task of memorialization, they do it quite differently. Herodotus overtly judges both his *logoi* and the people and events narrated in the *logoi*; Thucydides' judgment of people is more oblique, since the whole of his *logos* stands as his continuous considered analysis and judgment on the course of the war, while Xenophon accounts for the meaning of the ongoing narrative and the behavior of the people within it by privileging a technical military sphere of attention that also contains personal, moral, and ideological value judgments within it.

4   Deploying the Authorial Narrator's Voice

A third aspect of meaning in the early Greek historians is less easy to point to in the text than are memorialization and judgment, partly because it is so pervasive. Both our interest as readers in the remarkable things narrated and our trust in the judgments expressed in their texts rest, in fact, on a third element of meaning – the creation of a narrator-persona whose voice in the text conveys the ongoing narrative, and who seems to us both interesting and trustworthy as a narrator. Although they differ in memorialization and judgment, in this one area – the task of establishing the distinctive persona that claims to deliver the narrative – Herodotus, Thucydides, and Xenophon use the same kinds of techniques in conveying the very different flavors of their authorial temperaments. I list some of the more important of them here:

1   The overt narrator, acting sometimes like Homer, who has privileged access to the thoughts and emotions of the actors inside the narrative. This is the voice de Jong (1987) calls external, omnipotent, and omnipresent – the stage-manager who has outfitted the unrolling narrative in all its distinctive colors.

2   The organizer-narrator, explicitly managing the direction of the text, controlling where it will begin or end, interrupting with something new, explaining something, or engaging in more complicated movements like analepsis or prolepsis in order to render in meaningful linear form events that have happened simultaneously in different locations.

3   The knowledgeable and helpful narrator, sometimes importing, either in the first person or in neutral third-person description, supplementary background information necessary in his judgment if we are to understand the ongoing narrative.

4   The modest or hesitant narrator, stressing the human limitations of his knowledge. Herodotus is especially good at this, but even Thucydides in the later books occasionally signals such doubts (7.44, 8.87; Hornblower 1994a: 156). Xenophon has an affect of soldierly modesty in his deceptively straightforward prose and refusal of embellishment (cf. the extreme simplicity of the *Hellenica*'s beginning and end). He has not constructed a narrator who presents himself as straining to find things out or think deeply and critically about them (cf. Agesilaus' comment at 4.3.2), but rather implies that he has simply written down what he knows and left the rest aside.

5   More impressionistically still, perhaps, the narrator-as-genial-host, inviting in selected secondary and reported embedded narrators to have their say – Herodotus is famous for this, but Thucydides and Xenophon also do it. Thucydides includes speeches, but also a variety of letters: Themistocles' to Artaxerxes (1.137), the Persian king's intercepted letter to the Spartans (4.50), Nicias' to the Athenian assembly (7.11–15). While Herodotus is a master of depicting conversation among the actors in his text, one also thinks of the constitutional debate (3.80–83) or the council scene that opens Book 7 (7.8–11). Xenophon too likes to make room for his commanders' speeches, though it has to be said that many of them sound more like Nicias just before the battle of the great harbor in Syracuse than like Pericles or even the Cleon of the Mytilenean Debate (Thuc. 7.69; 3.37–40). Each time the historian lets the actors inside the narrative express themselves, he is tacitly telling us information about his own take on the world and his idea of the people in it, but he is also dialogically reminding us that the decisions and actions of the individuals within the narrative create the unfolding of events.

All three of our narrators convey their persona as historian by giving us, through-out their texts, some hint of their own lively ongoing engagement in its management. Of the three, Xenophon is the least vividly present as an expressive persona; Gray (below, Ch. 30) shows that this is an active, deliberate reticence, chosen because the narrative itself conveys so much of his own moral judgment in little quasi asides. Occasionally, however, even Xenophon exhibits flashes of personal narrative affect as when he dryly remarks that in defeat, the Mantineans at least learned not to let the river run straight through their walls (5.2.7), or when without comment he transmits the vivid Laconic cry for help sent to Sparta by a beleaguered commander (1.1.23): "Ships gone, Mindarus dead, men starving, what to do?"

The persona of the author-as-narrator conveys an important aspect of the meaning of the text, because it is in large part the quality of this voice that makes us believe that what we are reading is likely to matter to us. Each of the three authors speaks to us as someone who has put considerable effort and thought into the narrative. Their personas are different: Herodotus is genial and vividly discursive, Thucydides severely analytical, and Xenophon earnest and direct in the apparent transparency of his narrative. But in each case, it is the thoughtful management of the authorial voice that will make us, as readers, want to attend to this particular record of the past, and the judgments expressed about it, because we trust the author-as-narrator.

5   Recounting Narrative: "One Damn Thing after Another"

We come to the final and most important aspect of meaning in the histories of Herodotus, Thucydides, and Xenophon: their diachronic shape as a specific and idiosyncratic kind of narrative.

Each of the three writers under consideration here conveys what he thinks needs memorializing in his history, his judgment about the matters mentioned in it, and the flavor of his own authorial attention to the process, in a distinctive narrative form that identifies the genre itself as an ongoing account of events unrolling in time: in Meier's phrase (1987: 44), "a multi-subjective, contingency-oriented account," in which human beings, both individually and in groups, think, decide, and do things, with varying degrees of success; these lead in turn and over time to other things.

Another word for this process is "story" and, of course, this is where historical narrative is most vulnerable to the academics' cry of "we are losing!" For story is, as Mink has said and we have already amply seen, "a product of imaginative construc-tion." But is Mink right to add "which cannot defend its claim to truth by any accepted procedure of argument or authentication"?

If one properly understands the kind of truth that historiography claims for itself, one also understands that narrative of this sort – "one damn thing after another" – is precisely the vehicle through which historical meaning *per se* can emerge. For a multiply peopled, causally connected narrative *performs* the historian's truth. In the unrolling narrative of events in time the historian enacts his recording of important things from the past, records his judgment, and delivers us a sense of why he is a trustworthy narrator, showing us as readers what White (1987) calls "the content of the form." It is from reading, i.e., from re-performing the unrolling narrative that as readers we know (1) what the historian thinks real or true; (2) what he thinks important and why; and (3) how he sees individuals and groups fitting together, forming and reforming patterns of behavior in the ever-changing interplay of causality and unexpected contingency that it is his task as a narrative historian to observe. It is through this narrative performance that the historian mediates his own understanding of the behavior of human communities through the working of time.

How does each of our three narratives enact its claim to be (1) communicating real information, (2) emphasizing what is important, and (3) depicting how causes (*aitiai*) work, exploring exactly how "one damn thing" becomes another?

Herodotus does it by indirection. He begins with deflated myth – retold, he claims, by Persian *logioi* – and then dismisses the abduction accounts as effectively *exitēloi*, now lying beyond his ability to assess as history. He turns instead to Croesus and the *spatium historicum*, stating firmly, "I know this was the man who was the first to outrage Greeks" (1.5).

The whole of Herodotus' *Histories* unrolls as *logoi* or stories that we are to trust (or not!) because, precisely, in his narration of them Herodotus has resisted the temptation to channel the muse, to claim for his narrative more than the status of real stories from the past. If we are to come up with a metaphor for his procedure, we can think of him as a speaker with a slide show, or discrete little film clips. The individual accounts (*logoi*) are the slides or clips, and he and we together look at them in the sequence he has assembled.

What makes this distinctively history rather than myth or novel is the articulation of the process of his narration as one that privileges reality. As much as he can, he shows us the stories themselves as data, real accounts from the past, that are still around and so hopefully have not yet become *exitēloi* through the workings of time. People within his narrative repeatedly fail at their plans precisely because they have not paid attention to aspects of the unrolling narrative of events that Herodotus as author and we as readers see all too clearly. Without Herodotus having to lecture, or even too often to employ "warner figures," the narrative itself shows us how useful it is to take reality in all its unexpected contingencies very seriously.

Thucydides, as we would expect, undertakes narration quite differently. Where Herodotus constantly interrupts the interplay of causality and contingency by reminding us that we are looking at narrative fragments initially constructed by someone else, Thucydides has placed himself up in the projection booth, running the film that he himself has made. Book 1 performs the run-up to the Peloponnesian War: we are shown a variety of angles from which the past can be understood: in the largest temporal sweep of the "Archaeology" (1.1–19) and the smaller but still impressive one of the *Pentecontaetia* (1.89–117); in the biographical, almost Herodotean narratives of Pausanias and Themistocles (1.126–138); and in the detailed and dramatic accounts of doings at Epidamnus, Corcyra, the Spartan assembly, and the final meetings at Sparta and Athens (1.24–88, 118–125, 139–146). In the details of his unrolling narrative arrangement Thucydides shows his audience how events that began long ago and far outside either Athenian or Spartan control finally suck the major powers in, so that war begins. More overtly than Herodotus, Thucydides baldly claims that the attention to detail that he as author and we as readers engage with allows a kind of understanding that will be useful (*ophelimos*, 1.22).

His narrative, like Herodotus', is imaginative construction. Almost certainly, had we been there, we would not have written up the first steps of Thucydides' war as he has done. But such a focus misses the meaning of the kind of truth that historical narrative conveys. The careful, dispassionate narrative segments of Book 1 set up an expectation on our part as readers that in his sequential performance of summers and winters from 431 to 411 BCE Thucydides will give us the best, most accurate account of which he is capable. The way the narrative is constructed shows us that, like Herodotus, Thucydides believes in and respects facts. He too lets emerge in the ongoing narrative that the things of which one remains unaware will eventually do injury. Where he differs from Herodotus is in his notion of what constitutes a fact, and the appropriate relation of facts to narrative.

Xenophon's notions of fact and its relation to narrative are more different still. To understand properly the kind of truth that emerges from Xenophon's narrative, we have to change venues – out of the lecture hall or movie theater, and instead to an old-fashioned gentleman's club. There Xenophon will be seated by the fire, brandy snifter in hand, still dressed in riding clothes. He will speak to us as one fourth-century aristocrat to another, sometimes elliptically or even possibly in code, about how various of his acquaintances survived in the chaotic, often threatening world of the first half of the fourth century BCE. As he tells us what he has heard from his like-minded friends from all over the Greek world, he will also, as an officer and a gentleman, leave out the things he thinks unbecoming, in particular the appalling successes of those damn' Thebans. Xenophon does not offer a comprehensive survey of the politics of the Greek world; the understanding he offers is much more limited. But as the history of his reception over two millennia shows, Xenophon's narrative too conveys in its attention to military craft the same kind of alertness and effort to be precise as do the narratives of his two predecessors. This is more modestly and narrowly conceived history, but we can discern here too a desire to make causal connections clear, and to pay attention to facts, particularly military facts, that influence the unrolling causal sequence of events. We may (indeed, we do) criticize his judgment about *what* was important in the history of early fourth-century Greece. Nonetheless, comparable kinds of meaning emerge from the narrative. The historical narratives of Herodotus, Thucydides, and even Xenophon perform their ideas of truth, and, as they do so, they also show the nature of these authors' belief in the importance of understanding how particularities in the past fit together into patterns of causally connected meaning.

6 Conclusion

These four categories constitute important kinds of meaning found in early Greek historical narration. The basic task, as Herodotus, Thucydides, and Xenophon conceived of it, was to memorialize great events of the past; its second was to justify the memorialization in terms of an open exercise of judgment on the part of the historian: in all three authors we've seen an effort made to test and certify that process, which memorializes real things and does so using criteria of selection that will make sense to the historian's intended audience. Aristotle's categories of probability (*to eikos*) and appropriateness (*to prepon*) are certainly relevant here, to the historian as well as the budding orator, but his distinction in the *Poetics* between history and poetry (1451a36ff.) is even more important: the historian must take seriously not just the things that make intuitive sense to his readers, but also, in his exercise of judgment, the things that remain true but hard to make sense of together, what I have called here the arbitrary and contingent parts of "one damn thing after another." This is the category where the severest charge against Xenophon can be brought, but if one remembers that his judgment represents the ethical world of the fourth-century aristocrat and pro-Spartan military man, at least one sees why some of his odder principles of selection prevail. After Xenophon, at least to the extent we can make judgments about a largely missing sequence of Hellenistic historians, the goals and duties of the narrative historian underwent some changes, as history itself became part of a larger rhetorical project, and historians became useful because they supplied material for persuasive argument.

The argument as I made it here really works only for that early generation of historians in the fifth and fourth centuries who collectively began the process of accounting for the way the recent Greek past unrolled. As such, they bear a particular meaning for us today. At the outset of this essay I referred to the present as a time of uncertainty for history itself. We have perhaps too much to remember, to memorialize, and we have lost collective sight of why it is especially important to remember real things. This is something that all three of our ancient historians understood well, although they understood it differently from one another. All three thought that telling things intended to be true would be instructive, and that the more true things in their multiple interconnections one knew, the better one dealt with one's own time. But they also saw that uncomfortable aspects of reality tend always to be neglected, until we can no longer evade them – and in point of fact, Thucydides' Athenian soldiers, the would-be conquerors of Syracuse, did not make it home. Many of them died in a Syracusan quarry, on a cup of water and two cups of grain a day.

FURTHER READING

Important studies that contain further useful bibliography are: for Herodotus, Gould 1989; Lateiner 1989; Bakker et al. 2002; and Dewald and Marincola 2006; for Thucydides, Hornblower 1994a; Rood 1998; Greenwood 2006; for Xenophon, Anderson 1974; Gray 1989; Tuplin 1993; Dillery 1995. For modern historiographical issues and especially their contemporary developments, see Appleby et al. 1994; Berkhofer 1995; Munslow 1997, 2000; Jenkins 1999; and for ancient historiography as a literary undertaking, Hornblower 1994b; Marincola 1997; Kraus 1999a; Pelling 2000; Marincola 2001; and Dewald 2005.

CHAPTER EIGHT

Characterization in Ancient Historiography

L. V. Pitcher

For we are writing not histories, but Lives, and by no means is virtue or vice clearly delineated in deeds of the greatest note; rather, a little thing or a saying or a joke has captured character better than battles with titanic casualties, the mightiest confrontations, or the sieges of cities.

(Plut. *Alex.* 1)

1 Introduction

Plutarch's eloquent statement of generic distinction has often been quoted. It is a salutary warning against demanding from the biographer emphases and concerns which one might expect in a historian. Viewed from the other end, though, the remark is equally illuminating. Plutarch's dictum might be taken to imply that the depiction of human personality and idiosyncrasy – integral to the modern notion of "characterization" – is a distraction from the narration of great events that is the primary concern of the classical historians. Indeed, the idea that biography and history are not only different but mutually inimical is one that has found purchase in the works of some of the ancient world's modern inheritors.

As well as considerations of genre, the student of "character" in ancient historiography faces a more fundamental problem. This is the extent to which modern concepts of character or personality are relevant to the works of Greco-Roman antiquity. The word *kharaktēr* did not have its present-day meaning in classical Greek. It signified rather an impression, an engraving, or a distinguishing mark. The term translated as "character" in the passage above is *ēthos*. This covers some of the same ground as the English "character," but by no means offers an easy equivalency. If by "characterization" one means the analysis of complex psychological drives, the delineation of quirk and foible, and the evolution and development of personality under the influence of external pressures, one has to be aware that the applicability of these ideas to the works of the classical past is both debatable and debated. *A fortiori*, their applicability to works of ancient history is debatable as well.

A final preliminary warning, most pertinent to an enterprise of the present kind, must be sounded. "Classical historiography" covers a diverse range of authors, writing in different languages and subject to different environments and influences, over a period of almost a thousand years. Sweeping statements about the nature of characterization in the ancient historians run a serious risk of imposing homogeneity where none exists. Herodotus' way of handling character is in many respects different from Xenophon's, while both are markedly dissimilar from Tacitus'. In what follows, I have attempted to give some sense of the variety of the relevant texts and what distinguishes the use of "characterization" in each of them, as well as the traits which they share. It is worth remembering, though, that a discussion of this compass can only begin to scratch the surface.

Despite all these caveats, however, the subject of characterization in ancient historiography is an endlessly intriguing one. As we shall see, it is bound up with many other topics that are addressed elsewhere in this collection: the assessment of evidence, the significance of style, divergencies of focalization, and the significance of narrative structure. And for all the difficulties acknowledged above, the study of how and why the historians characterize the agents of their histories is by no means an idle or a fruitless one.

2 Consistency in Characterization

Since the applicability of modern notions of "character" to the texts of classical antiquity has come under scrutiny, it is perhaps helpful to establish certain *minima* from the outset. Can the idea that an individual has a consistent set of traits and patterns of behavior be identified beyond a doubt in Greco-Roman historiography?

The answer to this question is a definite "yes." Throughout the works of the classical historians, one finds instances of both the narrator and individuals within the text basing inferences and speculations on the assumption of a consistent character. Consider the following extracts:

> [Xerxes on Demaratus:] I will not accept that he is not well-disposed towards my affairs, judging from his past speeches . . . (Hdt. 7.237.1)

> [On the importance of taking precautions before surrendering:] It is unexceptionable to behave rationally when one has received adequate pledges – these being oaths, wives, children, and above all the past life of the individual in question. (Pol. 8.36.2–3)

[Of Hannibal's father, Hamilcar:] He then spent nine years in Hispania increasing Punic influence in such a fashion that it was clear that he was gearing up in his mind for a war greater than that which he was presently conducting, and that, if he had lived longer, the Carthaginians who waged war on Italy under Hannibal's command would have done so under the leadership of Hamilcar. (Livy 21.2.1–2)

[Rejecting a version of events in 69 found in "certain authors":] I do not believe that Paulinus, with his practical good sense, ever hoped for such moderation on the part of the people in that most corrupt age that the very men whose passion for war had destroyed peace would now abandon war for love of peace. (Tac. *Hist.* 2.37)

[On the assertion that Augustus had planned the murder of Agrippa Postumus:] Beyond a doubt, Augustus had made many harsh complaints about the ways of the young man, and had seen to it that his exile was sanctioned by decree of the Senate, but he did not show indifference to the death of any of his own, and it was not believable that he had brought death upon his grandson in order to assure the well-being of his stepson. (Tac. *Ann.* 1.6)

These extracts do not just assume consistency of character; the assumption makes possible the drawing of various conclusions. Xerxes in Herodotus deduces Demaratus' present goodwill towards him from the way in which the latter has acted towards him previously, and Polybius sees the way someone has behaved in the past as being as sure a guarantee of reliable conduct in the future as actual hostages. Tacitus uses the conception of the characters of Paulinus and Augustus which he has built up from elsewhere to adjudicate the more likely, the more "characteristic," one might say, from differing accounts of events. Livy, yet more ambitious, uses his sense of what drove Hamilcar to plot a contrafactual scenario, a history which never happened. All such pieces of ratiocination function from the premise that an individual's behavior is, or can be, consistent and (within limits) predictable.

The passage from Herodotus leads us to a further point. From the outset of the extant historiographical tradition, it is not merely the narrator who manifests an interest in determining individual character and making deductions from it. Agents within the text are equally adept at the same maneuvers. One might adduce another example from Herodotus: Cleisthenes, who makes trial of the potential suitors of his daughter to determine their "virtue and temper and breeding and way of life" (6.128.1). The characters of others can also be revealed or demonstrated, through a skillful manipulation of circumstances. Theramenes, in Xenophon's *Hellenica*, dramatically seeks sanctuary from his destroyers, not in the belief that the sanctity of the altar will actually ward them off, but because, as he himself puts it, "I wish to demonstrate this: that these people are not only most unjust towards men, but also most impious towards the gods" (2.3.53).

A notion of consistency in individual human behavior is, then, prevalent in ancient historiography. But what sorts of individuality are explored by the ancient historians? Is there any change or development in the capacity to articulate the nuances of human personality as the historiographical tradition progresses? And do particular historians have different ways of bringing these nuances out?

3   The Expression of Personality

Dr. Johnson described the delineation of characters in Xenophon's *Anabasis* as "the first instance of the kind known." The proposition is, at best, arguable, as well as somewhat imprecise in its original expression (Lane Fox 2004a: 2). One might argue that this distinction belongs instead to the dissolute and engaging parvenu pharaoh Amasis (Hdt. 2.172f.), with his adroit ripostes to criticisms of his background and drinking habits, or to some other individual in Herodotus. It is, however, worth exploring the possible grounds for Johnson's implicit statement that Herodotus and Thucydides, Xenophon's predecessors, do not offer vivid delineations of personalities.

It is revealing to compare Xenophon's expatiation on the personality of Cyrus with the explicit statements about the characters of individuals which the narrator offers in Herodotus and Thucydides. The comments of the Herodotean narrator about particular people are terse, and almost invariably limited to their endowment or deficiency in two areas: virtue and intelligence. Particular quirks, foibles, traits, or proclivities are not highlighted. There are exceptions to this tendency. We learn of Amasis, for example, that he was "fond of a drink and a joke and in no way a serious-minded man, even when he was a private citizen" (Hdt. 2.174.2). This is the exception, though, and not the rule.

Thucydides, likewise, is sparing with direct comments on the personalities of the individuals with whom he deals. Indeed, the focus is in some ways even narrower than that of Herodotus. Thucydides' narrator directly addresses the subject of individual virtue more rarely, and shows much more interest in analyzing the nature and forms of intelligence and competence. This is most clearly visible in his remarks on Themistocles (1.138.3): "for by native perception and without any prior or subsequent study, he was most sagacious in his snap judgments on what was happening and the best and most forward-looking predictor of future events." As before, one should note that there are certainly exceptions to this general rule of attention to competence rather than virtue. Nicias' demise, for example, extorts from the narrator a note of regret "on account of his whole way of life, utterly devoted to virtue" (7.86.5). The fact remains, however, that the narrator is generally sparing of explicit commentary upon the characters of his protagonists.

The lavish obituary for Cyrus which Xenophon places in *Anabasis* Book 1 certainly presents a signal contrast to this austerity. The reader does not learn merely that the leader of Xenophon's expedition was virtuous and capable. In fact, the nature of his virtues and capacities is set out in loving detail, from his skill and bravery when hunting (*Anab.* 1.9.6), to his punctiliousness in the observation of treaties (*Anab.* 1.9.8), to his sternness towards transgressors (*Anab.* 1.9.13).

It is also notable that, while Cyrus receives the most attention in this regard, he is by no means the only individual in the *Anabasis* to whom the narrator devotes a passage on his personal traits, attitudes, and proclivities. Clearchus' doggedly martial nature (*Anab.* 2.6.6) and regretted outbursts of rage (2.6.9) are likewise brought under the spotlight, as are the greed, megalomania, and deceitful character of Menon (2.6.21–22).

This difference in narrative technique, perhaps, helps to explain why the portrayal of Cyrus impacted upon Johnson's sensibility in a way in which the portraits of individuals in earlier authors did not. As we shall shortly see, explicit commentary on an individual's character from the narrator was by no means the only way in which an ancient historian might bring out the individuality of his protagonists, and many of the various methods by which individuation was achieved preceded the work of Xenophon. Nonetheless, overt authorial assessment and analysis of a person's traits and behavior are the most obvious manifestations of "characterization" in antiquity.

Authorial assessment of character does not, of course, perish with Xenophon. As far as history in Latin goes, Caesar, for the most part, shows a reversion to the spareness of Herodotus and Thucydides. The most overt comment on character that can be wrung out of the lengthy introductory piece concerning Vercingetorix, for instance, is the comment that "he wedded the utmost severity in his exercise of power to his outstanding activity" (Caes. *BG* 7.4.9).

Thereafter, however, the Roman historians make particular use of the device. In the Roman tradition, too, one sees a developing fascination with paradoxical characters, individuals in whom great virtues and great vices coexist, or in whom evil is accompanied with remarkable mental or physical abilities. The most celebrated example of the latter tendency is perhaps Sallust's analysis of the insurgent Catiline (*Cat.* 5.1–5):

> Lucius Catiline, born of a distinguished family, possessed great force of mind and body, but had an evil and vicious character. From his youth, civil wars, slaughter, rapine, and discord within the State gave him pleasure, and in them he spent his young manhood. His body could endure starvation, pain, and sleeplessness to an incredible degree; his mind was bold, tricky, and subtle, capable of concealing or feigning whatever he wanted, greedy for the property of others, profligate with his own, blazing in its desires, with a sufficiency of eloquence, but too little wisdom. His immense intellect continually craved the excessive, the incredible, and the transgressive.

Livy's Hannibal is likewise characterized by the narrator at the outset of his career as a creature of extremes. His military prowess and frugality are commended, but "huge vices equalled these virtues, great as they were: monstrous cruelty; treachery surprising even in a Carthaginian; no truth; no piety; no fear of the gods; no respect for oaths; no religious observance" (21.4.9). The same might likewise be said for Appian's Mithridates (App. *Mith.* 546–550), or Tacitus' Sejanus (Tac. *Ann.* 4.1). In Tacitus, however, the narrator's assessments of individuals – which are many and memorable – often go beyond this rather obvious paradoxography into more subtle explorations of character and its perception, but Tacitean characterization is in any event a subject which demands fuller treatment (§§4, 7).

Overt assessment by the narrator is, then, the most obvious place to look for characterization in ancient historiography. Some further observations upon the technique are in order, however. The first concerns its limitations in a work of narrative (which the historiography of the ancient world, almost by definition, is).

There is a monumental and somewhat static quality to this mode of pronouncement. The action comes to a standstill while such assessments are enunciated, with a consequent suspension of narrative flow. As a result, these analyses usually give the impression of being somewhat semi-detached from the contexts in which they stand. It is no coincidence that the longer, "set-piece," analyses of an individual's character which are collected above (pp. 105–106) all take place at obvious points of opening or closure in the narrative. In the cases of Cyrus, Menon, Clearchus, and Mithridates, the point in question is the death of the individual concerned, while Hannibal and Catiline receive this attention at the moment of their first introduction. Often, too, the assessment coincides with a division in the text itself, such as the beginning or end of a book.

These tendencies are not invariable, and the static quality of authorial assessment is not necessarily a bad thing. The foregoing does mean, however, that the wedding of characterization to action has to be achieved by other methods. In the next section, we shall examine the various means by which the historians of antiquity accomplish this feat.

4   Indirect Characterization

There are more and subtler ways for an author to convey what is important in someone's character than simply stating outright the narrator's own assessment. The most obvious of these is perhaps also the most prevalent: the contribution made by speeches. The narrator *in propria persona* is not the only voice that talks about and assesses the traits of individuals or groups in ancient historiography. Individuals within the narrative do so as well.

Examples of this technique are many and obvious. One famous instance would be the assessment of the collective characters of the Athenians in the first book of Thucydides (1.70), which comes not from the narrator but from the mouths of Corinthian ambassadors. It is found already, however, in Herodotus, and deployed with considerable adroitness. Consider the exchange between Harpagus and Astyages, after the former had engineered the latter's fall from power on behalf of Cyrus (1.129.3):

> And Harpagus declared that the achievement was justly his, because he himself had done the writing. But Astyages explained to him that he was the most foolish and unjust of all mankind: most foolish, because if he had indeed engineered the present situation, he had handed over the kingship to someone else and not kept it for himself, when he had had the chance to become king; most unjust, because on account of the dinner [at which Astyages had fed Harpagus his own son] he had enslaved the Medes.

In this passage, Astyages is offering up his own assessment of Harpagus' character. Note that he does so in the terms which we have already seen (p. 105) to be usual for the Herodotean narrator: virtue and intelligence (or, as here, the absence thereof). Nor is this just the name-calling of a defeated tyrant. The reasons for Harpagus' description as both unjust and stupid, coolly enumerated in a balanced antithesis, carry undeniable weight.

The subtlety of Herodotus' narrative art here is compelling. The reader comes into this scene expecting to be invited to rejoice in Harpagus' victory, on account of the cannibalistic humiliation his victim had previously forced upon him. In fact, the dignity of Astyages' bearing in defeat and the clarity of vision that he brings to the task of telling Harpagus a few home truths greatly increase the impact of the analysis. This piece of characterization has much more force coming from the deposed Median than it would have done from the narrative voice.

Characterization within a speech, then, can be a useful tool. It is one which Herodotus' successors deploy in numerous and ingenious ways. One such development, for instance, is characterization offered within a speech (or within the thought processes of an individual or group) that says as much, if not more, about the speaker than about the ostensible target of the characterization.

The most obvious form of this technique appears when an individual within a narrative makes an assessment of another individual that data from elsewhere in the text indicate to be partial, misconceived, or simply wrong. In the first book of the *Gallic War*, for instance, Caesar reports how he criticized those who assumed too readily that Ariovistus had gone rogue (*BG* 1.40.2): "Ariovistus (Caesar said) had most eagerly sought out the friendship of the Roman people while he himself was consul; why was anyone assuming that he would so recklessly deviate from his duty?"

The text will go on to show that the assumption of Ariovistus' treachery is correct, and so that this opening sally of Caesar's is wrong. The way in which this incorrect assessment is phrased, however, skillfully builds up a picture of the individual who is making it. Caesar is shown to be a person who expects people, in the absence of data to the contrary, to show consistency of behavior and to stand by their obligations. An honorable man, but nobody's fool; the rest of this speech goes on to analyze what will happen if it *should* transpire that Ariovistus has gone to the bad (which he has). Caesar the general's momentary misreading of Ariovistus is used by Caesar the historian, paradoxically enough, to shed a flattering light upon his own character. And, of course, Ariovistus' betrayal of Caesar's expressed faith in him, and the discreet note that this lets down Ariovistus himself and the Roman people as well, makes the picture of Caesar's foe all the more damning.

Further interesting complications can arise when the reliability of the indirect characterization is a little more ambiguous. A sophisticated instance of this may be found, again, in *Gallic War* 1, as Caesar's troops become agitated about the foes that they must soon face (*BG* 1.39.1):

> From questioning of our troops and the words of Gauls and merchants, who repeatedly declared that the Germani were physically huge, with astonishing prowess and experience in arms (they said that often they had not been able to endure even the expression or the stare of the Germani, when they had met with them), so great a fear suddenly overtook the whole army that it shook the minds and spirits of all exceedingly.

The neurasthenic prostration with which the soldiers greet the reports of their informants ("so great a fear...") does not inspire faith in their stability of critical judgment. This, in turn, induces a certain amount of skepticism in the reader as to the reliability of the merchants' description of the Germani, which is in any event suspiciously hyperbolic. Caesar's men, through their aptness to lose their heads over these unconfirmed and perhaps exaggerated reports, emerge as somewhat skittish, and in need of strong leadership. It is no surprise that this is almost immediately supplied by Caesar himself, who, in a speech from which we have already quoted (p. 108), swiftly brings them back to the straight and narrow.

Caesar the historian, however, is doing something rather more unusual than merely painting a picture of windy troops. In his own speech, he does go some way towards correcting the hysterical overestimation of the Germani that has panicked his men, but the fact remains that one of the first proper (though second-hand) pictures of the Germani which the reader is afforded in the *Gallic War* suggests formidable adversaries. Caesar the historian needs the events he describes to be significant, and Caesar the politician needs his own achievements to look as imposing as possible. Both imperatives demand a formidable adversary. Thus, although Caesar will temper the original portrait of the Germani as well-nigh superhuman, it does suit his narrative strategy to have a source theoretically independent from himself build them up as opponents.

Indeed the "building up" of an individual or group by depicting other people earnestly discussing their nature before their first appearance in person is a recurring and effective tactic in ancient historiography, and, indeed, elsewhere: from Shakespearean tragedy (Bradley 1905: 32) to contemporary cinema (as in the opening frames of the 2005 comic-book adaptation *Elektra*). To revert to historiography: Livy's authorial characterization of Hannibal, discussed above (p. 106), is not the first thing that the reader hears in Livy's text about the young man; it is preceded by a worried discussion in Carthage about what the young man might bring upon his city (Livy 21.3.3–6). In like manner, Xenophon subjects the nature of Jason of Pherae to extended analysis in a speech (*Hell.* 6.1.4) some time before the man himself actually appears in the narrative.

However, the most complex manifestations of this "indirect introduction" technique are probably those that the reader encounters in the works of Tacitus. The introduction of the emperor Galba at the beginning of the *Histories* is a case in point (1.5):

> There were also those who carped at Galba's age and miserliness. His austerity, once praised and spread about through his military reputation, was galling to those who recoiled from the discipline of former times and who had become accustomed under the influence of Nero over the course of fourteen years to love the vices of the emperors as much as they once feared their virtues.

Again, the final impact of this passage is complicated. The first thing one reads in the work that proffers a characterization of Galba is reported criticism of his age and stinginess. At least one of these criticisms finds confirmation almost immediately from the narrator, who opens the next chapter with the words "Titus Vinius and Cornelius Laco ... were destroying the weak old man" (*Hist.* 1.6). In the Latin, the words for "weak old man," *invalidum senem*, are even put at the beginning of the sentence for emphasis. Moreover, references to Galba's senescence continue to crop up throughout the subsequent narrative.

Thus far, Tacitus seems to be proceeding comfortably along the lines of his later introduction of Tiberius. The earlier emperor's alleged failings ("subject to the traditional deep-seated arrogance of the Claudii, bursting with many indications of savagery, despite attempts to suppress them": Tac. *Ann.* 1.4) are a matter for public debate in what seems at first a similar fashion at the beginning of the *Annals* even before the death of Augustus. Closer attention, however, quickly determines that something more subtle is going on in the debate concerning Galba's fitness to rule.

Even in the first sentence, alarm bells begin to ring. Tacitus often deploys forms of the word *increpantium*, which is translated as "carping" above, with a pejorative sense towards the complainant. Later in the *Histories*, for instance, it is used of those who accuse Vedius Aquila of being a deserter and traitor, "not on any grounds to do with him personally, but with each man foisting his own offense upon others, as is the way with mobs" (2.44). The next sentence strengthens suspicion about motives of the nay-sayers. Discontent with the emperor's austerity is explicitly attributed to the deterioration of morals under the fourteen years of Nero's reign ("accustomed to love the vices of the emperors as much as they once feared their virtues").

The final effect of Tacitus' initial indirect characterization of Galba is, then, a layered and subtle one. The emperor's failings are genuine (although, as Tacitus goes on to make clear, he has accompanying virtues as well), but the capacity of his critics to notice them does not redound to their own credit. Rather, it serves to confirm the corruption of their judgment. They disapprove of the right man, but do so for the wrong reasons. This nicely introduces a narrative which repeatedly highlights not just the readiness of people to analyze the characters of their fellow men, but also their tendency to misidentify what they see there, whether through foolishness or with the intent to mislead others. This is a world where Vitellius' profligate spending of his own and others' resources is labeled generosity – "on account of the greed for power, his very vices were taken as virtues" (Tac. *Hist.* 1.52) – and Domitian's gaucheness is mistaken for modesty (4.40).

Assessments essayed by people within the text are, then, every bit as useful as outright statements by the narrator for building a sense of individual character in classical historiography. Moreover, as we have seen from our analysis of Tacitus at work, this technique also opens up the possibility for more general points about the possible unreliability of the person doing the assessing, and the factors which might color his or her perception. There are, however, yet further ways in which the historians of antiquity can characterize the individuals with whom their narratives are concerned.

5   Characterization by Word and Deed

And I am not unaware that these utterances are insignificant. But I judge this to be admirable in the man, that when death was at hand neither his good sense nor his playful wit deserted his spirit.

(Xen. *Hell.* 2.3.56)

Thus does Xenophon defend his inclusion of various witticisms uttered by Theramenes on his way to execution under the tyranny of the Thirty Tyrants. The remark confirms, if confirmation were needed, that the historiographers were every bit as aware as Plutarch (cf. the opening quotation) of how useful small deeds, sayings, or jokes can be in establishing a picture of an individual. Individuals may be characterized as much by what they say or do as by overt commentary on their personalities from others, whether the narrator or others in the text.

It comes as no surprise that Xenophon himself is a notable exponent of this approach. He has a particular knack for catching what he sees as a person's essential characteristics from the way in which they behave on a first or early appearance in his narrative. A vignette concerning Clearchus from the first book of the *Anabasis* is a case in point (1.5.11–13):

> When a dispute arose between one of Menon's men and one of his own, Clearchus, judging the former to be in the wrong, beat him...One of Menon's men, who was chopping wood, saw Clearchus riding past, and threw his axe at him. He missed, but one started throwing rocks, then another, and soon there was an uproar. Clearchus fled to his own camp, and issued a call to arms.

In due course, Cyrus himself has to resolve the resulting mess. Xenophon thus succeeds in making some important points about Clearchus' character, without passing any overt judgments himself as narrator (Braun 2004: 101). The general is decisive and harsh in his judgment of situations, characteristics which can be productive of trouble, and which the narrative voice does eventually spell out in his "obituary" (*Anab.* 2.6.9; mentioned above, p. 105). In a similar vein, Menon, whom the narrator ultimately condemns for his untrustworthiness and lust for power (*Anab.* 2.6.21–22 and p. 105 above), is glimpsed early on (1.4.14–15) exhorting his troops to steal a march on their comrades in an effort to curry favor with Cyrus.

Although the *Anabasis* is in any event a work where the personalities of individuals and clashes between them bulk large, this technique of introductory characterization by word or deed may be seen operating in the *Hellenica* as well. The Spartan admiral Callicratidas is a fine example of this. He is presented from the outset as a blunt and no-nonsense individual by his sharp comments at the expense of, first, his predecessor Lysander (*Hell.* 1.6.2), and then Cyrus (1.6.7).

Personality and character can also be expressed not only in what is said or done, but *how* it is said or done. The speech of Sthenelaidas at the debate in Sparta just before the outbreak of the Peloponnesian War (Thuc. 1.86) is a celebrated instance of this: opening with a sneer at the "many words" offered by the Athenian ambassadors before it, it is itself notably short, at less than a sixth of the length of the speech by Archidamus which immediately precedes it. Brevity and terseness were famous Spartan virtues; with a speech of this concision, Sthenelaidas presents himself as a guardian of true Spartan values.

Less well known, but equally effective in its own way, is the speech that Xenophon puts into the mouth of Critias in the *Hellenica* (2.3.24–26), which speaks volumes about the character of the most cerebral of the Thirty Tyrants through its combination of ostentatiously displayed rationality – note the plethora of words indicating reasoning, recognition, causation, or deduction (italicized below) – and sinister euphemism (likewise italicized):

> If any of you thinks that more are dying than is appropriate, let him consider that *these things happen* everywhere where there is a change of constitution. And it must befall that very many are hostile to those engineering a change towards oligarchy, *on account of* this being the most populous of Greek cities and *on account of* the people having been nurtured in freedom for the longest period. But *having recognized*...that the people would never be well-disposed to the Spartans who had saved us, but that the best sort of people would by contrast always remain trustworthy, *on account of this* we are putting into place this constitution with the approval of the Spartans. And if we *perceive* that anyone is opposed to oligarchy, we will *expedite the inconvenience* to the best of our ability.

Manner of action can be as significant for the delineation of character as manner of speech, although its effects tend to be more diffuse, and so not susceptible to abbreviated treatment here. One example to note in passing is Appian's penchant for the use of verbs with the prefix *pro-* (indicating, amongst other things, the doing of things beforehand, in anticipation, or in advance) when speaking about the activities of Julius Caesar. While the collective impact of lexical choices such as these is subtle, their effect is undeniable. Appian uses them to build a picture of the dictator as ever active, preemptive, insightful and alert, a trick which Caesar himself achieves in his narratives of his campaigns through rather different means (below, p. 114).

In summary, then, the classical historians had numerous resources at their disposal to offer up characterizations of individuals within their works, through the selection of telling words or deeds and the style in which they were executed. One other such technique, however, calls for special consideration. This is arrangement and manipulation of the structure of the text itself, in order to highlight particular aspects of the individuals within it.

6 Structural Characterization

> But because he thought that in a war-like city there would be more kings like Romulus than there would be like Numa and that the kings themselves would go to war, he instituted the *flamen Iovis* as a perpetual priesthood, so that the sacred rites of the kingly office would not be neglected.
>
> (Livy 1.20.2)

Livy's description of the policies instituted by the second king of Rome, Numa Pompilius, furnishes a good example of "structural characterization" in action. Livy's narrator explicitly comments upon Numa's attainments as a man of peace when he is first introduced into the narrative, in accordance with the tendencies we have noted above (p. 107): "at that time the justice and piety of Numa Pompilius were celebrated" (Livy 1.18.1). Quite apart from authorial insistence, however, Numa's peace-loving characteristics are also thrown into relief by his position in the narrative. His traits stand out the more clearly for being juxtaposed with those of his martial predecessor, Romulus, and his yet more aggressive successor, Tullius Hostilius.

Livy, of course, had no control over the order in which the tradition held that the early kings of Rome had reigned. It did, however, lie within his capacities as narrator and literary artist to point up the contrast between Numa and the kings between whom he was sandwiched. This is exactly what the reader sees him doing above. Note the nice touch whereby it is Numa himself who perceives the disparity between himself and Romulus; once again, an observation is sharpened by originating from a character within the text rather than the main narrator.

The subtleties do not end there. Observe that the sentence does not run "he thought that . . . there would be more kings like Romulus than . . . like *himself*," but rather "he thought that . . . there would be more kings like Romulus than . . . like *Numa*." The point is small, but telling; "Numa" is already beginning to stand as a metonym for a particular set of values distinct from those which attach to the name of Romulus, even in the mind of the second king himself. Livy's structuring of his narrative of the early monarchs of Rome enables him to present them as embodying a comprehensive gallery of civic possibilities.

The delineation of character by means of significant juxtaposition is not a phenomenon limited to Livy. One of ancient historiography's particular delights is pointing up through proximity in the narrative the difference between good and bad generalship. Again, Xenophon's *Hellenica* furnishes a convenient example, where the narrator hammers the point home through his commentary (3.2.1):

> Dercylidas, having achieved this and taken nine cities in eight days, took care that while he spent the winter relying upon good relations he might not become a grievous burden to the allies, *as Thibron had* . . .

Dercylidas' competence is all the clearer for the contrast between his diplomacy and Thibron's poor management. The stage is therefore set for the embarrassing fiasco, later in the narrative (4.8.18–19), wherein Thibron finally meets his end. For further instances of good and bad generalship juxtaposed, one might also look at Appian's accounts of the doings of the Scipiones on campaign (*Iber.* 367; *Pun.* 554), where the contrast between the discipline demanded by the new broom and the parlous state to which matters had been reduced under his predecessors is highlighted by initial expulsions of undesirables from the Roman camp.

Juxtaposition need not, of course, play only upon the placing side by side of opposites: good and bad diplomacy, war-like and peaceful kings. The technique likewise thrives upon the setting together of good and better (or, more commonly, of bad and worse). Marius' assault on Capsa is attributed by Sallust to his desire to out-Metellus Metellus, his predecessor in command: "A very great desire to capture it had overcome Marius, both because of its strategic usefulness and because the labor was a tough one and Metellus had taken the town of Thala, similarly situated and fortified to Capsa, to great acclaim" (Sall. *Jug.* 89.6). Almost all of the narratives of the later Roman civil wars, for example, see to it that their protagonists are haunted by the shadows of their predecessors in internecine strife: Julius Caesar's behavior on his victory is anxiously monitored for adherence to or deviation from the pattern set by Sulla (App. *BC* 2.448); the triumvirs strenuously affirm the alleged distinction between their own proscriptions and the ones that preceded them (App. *BC* 4.39); Otho and Vitellius find themselves judged against the yardstick of Julius Caesar and Pompey, or Octavian and the Liberators (Tac. *Hist.* 1.50).

The juxtaposition of individuals, then, is the most obvious way in which the structure of a narrative can heighten or draw attention to particular traits and characteristics. It is, however, by no means the only one. Close study of the ancient historians reveals an armory of techniques whereby the manipulation of narrative flow, the order in which events are narrated, makes subtle points about individual character without a single word of overt comment being passed.

Caesar in particular, whose general reluctance to engage in overt characterization has already been a matter for comment (p. 106), affords numerous instances of these methods in operation. It was noted above (p. 112) that Appian creates an impression of Caesar as foresighted, preemptive, and quick off the mark through careful choice of verbs to describe his behavior. Caesar's own method of highlighting these traits in himself, by contrast, turns upon a mannerism not of lexis but of tense. Consider the following extracts, all from the *Gallic War*:

> When this matter was reported, Caesar burned the gates, sent in the legions *which he had ordered* to be ready, and took the town. (7.11.8)

> Since his own men were now in trouble, Caesar sent to their assistance around three hundred German horsemen, whom *he had decided to have with him from the beginning.* (7.13.1)

> Suddenly the Aedui appeared openly to our men on the flank, whom Caesar *had sent up* on the right by a different route to draw the band apart. (7.50.1)

> Everyone agreed what Caesar himself *had already ascertained* through scouts. (7.44.3)

Through parenthetical uses of verbs in the pluperfect (italicized in the passages above), Caesar repeatedly stresses the extent to which what unfolds in the course of the narrative is ordered and controlled by his own prior planning. Caesar already knows what everyone else is now finding out; Caesar has already sent men elsewhere to spring a surprise; Caesar has already arranged for the possibility of reinforcements.

The adroit general sees things coming in advance. It is telling to observe the terms of the narrator's indictment of the hapless Titurius (one of various incompetent commanders who get to play Thibron to the author's Dercylidas in the course of Caesar's works, though here he is the foil not so much for Caesar as for Cotta): "then at last Titurius, who had not seen anything coming beforehand, panicked and rushed around...which usually happens to people who have to do their planning in the middle of the action itself" (*BG* 5.33.1). Even something as simple as the use of a particular tense, then, can help to build the impression of a sagacious and perceptive character.

The manipulation of when something is revealed is a useful tool in historiographical characterization. The manipulation of whether it is revealed at all is likewise a potent ploy. It has often been remarked that a significant element in the impression of an Olympian and statesmanlike character that is produced by the Pericles of Thucydides stems from a structural consideration: none of his various speeches in the course of the work (Thuc. 1.140–144; 2.35–46; 2.60–64) is ever answered or contradicted by another speech from someone who opposes him. Being associated with some element of formal uniqueness or peculiarity within a text can be an effective means of conveying an impression of a character invested with capability and stature. For example, the volume of extended *oratio obliqua* granted to Vercingetorix greatly exceeds that allotted to any of the rest of Rome's enemies in Caesar's *Gallic War* (e.g., 7.14, 20). By such means does Caesar the historian make the last enemy of Caesar the protagonist appear forceful, sagacious (note his extended point-for-point rebuttals of the slanders of his opponents at 7.20), and so appropriately climactic.

7   Character Change and Development; Character and Behavior

The foregoing discussion has restricted itself to cases where the ancient historians deal with a character or personality that is essentially static. This, however, begs a question. Does ancient historiography ever entertain the notion that a person's character can change or develop? And if it does, how does it cope with this possibility?

It has on occasion been stated that ancient literature in general has no concept of character development or change (Wilamowitz 1907: 1109–1110). *A fortiori*, one would therefore expect such a possibility to be absent from the pages of classical historiography as well. The doctrine is, however, quite wrong. Consider, for example, this extract from Appian's *Macedonica*, in which the narrator discusses the behavior of Perseus (*Mac.* 16):

> He killed without measure or restraint, and from this point he immediately changed into being savage and hateful towards everyone, and there was no longer anything sound-minded or rational in him, but the man who had been most persuasive in the cause of good sense and sharp in reasoning and most brave in battle ... then turned completely and inexplicably to cowardice and foolishness, and became skittish and fickle and maladroit towards all, as his good fortune began to run out. This can be seen in many: that as their fortunes change, they become shadows of themselves.

The last clause (which might more literally be rendered "become more foolish than themselves") might be taken as indicating a residual notion of a "true self" from which the current state is an unhappy declension. Nonetheless, the general thrust of this passage is clear. Appian's narrator states clearly that Perseus' character *did* change, and for the worse. Other examples may be multiplied (Gill 1983: 481–487).

On the whole, it is true that the notion of character change or development is not often encountered in the ancient historians. Passages such as the one from Appian quoted above are the exception rather than the rule. Nonetheless, the Appianic extract should serve as a salutary reminder that ancient historiography, rather than contenting itself with a bland doctrine that people are what they are, and that is that, does engage with the conundrum of individuals who indulge in behavior seemingly inconsistent with other apparent aspects of their character. It does so, moreover, in a number of interesting ways.

Character change is only one possible explanation for such a problem. A more favored explanation is that certain aspects of the individual's character which had always been there already, but had formerly been concealed, came out into the open at a particular point. The most celebrated instance of this reasoning is that applied to Tacitus' Tiberius, which we have already quoted in another context (p. 110): "many indications of his savagery, although they were suppressed, burst forth" (Tac. *Ann.* 1.5). Revelation of hidden tendencies is not the whole story here (Woodman 1998: 155–167), but it is an important part. Such an analysis not infrequently identifies a particular external stimulus as prompting the requisite revelation. Once more, Tacitus provides a good example of this, in the form of the speculation that the reprehensible behavior of Antonius Primus might have come about because "success *revealed* in that sort of character greed and arrogance and other *hidden* evils" (*Hist.* 3.49).

This notion of "external stimulus" is an important one. In the ancient historians, the interaction between what might perhaps be described as an individual's "root tendencies," the impact of particular ideas or emotions, and changing external factors is often presented with considerable sophistication. The interaction can take many forms.

An individual or particular group may, for example, have characteristics that are determined or reinforced by their native environment, a notion particularly associated with Herodotus (1.71, only one amongst many examples), but which persists in the later tradition: witness Caesar's linkage (*BG* 1.1.3) between the valor of the Belgae and their inaccessibility and lack of communication with merchants. An individual's behavior may demonstrate the force of a particular notion or impulse operating upon his or her own deep-seated characteristics: thus, Tacitus can say (*Hist.* 4.55) of foolish behavior on the part of Julius Sabinus that "the glory attaching to a false lineage was spurring on his innate vanity." Innate characteristics may be reinforced, or overridden, by the intervention of others: so Vitellius becomes "more arrogant and cruel" on the arrival of his brother, while Flavius Sabinus' characteristic mildness is overriden by his equally characteristic tractability and the influence of L. Vitellius' wife (*Hist.* 2.63). Polybius, with his customary methodological exactitude, announces plainly his intention to grapple at length with the question of what turned the talented Philip V into a despicable tyrant (4.77.4); this promise the historian subsequently makes good with his nice discrimination between the elements of Philip's character that were inborn, part of his *phusis*, and those which the king developed as he aged: "it seems to me that his good aspects were a part of his nature, whereas his bad came upon him with his advancing years, as happens to some horses when they get old" (Pol. 10.26.8; cf. also Walbank 1972: 92–96).

Character, then, rarely manifests as a monolithic fixity in the ancient historians. The interplay between tendency, impulse, and environment is not something which they invariably sidestep. Rather, it is delineated with subtlety, grace, and perception.

8   Conclusion

It is possible, then, to draw certain conclusions about the role of characterization in ancient historiography. It has emerged that this is not a non-subject, or a mere matter of rhetorical embellishment. A notion of what drives individuals is fundamental to any attempt to work out why these individuals do what they do.

We have also seen, however, that characterization in ancient historiography is a matter that goes well beyond labels of virtue or vice attached to particular people by the narrator. Characterization can also be a matter of style, of inflection, or of structure. As so often in the study of ancient narrative, it transpires that the twists and turns of narration – why a particular matter is handled at this point, and in this particular way – are almost as important as the author's overt commentary. For an adequate appreciation of how characterization works in the classical historians, it is necessary to trust the singer *and* the song.

FURTHER READING

Although much work has been done on character and characterization in ancient literature, comparatively little of it has focused upon how this relates to historiography since Bruns 1898. The essays collected in Pelling 1990c are the place to start in coming to grips with the general issues, and the editor's concluding piece therein (Pelling 1990a) draws conclusions relevant to historiography. Gill 1983 magisterially refutes the notion that the ancients had no concept of character development.

Beyond this, the most profit is to be had in works that deal with individual historians. Ash 1999a is illuminating on characterization in Tacitus' *Histories*. Many of the contributions in Lane Fox 2004b, particularly those by Cawkwell, Braun, and Rood, make useful points about Xenophon's presentation of his protagonists. Walbank 1972 analyzes the views on character of one of the most methodologically explicit of ancient historians; Woodman 1998 tackles, among many other matters, Tacitus' haunting portrait of Tiberius.

Most profitable of all, however, is simply continued engagement with the texts of the ancient historians themselves. Recent commentaries have increasingly examined the contribution made by style and arrangement to the pictures presented of key historical figures. Hornblower, *CT*, for example, has a great deal that is pertinent to this topic in relation to Thucydides. With regard to most historians, however, much still remains to be said.

CHAPTER NINE

Speeches in Classical Historiography

John Marincola

1 Introduction

It would be difficult to over-emphasize the importance of speech in Greek and Roman life. Classical societies were dominated by the spoken word: facility and accomplishment in speaking were, after military achievement, the greatest glories one could win, and assured the way to success and renown. Already in Homer, the heroes are "speakers of words and doers of deeds" (*Il.* 9.443), and figures such as Nestor and Odysseus embody the communal value of effective speaking. With words one gave advice to friends, allies, fellow-citizens, or even kings and despots; one supported others in the courts either by composing speeches for those on trial (as in Athens) or taking the position oneself of being prosecutor or defender (as in Rome). From the earliest period of Greek literature poets were enamored of the word and its ability to influence events, and with the systematic study of rhetoric, "specialists" sought to provide, by means of rules, assistance for those embarking upon public life. The word, of course, both in Greece and Rome, flourished most in those periods when the people or the elite had a measure of political freedom, and matters were debated and explored openly. Closed societies and autocratic governments, by contrast, provoked a crisis in the aristocracy, precisely because free speech had to be curtailed and speakers needed to be careful lest they give offense to the powerful.

Thus it is no surprise that ancient historiographical works are full of speech – it is already in Hecataeus (*FGrHist* 1 F 30) – and not only brief remarks, intimate dialogues, and individual conversations but also (and perhaps especially) full-scale public debates. There were, to be sure, criticisms about the inclusion of speeches, but these were mainly aesthetic, having to do with the frequency of long speeches in direct discourse: these were judged to impede the action and break up the unity of a historical work (Cratippus, *FGrHist* 64 F 1; Diod. 20.1.1–2.2; Trog. F 152 = Just.

38.3.10; Gran. Lic. 36.30–32). It would never have occurred to any historian to write a narrative history wholly without reported speech.

Although oratory and history were seen as formally distinct genres (Brunt 1980), there was nevertheless a close correlation between the orator and the historian, for at least two reasons: first, the basis for all education in antiquity was rhetorical, i.e., geared towards giving public men the tools by which they could effectively address their colleagues and fellow-citizens, and also create works of literary merit. Second, and perhaps no less important, historians as public men themselves will often have given actual speeches: when Thucydides, Polybius, Xenophon, Sallust, Tacitus, Arrian, or Ammianus set pen to papyrus, it was not the first time that they were "composing" speeches. Even historians without a political career will, as members of their city-state, have listened to and been involved in discussions. Yet whether experienced or not, at the point where he introduced a speech into his history, the historian became (or became once again) an "orator."

The uses of speech in history were as great and as far-reaching as in real life, although certain uses tend to predominate. Speeches indicated the reasons and rationale of the historical characters, why they did what they did and with what aims, goals, and expectations. In a genre that relied greatly on sequential narrative, speeches could also provide a more abstract analysis of the underlying issues at stake in actions that were seen as important or distinctive. In Thucydides, for example, the debate of Cleon and Diodotus (3.37–48) treats not just the particular fate of the Mytileneans but also the issues at stake in how any state should treat its subjects, and how it should conceive of its own self-interest. In a different historical milieu, Sallust's Cato and Caesar likewise (and in imitation of Thucydides) debate the issues at stake in a state divided by civil war, discussing not only the fate of the current captives, but also the precedents they will establish, and how that will affect the future (*Cat.* 51–52). Debates might even be framed in such a way as to approach deliberately a kind of "universal" relevance: the analysis of monarchy, oligarchy, and democracy in Herodotus' Constitutional Debate (3.80) or the contrast between monarchy and oligarchy voiced by Maecenas and Agrippa in Cassius Dio (52.1–40) are examples of how historiographical speeches could become political, almost philosophical, analyses in miniature. For the Romans, often criticized for the provinciality and one-sidedness of their historiography, speeches attributed to enemies provided an opportunity to present the viewpoints of Rome's opponents, and thereby engage in a form of critical political analysis relevant to both the particular situation and the more general issues involved with empire and imperialism (see, e.g., Sall. *Hist.* 4.69 [Mithridates]; Livy 9.1 [Herennius Pontius]; Tac. *Agr.* 30–32 [Calgacus]; *Ann.* 12.37 [Caratacus]; cf. Balsdon 1979: 182–185).

Quite aside from this, speech also characterizes the speaker, by indicating his or her frame of mind and disposition. "As is men's speech, so is their lives" (Sen. *Ep.* 114.1; cf. D. Hal. *AR* 1.1.3) was a truism for the ancients, and the historian could reveal a character's nature by the type of speech he composed for him. This aspect might especially come to the fore in those times and under those political systems in which liberty was curtailed, and in which the effectiveness of speech as a motivator for action was impaired. If the Roman Senate of the empire lacked real power to influence events in the way that their ancestors had, a historian might nevertheless record their speeches as a way of both characterizing the individuals who spoke and illuminating the relationship between this elite class and the emperor who wielded the power (cf. Tac. *Ann.* 3.65.1 where he claims he will record only those speeches "distinguished for honesty or of notable shamelessness"). And one did not need a full-dress speech for this: short and pithy remarks could also indicate a man's nature. Plutarch's belief (*Alex.* 1.2) that a jest or phrase reveals more about character than victory in battles was already known and exploited by historians. Theramenes' witty remarks before his death revealed his self-possession (Xen. *Hell.* 2.3.56), while Arrian often relates brief conversations that illuminate Alexander's nature (e.g., 4.20, 5.18, 7.1.5–6, and esp. 2.12.8). The use of speeches served aesthetic ends as well: they marked out dramatic moments, the crucial points when important matters hung in the balance, or they built up suspense by retarding the forward movement of the narrative.

2   Writing Speeches: Truth vs. Probability?

Moderns naturally ask to what extent the speeches in the histories we have represent what was actually said. On the one hand, of course, exact verbal fidelity was not possible. In an age that lacked the technology to reproduce speech verbatim, a speaker's words will have been remembered differently by different listeners. The historians generally indicate the approximate nature of their speeches by the various expressions introducing them: a character spoke "such things" (*toiauta*) rather than "these things" (*tauta*: Gomme 1937: 166–167 on the difference, but some historians use them interchangeably: cf. Buckler 1982: 188 for Xenophon's procedure), or "a speech of this sort" (*huiusce modi orationem*, Sall. *Cat.* 50.5), or "these and similar things" (*tauta kai toutois paraplēsia*, Pol. 18.11; cf. Arr. *Anab.* 5.27.1: *tauta kai toiauta*; Tac. *Hist.* 1.15–16: *haec ac talia*). Sometimes the emphasis is on the tradition: "he is said to have spoken in this manner" (*in hunc modum locutus fertur*: Livy 37.45.11; Tac. *Agr.* 29.4; *Hist.* 1.15–16, cf. Livy 3.67.1). Only on rare occasions will a historian emphasize reproduction of the actual words, and these, not surprisingly, are brief remarks (cf., e.g., Tac. *Ann.* 14.59.4; 15.67.4), which will have been more easily remembered (e.g., Callisthenes' memorable departure "poorer by a kiss": Arr. *Anab.* 4.12.5 and Plut. *Alex.* 54.6, virtually identical).

The question of content, on the other hand, raises numerous issues of interpretation. As so often, we are hampered by the absence of theoretical discussions except those that we meet in historiographical polemic (which we must always approach warily), but it is questionable whether such discussions would have told us much about actual practice, which may have differed not only from historian to historian but sometimes also from speech to speech within an individual historian. Some scholars (e.g., Walbank 1965; Fornara 1983: 142–168) have postulated two approaches to the content of speeches, one that sought to discover and reproduce what was actually or truly said, and the other concerned not with what was said but only with what was "appropriate" to the person and circumstances. Yet it may fairly be questioned how far such a dichotomy advances our understanding of the problem, since in almost every historiographical speech there will have been a mixture of what was actually known and what could be surmised. It may be more profitable to approach the matter somewhat differently, taking account both of the literary quality of historiography in antiquity and of the various functions that history served in the ancient world.

For already in Thucydides' famous formulation of the procedure he followed in composing speeches, there are indications both of fidelity to what was "actually" said and simultaneously a reliance on notions of appropriateness (1.22.1):

> And as for all the things which each side said in speech either when they were about to go to war or when they were already in it, it was difficult to remember precisely the exactness of what was said (*tēn akribeian autēn tōn lechthentōn*), both for me, regarding the things I myself heard, and for those reporting to me at one time or another from elsewhere. But as it seemed to me that each would have said especially what was necessary (*ta deonta malist'*) for the given occasion, so it has been written by me, holding as closely as possible to the entire argument of the things that were truly said (*tēs xumpasēs gnōmēs tōn alēthōs lechthentōn*).

On the one hand, the historian is not talking about pure invention, for in that case there was no need of informants, nor would there be anything to hold "as closely as possible" to. Thucydides says not that it was "impossible" to remember the exact content of the speeches, but rather that it was "difficult" – an important distinction, and one that suggests that he really tried to find out and reproduce what was said. On the other hand, because it was difficult to remember the precise content of a long and complex speech, Thucydides allows himself an interpretive or re-creative element with the words "as I thought" (*hōs d'an . . . edokoun* – contrast this with his procedure with deeds: "not as I thought" [*oud' hōs emoi edokei*, 1.22.2]), and with the notion of *ta deonta*. *Ta deonta* are the "necessary things," i.e., the arguments that one needs to present one's case effectively (cf. Macleod 1983: 52: "what rhetoricians try to impart and orators to display"). This is not, of course, what Thucydides himself thought necessary given a particular situation – his speakers often present contradictory advice – but rather what he imagined the speakers, given their particular aims in their particular situations, would have needed to say to make their point as effectively as possible.

Thus elements both of fidelity and invention are present here. Moderns, not surprisingly, tend to choose one strand over the other, although Thucydides does not. Yet in some sense this is beside the point: for whatever relationship Thucydides' speeches bear to the actual speeches delivered, they are contextualized within a particular and highly developed literary form. No history is *the* representation of the past but rather *a* representation, and such literary "representations" of the world, whatever their genre, demand criteria of inclusion and exclusion (Conte 1994: 106–108). Thucydides' narrative of events, for example, does not cover all or even most of what happened to Athens, Sparta, and their allies between 431 and 411: everywhere there is a selective mentality at work (what was considered *axiologos*, "worthy of record"), recording this event, passing quickly over this one, writing this one up in detail. So too in the speeches: they are highly formalized, certainly in language (which is that of Thucydides' Attic Greek, no matter the speaker) but also in other areas: certain themes consistently and prominently recur (fear, honor, self-interest, resources, imperial conduct); speakers in different times and places "respond" to the arguments of others or echo earlier speeches; even when many speakers are reported to have spoken, Thucydides presents only one or two of these, and usually in a particular order (the second speaker usually prevails here as elsewhere in formalized debates). It is precisely because of this that we cannot use the speeches as reproductions (either more or less faithful) of what was actually said, even though Thucydides will have often reproduced some of the actual arguments used. Because the orientation and the shape of the speech, especially in what it emphasizes and what it omits, are the work of the historian himself, our impressions and understandings of a speaker are directly mediated through the historian's, not the original speaker's, words: selection and arrangement already carry with them interpretation. It is not a question of mendacity, but rather that the historian focuses on the things that *he* has decided are important and conducive to a "proper" interpretation.

Thus when we consider the remark of Callisthenes that "anyone attempting to write something must not fail to hit upon the character, but must make speeches appropriate (*oikeiōs*) to the person and the circumstances" (*FGrHist* 124 F 44), we ought not to posit a vast gulf separating this approach from that of Thucydides, nor assume that it reveals a "rhetorical" conception of constructing speeches as opposed to Thucydides' "historical" notion of what was actually said. Notions of appropriateness and probability reside at least partially behind Thucydides' understanding of *ta deonta*: his inability on occasion to learn the actual words spoken will have necessitated a certain measure of imaginative reconstruction, which, though *focalized* from the speakers' point of view, surely could only be based on what Thucydides himself deemed *appropriate* given what he knew of the character who spoke and the circumstances in which he spoke. So, for example, Nicias' last speech to his defeated army (7.77) – a speech not likely, given the situation, to have been remembered, much less reported to Thucydides, with much clarity, and which has a slew of ironic responsions to the Melian Dialogue (Connor 1984: 201–204) – must have been composed by Thucydides based on what he believed he knew of Nicias' character (cf. 5.16.1, 7.50.4) and on the situation of utter desperation in which Nicias found himself: in other words, what he *must* have said. Surely what is at issue here is not imaginative reconstruction in itself – this features in all historiography, ancient as well as modern – but what relationship such reconstruction has to the investigative aspect of history. In other words, we might accord greater trust to the substance of Pericles' speeches in Thucydides, not necessarily because they contain the actual words of Pericles spoken on that particular occasion (though they might to some extent) but because Thucydides as a contemporary and (we believe) conscientious researcher will have based his speeches on what was actually known of Pericles' policies and remarks.

The issue is thus not probability or appropriateness *per se*, but how such concepts were understood in antiquity and how they were related to the investigative aspect of the historian's task. Crucial here will be the change that occurs with the systematic study of rhetoric from the fifth century onwards, where there is a movement towards rules and *types*, as can be seen clearly in something like Theophrastus' *Characters*, where we find a highly stereotyped gallery of such figures as the coward, the braggart, the slanderer, and so forth. In the business of persuasion – i.e., in oratory's task – the ability to appeal to the audience's notions of probability became paramount, and drove all before it (cf. Arist. *Poet.* 1460a26: probable impossibilities are preferable to implausible possibilities). Such notions of types and stereotypes are opposed to the individuality and uniqueness of historical events (as we might understand them today), a point to which we shall return below (§4).

It is clear that Thucydides' approach stands behind Polybius' later remarks on speeches in histories (Nicolai 1999), but Polybius has, as usual, given a more detailed and more elaborately argued set of standards. Polybius' remarks about speeches appear throughout his history (2.56.10; 3.20.1–5; 29.12.2–10; 36.1), but the fullest treatment is found in his polemic with Timaeus, who, as in other matters, serves as Polybius' foil. The historian's duty, says Polybius, is to record the truth of what was spoken: history is not "to seek after men's probable utterances" (2.56.10) but rather its "particular function . . . is first to learn what words were actually spoken [*tous kat' alētheian eirēmenous . . . logous*], whatever they were" (12.25b.1), and consequently "it is the proper concern of the historian . . . to find out by diligent inquiry and report . . . what was actually said" (36.1.7). Timaeus, however, recorded "neither what was said nor the real sense of what was said" (*ta rhēthenta . . . hōs errethē kat' alētheian*: 12.25a.5 with Walbank, *HCP* II.385–386). Rather than select the appropriate arguments, Timaeus used his speeches to display his rhetorical talents, giving on every occasion all possible arguments (*pantas . . . tous enontas logous*, 12.25i.4), inserting "false rhetorical exercises and discursive speeches (*pseudē . . . epicheirēmata kai diexodikous logous*)," employing puerile antitheses, adducing extensive quotations from the poets, and having his speakers use over-clever interpretations, such as philosophers are wont to employ (12.26.1–26c.4). His speeches are thus pedantic and absurd.

Polybius postulates a close relationship between words and deeds in history, indeed much closer than did Thucydides (Sacks 1981: 79–96). For if the historian's first duty is to find out what was actually said, his second duty is to ascertain the cause "why a deed or speech succeeded or failed" (12.25b.1). The addition of "speech" here is noteworthy: Polybius indicates that a historical character's advice (what Thucydides might have called his *gnōmē*) is bound up in a causal relationship with the action that follows from that advice: the advice, that is, *explains* the action, and if one fails to give what was actually said and resorts instead to one's own invention, one removes the readers' ability to *understand* why certain actions were taken. If, that is, "Hermocrates" in Timaeus speaks using schoolboy antitheses and quotations from the poets, the reader cannot understand why the Sicilians took the action they did, nor why such action had a particular outcome. Word becomes divorced from action. Only Polybius, of surviving historians, makes this connection of *logoi* with utility, which in turn drives his insistence on having the actual words spoken (Sacks 1986: 395 n. 65).

For Polybius, then, not surprisingly, the truthful report of speeches is closely allied with the *pragmatic* function of history, namely, to teach lessons to political men of the future (12.25b.2–4):

> For the mere statement of a fact may delight us but is of no benefit to us [an echo of Thuc. 1.22.4]: but when we add the cause of it, the study of history becomes fruitful.

> For the mental transference of similar circumstances to our own times gives us the means of forming presentiments of what is about to happen and enables us at certain times to take precautions and at others, by reproducing former conditions, to face with more confidence the difficulties that menace us.

If we thus *understand* the attendant circumstances of an action – and this is provided mainly by speeches – then we have a "true" and useful history. That is why Polybius says that speeches "in a sense sum up the whole history and hold it together" (12.25a.3).

Thus Polybius is not so much defending history from rhetoric as postulating a certain relationship between the orator and the historian. A constant theme of Polybius' historiography is the close correlation between the historian and the man in political life. He sees such a person as his main audience (9.1.5), so it is probably not coincidental that such a character comes to the fore even in the discussion of speeches. Attacking Timaeus for using all possible arguments in his speeches, Polybius writes (12.25i.4–9, Paton, trs. with modifications):

> Few occasions allow for all possible arguments (*pantas... tous enontas logous*) to be rehearsed; the majority allow only for some – and those are brief – of the arguments that occur to one, and of these arguments some are acceptable (*prosientai*) to men today, others to men of the past, some to Aetolians, some to Peloponnesians, and some to Athenians. (5) But to invent all possible arguments for everything, without point or occasion, as Timaeus does in relation to every proposal ... is completely untrue, and full of affectation and pedantry: at the same time it has been the cause of failure and exposed many to contempt. What is necessary is on each occasion to choose those arguments that are suitable and timely (*tous harmozontas kai kairious... lambanein*). But since the needs of the case vary, (6) there is need of an unusual degree of attention and clarity of principle in judging how many and which of the possible arguments we should employ, that is to say if we mean to do good rather than harm to our readers. Now it is difficult to formulate what is opportune or not in all instances, (7) but it is not impossible to be led to a notion of it by precepts based upon personal experience and practice in the past. In the present case the best way of conveying my meaning is as follows. (8) If writers, after indicating to us the situation and the motives and inclinations of those deliberating report in the next place what was actually said and then make clear to us the reasons why the speakers succeeded or failed, we shall arrive at some true notion of the actual facts, and we shall be able, both by distinguishing what was successful from what was not and by transferring our impression to similar circumstances, to treat any situation that faces us with hope of success. (9) But it is, I think, very difficult to assign causes, and very easy to string together phrases in books, and while it is given only to a few to say a few words at the right time and discover the rules governing this, it is a common accomplishment and open to anyone to compose long speeches to no purpose.

The passage has puzzled scholars: is Polybius talking here about politicians or historians? It seems the former, but then (§6) he refers to "readers." Walbank (*HCP* II.397–398; *contra*, Ziegler 1952: 1527; Musti 1973: 211–214) believes that, despite the poor way in which he has expressed himself, Polybius here is talking about politicians *choosing* arguments and the historian *recording* those they chose

(§8). But surely the conflation of roles is what is most interesting. Polybius' argument, like all of the attacks on Timaeus, springs from a contrast between the man of public life and the intellectual in his study far away from the action. Just as a person who has not participated in public life cannot write in a way true to life (with *emphasis* and *enargeia*: see Schepens 1975b), so too a bookish man like Timaeus does not know the difference between philosophical and public life – lacking experience, he lacks the ability to compose an effective speech for the people or an army or even for an ambassador. Polybius, by contrast, having had a public career, could, and he moves easily between the politician and the historian in this passage because he sees their approach to public matters to be essentially the same. (Dio Chrysostom, interestingly enough, takes the same approach towards Xenophon, arguing that Xenophon's speeches are "most persuasive" because he did not rely on hearsay or copying, but actually participated in events and gave speeches [*Or.* 18.14–17].)

So Timaeus' speeches are at bottom rhetorical and Polybius' truthful? Not quite. We can pass over the unintentional irony that Polybius' criticism of Timaeus' speeches relies at bottom on the (rhetorical) argument from probability: Hermocrates as a great statesman *would not have spoken like that* (12.25k.6–26.9). Let us note, however, that Polybius acknowledges a "rhetorical" approach both in the idea that one must choose "appropriate" arguments and that certain arguments are "acceptable" (*prosientai*) to different audiences (the latter idea in particular relying in some measure on stereotypes: the Athenians like this, the Spartans that, etc.). Polybius is no stranger to appropriateness in speeches: L. Aemilius Paullus before Cannae speaks "words fitting to the present circumstances" (*ta preponta tois parestōsi kairois*, 3.108.2) and Scipio before Zama addresses his men in a few words "suitable to the theme and occasion" (*oikeiōs* – the same word used by Callisthenes – *tēs hupokeimenēs peristaseōs*, 15.10).

Moreover, Polybius reveals his reliance on notions of appropriateness through the predictably regular and template-driven patterns of speeches. It has been pointed out, for example, that the speeches Polybius assigns to ambassadors have a consistent form: they generally pursue a single argument, are rich in commonplaces, have *prooemia* that follow the stipulations of rhetorical textbooks, have perorations that are always recapitulations of the arguments, and are strongly modeled on the oratory of Demosthenes (Wooten 1974). Given that such speeches occur over the course of many years and in different places, it seems very unlikely that this was simply the style of the age (as Wooten suggests), and far more probable that Polybius, like Thucydides (but perhaps without the genius of his predecessor), chooses to reproduce speeches in his own particular way. Surely some speakers in their actual orations occasionally pursued several arguments or concluded not only with recapitulation but also with emotional appeals. Yet Polybius imposes a particular "rhetorical" form on all of them.

Even Polybius' attack on Timaeus for using all the arguments for every situation should not be considered an attack on "rhetorical" historiography, since rhetoric itself disapproved of such techniques: the orator was expected not to use all the arguments at his disposal, but only those that were appropriate to the situation, just as Polybius says (see, e.g., Cic. *Orat.* 70–71; *De Or.* 2.130; Sen. *Contr. 7 praef.* 1

[on Albucius, who on every occasion "wished to say not what ought to be said but what is capable of being said"]; Quint. 5.12.8). Polybius' attack is, therefore, a reassertion of the right of political men, rather than reclusive "scholars," to write history, and to write it, including its speeches, in a narrowly defined way.

But, as Polybius recognized, this was not the only purpose for history in antiquity. Political-military history written by participants was practiced throughout the centuries, but it coexisted with other, more antiquarian, types of history. Dionysius of Halicarnassus, for example, seems to echo Polybius in his understanding of the relationship between words and deeds (*AR* 11.1.3–4):

> When [people] hear of political events, they are not satisfied with learning the bare summary and outcome of the events, . . . but they demand also to be informed about the arguments by which they were persuaded and what men made those arguments, and all the circumstances that attended those events. Men who are engaged in the conduct of civil affairs . . . have this advantage, that in difficult times they render great service to their countries as the result of the experience thus acquired and lead them as willing followers to that which is to their advantage, through the power of persuasion.

As with Polybius there is an emphasis on the experiential and pragmatic value of history, and the relationship between speech and action, a point made even more explicit elsewhere (7.66.2–3):

> everyone, upon hearing of extraordinary events, desires to know the cause that produced them and considers that alone as the test of their credibility. I reflected, accordingly, that my account of this affair would gain little or no credit . . . if I left out the motives . . . , and for this reason I have related them all. And since they did not make this change in their government by using compulsion upon one another and the force of arms, but by the persuasion of words, I thought it necessary above all things to report the speeches which the heads of both parties made upon that occasion.

Dionysius, like Polybius, links word and deed closely here, giving speeches nearly the status of causes (Schultze 1986: 127), and seeing that same nexus between speech and action. And yet Dionysius is generally thought to be the most rhetorical of historians, filling his history of early Rome with page upon page of speeches that are thought to bear no resemblance to anything that could actually have been spoken (if indeed anything at all was spoken). How to reconcile this with his emphasis on the historian's truthfulness?

The answer comes from Dionysius' evaluation of Thucydides, where two aspects of that historian's speeches stand out. First, the appropriateness of the remarks made by Thucydides' speakers. Dionysius finds fault with Thucydides' portrayal of Pericles' defense of himself before the people, because Pericles does not, as one would in such a situation, conciliate the angry crowd or appeal to its pity. Similarly, in the Melian Dialogue, Thucydides attributes sentiments to the Athenians more appropriate to barbarian kings and entirely out of keeping with the acknowledged humanity and love of freedom of the Athenians. The Melians, too, are made to behave inappropriately, since their heroic resistance is out of character for a people never known to have done anything great; it is much more likely that they would have chosen acquiescence. For Dionysius, these speeches are simply not true to life, not true to what tradition has handed down about Pericles, the Athenians, and their enemies. That is one aspect.

The other aspect of importance to Dionysius is Thucydides' deployment of speeches, and in particular places where Dionysius believes Thucydides has omitted important debates that must have been held (*Thuc.* 14–15, 18). These omissions surprise Dionysius, not least because Thucydides surely had the ability to "discover the inherent arguments" (*tous enontas heurein…logous*, the same phrase used by Polybius for Timaeus) that were made on those occasions, especially as he was particularly gifted in the use of striking and novel arguments (34).

The reliance on the truth of tradition and the discovery of arguments shows how Dionysius arrived at the truth of his own account of early Rome. Having satisfied himself by investigation that the early Romans were in origin Greek and having learned, from his literary predecessors, how events turned out, Dionysius could then presume, from his expert knowledge of tradition and of Greek political philosophy, to expound what was said on both sides of a given issue (Gabba 1991: 72–74). This approach, it is true, minimizes the distance between past and present, yet it was not a difference in method *per se*, but rather an approach conditioned by the fact that Dionysius was writing non-contemporary history and was basing it on literary predecessors. As we shall see (§4), Dionysius, by conjoining past and present, is in the mainstream of classical historiography.

3   Conventions

As a literary genre, historiography developed a set of formal conventions that, while not iron-clad rules to be applied to every historian in every situation, nonetheless reveal certain patterns, approaches, and/or habits of thought in the ancient historians. For example, debates and speeches are nowhere near as long as what they must have been in the actual situation; nor does the historian catalogue the welter of speakers and their arguments, but rather limits himself usually to two (or at most three) speakers. And although no doubt many actual speakers will not have spoken well or to the point, the speakers in a history generally debate the issue with clarity, directness, and symmetry.

Ancient rhetoric divided speeches into three types: forensic (speeches of accusation or defense in the courtroom); symbouleutic (in which advice is given to individuals or public bodies on which course of action to take); and epideictic ("display" rhetoric, in which nothing was to be decided and what mattered was the prowess and ability of the speaker, and which often had as their goal praise and blame). Of these three types the vast majority of historiographical speeches are symbouleutic, as we would expect, since these speeches occur in relationship to actions taken by individuals or groups. Polybius (12.25a.3, cf. 25i.3) speaks of three classes of speeches, addresses to the people (*dēmēgoriai*), speeches of ambassadors (*presbeutikoi logoi*), and harangues of generals (*paraklēseis*), and these can all be considered forms of symbouleutic speech.

There are quite a few examples, however, of forensic rhetoric in historiography. The earliest example is that of the Plataeans presenting their case to the Spartans when on trial for their lives, and the Theban response (Thuc. 3.53–67). Other examples include Critias and Theramenes arguing their cases before the Athenian Council (Xen. *Hell.* 2.3.24–49), M. Manlius' defense before the dictator Cornelius Cossus (Livy 6.15.1–16.4), and Perseus and Demetrius pleading their cases before their father Philip (Livy 40.8.7–15.16). Curtius Rufus has a particular fondness for this type of speech (6.9.2–10.37; 7.1.18–40; 8.7–19), since it helped him dramatize the growing rift between Alexander and his men (Baynham 1998: 47). In Tacitus, Cremutius Cordus defends himself before the Senate, while delivering a striking call for the historian's freedom of speech (*Ann.* 4.34.2–35.4; Moles 1998).

The presence of epideictic oratory was more problematic; history's association with praise and blame allied it with epideictic's aims, and at least for some theorists the two genres shared a style (e.g., Cic. *Orat.* 207). Its close association can also be seen in the fact that Ephorus, Timaeus, and Polybius all discussed the *differences* between epideictic and history (Pol. 12.28a.8–10), which suggests that many saw the similarities. And Diodorus reveals an epideictic leaning when he identifies speeches of praise and blame (*enkōmia kai psogoi*, 20.1.2) as one type of historiographical speech. While we do have examples of epideictic speech in historiography (e.g., Thuc. 2.35–46 [Pericles' Funeral Oration]; Dio 36.27–29 [encomium of Pompey]), it is more common for historians to use elements of epideictic in their speeches, such that even symbouleutic speeches can display elements and *topoi* from epideictic (see Burgess 1902: 202ff. for examples).

Much attention has been given recently to the general's speech before battle (*paraklēsis/paraklētikoi logoi, cohortatio*), a type that goes back ultimately to Homer (Keitel 1987). A good deal of scholarly ink has been spilled in the debate over whether generals in antiquity really delivered formal (and at times lengthy) harangues to their troops. There is no doubt that generals addressed their troops before battle (see Caes. *BG* 2.20.1–2 with Erhardt 1995), but this does not mean that the historiographical speech is either what they said or how they said it. It seems most likely that the general rode along the line exhorting his men with words of encouragement, but these are likely to have taken the form of brief exhortations rather than lengthy and carefully constructed formal speeches (cf. Pol. 15.10.1 for both aspects; Plut. *Mor.* 803A for criticisms of lengthy harangues when men are armed and drawn up for battle). That is to say, the speech before battle is – as with other speeches – a formal convention that serves certain purposes. It allows the audience to understand the issues at stake, the strategy that lies behind the actions, and/or the decisive importance of the moment. When, for example, Scipio tells his men before Zama that the victor in the coming battle will have undisputed sovereignty over the world (Pol. 15.10–11), that can only have been known in hindsight (Walbank 1965: 12), but it marks the moment for the audience as the important turning-point in Rome's rise to empire. Such speeches have certain recurring and identifiable *topoi*: necessity, honor, the ease of victory, the support of the gods, the cowardice of one's opponents, and so forth (Burgess 1902: 212–213; Keitel 1987: 154–160). Readers were on the alert, however, for speeches that "smelt of the lamp" and seemed inappropriate to a military situation or common soldiers. Polybius (12.26a) criticizes Timoleon's harangue in Timaeus because a general before battle does not try to encourage his men by clever interpretations or learned allusions, and Plutarch dismisses the rhetorical effects and grand periods of the battle speeches of Ephorus, Theopompus, and Anaximenes with a line from Euripides: "none talks so foolishly when near the steel" (*Mor.* 803B).

We mentioned above the convention that speakers use the dialect and style of the narrator himself (Xenophon's inclusion of Doric Greek in his *Hellenica* [e.g., 1.1.23] seems not to have caught on), which means, of course, that Persians and Romans will speak Greek or Greeks and Carthaginians will speak Latin. At the same time, the historian might by subtle means try to individualize his speakers either by the form in which they speak (Tompkins 1972; Francis 1991; Debnar 1996, 2001) or by the language they use (see, e.g., Miller 1968 on Tacitus' Tiberius), though for the latter they do not imitate the style of a speaker so much as perhaps use a few phrases or idioms which would remind the audience of the speaker (Adams 1973; Briscoe 1981: 40–42). Perhaps this too hearkens back to Homer who, while everywhere using the same epic diction, nonetheless individualizes figures by assigning them distinctive vocabularies (Griffin 1986).

A more complicated convention is the attitude towards predecessors. A historian generally avoided including a speech in his history that was already published in literary form and available to the public (the evidence is convincingly displayed and interpreted by Brock 1995), though one might assign a famous orator a speech on an occasion where there was no surviving speech, as Livy does with Cato and the debate over the Oppian Law (34.2–7). When treating the same time period, the historian might avoid speeches where his predecessor had them and concentrate on those areas where speeches are absent (cf., e.g., Diod. 13.19–33, a debate, not in Thucydides, on the fate of the Athenian prisoners in Sicily), though on what basis he did so cannot be known. The famous example of Tacitus' version (*Ann.* 11.24) of Claudius' speech known from the Lyon inscription (*ILS* 212) suggests that historians did not feel the same hesitations towards inscriptions as towards published speeches (Brock 1995: 210–212).

When a speech already existed in a predecessor's work, it seems clear that the ancient historian felt himself bound in some measure by the content. He felt free – indeed he may have felt obligated (below, §4) – to modify it, recast it, "improve" it, and recontextualize it based on his own approach and the needs of his own history. When Livy is following Polybius' speeches, for example, he rearranges the form (adding *exordia*, conclusions, and sometimes his own *exempla*), elaborating on matters only implied in his predecessor's version, yet at the same time not traveling off in unharnessed flights of fancy. The same is true for Tacitus' reworking of Claudius, which, while producing a stylistically superior speech, keeps the general point and even some of the arguments used in the inscription. Even Dionysius, the rhetorical historian *par excellence*, can be seen to respect the tradition in a certain measure (Usher 1982: 835–836). A predecessor seems, therefore, to have kept the historian from composing a *wholly* free composition. At the same time, it would be naïve to suggest that his approach was the same as with deeds, since it seems clear that many historians invented speeches for particular occasions where none existed in his sources. Both in the wholly "invented" speeches (i.e., those for which there was no precedent) and in the level of detail, argument, and adornment, historians were virtually creating a new speech – they were, that is, engaging in literary *aemulatio*, both with immediate predecessors and with the whole tradition of ancient historiography. Which brings us to our final observations.

4   Past and Present

The speech in ancient historiography mediates between past and present (as does narrative history itself), and this mediation manifests itself in at least three ways. First, speeches in later writers allude to or are modeled on those of predecessors; second, many historians have their speakers use historical *exempla*; and third, many speeches display anachronisms and what we might call "modernizings," updatings that are more about the historian's own time than the putative era he is recreating. Let us take each of these in turn.

On the first topic, it should be no surprise that a historian's speech would be modeled on that of a distinguished predecessor. Historiography was, after all, a literary genre, and as such it partook of all the elements of competition and display that were inherent in other genres. Polybius himself makes reference to such expectations when he refuses to "enter the contest" (*enagonismati*, 36.1.1) by including the speeches made before the Third Punic War, and his hesitance stands in strong contrast to that of Diodorus, who claims it would be false modesty for a historian not to engage in such contests (20.2.1). The "contest" involved not only the creation of an appropriate speech for the character but also the display of an acquaintance with the tradition and an ability to build on, refine, and allude to one's predecessors. As always, slavish imitation was to be avoided; the writer was expected to recreate imaginatively in a new context what his predecessors had done (Russell 1979). Thucydides' Sicilian debate (6.9–18) reenacts and reanalyzes the arguments about empire and imperialism rehearsed by Mardonius and Artabanus in the Persian decision to invade Greece (Hdt. 7.8–10; Raaflaub 2002b). Sallust's debate between Caesar and Cato (*Jug.* 51–52) owes much to Thucydides' Mytilenean Debate (3.37–48); the Campanians' request for Roman assistance at Livy 7.30–31 is modeled on Thucydides' Corcyrean debate (1.24–45; Oakley, *CL* II.293–294); and Tacitus' account of the debate on governors' wives accompanying husbands to their provinces imaginatively recasts some of the same issues that Livy explored in his debate on the repeal of the Oppian Law (Ginsburg 1993: 89–96; Santoro L'Hoir 1994/5). And such an approach may not have been exclusively "literary": Claudius' speech to the Senate recorded in the Lyon inscription mentioned above is clearly indebted to the speech Livy attributes to the tribune Canuleius (4.3.2–5.6; Last and Ogilvie 1958).

As to historical *exempla*, they were sparsely used by Herodotus and Thucydides, but seem to have come into their own in the Hellenistic world. In Polybius' account of the congress at Sparta in 211 BCE (9.28–39), Chlaeneas rehearses the deeds of the

Macedonians from Philip II to Antigonus Gonatas so as to encourage the assembly to resist Philip V, while Lyciscus refutes Chlaeneas by going through the same events offering different historical interpretations and adding other events not treated by Chlaeneas. Sallust has Licinius Macer remind the plebs of their own history, recalling their earlier victories against the patricians (*Hist.* 3.48), and Mithridates uses historical *exempla* to bolster his argument against trusting the Romans (*Hist.* 4.69). Livy's work abounds in historical *exempla* (Chaplin 2000), and the conflict in Tacitus between past and present strongly suffuses all of his work (Ginsburg 1993).

Two points should be made about *exempla*. First, there is no doubt that orators in the real world employed historical *exempla* regularly as ways of swaying their audiences and buttressing their cases. Plutarch, in his *Political Precepts*, advises a speaker addressing the people to use "histories and tales" (*historias kai muthous*, 803A), and Quintilian explains more fully (3.8.66, tr. Russell):

> Almost everyone rightly agrees that this use of examples [i.e., historical] is particularly appropriate to this kind of speech [deliberative] because the future often seems to reflect the past, and experience can be regarded as evidence supporting theoretical reasoning.

Such actual use, however, was not by itself a guarantee that *exempla* would be reproduced in historiographical orations, since (as we noted above) histories were literary compositions that interpreted rather than simply mirroring the "real world."

What made the use of *exempla* in historiography valuable was the belief of historians themselves that the past was a teacher for the present and future. But not in a simplistic or nostalgic sort of way. Rather, the historian exploits the situation of the reader of history, who, unlike the deliberative orator, already knows the outcome of events, and by so doing the historian provides an additional analytical level: in light of his later knowledge, the reader can watch the debate unfold and analyze the deployment of *exempla* made by the speakers, and reflect upon which were accurate, which significant, which appropriate (for this dynamic see Chaplin 2000: *passim*). The reader must simultaneously evaluate to what extent the past can be a guide since innovations are always possible and later ages (including the reader's own time) also have much to offer (see, from very different viewpoints, Pol. 9.2.5 and Tac. *Ann.* 3.55.5). Recreating the drama of debate, then, the historian through speeches also examines the purpose and value of history itself.

We come, finally, to anachronisms and "modernizings." It has been noted that many speeches in the historians reveal more about the historian than the era of which he was writing. To some extent, this was the result of their use of probability and appropriateness, concepts that are, by and large, culturally determined (one need only consider what ancients thought it probable or appropriate for a woman to do): relying on such notions, the historian's ability to recreate the past imaginatively was limited, and this led to a type of "unhistorical thinking" (Wiseman 1979: 41–53). This is an enormous topic which cannot be treated here (for some starts see Marincola 2007), but it was not just rhetoric that led the ancients to view the world in this way. The ancient habit of seeing the past in the present and the present in the past – this sense of *continuity* with the past, characteristic of traditional societies – fostered an

approach that did not postulate a wide gulf between it and the historian's present (cf. Tac. *Ann.* 4.33.4; Griffin 1985: 188–191). Much of the process of "modernization" will have been unconscious, the result of each generation's examining those things of interest to it (this, after all, is still true of history). So it is no surprise that Livy chooses *exempla* with particular resonance for his Augustan audience (Chaplin 2000: 74–77, 80–82), or that the speech of Galba to Piso (Tac. *Hist.* 1.15–16) should be written in the light of Nerva's later adoption of Trajan (Heubner 1963: 47–49), or that Amyntas' defense before Alexander in Curtius (7.1.26–30) should have been influenced by the contemporary trial of M. Terentius (Tac. *Ann.* 6.8; Heckel 1994: 69–70) or that Dio's "debate" between Maecenas and Agrippa (52.1–40) represents not the Augustan age but the uncertain conditions of the third century when Dio was writing (Millar 1964: 102–118). If we want to call this a failure of historical imagination, we can, but it seems to me that this is putting the emphasis in the wrong place. Modern historians tend to look for the difference in the past, the essential uniqueness of an event at a particular time and place. The ancients were more concerned with what they thought of as timeless truths, and so they usually sought what connected them to the past. In their speeches, they made the past and its historical actors come alive with an immediacy that could not always be managed in the narrative itself. If their speakers echoed those of earlier times and earlier historians (precisely the things that we point to in arguing their essential falsehood), this was for them and their readers the guarantee that they had executed their task responsibly and faithfully – that they had told things not so much as they really were but as they really are.

FURTHER READING

For overviews of speeches in ancient historians see Scheller 1911: 50–56; Avenarius 1956: 149–157; Walbank 1965; Fornara 1983: 142–168; and Brock 1995. For generals' speeches see Albertus 1908; Keitel 1987; and (for their historicity) Hansen 1993, 1998 and Pritchett 1994, 2002.

Most treatments of speeches naturally focus on individual historians.

For Herodotus see (for starters) Deffner 1933; Hohti 1976; Lang 1984; and Pelling 2006. For Thucydides the scholarly bibliography is enormous: see Stadter 1973: 124–165 for the bibliography to 1972; Marincola 2001: 77 n. 77 adds more recent bibliography; see also below, Ch. 28. For his generals' speeches see Luschnat 1942 and Leimbach 1985. On Timaeus see Pearson 1986. On Polybius, see Pédech 1964: 254–302; Walbank 1965; Wooten 1974; and Nicolai 1999. For Dionysius see Flierle 1890; Usher 1982: 832–837; Schultze 1986: 127–132; Gabba 1991: 68–73, 83–84; and Fox 1993. For Arrian see Bosworth 1988: 94–134 and Hammond 1999; for Dio see Millar 1964: 49–55, 78–83, and McKechnie 1981.

On the Latin side there is much of value in the analyses of Ullmann 1927, even if the divisions of speeches are sometimes too arbitrary. Differently oriented but also worthwhile is Leeman 1963. See also Miller 1975 and, on the Latin use of indirect discourse (a topic I have not touched on here), see Utard 2004. For Sallust see Schnorr von Karlsfeld 1888 and Nicolai 2002. On Livy see Gries 1949b; Walsh 1964: 219–244; Luce 1993; Forsythe 1999: 74–86; and Chaplin 2000. For Tacitus see Miller 1964; Martin 1967; Ginsburg 1989; and Keitel 1991, 1993. Curtius' speeches are treated in Helmreich 1927 and Ammianus' in Pighi 1936.

CHAPTER TEN

Readers and Reception:
A Text Case

A. J. Woodman

In 18 CE the charismatic prince Germanicus – nephew and adopted son of the emperor Tiberius – became consul for the second time and embarked on a sightseeing tour of the Mediterranean world which took him to Greece, Asia Minor, and Egypt. It was evidently not until the following year that he reached Egypt, where, though bilingual in Latin and Greek, he found himself unable to understand the inscriptions on the monuments there: they were written in Egyptian characters, and a senior priest was ordered to translate them for him. From there he proceeded to Syria, where he came into conflict with the governor of the province, Calpurnius Piso, and shortly afterwards met his death at Antioch in mysterious circumstances. As news of this tragedy became known, there was an outburst of uninhibited mourning on a universal scale and the immediate upsurge of conspiracy theories as to the cause of his premature death. When Piso returned to Rome in 20 CE, he was accused among other things of having poisoned Germanicus and, halfway through his trial, was found dead in his bedroom, evidently the victim of suicide: he had been stabbed through the throat, and a sword was lying beside him on the ground.

The later stages of this compelling story have recently attracted intense scholarly interest because of two inscriptions discovered in Spain. The first of these, the *Tabula Siarensis*, sheds light on the honors which were paid to Germanicus after his death. The second, the *Senatus Consultum de Cn. Pisone Patre*, comprises the record of Piso's trial in the Senate. Yet even without this extra dimension of topicality, Germanicus' last journey constitutes an intrinsically attractive subject, falling, as it does, somewhere between pilgrimage and tourism, and including "sites of memory" on the way. The principal source for it is Book 2 of Tacitus' *Annals* (53–61, 69–73), beginning as follows (53.1–3):

> *Sequens annus Tiberium tertio, Germanicum iterum consules habuit. sed eum honorem*
> *Germanicus iniit apud urbem Achaiae Nicopolim, quo venerat per Illyricam oram viso*

fratre Druso in Delmatia agente, Hadriatici ac mox Ionii maris adversam navigationem
perpessus. igitur paucos dies insumpsit reficiendae classi; simul sinus Actiaca victoria
inclutos et sacratas ab Augusto manubias castraque Antonii cum recordatione maiorum
suorum adiit. namque ei, ut memoravi, avunculus Augustus, avus Antonius erant,
magnaque illic imago tristium laetorumque. hinc ventum Athenas, foederique sociae et
vetustae urbis datum ut uno lictore uteretur. excepere Graeci quaesitissimis honoribus,
vetera suorum facta dictaque praeferentes quo plus dignationis adulatio haberet.

The problem with this passage, as with the inscriptions themselves, is that it is written in Latin, a language which is understood by almost no one in the twenty-first century: most people today, if confronted with it, would find themselves in the same position as Germanicus himself when confronted by his Egyptian hieroglyphics. The problem is particularly acute for students of the ancient world, of whom there are significant numbers in colleges and universities and who these days constitute the largest single group of potential readers of Tacitus' *Annals.* How are students to gain access to Tacitus' text? The obvious answer is that they will consult a translation.

Here are four "standard" English translations of *Annals* 2.53 published at intervals of roughly two or three decades during the past 120 years:

(a)
In the following year Tiberius held his third, Germanicus his second, consulship. Germanicus, however, entered on the office at Nicopolis, a city of Achaia, whither he had arrived by the coast of Illyricum, after having seen his brother Drusus, who was then in Dalmatia, and endured a stormy voyage through the Adriatic and afterwards the Ionian Sea. He accordingly devoted a few days to the repair of his fleet, and, at the same time, in remembrance of his ancestors, he visited the bay which the victory of Actium had made famous, the spoils consecrated by Augustus, and the camp of Antonius. For, as I have said, Augustus was his great-uncle, Antonius his grandfather, and vivid images of disaster and success rose before him on the spot. Thence he went to Athens, and there, as a concession to our treaty with an allied and ancient city, he was attended only by a single lictor. The Greeks welcomed him with the utmost elaborate honours, and brought forward all the old deeds and sayings of their countrymen, to give additional dignity to their flattery. (Church and Brodribb 1884)

(b)
A.D. 18. CONSULS TIBERIUS CAESAR AUGUSTUS III. AND GERMANICUS CAESAR II.
Tiberius now entered upon his third Consulship, Germanicus upon his second. Germanicus entered upon office in Nicopolis, a town in the Province of Achaia, which he had reached by way of the Illyrian coast after paying a visit to his brother Drusus, then quartered in Delmatia. Having encountered bad weather in the Adriatic, and again in the Ionian Gulf, he spent a few days at Nicopolis to refit. From this place he visited the bay famed for the victory of Actium, where he inspected the spoils dedicated by Augustus, and the camp of Antonius. These scenes revived family memories in his mind; for as he was great-nephew of Augustus and grandson of Antonius, they called up before him many visions of triumph and disaster. Thence he passed on to Athens, where out of compliment to our treaty with that ancient and allied city, he contented himself with a single lictor.

He was received with extraordinary attentions, the Greeks parading the exploits and sayings of their forefathers to add importance to their flatteries. (Ramsay 1904)

(c)
The following year found Tiberius consul for a third time; Germanicus, for a second. The latter, however, entered upon that office in the Achaian town of Nicopolis, which he had reached by skirting the Illyrian coast after a visit to his brother Drusus, then resident in Dalmatia: the passage had been stormy both in the Adriatic and, later, in the Ionian Sea. He spent a few days, therefore, in refitting the fleet; while at the same time, evoking the memory of his ancestors, he viewed the gulf immortalised by the victory of Actium, together with the spoils which Augustus had consecrated, and the camp of Antony. For Augustus, as I have said, was his great-uncle, Antony his grandfather; and before his eyes lay the whole great picture of disaster and triumph. – He next arrived at Athens; where, in deference to our treaty with an allied and time-honoured city, he made use of one lictor alone. The Greeks received him with most elaborate compliments, and, in order to temper adulation with dignity, paraded the ancient doings and sayings of their countrymen. (Jackson 1931)

(d)
In the following year Tiberius was consul for the third time, Germanicus for the second. The latter assumed office at Nicopolis in the province of Achaia, which he had reached along the Adriatic coast after visiting his brother Drusus, then stationed in Dalmatia. Since both the Adriatic and the Ionian seas had been stormy, he spent a few days at Nicopolis overhauling the fleet. He employed this opportunity to visit the gulf famous for the victory of Actium, and its spoils dedicated by Augustus, and Antony's camp. The place brought memories of his ancestors, for (as I have pointed out) he was the grand-nephew of Augustus, and the grandson of Antony. Here his imagination could re-enact mighty triumphs and mighty tragedies.

Then he visited Athens, contenting himself with one official attendant, out of regard for our treaty of alliance with that ancient city. The Greeks received him with highly elaborate compliments, and flattery all the more impressive for their emphasis on the bygone deeds and words of their own compatriots. (Grant 1956)

If students were to compare these translations with one another, however, they would soon note the many mutual discrepancies and would quickly be asking themselves which, if any, is an accurate representation of Tacitus' Latin. Wanting an answer to this question, and having no Latin themselves, they would perhaps think of taking advice from one of their teachers – that is, from a professional classicist, just as Germanicus applied to a senior priest. Unfortunately, however, some scholars believe that the Egyptian priest was himself unable to understand the inscriptions of his native land and that he simply invented an elaborate narrative to impress his royal visitor. But surely the same cannot be said of today's professional classicists?

*

The answer to this question has two distinct aspects. Reviewing a recent book written by a university classicist and published by a distinguished university press, a scholar expressed himself amazed by some of the author's ideas of Latin and confessed that he had little faith in the author's accuracy or his capacity to understand at the most elementary level the Latin texts he discusses in the book. Though the author describes himself as a specialist in "historiography," he would evidently not be an appropriate source of advice for students wishing to know something of the Latin text of Rome's greatest historian. In another recent book, written by a prolific professor of classics and described by its learned reviewer as one that "Every classicist should read," Butler's then standard Loeb translation of Quintilian 10.7.30 was quoted as follows: "the notes of other orators are also in circulation [*quoque*]." As seems clear from her insertion, this author thinks that *quoque* ("also," which appears earlier in Butler's sentence) means "in circulation" or, as she puts it in her elucidation of this passage, " 'here and there' (*quoque*)." This error leads her to misunderstand the passage of Quintilian and hence to misuse his evidence in her subsequent argument. Clearly this author would not be the ideal scholar with whom to discuss the celebrated crux (34.3) in Augustus' *Res Gestae*, one of the most important inscriptions to have come down to us from antiquity, where the issue revolves around whether Rome's first emperor wrote *quŏque* = "also" or *quōque* = "each" (Adcock 1952).

Although the extent to which these scholars are representative of contemporary classics is perhaps hard to say, they are certainly not isolated examples. Of course no one is immune to the occasional error, and few scholars would claim that their linguistic knowledge is faultless, but it appears to be the case that significant numbers of professional classicists have a less certain knowledge of Latin than one would expect. Yet that is only one aspect of the problem. No less worrying is the fact that there are, at least in Britain, classicists who know no Latin – who indeed see no need to know Latin – but who are employed in university departments of classics as teachers of students. Such scholars would obviously be quite incapable of helping any well-intentioned but Latinless student with the text of Tacitus' *Annals*. And, in case one is tempted to ask whether this matters, how would one react to the knowledge that a specialist on the Third Reich was ignorant of German? Or a cardiologist ignorant of basic anatomy? Yet no one gives a second thought to the fact that national accreditation agencies in Britain can award top ratings for teaching procedures and for research to university departments of classics in which students are routinely taught Greek and Roman history by scholars who themselves cannot read a single word written by a Greek or Roman historian.

Such ignorance is symptomatic of a wider malaise. The chairman of a classics department in Britain was recently quoted as saying during an interview that classics is "the ultimate interdisciplinary subject. It's literature, history, archaeology, political philosophy and art, all rolled into one. You can get a grounding in the latest literary critical techniques, the most up-to-date archaeological theories, and the trendiest historical approaches." The reaction of his interviewer to this claim was to assure her readers that "Not all universities have fizzing classics departments" like that of the featured professor; his, she explained, "is lively partly because it has changed so much. Gone is the emphasis on learning ancient languages. Instead you take degrees in classical civilisation and ancient history and read translations rather than original texts." The message is absolutely clear. The less the emphasis on Latin and Greek, the more "fizzing" and "lively" your subject and department will be. Yet how students are expected to apply "the latest literary critical techniques" to texts they cannot read was not explained.

The fact is that students who have no Latin or Greek are paralyzed by a linguistic ignorance which in most cases is not their own fault. They are educated in a culture in which they are assured both explicitly and implicitly that reading translated texts is an adequate form of study; yet they are inhibited from making any pronouncement about their texts because, not knowing what the originals say, they can never know whether there is any basis for their pronouncements: they are forever obliged either to take their translations on trust or to be dependent on the superior linguistic knowledge of others. Not only does this represent the very opposite of the intellectual skepticism and independence which are regarded as the desirable goals of modern education, but it means also that they cannot subject to informed questioning any teacher who happens to know the original language.

Another professor of classics, surveying recently the ways in which his subject has been taught over the decades in the United Kingdom, referred condescendingly to those who have tried to champion "the defence of linguistic standards for the few." This seems less than appreciative of those devoted schoolteachers who over the course of many years surrendered their lunch hours and other free time in order to preserve, often in the face of determined opposition from their superiors, the languages of Greece and Rome and to pass on their love of them to future generations; but this scholar evidently subscribes to the view expressed recently by a specialist in ancient history, namely, that in traditional classics the "emphasis on dead languages makes it too difficult for wider appeal" and that its "elitism is against the spirit of the age and is undemocratic" (Toner 2002: 129). According to this warped, pernicious, and solipsistic logic, linguistic knowledge represents a distinction, and any form of distinctiveness offends the sensibilities of those who parade themselves, however improbably, as champions of "equality." Curiously, these same persons do not complain about the "undemocratic" knowledge of the pilot who transports them to their international conferences, or about the "elitism" of the pediatrician who cares for their sick child in hospital. But students are fair game for their vicarious egalitarianism, and, since not all students can know Latin or Greek, it is more "democratic" to insist that classical texts are read through the medium of English translations. Such self-indulgence on the part of their teachers represents an abrogation of responsibility towards generations of students.

*

Since translations are in such common use, let us return to the four translations quoted above and see how they compare with what Tacitus actually wrote. Tacitus' first sentence is – astonishingly – translated by Ramsay *twice*, the first time in the form of a heading. Ramsay's policy was always to place such a heading at what he perceived to be the start of each narrative year. If Tacitus begins a year with the consuls' names in the ablative case, as he regularly does, Ramsay converts this formula into a separate heading (as in the preceding and following years at 2.41.2 and 2.59.1, respectively). If Tacitus has no reference at all to the consuls but Ramsay thinks there should be one, he sticks one in (as at 3.1.1). If Tacitus begins with a reference to the consuls but does not use the ablative absolute, Ramsay will sometimes extract this reference from the opening sentence to form a heading (as at 3.52.1 and 6.1.1), while at other times he will retain the first sentence but duplicate its consular reference in the form of a heading (as here and at 3.31.1). It is of course a grotesque distortion to introduce headings where none exists in the Latin, but it is at least as unfortunate that readers of Ramsay's regularized headings have no way of knowing that, as has been shown so well (Ginsburg 1981), there is point to the varied ways in which Tacitus introduces each narrative year. It does not improve matters that Ramsay in the heading equips the consuls with extra names which are not in Tacitus, and in the first sentence uses the same verb ("entered upon") as he will use in the next, although Tacitus had himself used different verbs (*habuit . . . iniit*): such variation (*variatio*) is of course the principal hallmark of his style (Sörbom 1935). In fact only Jackson translates the first sentence with anything like accuracy, retaining the characteristically Latin idiom of *annus* ("the year") as subject of the sentence.

The second sentence is typical of Tacitus in that its main verb (*iniit*) occurs early and is followed by a series of appended clauses or phrases: first a relative clause (*quo venerat . . .*), to which are appended an ablative absolute (*viso fratre Druso*) and, in parallel, a nominative participial phrase (*Hadriatici . . . perpessus*), the former qualified further by a present-participial phrase (*in Delmatia agente*). Only Church and Brodribb preserve this typical arrangement. The three other translators slice Tacitus' single sentence into two, the second of which is attached by Ramsay and Grant to Tacitus' third sentence, thereby ruining the original sentence structure altogether; moreover, Grant is anticipated by Ramsay in the editorializing addition of "province of" before "Achaia," and by Jackson in omitting to translate the participle *perpessus* ("having endured"), which Ramsay mistranslates ("Having encountered").

After a brief sentence consisting of a mere six words, Tacitus next constructs a longer sentence which itemizes separately three sites which Germanicus visited (and which are reduced by Ramsay and perhaps also by Jackson to two). The first is the bays of Actium, in which the word order is: noun (*sinus*), ablative phrase (*Actiaca uictoria*), and adjective (*inclutos*). The second site is that of the trophies, in which the word order is: participle (*sacratas*, equivalent to an adjective), ablative phrase (*ab Augusto*), and noun (*manubias*). Thus the arrangement of the first two sites is chiastic (*a b c ∼ c b a*), a refinement which none of the translators attempts and which perhaps none was even aware of. Yet chiastic arrangement, common in verse and oratorical prose, is a sure sign that Tacitus is being deliberately artful. Let us follow the sign and see where it leads.

The bays of Actium, a plural expression found elsewhere in verse (cf. Manil. 5.52; Petron. 121.1, line 115) but rendered by each of Tacitus' translators as a singular, are described as *inclutos*, a compound adjective formed from the Latin intensifying prefix *in-* and an adjectival form which is identical with, and suggestive of, the Greek adjective *klutos*, meaning roughly "famous" (Maltby 1991: 299). *inclutus* is a relatively unusual word and is normally reserved by Tacitus for temples and other similarly sanctified places; but, as a "Grecizing" word, it is particularly apposite in the present context. The Roman Germanicus was more than conventionally Hellenized (in Egypt he adopted Greek dress, as Tacitus tells us later at 2.59.1); and not only is he here visiting Greece, but the city which Augustus had founded to celebrate his victory over Mark Antony had a Greek name: Nicopolis (which Grant names twice, as opposed to Tacitus' once) means "Victory City." This amalgamation of Greek and Roman elements was carried over to the memorial which Augustus constructed to commemorate his victory and where he displayed trophies taken from the enemy fleet. "In all respects," say the latest experts on the memorial, "the victory monument skillfully mixed Hellenistic with Roman forms and images" (Murray and Petsas 1989: 124). In such circumstances, *inclutus* is a most appropriate word.

The Greek adjective *klutos* derives from the verb *kleō*, which means "tell of," "celebrate," "glorify." From the same root comes the noun *kleos*, which means "fame" or "glory": that is the noun from which comes "Cleopatra," the name of the Greek (Ptolemaic) queen who together with Antony was defeated by Augustus at Actium. Her name means "Glory of her Country," and of course Actium is the very site which Germanicus is at present visiting. Whether Tacitus was playing on these associations must remain uncertain, although it should be noted that he frequently capitalizes on the etymology of proper names; at any rate, to translate *inclutos* by the English "famous," as do Church and Brodribb and also Grant, seems quite inadequate. Jackson's "immortalised" is a great improvement, but does not have the rarity value of *inclutos* and naturally carries no suggestion that Tacitus may be punning on the name of one of the defeated parties.

inclutos is paralleled, as we have seen, by the participle *sacratas*, a simple form which is frequent in poetry and which Tacitus much prefers to the more normal compound *consecratus*. An English translation ought to bring out this poetic flavor, but, before we discover whether the translators have found a suitable word, we should look ahead to the third site which Tacitus itemizes: Mark Antony's camp. (Antony had two campsites, one on each side of the entrance to the Ambracian Gulf [Pelling 1996: 60, fig. 1]; it is impossible to know which of the two Tacitus means.) The Latin word for "camp," which is followed by Antony's name ("**castra**que Antonii"), is an anagram of the first two syllables of the word which we have just been considering and which in turn is followed by Augustus' name ("**sacra**tas ab Augusto"). Such word play is extremely frequent in Latin authors and is a very regular feature of Tacitus' style: e.g., *Ann.* 3.67.2, "non **temper**ante Tiberio quin **prem**eret uoce, uultu" ("Tiberius not refraining from pressuring with language and look"); 6.41.2, "come Tiridatis ingenium Romana**s per** artes **spera**bant" ("they hoped that Tiridates' disposition would be affable because of his Roman attainments"): it therefore seems worthwhile trying to reproduce it, if only to correct the general misapprehension, encounted in many handbooks and works of reference, that Tacitus is an "austere" author. But the word play is in fact impossible in English, even without the extra incorporation of a poetic equivalent of *sacratas*.

Tacitus concludes the present sentence by saying that Germanicus visited all three sites "cum recordatione maiorum suorum." It is important to keep this reference to Germanicus' ancestors to the end, since it is explained by the following sentence, which indeed begins with the explanatory word *namque* ("for"); but only Ramsay and Grant manage to do this, and each has been obliged to make two sentences out of Tacitus' single original. Their renderings of the Latin phrase (respectively "These scenes revived family memories in his mind" and "The place brought memories of his ancestors") are perhaps closest too to Tacitus' meaning. Tacitus does not say that Germanicus himself "evoked" memories of his ancestors, as Jackson expresses it, nor does he say that the prince visited the sites "in remembrance of his ancestors," as Church and Brodribb put it, as if his primary purpose had been to pay respect to his family. Since *cum* means "in accompaniment with," something like "accompanied by memories of his own ancestors" would be appropriate – except that Tacitus has avoided the plain word *memoria* ("memory"), which elsewhere he uses many times, in favor of the less usual *recordatio*, which he hardly uses at all.

Tacitus' avoidance of the noun *memoria* here may constitute a further example of his love of variation, since the next sentence begins with one of his favorite parenthetic remarks, *ut memoravi*. Given that the context is a visit to historical sites, it is surely significant that Tacitus has deployed a phrase whose verb has a root which comes from, and suggests, "memory." Yet Grant produces "as I have pointed out," Church and Brodribb (like Jackson) prefer "as I have said," while Ramsay – again astonishingly – omits to translate the phrase altogether, despite the fact that cross-references are a feature of Tacitus' style. The sentence ends thus: "**mag**naque illic **imag**o tristium laetorumque." It will be seen that the adjective *magna* is mirrored in the noun which it qualifies and which itself means "image," a subtlety which is first found in Vergil's *Aeneid* (4.654) and occurs elsewhere only in poetry. Whether Grant noticed this must remain doubtful, but his reference to "mighty triumphs and mighty tragedies" brilliantly suggests that there is something special about the Latin. His choice of the word "imagination," on the other hand, seems mistaken: *imago* here denotes that which makes contact with, rather than is produced by, one's physical or mental vision.

Each of the four translations attempts in its own way to render the variation of adjectives meaning "old" in the last two sentences (*vetustae* and *vetera*), yet none of them quite catches the relative unusualness of the former or manages to indicate that both words share the same root. Grant, however, diverges radically both from Church and Brodribb and from Ramsay in placing a new paragraph at the beginning of the penultimate sentence (Jackson inserts a dash instead). There is much to be said for this suggestion, but it ignores the fact that four of the "colorless" words in the last two sentences (*ventum ... urbis ... honoribus ... haberet*) pick up the same four in the two opening sentences (*habuit ... honorem ... urbem ... venerat*); and, since this repetition is chiastically arranged, it seems that we are presented with an example of "ring composition," indicating closure rather than inception.

*

From this discussion it should be evident just how wide a gap there is between each of the four translations and Tacitus' Latin; indeed it may be doubted whether any of the translators was even aware of many of the various phenomena which characterize the style of this passage and which in many cases are quintessentially Tacitean. It is also worth bearing in mind that this is a relatively straightforward passage of Tacitean Latin and that it represents less than one thousandth of the total text of his *Annals*. Nevertheless, since it is clear that some translations (such as Jackson's) are better than others (such as Ramsay's), in what position would readers be if they were to use a translation which tried to accommodate all the issues raised in the above discussion? Can a "good" translation ever take the place of the original text?

Just as we cannot communicate our own experiences to someone else except by language, so we have no access to history – that is, to past events – except through texts. History has no existence, other than in some metaphysical sense, without language: the events of the second decade of our era would not exist for us if we did not possess the *Annals*, inscriptions, and other texts. Yet it is common these days to maintain that there is no simple correspondence between a text and what that text represents (see, e.g., Clark 2004: *passim*). A historical narrative may present itself as a mimetic text, and it may do so successfully, but it will not in fact represent "reality" or "events" or "how things really were." If one accepts this proposition, as many scholars do, one will acknowledge that Tacitus' Latin, so far from offering a window on reality, acts more in the manner of a bull's-eye pane of glass, distorting the view beyond to a greater or lesser degree.

This distortion is doubly compounded by the act of translating, as if the bull's-eye pane were made of glass that is not only frosted but colored too. In the first place there is no such thing as a "neutral" translation. Translation is inseparable from interpretation, and translators are obliged to make numberless decisions of interpretation on every page that they translate, decisions which will multiply in the case of a multifariously suggestive text such as Tacitus' *Annals*. Each decision will close off one or more interpretations of which the original is, *ex hypothesi*, capable; and one translator's interpretation will differ from another's, and neither may coincide with what the author originally meant. But, even on the assumption that a translator were consistently on the same wavelength as the author's intention, there would still remain the insuperable fact that the author, by being translated, is made to say what he did not say. And no attempt at transposing linguistic or literary or rhetorical phenomena from one language to another will be able to deal with *all* such phenomena, even supposing the translator to be aware of them all (which in itself is improbable). For practical purposes, therefore, readers who rely even on "good" translations have no hope at all of even approximating to the experience of those who can read Tacitus' original text.

It is often maintained that the relationship between the style and content of historiography can be seen in terms of icing on a cake or embroidery on a piece of cloth: if you remove the icing/embroidery/style, you are at least left with the cake/cloth/content. If these analogies were true, it might be argued that the division between style and content is applicable to a translated text: the four translations of Tacitus inevitably dispense with the icing/embroidery but one can still extract from them some content, namely, the facts that Germanicus had a bad voyage down the Illyrian coast, inspected the evocative site of Actium, and then moved on to Athens, where he was given a friendly reception. Yet the above analogies are misleading, for two reasons.

In the first place they imply that style takes second place to the "real" business of historiography, which is content. This completely contradicts the priorities of antiquity, when the reception of historical texts focused on the style in which they were written. When Dionysius of Halicarnassus in his essay *On Thucydides* discusses his author's text, it is the minutest details of language and rhetorical devices with which he is principally concerned. Collingwood (1946: 29) famously asked of Thucydides, "What is the matter with the man, that he writes like that?" This question would have seemed utterly natural to Dionysius, yet it is meaningless to many modern scholars: after all, Rex Warner's English in the Penguin Thucydides is much like Michael Grant's in the Penguin Tacitus; both of them read perfectly easily and there is nothing remotely distinctive about either of them, let alone something so peculiar about the Thucydides that it deserves to be questioned. Hence readers who rely solely on translations not only operate with the wrong priorities but also are in no position to investigate the very aspect of a historian's work which was the ancients' principal concern.

Second, the above analogies assume the separability of style and content, whereas a truer analogy would be a knitted pattern: knitting and pattern are each constitutive of the other. Ancient writers themselves defined historiography in terms of oratory (Cic. *De Or.* 2.62–64; *Leg.* 1.5) or poetry (Quint. 10.1.31) or as falling between the two (Aristid. *Orat.* 28[49].68). These definitions, which to the modern reader seem individually strange and mutually contradictory, come about because the writing of history was regarded as an entirely rhetorical procedure (Woodman 1988: 78–116, esp. 98–101). Some of the effects of this have already been seen in our analysis of Tacitus' passage: elaborate word order (including chiasmus), deployment of poetic vocabulary, etymological and bilingual word play, and assonance (both anagrammatical and symbolic). This concentration of rhetorical devices underlines the essential difference between Tacitus' text and that of a modern historian. The point is not that these devices are important in themselves (although they are), but that they are diagnostic of the rhetorical nature of the text. If these devices are absent, as they are when the text is translated, there is nothing intrinsic to the text to alert the reader to the fact that the text is the product of a completely different mindset from that of a modern work of history: a page of a Loeb or Penguin translation can look deceptively like a page of the *Cambridge Ancient History*. Conversely, it is only by being able to read and understand Tacitus' poetic Latin that key questions concerning Germanicus' relationships with his troops and with Tiberius can be grasped (see Woodman 1998: 218–219, 226–228): style and content are indivisible. Thus readers of translated texts are never in a position to understand the nature of the evidence offered to them by the Greek and Roman historians, and those who teach on the basis of translated texts will be forever basing their teaching on a false premise. But this is only part of the story.

The sequence of events attributed to Germanicus in our passage is not unlike that experienced by the hero in Book 1 of the *Aeneid*, where Aeneas lands his fleet after a storm, visits a commemorative site and relives a famous military engagement of special significance to himself, and finally is given a royal welcome in a foreign city. Indeed elsewhere in the story Aeneas visits Actium itself (*Aen.* 3.278–288). Since some scholars have argued that Tacitus depicts Germanicus in terms of Aeneas (e.g., Savage 1938–1939 and 1942–1943; see Goodyear 1981: 243–244), the relationship between these texts is worth considering. Has Tacitus borrowed from, or alluded to, Vergil? Latinized scholars can try to answer this question by comparing the texts for verbal and phraseological similarities. If the evidence is sufficient, they may conclude that Tacitus has (as it were) borrowed from the story of Aeneas and applied his borrowing to Germanicus. If that is the case, there is in fact *no* content (in a historical sense) to Tacitus' narrative at all. The translation – by the very fact of its being a translation – gives spurious authenticity to a sequence of "events" which, in the original Latin, can be shown not to exist. Latinless scholars cannot conduct such tests because they are at the mercy of translators: unless they happen to use translations of the two quite different texts which each happen consistently to translate the same Latin words by the same English words (and there is no likelihood of this whatsoever), there will be no similarities on which to base a judgment.

Forty years ago M. I. Finley complained that classicists knew Latin and Greek but did not know how to do history (see Dorey 1965: v; cf. Finley 1975: 71–72); today the situation is reversed: classicists may think they know how to do history but many of them know no Latin or Greek. But do they even know how to do history? Modern historians are taught that one of their most essential tasks is always to question the evidence with which they are presented. But scholars without Latin or Greek cannot question the evidence of an ancient historian such as Tacitus or Thucydides because they do not know what that evidence is: they cannot understand what he wrote. This means that vast tracts of evidence – in fact a high percentage of the evidence on which our knowledge of the ancient world depends – must remain a closed book to them. It is of course true that not every scholar of ancient history will be concerned primarily with the interpretation of texts. But Latinless scholars cannot even join in the debate. Some classicists devote substantial time and labor to the close reading of historical texts and to the reinterpretation of familiar passages, operations which in turn can have significant implications for "history." Yet Latinless scholars will not be able even to judge for themselves whether an old or a new interpretation is the more plausible, since they lack the common currency in which the exchange of ideas is conducted.

*

Historiography differs from other forms of writing in that it *matters*. Some "translators" of Greek tragedy know not a single word of Greek but simply rephrase in their own words an existing translation such as those available in the Loeb or Penguin series. Not only do they get away with this but their versions, although not qualifying as translations at all, can be acclaimed by critics with impunity, because nothing depends upon them: both their authors' reception of "Greek" tragedy and this reception's subsequent reception by critics are entirely self-referential. But historiography purports to tell us "facts," and facts are important because upon them depends the reconstruction of the past. Historical texts, in other words, not only have a similarly intrinsic interest to that of other literary texts but also declare themselves as referring to external events, to "reality."

Moreover, our knowledge of the Roman world is reliant on these texts to a very large degree: if we want to know about the history of the Roman republic or the early empire, our automatic reaction is to consult Livy or Tacitus. Now the history of Rome is not only important in the way that any serious history is important, but it also constitutes, more formally, a substantial and essential element in degree programs in ancient history or classical civilization. Thus the study of Livy or Tacitus is correspondingly important. No worthwhile study of Roman history can be conducted without reading what was written by these authors. Yet the nature of their texts, our understanding of which has been revolutionized over the past twenty-five years or so, cannot be grasped without a knowledge of the language in which they were written. The very referentiality of the texts – and hence the extent to which they may be used as evidence for "events" – is at issue. If they are read in anything but the original Latin, the reader will be unable to distinguish actual historical information from the author's imaginative constructions. And the study of history itself becomes impossible if readers do not acquire the means to distinguish fact from fiction.

FURTHER READING

General introductions to Tacitus are Martin 1981 and Mellor 1993. Every classical text should be read with the aid of a good commentary, if one is available: for Book 2 of Tacitus' *Annals* there is Goodyear 1981. Tacitus' presentation of Germanicus has been much discussed: see especially Pelling 1993. The standard discussion of Tacitus as a literary artist is Walker 1952, which takes for granted a knowledge of Latin. Though "translation studies" are very much in vogue at the moment (see, e.g., Venuti 1995 and von Kittel et al. 2004; note also Possanza 2004), not much attention seems to have been paid to the use of translated Greek and Latin texts in scholarly contexts, the problems of which are either unappreciated, ignored, or swept under the carpet; note, however, Hardwick 2000. The difficulties of rendering Tacitus in particular into English have recently been discussed in a new translation of the *Annals* which aims to keep as closely as possible to the Latin text (Woodman 2004); note also Martin 2000. On the nature of Latin historiography, anything by Wiseman will be stimulating and well worth reading: his classic text on this subject is Wiseman 1979; note also Woodman 1988 and Kraus and Woodman 1997. Differently focused but also excellent is Marincola 1997.

PART II

Surveys

CHAPTER ELEVEN

The Development of the War Monograph

Tim Rood

1   Introduction

Attempts to understand the origins and development of Greek historiography are constantly thwarted by the paucity of information available to us. But if we turn to the development of one branch of Greek historiography, the war monograph, we seem to be in a slightly more fortunate position. We have in full the histories of both Herodotus and Thucydides. Herodotus' work covers a vast temporal and geographical spread, but it comes to a climax with a detailed narrative of the Persian expedition to Greece in 480–479 BCE (Books 7–9). Fifty years after the successful resistance to Persia, the two Greek states that had played the leading role in that resistance, Athens and Sparta, found themselves at war, and the war on which they were engaged found its historian, Thucydides. Thucydides' *History* provides a detailed season-by-season narrative of the Peloponnesian War down to 411 BCE (it was left incomplete, probably owing to the author's death). As we assess Thucydides' concentrated focus on a single Greek war against Herodotus' more diffuse interests, it is tempting to plot a development from the earlier to the later historian: a prominent modern critic of historiography has written that "the war monograph implicit in Herodotus emerged perfected at Thucydides' hands" (Fornara 1983: 32). That is to say, Thucydides realized that Herodotus' detailed account of Xerxes' expedition was a potential model for a work devoted to a single war.

Fornara's account of the development of the war monograph rests heavily on Jacoby's view of the development of Greek historiography (above, p. 5). Jacoby argued (1956: 37–39) that as Herodotus' understanding of the significance of the Persian Wars developed, his increased understanding led him to expand on the mythographic and ethnographic interests of his predecessor Hecataeus and to develop a form of historical writing that would enable him to present his investigations into the great clash between Greece and Persia.

There are various problems with Jacoby's view of the development of Greek historiography, and these problems complicate the view of the development of the war monograph that Jacoby posited. Jacoby operates with a seemingly static notion of the different genres; his view is excessively focused on individuals and suspiciously teleological as it plots a development from Hecataeus to Herodotus and then from Herodotus to Thucydides (Marincola 1999); and he does not set the changes he outlines in relation to changing philosophical notions of the cosmos or to conceptions of temporality or space (Humphreys 1997).

In this chapter we shall focus not so much on the broader intellectual context in which the monograph developed as on the main problem posed by the form of the monograph – the temporal and spatial demarcation of its subject. But first we have to address a further difficulty in Jacoby's model – the relation of his categories to ancient terminology.

The problem of terminology is particularly acute when we have to deal with the war monograph. Fornara, as we have seen, was prepared to speak of the war monograph implicit in Herodotus. Alonso-Núñez, by contrast, claimed that both Herodotus and Thucydides did in fact produce "historical monographs": "the war between the Persians and the Greeks was the subject of the former, the struggle between Athens and Sparta the theme of the latter" (1990: 174). The main problem in using the term "monograph," however, is not the differences that may arise in the scholarly community, but the fact that the term itself is modern and misleading. The Greek word *monographos* is found on Hellenistic papyri, but it means "a notary." Our term "monograph," by contrast, dates from the eighteenth century, when it was used to describe a separate treatise on a single species of plant or animal, and it still suggests a specialized and technical work; in modern English at any rate the phrase "war monograph" has an odd ring to it.

How then did writers in antiquity conceive the task of composing a work on a single war? In *FGrHist*, Jacoby defined war monographs more precisely by glossing them with the Greek term *kata meros suntaxeis* – a term taken from Polybius, the Greek historian of the second century BCE. That Greek term, however, does not really correspond to our term "war monograph." To understand its implications, we have to look at how Polybius uses it in polemical contexts as a means of bringing out the advantages of his own (universal or general) history: we can then weigh the sort of war narratives about which we do have sufficient information against the principles laid down by Polybius.

2   Polybius, Monographs, and Universal History

When Polybius conceived of his own work as a universal history he was thinking partly in geographical terms. Unlike former historians who dealt with "the history of one nation, such as Greece or Persia," Polybius himself had "undertaken to describe the events occurring in all known parts of the world" (2.37.4). Indeed, he seems to imply that a genuine universal history was impossible before the rise of the Roman empire. He does at one point acknowledge that other historians have made "the same boast as myself, that they write general history (*ta katholou graphein*) and have undertaken a vaster task than any predecessor" – and he is prepared to make one exception, Ephorus, "the first and only writer who really undertook a general history" (5.33.1–2). But in the introduction to the work as a whole Polybius claims that "previously [before 220 BCE] the doings of the world had been, so to say, dispersed, as they were held together by no unity of initiative, results or locality; but ever since this date history had been an organic whole (*somatoeides*), and the affairs of Italy and Africa have been linked with those of Greece and Asia" (1.3.3–4). The implication of this passage is that even a work of Ephorus' breadth (covering some 700 years: below, p. 172) does not have the same universality as Polybius', since the geographically separate events treated by Ephorus were not causally interconnected. Indeed, the word Polybius uses for the affairs of the world before the rise of Rome – "dispersed" (*sporades*) – is common in anthropological accounts of humankind that trace a progression from the life of primitive men living in scattered dwellings to the creation of the earliest settlements and ultimately of fortified cities. Polybius implies that historical works covering events before the rise of Rome are primitive by comparison with his own historiographical project.

Polybius offers further criticism of historical monographs when he explains that only a universal history can bring out adequately the workings of *Tychē* (1.4.7):

> He indeed who believes that by studying isolated histories he can acquire a fairly just view of history as a whole, is, as it seems to me, much in the case of one, who, after having looked at the dissevered limbs of an animal once alive and beautiful, fancies he has been as good as an eye-witness of the creature itself in all its action and grace.

The severed limbs of monographs contrast, it is implied, with the organic unity of Polybius' work – a unity made possible by the fact that history had become an "organic whole" (*somatoeides*) with the rise of Rome. Indeed, when Polybius concludes that the benefit and pleasure of his universal history lie in the "study of the interconnection of all the particulars" (*tēs hapantōn pros allēla sumplokēs*, 1.4.11), he again hints at the link between the form and the content of his work: the task of "interconnection" (*sumplokē*) here enjoined upon the reader mirrors the "interconnection" (*sumplokē*) of historical events brought on by the rise of Rome.

Polybius' defense of his universal history offers valuable evidence for the types of argument used to defend war monographs. Polybius' critique of the dissevered limbs of the monograph is a response to the claim that the more limited scope of war monographs gave them a greater unity. The attractions of the unified war monograph do nonetheless make themselves felt within Polybius' work. He does sometimes break his usual structuring principles – and on one occasion he breaks them precisely for the sake of the organic unity that he claims for his work as a whole (14.12.4–5):

> It struck me that my narrative would be easier both for me to write and for my readers to follow if I performed this part of my task not by merely alluding every year to small

events not worth serious attention, but by giving once for all a unified picture so to speak of this king's [sc. Ptolemy Philopator IV's] character.

Here Polybius uses of a section that breaches his normal rules the same adjective *sōmatoeidē* ("unified") that he had applied to the contents of his work as a whole (1.3.4). And this unified section on Ptolemy IV did presumably include a coherent account of a native revolt ("a war which, apart from the mutual savagery and lawlessness of the combatants, contained nothing worthy of note, no pitched battle, no sea-fight, no siege") that would have seemed negligible if split up according to Polybius' usual principles.

While his own conception and execution of universal historiography is not free from tensions, Polybius had further criticisms of monographs. It is not just that monographs lack the virtues of universal histories: they are also liable to distinctive faults of their own. Polybius argued that "those who write narratives of particular events (*hoi tas epi merous graphontes praxeis*), when they have to deal with a subject which is circumscribed and narrow, are compelled for lack of facts to make small matters great and to devote much space to matters really not worthy of record" (7.7.6). So too later he claims that they work up elaborate set-piece descriptions of battles, sieges, and places (29.12). The greatest weakness of particular historians lay, however, in their treatment of causation: "it is impossible to get from writers who deal with particular episodes (*tōn tas kata meros historias graphontōn*) a general view of the whole process of history (*tēn tōn holōn oikonomian*)" (8.2.2). Here we do find Polybius using one of the terms picked up by Jacoby – *kata meros* – though the noun attached to the phrase is *historiai*, not *suntaxeis*. More significant, perhaps, is the fact that Polybius here uses a word for the process of history – *oikonomia* – that was commonly used for the arrangement of individual histories. The implication is that a particular arrangement of a historical text is required to bring out the arrangement of the historical events described within it. This is borne out by Polybius' argument that readers of particular histories can learn how the Romans took Syracuse and how they occupied Spain, but not the circumstances that led to their acquiring universal empire: readers who "study separate histories" (*dia tēs tōn kata meros suntaxeōs*) cannot hope to become familiar with "the general history of the world as a whole" (8.2.11).

Why did Polybius fail to devote any attention to the critical problems posed by the war monograph? One reason may be that there were in fact few historians who devoted works to a single war. We have seen that Thucydides wrote a history of a single war. But he had surprisingly few followers. More commonly different wars and battles would be thrown together in a narrative of contemporary Greek affairs – on the model of Xenophon's *Hellenica*, which starts as a continuation of Thucydides' work but then extends down to 362 BCE. It is telling, indeed, that some of the accounts of specific wars known to us were written by poets: Choerilus of Samos wrote a verse account of the Persian Wars towards the end of the fifth century BCE; Hegemon of Alexandria wrote a *Leuctrian War* (*FGrHist* 110); and the Simonides of Magnesia who wrote *The Deeds of Antiochus and the Battle against the Galatians* (*FGrHist* 163) is, like Hegemon, described as an *epopoios* (writer of hexameter verse).

One war that did attract treatment in prose was the Third Sacred War (356–346 BCE): accounts were written by Cephisodorus (*FGrHist* 112), Leon of Byzantium (*FGrHist* 132), and Callisthenes (*FGrHist* 124), who also wrote a ten-book *Hellenica* covering 386–356 BCE and an account of the early stages of the expedition of Alexander, whom he accompanied as historian until his execution in 327 BCE. Perhaps, however, one reason for the popularity of this war was precisely its epic resonances: like the Trojan War, it lasted for ten years and could be presented as arising from a dispute over women.

The claim that it was their rareness that made Polybius neglect the specific problems posed by war monographs will not quite do. The next major wars to attract monographs were both wars that Polybius described himself – and his descriptions show that he made use of the available monographs: the First Punic War, treated by Philinus of Acragas (*FGrHist* 174), and the Second Punic War, handled by another Greek historian from Sicily, Silenus of Caleacte (*FGrHist* 175) as well as by Coelius Antipater, author of the first Roman monograph (*HRR* I.158–177). Polybius was also familiar with the works of the Sicilian historian Timaeus, who wrote a separate work on Pyrrhus in addition to his long Sicilian history; presumably Timaeus' work on Pyrrhus was not, however, a strict war monograph but rather focused around Pyrrhus' foreign expeditions (compare Zeno's work entitled *Pyrrhus' Expedition to Italy and Sicily*, *FGrHist* 158), on the model of Xenophon's *Anabasis* and the Alexander historians as well as the early stages of Herodotus' account of Xerxes' expedition against Greece. Even if one discounts Timaeus, Polybius' silence on the war monograph may seem even more surprising when one considers that he himself later wrote a monograph on the Numantine War (143–133 BCE).

It seems more likely that the reason Polybius did not analyze the specific elements of war monographs is that he did not distinguish between war monographs and other forms of contemporary history writing. Like Thucydides' account of the Peloponnesian War, the "monographs" mentioned above were all written by contemporaries (though there is some danger of circularity in making this assumption for writers about whom we have no clear biographical evidence). The monograph treating a past event was a later development, best represented among surviving works by Arrian's account of Alexander (for an earlier treatment of Alexander by an imperial author, note Potamon, *FGrHist* 147 – if this was a historical work) and in Latin historiography by Sallust's *Jugurthine War* and by Curtius Rufus' history of Alexander.

While Polybius does not expressly engage with the war monograph in his discussions of earlier historians, the treatment of specific wars does enter into his defense of universal history. In Book 3, after answering the charge that his book is more difficult to acquire and read than particular histories (3.32 – *tas tōn kata meros graphontōn suntaxeis* – again close to but not quite the phrase Jacoby favored for the monograph), and complaining that such histories "mostly give different accounts of the same matter," Polybius turns again to the advantages of universal history for the analysis of causation (3.32.7–9):

> I regard the war with Antiochus as deriving from that with Philip, the latter as resulting from that with Hannibal, and the Hannibalic war as a consequence of that about

Sicily...All this can be recognised and understood from a general history, but not at all from the historians of the wars themselves...unless indeed anyone reading their descriptions of the battles alone conceived that he has acquired an adequate knowledge of the management and nature of the whole war.

Without the proper analysis of causation, Polybius further argues, "what is left is a clever essay (*agōnisma*) but not a lesson (*mathēma*), and while pleasing for the moment (*parautika men terpei*) of no possible benefit for the future" (3.31.13). Polybius' criticism that looking at a war in isolation will lead to a misrepresentation of its place in broader causal patterns is particularly striking because his language echoes in various ways Thucydides' claims on the conflicting accounts given by different informants and on the utility of his history of a single war (1.22). Polybius uses Thucydidean criteria against the type of history written by Thucydides himself.

Polybius clarifies his criticism of the monograph further when he handles separate wars in his own narrative. The moment he chooses for the beginning of his work (220 BCE) is marked by wars in different parts of the world – the Social War in Greece, the war fought for Coele-Syria between Antiochus and Ptolemy Philopator, the Second Punic War in Italy, Africa, and neighboring areas – and in the early stages of his narrative Polybius does in fact devote long sections to single wars (Book 3, for instance, covers the origins and opening years of the Second Punic War). It is only when events in different parts of the world have become, in his view, causally related (the "interweaving" or *sumplokē*, which occurred in 217 BCE) that he starts to adopt a strict annalistic arrangement. This change of practice in the course of the work brings out how misleading it would have been for him to continue with the earlier arrangement. Yet Polybius still leaves open the possibility that monographs were fine for periods when there was not the same degree of causal interaction as at the time of the rise of Rome.

The potential advantages and shortcomings of the monograph form are still more clear from Polybius' preliminary account of events preceding the start of his history proper (the *prokataskeuē*, covering Books 1–2). Included in the introduction is a long narrative of the First Punic War (1.16–63) justified by the claim that "it is not easy to name any war which lasted longer, nor one which exhibited on both sides more extensive preparations, more unintermittent activities, more battles, and greater changes of fortune" (1.13.11, cf. the closing comment at 1.63.4). Focusing as it does on continuity and length, this explanation recalls Thucydides' criteria for judging the greatness of the Peloponnesian War (1.23). The narrative of the First Punic War is followed by accounts of the Carthaginian war against the mercenaries (1.65–88) and by Rome's war against the Gauls (2.1–36) that both close with narratorial claims about their greatness: the Mercenary War "far excelled all wars we know of in cruelty and defiance of principle" (1.88.7) while the Gallic War was "second to no war in history" in "the desperation and daring of the combatants and the numbers who took part and perished in the battles" (2.35.2). By making claims generally used to magnify a historian's overall subject in relation to wars that are only part of his introductory books, Polybius underlines the even greater importance of the subject of the main part of his work – and so further undermines the potentiality of the monograph.

Polybius' historiographical criticisms are notable for their lack of a historical dimension. He weighs up earlier historians against his own standards without exploring developments in history writing over time. His criticisms are notable, too, for their focus on historians writing in the second half of the fourth century BCE and afterwards – historians whose works do not survive intact and are in some cases largely known through the distorting lens of Polybius' presentation of them. How do Polybius' claims about "particular" histories work if we turn to the earlier historians whose works do survive – Herodotus, Thucydides, and Xenophon? Did Polybius present a skewed account of the potentialities of monographs or "particular" histories? To answer these questions it may be helpful to start by looking to one of the main inspirations for the early historians – the presentation of war in Homeric epic.

3   War, Homer, and the Historians

Historians' accounts of wars were all written under the shadow of the *Iliad*, an epic extraordinary for the complexity of its narrative portrayal of the Trojan War. The *Iliad* itself covers a period of fifty or so days in the tenth year of the war, but it indirectly offers a narrative of the entire war. This ambitious aim of getting the whole of the war covered within the compass of the narrower theme of the wrath of Achilles is achieved in a number of ways. In Book 2, Odysseus recalls Calchas' prophecy at the start of the war that the war would last ten years. Again in Book 2, the catalogue of ships shows signs of having been adapted from a catalogue at Aulis (hence the need to explain the absence of Achilles, Protesilaus, and Philoctetes from the fighting). The *teichoscopia* in Book 3 and Agamemnon's review of Achaean warriors in Book 4 also have an introductory purpose that would not be out of place in a poem about the whole war. Even more pointedly, the duel between Menelaus and Paris in Book 3 – which ends with Paris being whisked off by Aphrodite to Helen – replays the cause of the war, while Trojan culpability in the war as a whole is underscored by the fact that it is a Trojan, Pandarus, who breaks the truce in Book 4. And just as the early books of the *Iliad* look back to the early years of the war, so too the closing books anticipate both the death of Achilles and the end of the war itself, the sack of Troy: Hector comes to stand for the defense of Troy as a whole, and the lamentation at his death is compared with the cries that would be uttered at the burning of the city (22.410–411).

The handling of time and perspective in the *Iliad* raises uncomfortable questions for the writer of the war monograph. If a poem on the narrower theme of the wrath of Achilles can at the same time be a satisfying presentation of the Trojan War as a whole, why offer a narrative of all ten years? Similar questions are raised by the handling of war in another genre – Athenian tragedy. Like the *Iliad*, Aeschylus' *Persae* (performed in 472 BCE) can be read as a reflection on the narrativization of war. The play starts with the chorus of Persian elders in Susa looking back to the departure of Xerxes' expedition to Greece. It includes a passage in which the queen asks questions about Athens – a passage that provides the ethnographic and political background necessary for understanding the Athenian victory, and reveals, indeed, the importance of ethnographic investigation for historical explanation. Aeschylus' play also includes a messenger speech devoted to the battle itself and a scene where the previous Persian king, Darius, is raised from the dead to provide both a sketch of earlier Persian history and a prophecy about the battle of Plataea the following year.

Not all poets were as versatile in their treatment of time as Homer and Aeschylus. In the *Poetics* (1451a22–30), Aristotle stressed the narrowness of the plots of the *Iliad* and *Odyssey*, contrasting the more episodic Heracles and Theseus epics. He later argued that only one or two tragedies can be made from the *Iliad* or *Odyssey*, but that many can be made from the cyclic epics like the *Cypria* and the *Little Iliad*, which dealt with events in the Trojan War earlier and later than the events covered in the *Iliad* (1459a29–b7). Other epic poets, in Aristotle's view, were more like historians in their episodic arrangement.

When we turn to Herodotus, however, we find a thoughtful experimentation with the possibilities of the war narrative that is similar to the complexities found in Homer and Aeschylus. It has been claimed, as we have seen, that the form of the war monograph is implicit in Herodotus' work, and at first glance this claim seems plausible. Herodotus' account of Xerxes' expedition against Greece sets the mold for many later accounts of wars: it features a council of war, a catalogue of forces, a comparison with previous expeditions, and dreams and other portents. At the same time, however, the debate in the Persian court points to important continuities with Herodotus' presentation of previous Persian kings. Xerxes inherits from his predecessors the urge to expand – or rather, it is because he feels the need to match his predecessors that he follows their expansionist path. To divorce the account of Xerxes' expedition from the rest of the work is to do violence to Herodotus' historical thought.

There are many other accounts of wars in Herodotus that could be read as self-standing pieces inserted into the account of the development of Greco-Persian hostilities. Yet Herodotus' very justification for introducing, say, an account of hostilities between Athens and Aegina undermines any superficial impression of possible textual independence: Herodotus conceives of such hostilities as part of an ongoing pattern of hostility grounded in patterns of reciprocity and revenge. The closer attention to linear temporality in the account of the Ionian Revolt (e.g., indications by year at 6.18, 31.1, 40.1, 42.1, 46.1) may give that narrative an even greater appearance of self-sufficiency. Yet the original Athenian decision to send ships in support of the revolt is a "beginning of evils" (5.97) that looks well beyond the immediate context to the Persian invasions of Greece and beyond. So too the portent – an earthquake at Delos – that accompanies the first Persian invasion of Greece in 490 BCE heralds troubles for both Greeks and Persians that embrace within their scope the Peloponnesian War itself (6.98).

What then of Herodotus' overall demarcation of his topic? Dionysius of Halicarnassus (*Pomp.* 3) praised Herodotus for his choice of a beginning – the first wrongs committed by non-Greeks against Greeks – and an ending – the Greek victories at Plataea and Mycale in 479 BCE. But Herodotus in fact continued his story of Greek–Persian hostility beyond those battles by narrating the events of the rest of that year, as the Athenians – under the generalship of Xanthippus, father of Pericles – start to assume the leading role in pressing the war against Persia in the eastern Aegean. Herodotus concludes with the statement, "Nothing further happened for the remainder of the year" (9.121), followed by an analepsis to the proposal put to Cyrus by Artembares (an ancestor of the Artaÿctes whom the Athenians have just crucified at the richly symbolic setting of the Hellespont – on "the shore on which Xerxes' bridge across the straits had ended" [9.120.4]) that the Persians should move to a less rough land. Herodotus' story ends with strong hints that a new story of the Athenian rise to power is starting: nothing further may have happened in that year, but the story of the Athenian rise to naval hegemony would continue – a story prefigured indirectly in the tensions among the Greeks in their hour of triumph and directly by various external prolepses.

At the same time, Herodotus' ending complicates his choice of an opening for his story. The fact that Artaÿctes is punished for despoiling the shrine of Protesilaus (9.116, 120.4) provides a sense of an ending by looking back to the Trojan War – the beginning of Greco-barbarian hostilities highlighted by the "learned Persians" at the start of the work, but then dismissed as Herodotus turned to another starting point, Croesus' conquests in Ionia. Herodotus seems to be suggesting that the Trojan War might after all have been an appropriate beginning. Indeed, towards the start of his great account of Xerxes' expedition he had compared the size of Xerxes' army with Agamemnon's and described how Xerxes visited Troy on his way to Greece (7.20.2, 43.1).

Herodotus' stress on the openness of his ending as well as the intricate links between the narrative of Xerxes' expedition and the earlier portions of the work both point to the tendentiousness of Polybius' criticism of earlier non-universal historians. Nor was Herodotus alone in implicitly setting the events covered in his own work in the context of a wider historical narrative. The openness of his ending was picked up in the fourth century BCE by Xenophon. Xenophon's *Anabasis* – an account of the adventures of a mercenary army in Asia – ends with the army attaching itself to the Spartans and departing for a new war on two Persian satraps. More self-conscious is the ending of Xenophon's *Hellenica*. The work starts as a continuation of Thucydides' incomplete history of the Peloponnesian War ("and after that" [*meta de tauta*]), and ends with the battle of Mantinea in 362 BCE – a battle that leaves "even more uncertainty and confusion in Greece than there had been previously." Xenophon continues: "Let my account conclude at this point. What happened after that (*ta de meta tauta*, echoing the opening *meta de tauta*) will perhaps be a concern for someone else" (7.5.27). Xenophon, then, was positioning himself as a continuator of Thucydides while also expressing the wistful hope that someone else would do him the service he had done Thucydides. At the same time, he "reveals the topic of confusion in the Greek world as a thematic preoccupation" (Tuplin 1993: 39), and his text's emphasis on its own lack of resolution is vital to our reading of it: the claim of greatness that Xenophon makes for his subject is not the greatness of any particular war, but the greatness of the confusion caused by the failure of wars to produce any long-lasting solution of the internal problems of Greece. Unlike Thucydides' opening claim about the greatness of the Peloponnesian War, this is a claim that has to be made at the end of the work: the unconventional placement suggests that the presentational strategies favored by Thucydides can no longer do justice to the texture of a Greek world that has moved beyond a bipolar structuring of power.

It is telling that Xenophon was composing the *Hellenica* at roughly the time that the concept of the epic cycle was being established. By the second half of the fourth century BCE, it is likely that the various early epics on the Trojan War had been arranged in a chronological sequence, with alternative beginnings and endings supplied to mark their place in a sequence (Aristoxenus knew an alternative beginning to the *Iliad*). At the same time, there may have been some alterations to the poems to create a neater chronological continuity: the last part of the *Little Iliad*, for instance, had originally overlapped with the *Sack of Troy*, but the overlap may have been removed when they were joined together as part of the cycle. It seems that the creation of a linear and episodic account of the Trojan War and its aftermath reflects the same intellectual endeavor as Xenophon's placing of himself in a sequence of past and future historians.

What then of the work identified by Fornara as the perfection of the war monograph – Thucydides' history of the Peloponnesian War? In focusing on the history of a single war Thucydides was, it seems, inventing a form that had already been deconstructed by Homer. And by leaving his history incomplete Thucydides laid his own construction of the Peloponnesian War open to the rewriting of his followers. Xenophon, as we have seen, picked up where Thucydides left off – but went well beyond the ending that Thucydides had projected for his own work. Thucydides had suggested that he would end his work with the destruction of Athens' walls (5.26.1) – a fitting end given the stress in the "Archaeology" on walls as an emblem of power and the link in the *Pentecontaetia* (the account of the fifty years between the Persian and Peloponnesian Wars) between Athens' walls and Themistocles' imperialist foresight. That scene does feature as a prominent internal closure within Xenophon's *Hellenica* (2.2.23): "Lysander sailed into the Piraeus, the exiles returned and they pulled down the walls with great enthusiasm to the music of flute girls, thinking that that day was the beginning of freedom for Greece." The sense of closure is strengthened by the echo of the Spartan envoy Melesippus' famous words at the start of the Peloponnesian War: "this day will be the beginning of great troubles for Greece" (Thuc. 2.12.3). The end that was thought of as a beginning of freedom proved, however, to be no beginning at all: Xenophon's focus on thoughts that were soon to be disappointed undermines the sharp delineation of the end of the war. Before long Xenophon will be showing the resurgence of Athens' imperial ambitions.

Xenophon is not alone in questioning the very foundation of Thucydides' construction of his war. Thucydides' apparently natural demarcation of the Peloponnesian War has been questioned by some modern historians: Geoffrey de Ste. Croix, for instance, complains that "*his* war began only in 431, and not (as it should have done) some thirty years earlier" (1972: 3). Thucydides' structuring of his war (or *taxis*) was earlier berated by Dionysius, who argued that Thucydides "might have begun his narrative not with the events at Corcyra, but with his country's splendid achievements immediately after the Persian War," and that he should have ended his history "with a climax, and one that was most remarkable and especially gratifying to his audience, the return of the exiles from Phyle, which marked the beginning of the city's recovery of freedom" (*Pomp.* 3) – a genuinely new beginning, in Dionysius' rosy reading of Athenian history.

How circumscribed, then, is Thucydides' own definition of the war that was his subject? At times it seems that his war is indeed a natural self-sufficient entity. At the start of his work, Thucydides starts by saying that he "wrote up the war of the Peloponnesians and the Athenians," starting when the war itself began (1.1). He also claims that the narrative of the war itself will prove its superiority to all earlier wars (1.21) and that the war starts with the Theban attack on Plataea (2.1). And later he confronts claims that his twenty-seven-year war was in fact composed of separate wars with an interlude of peace (5.26). Thucydides, then, was at least aware that there were other ways of splitting up his war – just as he was aware that there were other ways of naming it (from the Peloponnesian perspective, it is the "Attic war"). Elsewhere we get a sense of other possible demarcations: the Spartan envoy Melesippus' remark on the beginning of evils (quoted above) suggests that the Athenian rejection of the final Spartan envoys could be defined as the beginning. And Thucydides' own choice of the attack on Plataea as a beginning points to a contrast with the united Greek victory at Plataea – and so suggests that the war between the two great victors over Persia was grounded in the tensions that developed from that victory. Indeed, Thucydides' elaborate organization of his material in Book 1 (including the postponed narrative of the *Pentecontaetia*) constantly raises the question of beginnings: it hints that the Peloponnesian War was rooted in the Athenian expansion after the Persian Wars – and that Thucydides' work can be seen as a sequel to Herodotus'.

While we can see that Thucydides does complicate the apparently fixed starting point for his war, we can only speculate on how Thucydides would have treated the end of the Peloponnesian War. His account of the Athenian and Spartan motives for making peace in 421 BCE is constructed so as to hint already at the fragility of the peace (Rood 1998: 84–88). But there Thucydides was confronting the need to persuade his readers that the end of the first ten-years war (431–421 BCE) was not a real ending – that the years of the Peace of Nicias deserved their place in the war. Thucydides, by contrast, insists on the collapse of Athens in 404 BCE as the real end of the war. And yet scholars have seen hints in Thucydides' opening book (warnings in the Athenian speech at Sparta, the excursus on the haughty Spartan regent Pausanias) that he was writing in the knowledge of the unpopularity of the Spartan hegemony established at the end of the war. Thucydides too may have been aware that his war was part of a continuing story.

Thucydides breaks down any simple definition of the war monograph still more profoundly when he claims that his narrative of the Peloponnesian War will be useful to "any who wish to look at the plain truth about both past events and those that at some future time, in accordance with human nature, will recur in similar or comparable ways" (1.22.4). Thucydides collapses together the events of the Peloponnesian War with those of all later wars. Far from being a simple war monograph, Thucydides' whole narrative is an account of events that occurred once and of events that occur many times. Thucydides saw himself as a universal historian. And a universal historian

of conflict in general: the claim of recurrence made for the account of the Peloponnesian War recurs in his generalizing analysis of civil war (*stasis*) that builds on his
account of the Corcyraean civil war (3.82), and that analysis is itself a prism for
understanding the outbreak and development of conflict between states as well as
within states (Macleod 1983).

4 Conclusion

The works of Herodotus, Thucydides, and Xenophon suggest possibilities for the
form of the war monograph (or for "particular" histories) greater than Polybius
claimed possible – precisely because these historians challenge the very parameters of
the genre. The war monograph did not develop: it was at most an idea towards which
historians – and poets – could fruitfully gesture, a genre conceived precisely in order
to highlight its own limitations: limitations that, in the mind of a Thucydides at least,
were a spur to the creation of a work that is demeaned by being seen as the first and
perfect example of its genre, springing out from the head of Herodotus like Athene
from the head of Zeus.

FURTHER READING

The most influential account of the development of the monograph (and of historiography in
general) has been Jacoby 1909; see also Fornara 1983. For criticisms of Jacoby's approach,
see Marincola 1999 and Humphreys 1997. A stimulating modern overview is provided by
Hornblower 1994b. Strasburger 1982 remains the essential discussion of Homer's significance for historiography; on the epic cycle, see Canfora 1999 and Burgess 2001a, b. For a
wide-ranging approach to the shifting conceptions of temporality which paved the way for
the development of historiography, see Csapo and Miller 1998. Marincola 2005 offers a
good overview of the way historians delimited their subjects in their endings; on specific
historians, see Boedeker 1988, Dewald 1997, and Pelling 1997b on Herodotus; Rood 1998
on Thucydides; and Tuplin 1993 and Dillery 1995 on Xenophon. Polybius' methodological
remarks are an essential source for ancient views on monographs and other genres of ancient
historiography: they are lucidly discussed by Walbank in his monograph on Polybius (1972)
as well as in his collections of essays (1985, 2002) and in the detailed notes on specific
passages in *HCP*. The development of the monograph by Sallust has been excellently
discussed by Levene 1992.

CHAPTER TWELVE

Continuous Histories (*Hellenica*)

Christopher Tuplin

1   Introduction

Our ability to provide a continuous account of the political and military history of Greece – to achieve something that would not be possible if we only had archaeo-logical, epigraphic, and numismatic evidence – depends upon direct or indirect access to the ancient authors who told parts of that story. The output of those authors (mostly only fragmentarily preserved) put on record memorable events from the past in various different ways in terms of literary style, choice of material, structure of presentation, and so forth. The present chapter deals with one particular sub-set – the writers of continuous history or *Hellenica*. Most ancient historians and classicists probably have a clear idea of the identity of some core examples of the genre. But the two terms are arguably in tension with one another, and the first is ambiguous: we need to resolve these tensions and ambiguities if the sub-set is to have a clear identity. I shall construct the chapter as an investigation of this issue of definition, while trying to ensure that basic information about what I take to be the crucial authors is put on record.

2   Definition

Membership of our genre (as conventionally conceived) seems to involve a number of criteria relating to literary texture, chronological scope, title, and geopolitical and thematic focus.

Literary Texture

We are dealing with a narrative stretching over some period of time, in which events appear in chronological order and in some sort of structure of cause and effect – i.e., a continuous piece of storytelling (this is one of the senses of "continuous" at stake), not simply a more or less random list of items. (I do not mean to suggest anything particular about the degree of sophistication of the causal structure involved; and the issue is not whether an author is or is not prepared to see the hand of God or fate in certain sets of events.) This is, of course, a pretty loose criterion: it is easily met by authors such as Ephorus or Polybius who, as authors of so-called "universal history" (albeit in different modes), are normally regarded as clearly outside the genre with which we are concerned – and who should be so regarded, if the genre is to have any useful content at all. But it excludes, for example, anything in which sets of events are assembled simply because they illustrate some moral or political or ethnographic proposition, and might be held to exclude certain types of biographically oriented text: the scale of Theopompus' *Philippica* keeps it in the fold of continuous history (in the sense used in this paragraph), but Stesimbrotus' work on Themistocles, Thucydides, and Pericles may well be another matter, and Ion's *Wanderings* would surely be.

Chronological Scope

The genre we are dealing with is (it may be claimed) for writers of contemporary or near-contemporary history. To be more precise: our authors produce narratives that cover a clearly delimited period of time which started in the comparatively recent past. (Some allowance has to be made for digressive material.) This, of course, immediately excludes all authors who, though they may have narrated contemporary or near-contemporary politico-military events (perhaps in some detail), did so within a discourse that stretched back to mythological times (e.g., Ephorus, Anaximenes, Zoilus, Nicolaus, Diodorus). How many more it excludes (among authors whose starting point we can identify) depends on what one means by "comparatively recent" and what marks the starting point. The latter question intersects with issues of thematic focus and will be dealt with under that heading. But the first point requires comment now.

Xenophon's *Hellenica* is a model-example of our genre, and all events narrated in it fell within its author's lifetime, perhaps even within his adult lifetime. But this cannot be a necessary or sufficient criterion. On the one hand, a corresponding claim could be made by authors conventionally outside our genre such as Thucydides, Hieronymus of Cardia, Athanas of Syracuse, or the first-generation Alexander historians. On the other hand, most authors conventionally included in our genre score less well than any of these. Cratippus *might* be an exception (D. Hal. *Thuc.* 16 says he "shared an *akmē*" with Thucydides, though this is a very inexact indication); but even on the chronology rightly espoused by Flower (1994), Theopompus' lifespan only just overlapped his *Hellenica* (which ended in 394) – whereas he was an adult through the period covered by the main narrative of *Philippica* (a work normally regarded as outside our genre) – and, although Callisthenes' lifespan intersected the thirty years covered by his *Hellenica* (387–357), it is hard to say by how much or whether any significant part of the overlap was with his adult years. In terms of contemporaneity, then, the most one can claim for authors like this is a concern with events that at least fell within the adult lifetime of their fathers' generation. In short, we can exclude those who wished to range back to mythological or near-mythological times, but no simple test of contemporaneity firmly identifies a distinct-ive genre within the category of those who are definitely writing narrative history.

Title

Nor is title a straightforward resource. *Hellenica* has come to be used as a category-identifier, so that to say of a work that it is a *Hellenica* is to affirm that it belongs to our genre. But ancient usage does not define such a narrow field. We cannot identify the timeframe or narrative character of Charon's *Hellenica* (all the surviving historical fragments can be assigned to his Lampsacene local history or his *Persica*), but Anaximenes' *Hellenica* (the first part of a tripartite *Historiai*) embraced mythology and certainly had a different chronological scope from the homonymous works of Xenophon, Theopompus, or Callisthenes, while Neanthes' *Hellenica* may well not have dealt systematically with a continuous piece of Greek history. Contrariwise, not only do we not have an ancient title for Cratippus or the so-called *Hellenica Oxyrhynchia*, but various other authors who have been or might theoretically be assigned to our genre did not use the title *Hellenica* (e.g., those of Daimachus, Duris [*pace* Diod. 15.60], Phylarchus, Euphantus, Demochares). Once again, then, we have a criterion which is neither necessary nor sufficient. It is, however, one that, as we shall see, may still prove useful.

Geopolitical and Thematic Focus

That modern parlance has developed as it has is, of course, due to the conjunction of title and perceived geographical scope in the works of Xenophon, Theopompus, and Callisthenes: the geographical scope is mainland Greece and the Aegean (with its northern and eastern seaboards), no single state or restricted geographical area or specific individual within that area completely dominates the selection of material, and material from further afield is only present intermittently and as demanded by the narrative thread of the central area. As in other cases there is more to be said about these criteria.

(1) Cicero (*Fam.* 5.12.2) distinguished *perpetua historia* from the writing of works about individual wars. The sense of "continuous" history here recalls the issue of literary texture, but is nonetheless separate. Passages from a war monograph need not read very differently from passages from a continuous history; the distinction lies in sharpness of thematic definition, leading to exclusion of peripheral material and shorter overall length; and in Cicero's model cases the distinction is very clear since the authors involved (Callisthenes, Timaeus, and Polybius) had also written continu-ous histories which abutted the relevant wars – though only one of them used the title *Hellenica* or would normally be put in the category of *Hellenica* writers.

(2) Among the alternatives implicit in the word *Hellenica* is *Sicelica*. When the Suda entry on Philistus remarks that "[*Sicelica* are] the account of hostile activities of Greek against Greek" we smile wryly, for *Hellenica* are surely exactly that. But, as a

result of the circumstances in which large-scale history writing emerged in the Greek world (which, as it happened, occurred in the Aegean basin) and the tendency for the historical experience of Sicilian Greeks to be relatively separate from that of mainland/Aegean Greeks, Sicily generated a distinct historiographical tradition and, although the historiographical apartheid eventually broke down to some extent, it did so in works that, for other reasons too, seem to fall outside our genre (e.g., Theopompus' *Philippica*, Ephorus). The fact that there could be Greek history in which Sicily only figured discontinuously is significant – and might even be treated as decisively definitive in generic terms. (I assume Sanders 1995 is right against, e.g., Shrimpton 1991: 36–37 that Theopompus' *Hellenica* had no significant treatment of Sicily.) For example, Diyllus' inclusion of Sicilian material (73 T 1) encourages us to see both parts of his *Historiai* in relation to Ephorus and the tradition of "universal history."

Some insist that *Sicelica* are simply the western counterparts of *Hellenica* (Fornara 1983: 38). There are ways in which this is true – viz. the clear geopolitical focus on a parallel multi-*polis* part of the Greek world, and the emergence of some degree of continuation (on which more below) – but also at least two in which it is not. First, the fact that Antiochus and Philistus incorporated contemporary history in a discourse that began with the very distant past constitutes a significant distinction, one that we have already used to separate, e.g., Ephorus from our genre. It is true that Ephorus' work was thematically organized and geopolitically "universal" in a way *Sicelica* were not, but that does not dissolve the distinction between Philistus and the *Hellenica* writers: choice of starting point is a telling feature of a work of historiography, and the difference here between the earliest *Sicelica* and *Hellenica* writers does reflect a difference in what prompted them to write. (More on this later.) Second, if the bulk of Philistus' work was focalized around the Dionysii (as Marincola 2001: 109 maintains), one might allege that it was more akin to Theopompus' *Philippica* than to the genre labeled as *Hellenica*. Of course, some who maintain that *Sicelica* are the counterpart to *Hellenica* also maintain that the *Philippica* is only a special kind of *Hellenica* (Fornara 1983: 34; Flower 1994: 149; cf. Will 1991: 117, who regards *Hellenica*, *Sicelica*, *Persica*, and *Philippica* as parallel types of *perpetuae historiae*, in contrast to Ephoran universal history). Given the work's scale, the scope of Philip's engagement with the Greek world and the contemporaneity of the main historical thread, that is an understandable proposition. But if we entertain this proposition without serious qualification it tends to undermine the exercise in definition in which we are currently engaged.

(3) So how do our authors select which bit of Greek history to write about? In some cases the point from which the narrative starts is the point at which an existing narrative ends. This was certainly true of the *Hellenica* of Xenophon and Theopompus, both of which began from the abrupt end of Thucydides' history: they continue an unfinished text, completing its original project (narrative of the Peloponnesian War) and carrying the story forward to a later point. It is a complicating factor that in Xenophon's work the completion may be a distinct compositional unit from the continuation, but for the moment we can leave that to one side. Instead let us note two further relevant texts. Cratippus wrote a history whose known content

postdates 411 (I assume 64 F 3 is a back-reference) and in which the author criticized Thucydides' composition of speeches and (perhaps) commented on his place of death (F 2). The phenomena are consistent with Cratippus having completed and continued Thucydides; similar things apply to the *Hellenica Oxyrhynchia* – known narrative does not predate 411 and uses Thucydidean seasonal dating, and the author refers to Thucydides (though to a particular piece of narrative, not a general historiographical feature) – and the same inference, that we are dealing with a completer-continuator, is universally drawn. This time the complicating factor is that Cratippus and the author of *Hellenica Oxyrhynchia* may be one and the same. More important, however, is the spread of the continuation principle beyond authors who began by completing Thucydides.

Callisthenes began his *Hellenica* in 387, and we do not know that any Thucydides-continuator ended then. Xenophon (362) and Theopompus (394) certainly did not, and this is probably true of Cratippus too (Plutarch's contents list ends in 393, and he would surely have continued it at least until Thrasybulus' expedition of 390/89 if he could have done so). About the *Hellenica Oxyrhynchia* (if distinct) we can say nothing. Of course, wherever existing narratives finished, the fact that the start date coincided with the King's Peace did not preclude a scene-setting review which might have embraced the gap since 393, but as it also seems that the whole of Book 1 was introductory to a narrative that only became detailed from the liberation of Thebes in 379/8 (Stylianou 1998: 94 n. 249, after Jacoby *FGrHist Komm.* IID.416–417), it looks as if the link between Callisthenes and his predecessors was in any case rather different from that between those predecessors and Thucydides, and that his starting point was as much the product of a historical watershed as a reflection of the existing historiographical landscape. Of course, we might say that this is unsurprising, since the situation facing the Thucydides-continuators was peculiar, and we might affirm that Callisthenes was at least contributing to a continuous multi-author record of "Greek history," and extending its lower limit (albeit only by a half-decade after Xenophon's terminal date). This does, however, involve introducing a fourth sense of "continuous history" – not a proposition about narrative texture or absence of monographic theme or neat provision of links in a continuous chain, but something a good deal more vague.

Callisthenes' work ended in 357/6 with the start of the Third Sacred War, a conflict whose epochal significance for traditional hegemonic states in central and southern Greece was patent by the time he laid down his pen. We can identify another work (Diyllus' *Historiai*) that took 357 as its start date, but at this point the generic issue becomes clouded again, for it was arguably more a continuation of Ephorus than of Callisthenes. To be more precise: Diyllus' work was in two sections (*suntaxeis*), starting in 357/6 and 341/0 (73 T 1–2). 341/0 was the date of the latest events covered in Ephorus' universal history, 357/6 the start date of the one major episode prior to 341/0 not covered when the author died, viz. the Third Sacred War. (Interestingly, Diyllus [73 T 3] could be said to have assembled "common affairs" [*tas koinas praxeis*], just like Ephorus: 70 T 11.) An exact grasp of the situation is impeded by our ignorance of the relationship between the date at which Diyllus started work and that at which Ephorus' son Demophilus wrote a book on the Sacred

War to supplement his father's *History*. But there is no substantive reason to say that Diyllus began as a *Hellenica* writer continuing Callisthenes (albeit one including Sicilian material) and then turned into a universal historian continuing Ephorus – and not much point, either, since to say such a thing would not conceal the fact that the prospect of continuation has ceased to be the preserve of so-called *Hellenica* writers.

Diyllus' twenty-six-book work ended in 297/6 and was continued by Psaon of Plataea in thirty books, an enterprise of which nothing is known save that Dionysius thought little of its style. Meanwhile a new chronological series had started. Hieronymus of Cardia's history of the post-Alexander world ran from 323 to 272, Phylarchus' *Histories* from 272 to 220/19, Polybius' main narrative from 220/19 to 146 (prefaced by a two-book introduction covering 264 onwards, which picked up from the endpoint of Timaeus' monograph on the Pyrrhic Wars), Posidonius' from 146 to the 80s, and Strabo's from 146 (again) to (perhaps) the 20s. (Fornara 1983: 46 notes an analogy with the " 'perpetual histories' of the Greeks [*Hellenica*]." But the 220/19 start point also picked up from Aratus' *Memoirs* [Pol. 4.1.9], 264 was "when the Romans first crossed the sea" as much as when Timaeus' *Pyrrhus* stopped, and there is a further summary history back to 387/6 [1.6–12].) None of these is plainly a representative of our genre, and that Phylarchus has been claimed to be owes more to the strong association of his work with Peloponnesian history created by accidents of survival than to objective reasoning. One might as well claim Hieronymus for our genre on the grounds of clear Thucydidean influence (Hornblower 1995: 59) – save that Thucydides is not (in conventional understanding) a representative either but at most the cause of its existence. (There is also the problem of Hieronymus' putative organization of material around individuals: Hornblower 1981: 79–80.)

Another prominent early Hellenistic historian does not quite fit into this (or any) chronological series. Duris' *Histories* ran from 370 to ca. 281. The end comes with the death of Seleucus I (the last of Alexander's generals-turned-kings) and the start surely has a similarly Macedonian focus – the death of Amyntas III ushering in the troubled decade that led to Philip II's accession. Duris performs a distinctive task in linking the early third-century Hellenistic world to a late classical watershed – but it is a link that initially covered ground fairly rapidly, since the start of the Third Sacred War is already reached in Book 2, and the fact that some authorities cite the work as *Macedonica*, even if it does not quite establish this as the official title against others who cite it as *Historiai* – or indeed Diodorus who calls Duris a writer of "the history of Greek affairs" (*hē tōn Hellenikōn historia*: 15.60) – is good evidence about the work's perceived focus (cf. Pédech 1989: 316). We might take the view that, by subsuming everything from before Philip's accession through Alexander's reign and the four decades of the Diadochoi into a single discourse, Duris was inaugurating a new Macedonian (or Greco-Macedonian?) strand of continuous history, a successor for the new age to the *Hellenica* tradition of those who wrote the history of the first half of the fourth century. But if so, the disregard of his end date suggests that in the next historiographical generation no one felt the distinctiveness of his project strongly enough for it to take precedence over the fact that Hieronymus had reached 272 – especially as he had set out from what one suspects people now thought a more natural starting point, viz. Alexander's death. In any case, to see Duris thus is only another way of admitting either that the original genre has died or that its scope has to be seriously redefined.

The practice of end-date continuation is rare outside Hellenic or Helleno-Macedonian history. Heracleides' *Persica* is a mysterious work, generically speaking, and Dinon's *Persica* certainly did not merely continue Ctesias or Heraclides but went back past Cyrus the Elder to Ninus and Semiramis, while the fifth-century writers of Persian history undoubtedly produced heavily overlapping narratives. In the west, on the other hand, although the first Sicilian historians, Antiochus and Philistus, each began in the distant past, the abrupt end of Philistus' history did prompt a continuation: Athanas' history was really about Dion's activities and their aftermath, but a prefatory book covered the seven years needed to link it with Philistus. But no one accorded him the same honor: Timaeus returned to a start point in the distant past, while Callias and Antandrus focused on Agathocles, and none of the other earlier fourth-century Sicilian historians (Hermias, Polycritus, Alcimus, Timonides) forms part of any sort of series.

It seems, then, that continuation was a distinctive feature of works providing narrative of the main thread of Greek history – but not strictly speaking of the putative sub-set of *Hellenica*. Where did it come from? Nothing of the sort is found at the start of Greek historiography. Charon's *Hellenica* and Damastes' *On Events in Greece* (*Peri tōn en Helladi genomenōn*) stand in splendid mutual isolation, and in any case neither they nor the other lost authors of the era (who do not even have specious titles) can be assumed to have provided the sort of narrative history we are looking for (there is mostly no question of such a thing), while Thucydides is in dialogue with Herodotus, but does not continue him in any solid sense.

What prompted continuation was two things: the accident that Thucydides' *History* was incomplete and a perception that, even if it were complete, it need not (perhaps should not) be the end of the story. As before, actual political developments matter. When Thucydides' text reached its final state it was already arguable (especially by those who absorbed the message of Thucydides' argument for continuity between 421 and 414) that 404 was just a stage in an ongoing struggle. Between then and the date at which the earliest fourth-century writers of *Hellenica* began work, every passing year made the point more clear.

It is true that the putative existence of two compositional units within Xenophon's *Hellenica* (1.1.1–2.3.10; 2.3.11–7.5.27) raises the possibility that he conceived of completion and continuation as distinct processes. This is not a problem for those who believe either that Xenophon was working with Thucydides' unpublished notes – in which case the project is so heavily determined by literary piety that wider issues of historical interpretation are not broached (Grigolon 2002 provides recent advocacy of the "Thucydides Papers" hypothesis; Rood 2004 discerns something different and much more persuasive, viz. intertextual allusions linking Xenophon and Diodorus-Ephorus with passages from Thucydides' *extant* work) – or that the linguistic and textural differences between the completion and continuation do not presuppose a significant gap in date of composition – in which case basic historiographical unity is intact (Gray 1991: 211–212 argues this case, not unpersuasively). But if Xenophon wrote the completion – entirely from his own resources and research – quite soon after Thucydides' text reached its final state and then did nothing more until late in life, it might be that (at work in the late 390s or early 380s) he did not initially think it wrong to see the war as a self-contained whole – though, if so, there would be no cause to berate him, since there is no evidence that Thucydides himself ever thought otherwise. (We must acknowledge that even now far more historians accept – even unreflectingly – Thucydides' view about the twenty-seven-year war than affirm that the Peloponnesian War did not really end until 387/6.) But, even granted a gap, there is no way of proving that Xenophon did not in fact see the historical continuity across 404 but fail to act upon it because of accidental distractions or other literary and historical priorities: entering the Socratic fray (another type of historical task) was perhaps more pressing than continuing Thucydides.

In any event, the failure of one author to move straight from completion to continuation does not alter the fact that sooner or later the hole at the end of Thucydides' text, the disorder of politico-military events in the fourth century and their inextricable causal connection with Athens' enforced surrender in 404 prompted others who wished to write the history of those events to pick up the story where it had been left off rather than starting entirely afresh. As Will (1991: 115–116) remarks, there is an element of accident here, but his imputation that continuators extended Thucydides' story merely in order not to be seen as slaves to someone else's project is surely unfair: historical and political judgment is involved, even if the precise shading of that judgment and of the reasons for wishing to write history at all may vary with personality and the precise timing of the decision to set to work. On the latter we can make no very fine evaluations: Cratippus surely precedes Theopompus but by an unknown and perhaps considerable distance (some or all of Theopompus' work existed by 343 [*FGrHist* 115 T 7], but it "plagiarized" Xenophon's *Hellenica*, completed in the mid-350s, and, while Badian [2004: 47] has *Hellenica* 4, which provoked a notable example, written before 362, and even unitarians must allow for a longish process of writing and pre-publication circulation, Porphyry [115 F 21] claims extensive plagiarism, so perhaps Theopompus consumed Xenophon's text whole), Xenophon is, as we have seen, controversial (though the final end date of mid-350s is firm), and the *Hellenica Oxyrhynchia* only fixable within fairly wide margins – after 387/6 (19.2) and before 346 (21.3) is the conventional, and only safe, formulation. On the former (author personality) we certainly cannot assess the four (or three) cases equally in the absence of contextual evidence about Cratippus and/or the author of the *Hellenica Oxyrhynchia*, but everything we know about Theopompus and Xenophon suggests prominent individuals who engaged with the public issues of their time and had a natural inclination to do so in a historical mode. Thucydides' assertion of the principle of writing contemporary history (and history in which the prime focus was the violent interaction of Greek *poleis*) validated the idea that others who were concerned by the contemporary situation of such *poleis* should pursue that concern through the writing of narrative history; as their contemporary situation was the direct result of Thucydides' contemporary situation (same actors, similar aspirations, different balance of power), continuous historical narrative turns out to be simply logical. (The power of form is clear in the continuation section of Xenophon's *Hellenica* which lies on the edge between historical record and contemporary commentary. Driven by an exemplary and [broadly] political agenda, its form is based on Thucydides and existing completion-continuations, just as elsewhere Xenophon develops other literary forms, more or less predicated on prior generic models, within which to work on a similar range of topics.)

But, if logical, will continuous historical narrative ever stop? Xenophon's answer in the 350s was "not yet," for *Hellenica* ended with an assertion that disorder was unresolved and a suggestion that someone else continue the story (no one did). This suits Xenophon's characteristically open-ended and question-posing frame of mind; but the same should in principle have been true of Theopompus and Cratippus, who also ended at points of non-resolution, viz. the battle of Cnidus and the restoration of Athenian naval potential. By the time Cratippus' text reached its final state, it was already obvious that Conon's triumphant return to Athens in 393 was but a moment in an ongoing tale. But it was certainly a highly symbolic moment (given what happened in 404) and, though Conon disappeared, Thrasybulus failed, and Athens was dragged into the King's Peace, the walls remained intact, and there were still triremes in the Piraeus. For a believer in continuous history (especially an Athenian one), 393 was a possible deliberate endpoint: we do not have to assume that Cratippus followed Thucydides' example and died in harness (though it could be so), but any hope he had that his text would be directly continued was disappointed. The case of Theopompus is, however, different. A positive interpretive gloss can perhaps be given to his focus on 410–394 (the theme is Spartan hegemony and its maritime aspect: see Shrimpton 1991: 36f. and Schepens 1993: 199, though the former's claim that non-maritime events were neglected is based on convoluted argument; for various views on his attitude to Sparta cf. Meyer 1909: 143–144; Momigliano 1931; Lane Fox 1986; Bruce 1987; Flower 1994: 73–74; and especially Schepens 2001c), but one reason for stopping in 394 was surely that a truly contemporary subject now seemed more important, readily researchable, and replete with literary potential. Just as the new conflict of 431 took precedence over any need to continue Herodotus, so the rise of Macedon – an entirely new phenomenon that fell outside the agenda created by the Peloponnesian War (*mutatis mutandis* something *not* true of the Peloponnesian War in relation to the agenda created by the Persian Wars) – took precedence over continuing inspection of the hegemonic rivalries of Athens, Sparta, and Thebes (cf. Flower 1994: 152–153). Theopompus will not have expected anyone to continue his *Hellenica* – and no one did.

In fact, no early exponent of continuous history secured a direct continuator, unless the true scope of Cratippus and/or *Hellenica Oxyrhynchia* was such that he/they were directly carried forward by Callisthenes. Even if so, the first book of his *Hellenica* merely linked Corinthian War narrative to what was in any event his main interest, viz. the collapse of Spartan hegemony in and after 379/8 and the concomitant rise of Athens and Thebes (cf. above, p. 163). Unlike Theopompus, and despite reaching adulthood during the reign of Philip, Callisthenes still considered that narrative of a previous era mattered; Xenophon's treatment was evidently found inadequate (Callisthenes' was longer and wider-ranging), and it was historical judgment, not pedantic continuity, that determined the starting point for a partial replacement whose influence upon the later tradition was marked (and apt to be undervalued) but whose political thrust remains debatable (see, e.g., Sordi 1958a: 194 ff.; Meister 1990: 105; Hornblower 1994d: 10; Stylianou 1998: 121). As we have seen, this way of choosing one's starting point does not rule out "continuous history" (provided that judgment about an era does not turn into selection of a monograph topic), but it makes its definition a bit more fuzzy at the edges. There was, however, one precise link Callisthenes did still have with Theopompus and Xenophon (about Cratippus we cannot tell) – the title *Hellenica*. Bland though it is, it makes a more significant thematic assertion than the Herodotean and Thucydidean *Historiai*: the reader is promised the doings of Greeks – not of one or two individual Greek cities but of a range of them (*de facto* those in the mainland/Aegean region that was the central battleground of Greek hegemony), and not (in their own right) of barbarian powers. (The usage reflects that of fourth-century orators: see, e.g., Aeschin. 1.64; Isoc. 5.107; 7.80; 8.55; 12.11; Dem. 3.25–26; 10.53; 13.7, 35; 14.38; 18.59; Hyp. *Dem.* col. 15.4.) Since none of the authors known to have used the *Hellenica* title was working (or, certainly, finished) before 387/6, the latter point has special resonance. Callisthenes perhaps bought into it with particular clarity (it would be nice to know how clear it was at the time Callisthenes started work that the standoff represented by the King's Peace was not going to last much longer), but his agenda was certainly like that of the others, even if his text variously overlapped or failed to link with theirs: his title guarantees this, and that is why "Continuous Histories (*Hellenica*)" can be a legitimate label – at least thus far.

But only thus far. There is no reliable evidence for continuing use of the title by any relevant author. (The only possible case is Menodotus' fifteen-book *Hellenikai pragmateiai*, known only from Diod. 26.4.) The reason is plain. Contemporaries of Philip and Alexander who set about describing their reigns knew that their subject could not be called *Hellenica* because, without prejudice to the niceties of ethnicity, there was a sufficient sense of distinction and historical dissociation to ensure that the activities of such rulers (especially aggressively successful activities at the expense of Greek states) were a Macedonian, not a Greek, thing. That Theopompus actually had no choice but to find another title (having already used *Hellenica*) does not alter this basic fact, though it must have served to stress it, as did the distinction within Anaximenes' historical work between *Hellenica* (albeit *Hellenica* that embraced the distant past) and *Philippica*: a line is being drawn between different eras of history writing (cf. Pol. 8.11). When Callisthenes embarked upon his *Hellenica* at a time at which Theopompus had (ostentatiously?) abandoned one, he was perhaps making a point: but in due course he turned aside to write a monograph on the Sacred War (was that a product of Delphic interests, or the realization that the conflict crucially changed the old political geography, or both?) and then to become wholly (and fatally) involved with Alexander. As time went on and a new world was born of Alexander's legacy, any diminution (and how much was there?) in the sense that Macedonian rulers were alien to "Greek" historical experience was more than compensated by the fact that some Macedonian rulers were firmly based outside the traditional mainland/Aegean theater. The broad-scale regional conflict between hegemonic powers involving

Greek city-states that is the early Hellenistic parallel for the conflicts of the first half of the fourth century was driven by powers based in Asia or Egypt in a way in which the Persian kings, however important in the formation of classical Greek historical experience, never achieved: the canvas of "Greek" history became hard to distinguish from that of universal history – and that (precisely) was not *Hellenica*. So Greek historians of the era (i.e., historians who themselves came from Greek cities) certainly adopted the principle of continuous record but (it could be felt) were not writing Greek history.

The principle of ensuring a continuous treatment of broad-scale history is a distinctive one: it marks off genuine exemplars of Jacobian *Zeitgeschichte* from all sorts of other things that can count as history writing. And it is distinctively Greek: at Rome, successive generations of annalists extended the historical record, but they kept on starting again from the beginning, even if later parts of the story got proportionally longer. This happened because of the abiding importance of the state's early history for Roman identity, both in general and for the manipulative purposes of individual families. There is nothing parallel or comparably peremptory in relation to the Greek world at large or, given a less coherently aristocratic environment, to individual cities; the contrast reflects the fact that Greece and Rome are incommensurate terms. But in assigning to Phylarchus and Duris the categorical description (but not the title) *Hellenica*, Marincola (2001: 106) ought to be not merely affirming that the principle of continuous record is alive (let alone reborn). That would be a weak or false claim, since the Philip and Alexander historians certainly ensured the maintenance of such a record: in this respect there is only a specious distinction between (on the one hand) the texts discussed above from the earlier fourth century and the early Hellenistic period and (on the other) narrative works on Philip and Alexander: once one allows (as one must) that continuous history does not require precise chain-link continuation at all points, the latter set (which have start and end dates just as much as the others) are part of the series. Flower (1994: 156) warns that Theopompus' boast (115 F 25) of having written 20,000 lines of epideictic oratory and 150,000 lines of prose in which "it is possible to find the affairs of both the Greeks and the barbarians being reported up to the present time" is not a claim to have created a *de facto* universal history; but it is a claim, of sorts, about continuous history.

Classification of Duris and Phylarchus as writers of *Hellenica* must be suggesting a more substantial qualitative link. But what can this be? The facts of style that used to fuel talk of tragic history and are now better understood (Gray 1987; Marincola 2003) did probably distinguish the experience of reading them from that of reading Xenophon or the Oxyrhynchus historian or (so far as we have any ground for supposing) Cratippus and the *Hellenica* of Callisthenes and Theopompus: that is, although vivid writing can be found all over the place (even in Thucydides or Polybius), Duris and Phylarchus were as a general rule more given to such things and did it more imaginatively – even inventively. But perhaps this is a surface matter, not inconsistent with more serious historiographical continuity. Unfortunately, nothing presents itself that plainly serves to distinguish the relationship of our two authors to their predecessors from that of their contemporaries and successors.

Of course, we are hampered by poverty of information. Where Kebric (1977: 21–22, 31, 47) affirms that Duris gave an anti-Macedonian color to his treatment of Macedonian hegemony, raising the possibility that Duris was an aggressively Hellenic historian, Pédech (1989: 347–348) can virtually claim the opposite, while conceding denunciation of particular bits of immorality, and no one can be sure which (if either) is correct. In any case to affirm a link between political "hellenism" and a distinctive inheritance from earlier writers of *Hellenica* (which neither Kebric nor Pédech does) would look like equivocation or an admission that Duris was operating in too different a world for the assertion of generic continuity to be helpful. On the other hand Pédech's attempt (1989: 492) to capture the difference between Phylarchus and Thucydides or Xenophon just takes us back to propositions about style, inevitably more colored by Polybian bile than by any ability to read much of the author at length. In short, I doubt we can see Duris or Phylarchus clearly enough to adopt anything but a rather brusque approach, in line with the earlier remarks about title choice. Bluntly, we must either remove the title *Hellenica* from our genre criteria, in which case Duris and Phylarchus are not the only continuous historians of the Hellenistic era (and the genre of continuous history becomes a touch amorphous), or – I think preferably – we must insist upon it, in which case our genre is a distinct sub-set of continuous history, has a brief lifespan from Cratippus to Callisthenes, and corresponds to the last generations of Greek freedom. (Which is not to say that the works involved only appear as reactions to the Macedonian threat – or are the only historiographical reaction to that threat: the Ephoran project could equally be seen in that light. Another perspective stresses Ephorus' origin in Greek Anatolia: cf. variously Will 1991: 127; Breglia Pulcia Doria 1996.) A byproduct of the Peloponnesian War and Thucydides' incomplete account thereof, they established the principle that the story of conflict between powerful states never comes to a stop. Originally the states involved are *poleis*, but the idea proved extensible to any version of the Greek world in which conflicting powers (of whatever sort) still existed. The ever more dominant power of Rome would in due course render the principle obsolete.

FURTHER READING

For presentation and critiques of Jacoby's generic analysis of historiography (in which *Hellenica*/continuous histories form a sub-set of *Zeitgeschichte*), see Fornara 1983: 1–46; Marincola 1999. In the latter's alternative analysis *Hellenica* fall into the category of texts focalized on the nation as a "group of city-states." Some of the modalities of Thucydides-continuation are discussed (in rather different ways) in Gray 1991; Schepens 1993; and Rood 2004. For treatments of relevant individual historians see: Chambers 1993 and Schepens 2001b (*Hellenica Oxyrhynchia*); Pédech 1970 and Lehmann 1976 (Cratippus); Lane Fox 1986, Pédech 1989: 17–254, Shrimpton 1991, Flower 1994, and Schepens 2004 (Theopompus); Prandi 1985 (Callisthenes); Hornblower 1981 (Hieronymus); Kebric 1977, Pédech 1989: 255–389, and Landucci Gattinoni 1997 (Duris); Pédech 1989: 391–493 (Phylarchus). There is much to be learned about Ephorus and other aspects of the historiography of the pre-Macedonian fourth century from Stylianou 1998 (esp. 85–131).

CHAPTER THIRTEEN

Universal History from Ephorus to Diodorus

John Marincola

1 Writing "Universally"

If universal historians are "those who study the history of mankind from the earliest times and in all parts of the world known to them" (Alonso-Núñez 2002: 117), then not all of the historians mentioned in this chapter can be considered such. Since, however, generic boundaries in antiquity were fluid and constantly capable of redefinition (Marincola 1999), the term may still be of some use in covering a wide range of Greek authors (for the Latin Trogus, below, p. 287) who, by their own admission or in the judgment of later writers, "wrote universally" (*ta katholou graphein*, Pol. 5.33.2) or treated "world events" (Green's felicitous translation of *koinai praxeis*, Diod. 1.4.6). In antiquity, to write universally comprehended at least two different types of history: first, histories that covered the entire known world (*oikoumenē*) from earliest recorded times to the author's own day, i.e., universal in time and space; second, histories that treated known events within a restricted time period, i.e., universal only in space. Although the seeds of such interest can be traced back as far as Herodotus (Burde 1974: 9–17; Vattuone 1998; Vannicelli 2001), it was the fourth century that saw the first truly universal historians, a genre that thereafter was attempted by many. The main Greek practitioners of the first type were Ephorus (§2), Timagenes of Alexandria (author of an *On Kings* that went from earliest times down to Julius Caesar: Jacoby, *Komm.* II.C.222), Diodorus (§4), and Kephalion (a history from Ninus and Semiramis to Alexander the Great: *FGrHist* 93 T 2). The most comprehensive history (and the longest written in antiquity) was that of Nicolaus of Damascus (*FGrHist* 90), tutor of Antony and Cleopatra's children, friend and advisor to Herod the Great, who in 144 books treated earliest times down to the death of Herod in 4 BCE (Toher 1987). Practitioners of the second type included Theopompus of Chios (§3), Polybius (below, p. 245), and his continuators,

Posidonius of Apamea (fifty-two books covering 146 to the mid-80s BCE: below, p. 250) and Strabo of Amaseis (*FGrHist* 91: forty-three books from 146 probably to 27 BCE; Dueck 2000: 70).

2   Ephorus

Ephorus came from Cyme in Asia Minor (*FGrHist* 70 T 1) but we know practically nothing about his life. He was probably born around 405 and died sometime after 330. His father's name is recorded as Demophilus (also the name of his son), and the ancients include him with Theopompus as a student of Isocrates (TT 3–6), though on both counts this is unlikely to be anything other than inference or guesswork (Jacoby, *Komm.* II.C.22–23; Flower 1994: 42–62).

Although he wrote several other works – including a work on his home town, treatises *On Inventions* (*Peri Heurēmatōn*) and *On Style* (*Peri Lexeōs*) – his most important work was the *Histories*, in thirty books, the last one brought out by his son Demophilus. It was on a scale not seen before, beginning with the Return of the Heraclidae (the sons of Heracles) and ending with Philip II's siege of Perinthus (T 10), i.e., from 1069 to 341/0. Ephorus treated not only Greek events but also those of the east (particularly Persia), of Sicily and the Greek west, and, from 360 on, of Macedon in the north.

Given that Ephorus was the first to attempt such a wide-ranging history (Pol. 5.33.2), his arrangement of such a large amount of material was crucial. Diodorus (5.1.4) says that he organized his work *kata genos*, the likeliest interpretation of which suggests an arrangement by individual topic, i.e., by grouping common events according to their geographical area rather than – like Thucydides – following an annalistic arrangement in which one ordered events strictly within a particular year (Drews 1963, 1976; but cf. the modifications of Vannicelli 1987). This arrangement facilitated comprehension (a story could be followed through to its conclusion) but also obviated chronological problems, since Ephorus could use whatever chronology was appropriate or traditional for each area, without having to work out a universal chronology (Schepens 1977a: 116). The first three books of the *Histories* dealt with the origins of the individual Greek city-states, a topic in which Ephorus seems to have had a particular interest and competence (T 18a), while Books 4–5 were geographical in nature. Book 6 commenced the history proper; by Book 11 Ephorus was already at the Persian Wars (490–479); by Book 21 he was in the early fourth century. Thereafter, as was to become standard for large-scale histories (perhaps because later historians actually followed Ephorus' example), the treatment became more detailed as he approached his own times: the last ten books covered just over forty-five years (387–340).

Despite the wretched state of the fragments, enough survives to show that Ephorus had much to say about the writing of history, and history itself. He divided his history into individual books, beginning each with a preface, where he most likely discussed arrangement and methodology. In the general introduction he took the Platonic line that *mousikē* was introduced for the purposes of deception and beguilement (F 8): Polybius (4.20.5) criticized him for this, but Ephorus was probably contrasting the deception inherent in poetry with the truth-value of history (much as Polybius was later to do in his own comparison of tragedy with history, 2.56). Perhaps, in conjunction with this, Ephorus spoke also of the difference between history and epideictic oratory, and said that the former required infinitely more effort than the latter (F 111), no doubt because of the need to collect sources and investigate places. He also made a methodological point by beginning with the Return of the Heraclidae, thus effectively skipping over the entire early "history" of Greece. Occasionally, however, in digressions or when it was apposite, he treated early times (FF 31–34, e.g.), but when he did, he used the tools of rationalization that had been employed from Hecataeus onward: in his narrative of Apollo at Delphi, for example, the Python whom Apollo slays is actually a beast-like man named Drakon ("Snake"). Such activity, however, should not be seen as essentially in conflict with his attitude towards myth, which he sharply distinguished from historical truth (F 31b).

Given the vast size of his work, Ephorus, not surprisingly, had to rely for much of his history on earlier writers, and, at least in the non-contemporary portions, he probably made no pretense to original investigations. F 9, probably from Book 1, explains one way in which he evaluated sources:

> Ephorus says that when writing about our own times (*kath' hēmas*), we consider those speaking most accurately (*akribestata*) to be the most reliable; but concerning things long ago (*tōn palaiōn*), those who proceed in such a way we consider most untrustworthy, since we assume that it is not probable, given the great distance in time, that all of the deeds or a majority of the speeches would be remembered.

Ephorus probably went on to say that he would use those "most accurate" (i.e., most detailed) sources – most likely those historians who were contemporaries of the events they described – in his own account (Schepens 1977a: 103–107; above, p. 50). He did not limit himself to historians, however, quarrying information also from poets, other writers (such as orators), and inscriptions to fill out his narrative (Barber 1935: 127–130; Sunseri 1997: 161–167; Flower 1998; Parker 2004 [2006]: 29–33). How Ephorus treated the events of his own time is not certain, but it seems that he used the Oxyrhynchus historian until about 386 (when that work concluded) and that thereafter (for the last forty years or so) he conducted his own researches for the contemporary portion of his work (Parker 2004 [2006]: 40–45, arguing against the *communis opinio* that he used Callisthenes for these later years).

Ephorus has sometimes been faulted for his provincial bias towards his home town Cyme (F 236), but he was also the man who first united western Greek history with its mainland counterpart, going so far even to assert that it was Gelon's victory against Carthage at the time of the Persian Wars that "freed not only Sicily but all Greece" (F 186). He has been sometimes faulted for explaining the outbreak of the Peloponnesian War by reference to the character of Pericles (F 196), but this probably indicates that he thought individuals of great importance in determining the direction of their cities. Indeed, like the whole community of fourth-century writers, he was strongly interested in moralism. The nature and extent of this moralism, nevertheless, seems to me an open question, although most scholars believe that it was presented in an ongoing and explicit form, and that it at times even led him to falsify history (an extreme application in Pownall 2004: 111–142). It certainly cannot be denied that Ephorus was interested in character, both of individuals and of nations: Polybius praises him particularly for his evaluation of historical actors (12.28.10), and we have quite a number of examples of his interest in the *mores* of peoples Greek and barbarian (e.g., FF 42, 54, 148, 149). But the question is one of *scale* and context (Ephorus' history, after all, comprised a vast amount of material), and it must be factored in with Ephorus' reputation for reliability and accuracy: even Polybius, who found fault with Ephorus' descriptions of land battles (12.25f, where, however, he praises his description of naval battles – a point often overlooked by scholars), nevertheless included him among "the most renowned of the older writers" (6.45.1). No doubt both for his moralism and his reliability he was much used and much praised in antiquity, becoming one of the canonical historians (Schwartz 1907: 24–26; Barber 1935: 157–159), inspiring continuators in the next generation (i.a. Diyllus and Psaon: Diod. 16.14.5; 21.5), and serving as a model in different ways for Polybius and Diodorus.

3   Theopompus

Theopompus was born around 378/7 on Chios, and as a young man was exiled with his father Damasistratos for pro-Spartan leanings. Thanks to the intercession of Alexander the Great, he returned to Chios in 333/2 at the age of 45, but he was exiled a second time after Alexander's death, and came eventually to Ptolemy's court. He died soon after 320. Theopompus himself says (*FGrHist* 115 F 25) that "there was no important public space or eminent city of the Greeks that he did not visit" and everywhere he left behind "great fame and the memory of his literary excellence." He claimed to have written more than 20,000 lines of epideictic speeches and 150,000 lines in which he treated "the deeds of Greeks and barbarians down to his own day" – the latter surely a reference to his historical works.

Those works began probably with an epitome of Herodotus, then a *Hellenica* (twelve books, continuing Thucydides to 394), finishing with his greatest achievement, the *Philippica*, so-called because of Philip of Macedon, the dominant figure of his age: "Europe," Theopompus claimed in the preface (F 27), "had never before produced such a man as Philip." Such an individual-centered history had important consequences for later writers (Fornara 1983: 34), but Theopompus also has a claim to be considered a "universal" historian: he wrote, after all, "the deeds of Greeks and barbarians," and did not limit himself to Philip or Macedon, but rather ranged far afield, including periods and places that had nothing to do with Philip. His excursuses included treatments of Persian history from ca. 394–344 (eight books), Asia Minor (four books), Sicilian history (three books), and Spain and Italy (two books), not to mention one on earlier Athenian history (for the arrangement of Theopompus' history see Pédech 1989: 73–206; Shrimpton 1991: 59–94). In Book 8 he devoted an entire section to marvelous occurrences (*Thaumasia*), which he introduced with the provocative claim that "he would narrate myths better than Herodotus, Ctesias, Hellanicus and the writers on India" (F 381) – but the very self-consciousness suggests that he did not take these stories seriously. Dionysius must be referring to this range when he says (*Pomp.* 6) that Theopompus "treated settlements of nations and foundings of cities, lives of kings and peculiarities of customs, and his work embraced whatever was marvellous or unusual in every land and sea." It is not, therefore, unreasonable to see Theopompus' history in some ways as a contemporary universal history, a kind of predecessor for Polybius' history, with the histories of various lands united not by Rome but by Philip (Bruce 1970: 108–109; Meister 1990: 91; Vattuone 1998: 78–84; *contra*, Flower 1994: 154–160) – even if the organization was looser and Polybius was to chastise him for centering his history around an individual (8.11.3–8).

As the author of a contemporary history, Theopompus engaged in the travels necessary to see sites and interview participants. Dionysius (*Pomp.* 6) says that "he was an eyewitness of many events and he met with many of the leading men of his day, generals, popular leaders, and philosophers" – and with kings, of course, since he spent time at Philip's court as well (T 7). Such close contact, however, did not lead Theopompus to flatter the subjects of his history – quite the contrary. His reputation in antiquity, borne out by the verbatim fragments that survive, was of a man scathing in his criticism of contemporaries (and non-contemporaries, as well), finding fault with his age for its physical and moral degeneracy. Unlike Ephorus, who seems to have shown both good and bad models of behavior, Theopompus focused relentlessly on what was corrupt and degenerate. His was a "history without heroes" (Connor 1967), treating even Philip to the same sort of criticism leveled against others. Democracies fared no better: Theopompus attacked the demagogues of Athens in a special digression which reached back to the earliest Athenian leaders (FF 85–100), and he called into question Athens' claims to greatness at the time of the Persian Wars (F 153 with Connor 1968: 78–89). For only a few men – the Spartans Lysander, Agesilaus, and Pedaritus – did he have words of praise: no wonder Plutarch says (*Lys.* 30.2) that Theopompus is more reliable when he praises than when he censures!

His style, some examples of which are preserved (e.g., FF 162, 213, 263, 291), was lively, at times even bombastic, but we should beware of assuming that it was consistently so. It is more likely that his general narrative style was rather evenly paced (Duris even complained that his work lacked effective imitation [*mimēsis*] and pleasure [*hēdonē*]: *FGrHist* 76 F 1, with Gray 1987), and that at certain crucial moments, where outrage was demanded, he raised the tone to effect his point (cf. D. Hal. *Pomp.* 6: "in some passages, when he gives free play to his emotions" – which suggests the occasional heightening).

Theopompus was much read in antiquity. Pompeius Trogus modeled his own history on him, and Dionysius valued him greatly. Polybius, however, criticized his battle descriptions and his excessively negative disposition (TT 19, 32), and Plutarch found fault with his overly rhetorical speeches (T 33). He was also taken to task for his censoriousness and bitter tone, which to some seemed more fitting to a prosecutor than a historian (T 25a). In the modern world his political and moral outlook have been very differently evaluated. He has been seen as everything from an intent Panhellenist (Bury 1908: 165) to a disengaged Cynic (Murray 1946). Yet Theopompus and his *Philippica* seem to defy categorization – perhaps exactly as he intended. Although not a universal historian in the strict sense, he shares with Ephorus (and indeed Herodotus) a catholic interest in men and *mores*, in lands and cultures, and in the relationship between character and achievement (see Flower 1994: 160–165 for Herodotus' influence).

4   Diodorus of Sicily

Diodorus' *Historical Library* (*Bibliothēkē Historikē*) is the only universal history to (largely) survive from antiquity. Diodorus was born in Agyrion (1.1.4), but spent a great amount of time in Rome, where he learned Latin and availed himself of the excellent research facilities there (1.4.2–4). He says (1.4.1) that he traveled through much of Europe and Asia to inspect the sites of his history, and he mentions (1.44.1) a specific visit to Egypt during the 180th Olympiad (i.e., 60–57 BCE). He worked thirty years on his history (1.4.1), and, although his birth and death dates are uncertain, it is likely that this activity lasted from approximately 60 to 30 BCE. His history was probably not fully revised at the time of his death (1.4.6; cf. Green 2006: 30 with n. 145).

Diodorus' history comprised forty books, from the origins of the world down to his own day, ending probably in the year 60 (Sacks 1990: 169–184; Green 2006: 237–241). Books 1–5 survive complete, as do 11–20, with the rest in fragmentary state, a situation that hampers our ability to see Diodorus' true worth as a historian since (as with Livy) we have mainly the earliest times and not the more contemporary portions of his work. Not surprisingly, he claimed (4.1) Ephorus as his inspiration, but felt he surpassed his predecessor by including the earliest "mythical" times (and, unlike Ephorus, he did not simply rationalize myth but placed original and rationalized versions side by side: Marincola 1997: 119–121; cf. Ambaglio 1995: 39–57). Books 1–3 treated earliest non-Greek history (Egypt, Assyria, Media), 4–6 that of the Greeks (Book 5 focuses largely on islands and the myths that surround them). Books 7–17 went from the Trojan War to Alexander (though early Roman history is included), 18–40 from Alexander's death to Diodorus' time. In Books 7 through 22, it was Greek history that stood in the foreground, while thereafter Roman history became predominant.

Diodorus followed a twofold arrangement. For events before the Trojan War, where accurate chronology was lacking (1.5.1), he arranged his material, like Ephorus, by category, treating events of this or that nation in this or that part of the world. From 776 onwards, however, Diodorus decided to arrange events annalistically, and what is more, he attempted to integrate different chronological systems within his history, dating events by Athenian archons, Roman consuls, and Olympic victors. For this he used Apollodorus of Athens (below, p. 522), among others, but it was perhaps inevitable that many errors would be made (though whether by Diodorus or his sources cannot always be known). For one thing, the Athenian archon-year began in mid-summer, while the Roman consuls took office on March 1 (January 1 from 152 BCE on). Add to this that Diodorus often succumbed to the temptation to tell a story from beginning to end in one place (even if the events took place over several years) and you have all the ingredients for chronological disaster. Diodorus recognized the problem, but only in a general way, not as it applied to his specific situation (20.43.7):

> [O]ne might find fault with history, when one sees that in life many different actions end at the same time, but that it is necessary for those who record them to interrupt the narrative and to parcel out different times to simultaneous events contrary to nature; and so the experience of the events contains truth, but the narrative account, lacking similar power, imitates the events, but falls far short of true arrangement (*mimeisthai men ta gegenēmena, polu de leipesthai tēs alēthous diatheseōs*).

This is an important point about historical narration, one that continues to be debated by historiographical theorists today, but Diodorus' is largely an aesthetic judgment, unconcerned with the pragmatic difficulties of combining sources in an era before a universal calendar existed.

Like Ephorus, Diodorus was dependent on written sources for the bulk, if not the entirety, of his work. The title of *Library* suggests a collection of excerpts from historians, and indeed, from the nineteenth century on, Diodorus has been thought a "scissors-and-paste" historian, one who, page after page, blithely and uncritically transcribed his sources, even when they contradicted one another. The style in which he cast his predecessors is certainly his own (Palm 1955), but even so, some scholars have held that his interventions in the sources are minimal, and that therefore he, more than any other historian, provides a window onto several lost historians. Indeed, in certain cases it seems fairly certain that this source can be identified: Hecataeus of Abdera for much of Book 1; Ephorus for the Greek history in Books 11–20; Hieronymus of Cardia for the history of the Diadochs in Books 18–19.

Two issues, however, complicate the matter. The first question is whether or not Diodorus followed a *single* source for long periods of time, a question to which some scholars give an unqualified yes (e.g., Hornblower 1981: 18–75; Stylianou 1998: 49–50, with reff. to earlier works). If this is the case, then we can be pretty certain that (to take one example) it is all pretty much Ephorus for the Greek history of the fifth and fourth centuries. But what if Diodorus used a primary source for long parts and consistently referred to one or more *secondary* sources? That would make the attribution of any particular passage more difficult (Drews 1962; Meister 1990: 178). The second issue is to what extent the opinions and evaluations expressed in the *Library* belong to Diodorus or his sources. Earlier scholars did not hesitate to attribute even the material of Diodorus' prefaces to his sources (Posidonius being the favorite for the general preface of Book 1). The matter is of importance not only for those who would use Diodorus to reconstruct lost histories, but also for those interested in the work of Diodorus that we actually have (admittedly, a far smaller number). For this question really concerns the extent to which Diodorus shaped his own work, giving (or trying to give) thematic unity to a vast account that embraced many different nations and many different types of action over a long period of time.

Although some scholars continue to believe that even the opinions expressed by Diodorus are those of his source (see, e.g., Meister 1973/1974; Canfora 1990), some now give Diodorus greater credit for the shaping of particular themes and interests in his work. In this approach, much of the narrative proper – the actions, motivations, even the speeches of the historical actors – is owed to Diodorus' source, while the selection of incidents for highlighting, the lessons drawn from the events, and the larger interpretive framework into which the events are slotted are those of Diodorus himself. The fact that certain themes recur with great frequency throughout Diodorus' work strongly argues against a single source for them.

Sacks, who has most energetically argued this position, has pointed out, for example, that Diodorus is concerned throughout his history with benefactors (*euergetai*) of mankind, and the ways in which they have helped humans to advance and prosper (Sacks 1990: 61–82). Perhaps not coincidentally, Diodorus sees the historian's work in this light (1.1.3):

> It is right that all people offer great thanks to those who compose universal histories (*koinai praxeis*), because they have tried to benefit by their individual efforts our common life (*koinon bion*). By offering an education without danger in what is beneficial they give their readers, by their presentation, an experience which is the finest. [...] As if servants of divine providence, they have tried to present in one and the same account all peoples, who, although separated by place and time, have a kinship with one another.

Another interest exhibited by Diodorus is in the nature and success of empires, an appropriately "universal" theme for such a long work. Here again Diodorus takes an independent line from his predecessors, arguing that kind actions by ruling states inspire loyalty in their subjects, but that when this turns to harsh or overbearing actions, disaffection arises, which eventually leads to the empire's downfall (Sacks 1990: 42–54; 1994: 216–220). Living, as he did, during the ravages of the late republic (Sacks 1990: 161–168), Diodorus does not hesitate to criticize the ruling power, Rome (32.4.5), and to assimilate her to this pattern of rise and fall of previous empires. Naturally, the format of universal history is ideal for creating patterns of just this sort, where later events and individuals can be interpreted in light of their predecessors.

5   Conclusion

Universal historians are often criticized for what they are *not*: not primary researchers, not keen political analysts, not discriminating in their use of sources. That, of course, is to misunderstand the nature of their work. Although they claimed to have bettered their predecessors in some things, they seem to have made no pretense to "original" research for the non-contemporary portions of their histories: but in this they were no different from all other ancient historians, whose "research" of the past consisted of the systematic study of, and incremental improvement on, their predecessors' works (Marincola 1997: 105–107; Bosworth 2003).

The benefits of their histories, as they saw them, were manifold. First, they provided for their audience a compendium of what was known about the world, all within the convenience of a single work. By writing a single-stranded history, so to speak, their works could be used by those without the time or money to procure and read the large number of histories on individual topics. Second, they provided such information in an up-to-date and uniform style, something that likewise assisted in the reading of earlier events. Third, such universal works facilitated the understanding of history, if not always in the Polybian sense of seeing the interconnectedness of causes and effects (above, p. 149), then in the more general sense of showing continuity and change, and discernible patterns – such as rise and fall – throughout all of recorded time, and of the variety of permutations that such patterns could take (Clarke 1999b: 256–261). Finally, and perhaps most importantly, they used the vast canvas of their narrative to create paradigms – predominantly, but not exclusively, moral – of the characters who had made history whether for good or ill. Such emphasis on moralism and paradigmaticism was (again) not unique to universal historians: but they could make the claim that their histories were superior because they contained the greatest number of such events and were therefore of the greatest use to their readers.

FURTHER READING

Useful overviews of universal history can be found in Breebaart 1966; Burde 1974; Momigliano 1982a; Alonso-Núñez 1990 and 2002; and Clarke 1999b.

On Ephorus, it is astonishing that the sole monograph devoted to this important author remains the ancient (and now rather outdated) Barber 1935. Schwartz 1907 is still worth reading; more recent studies of importance are Schepens 1970 and 1977a; Pownall 2004: 111–142.

Theopompus, by contrast, has been well served by recent books. Connor 1968 concentrates on Theopompus' treatment of Athens. Shrimpton 1991 is a substantial overview (with all of the testimonia and fragments translated), while Flower 1994 is more focused on Theopompus' place in the historiographical tradition, and on establishing how he was influenced by the contemporary intellectual climate. Other worthwhile treatments are Bruce 1970 and Pédech 1989: 17–254.

For Diodorus see Schwartz 1905 and Farrington 1947: 55–87. The scissors-and-paste Diodorus is defended most recently in Stylianou 1998: 132–139, while Drews 1962 and Sacks 1990 and 1994 emphasize Diodorus' independence of thought. To them can now be added Green 2006, which provides a judicious overview and spirited defense of Diodorus (cf. also below, Ch. 33), as well as a fine translation of Books 11–12.37.1, with copious annotation.

CHAPTER FOURTEEN

Local History and Atthidography

Phillip Harding

1   Introduction

In the volume of his collection devoted to histories of individual states, Jacoby lists more than three hundred works (*FGrHist* 297–607). Seventy-eight different cities or territories are represented from Achaea to Troezen, sometimes with multiple authors. It will be no surprise that the largest entry is for Athens (more that fifty authors and about 200 pages of fragments). By comparison, the second largest collection encompasses the whole area of Sicily and Magna Graecia (twenty-three authors and almost 150 pages of fragments). Most other places have much less, some with barely a fragment or two preserved. Many of the works listed are, in fact, mere names of authors or titles. This chapter will be similarly constrained to use the more abundant evidence from and about Athenian authors as the basis of its study of ancient Greek local historiography in general, though it will bring in parallel evidence wherever appropriate. The discussion will restrict itself to works that can reasonably be considered to have covered the whole of a state's history and will exclude monographs about some special aspect, as, for example, the constitution (*politeia*). But it must always be kept in mind that, whatever conclusions are advanced about the nature of the genre, they will always be based upon fragments (or *reliquiae*, as Brunt 1980: 477, prefers to call them) of the originals and that, consequently, they could be quite mistaken (cf. Harding 1994: v–vi).

2   Form and Style

Despite what has just been said, we have a fairly good idea of the form and style of the Athenian version of the genre (the *Atthis*), and no good reason to think that other states' histories were much different. We owe this knowledge not only to the fragments of the individual authors, but also to the comments of ancient scholars, especially Dionysius of Halicarnassus. At the end of the preface to his *Roman Antiquities*, he distinguishes the form of his history from others, specifically those that are exclusively about wars or constitutions and "the chronicles, which those who have written the *Atthides* have published" (*AR* 1.8.3). A later scholar elaborates on the nature of these "chronicles" in a note on one of the authors, Philochorus, stating that "he encompasses the deeds of the Athenians and their kings and archons" (Suda s.v. "Philochorus"). Finally, the surviving fragments of the authors of the *Atthides* (the Atthidographers: Hellanicus, Cleidemus, Androtion, Phanodemus, Demon, Melanthius, Philochorus, Ister) and the works derived from them clarify what is meant: the Atthidographers structured their work around the reigns of kings and the magistracies of archons (cf. Harding 1994: 3–6). Some idea of what this might have looked like in a bare-bones form, but with chronographic data added, can be seen from later chronologies that were in part derived from or based upon the *Atthis*, such as the Parian Marble (*FGrHist* 239), the *Chronica* of Apollodorus (*FGrHist* 240), or that of Castor of Rhodes (*FGrHist* 250). Castor preserves the only complete list of Athenian kings and his work was itself a source for Eusebius' *Chronica* (Mosshammer 1979: 130) and, probably through him, of Syncellus' great chronography of world history from the creation onward (Adler and Tuffin 2002: lv–lxix).

The relationship between a chronology and a local history (chronicle) can be illustrated by comparing the first entry in the Parian Marble with known fragments of an *Atthis*, that of Philochorus, since his work is the best preserved. In its heading the Parian Marble announces that it is recording "dates," starting from the time of Cecrops, "who first was king over the Athenians, down to the archonship . . . of Diognetos at Athens" (264/3 BCE). It then records as its first entry (*FGrHist* 239 A 1) that 1,318 years before Diognetos (i.e., 1556 BCE) "Cecrops became king of Athens and the land got the name Cecropia, which had previously been called Aktike, after Aktaios, the autochthon." Both king and archon are typical of the *Atthis*, as is the historical note, but the chronographic calculation is the result of Hellenistic Alexandrian scholarship. On the other hand, the local historian's entry under Cecrops was far more varied in its scope and detail. We know from FF 92–97 of Philochorus' history that he discussed Ogygos and Aktaios, the precursors of Cecrops, and, unlike the Parian Marble (the author of which had clearly used a different *Atthis*), denied the existence of the latter (F 92); that he attempted to rationalize Cecrops' nickname, "bi-form," by suggesting that he had an extra large body or that he spoke two languages (F 93); that he believed that Cecrops brought the people together into twelve communities (*poleis*), because the land was being attacked by the Carians and the Boeotians, and he has given us the names of the twelve cities (F 94); that he attributed a primitive form of census to Cecrops, by way of explaining a proverbial expression (F 95), and that he considered him the founder of the cult of Kronos and Rhea in Attica (F 97).

No doubt Philochorus had more to say about Cecrops, but this is all that remains. He proceeded to give similarly detailed entries under each successive king, listing them by name in family relationships (e.g., son, brother), in the manner of the genealogists (for the full list see Harding 1994: 4–5). There is insufficient evidence to show that he (or any Atthidographer) calculated the length of a reign any more precisely than by generations or subdivided it into separate years. By contrast, the chronographer claimed to know such data and listed his events by dates. In sum, the chronicler and the chronographer used the same material, but for different purposes. For the chronicler, the names of kings served as a framework upon which to develop a narrative of a state's mythical past.

This is no less true when we reach the time of annual magistracies. In Athens this took the form of the eponymous archons, whose names had been kept from the time of the first holder of the office (Creon in 683/2) and had been published on a marble stele sometime in the last quarter of the fifth century. In other states the eponymous office had different titles, but they were similarly preserved and served the same function. As Jacoby was at great pains to demonstrate (1949: 86–99, 169–176), these lists were merely names and were not accompanied by historical notes; nevertheless, they became the framework for what may be loosely termed the "historical" part of a local history (Harding 1994: 3). The format employed was that the heading for a given year was marked by the name of the magistrate, accompanied by some specific identification, wherever known. For example, in the case of Athens, archons' names are often accompanied by their demotic (deme-name), at least for the post-Cleisthenic period. Following that, the first entry under that name was introduced by the formula "in the term of office of this man. . . ." Other events of that same year were listed in chronological order. An excellent example of this format can be seen in Dionysius' first *Letter to Ammaeus* (9), where three separate parts of the Athenian response to Philip of Macedon's attack on Olynthus were cited verbatim from Philochorus' account of the year of Callimachus from Pergase (349/8). These were excerpted by Dionysius from an annual account that clearly contained intervening material that broke up the narrative of the Olynthian war, because it had to be inserted in chronological sequence. The passage is so important as an illustration of the method and style of the horographer that it deserves to be quoted in full:

> As Philochorus makes clear in the sixth book of his *Atthis*, writing verbatim as follows: "Callimachus from Pergase: In this man's term of office the Athenians made an alliance with the people of Olynthus, who were under attack by Philip and had sent ambassadors to Athens; as assistance they dispatched 2,000 peltasts and the 30 triremes that were with Chares, and they manned 8 others as well." Then after narrating a few intervening events he continues: "About the same time, since the Chalcidians in Thrace were being worn down by the war and had sent an embassy to Athens, the Athenians sent Charidemus, the general in the Hellespont, to assist them. With 18 triremes, 4,000 light-armed troops and 150 cavalry he joined the Olynthians in invading Pallene and Bottiaea and laid waste the land." Further on he writes the following about the third alliance: "Once again the Olynthians sent ambassadors to Athens and were beseeching (them) not to overlook the fact that they had been exhausted by war, but to send them help in addition to the forces already there. This help should not be composed of mercenaries, but of Athenians themselves. The Athenians sent them 17 additional triremes, 2,000 citizen-hoplites and 300 citizen-cavalry in horse-transports. Chares was the general in charge of the whole expedition."

This excerpt demonstrates not only how a chronicler organized his material within his annual entries but also how he showed their temporal relationship to one another (e.g., "about the same time") and connected two related incidents that had been separated by intrusive data (e.g., "once again"). It also shows that the chronicler did not write just notes but complete sentences with subordinate clauses. Nevertheless, at the same time it justifies Dionysius' criticism that the style of the chronicle was "monotonous and hard for the reader to stomach" (*AR* 1.8.3).

3 Content and Sources

The contents of a local history covered a large variety of topics, ranging from the origins of names of places and topographical phenomena, of families, of cults and religious sites and festivals, of political, administrative, and legal institutions, of famous sayings (proverbs) and traditional tales to precise details of recorded or contemporary events. The accounts and explanations (*aitia*) of origins were usually found in the early books of a state's history and their function was surely to lay the foundation for a people's identity. In part, they set the stage for the interpretation of the more immediate events recorded in the later books. But the reverse is also true, namely, that the past was revisited and reviewed through the eyes of the present (Thomas 1989: *passim*). In the case of Athens the introduction of democracy exerted a dominant influence over the interpretation of its early history, though not to the extent we find in the *epitaphios logos* (Loraux 1986: *passim*). It is not uncommon to distinguish the different narratives as "mythical" and "historical" and from our perspective these terms may not seem inappropriate. So often the early books contain accounts that seem fabricated and blatantly self-serving: what might be called "the politics of myth" (Loraux 2000: 29). It is well to remember, however, that for the authors of local histories these "mythical" accounts were embedded in oral tradition, which for their community was its "history." Similar material, often colored by their experience after contact with Europeans, can be found in the narratives of First Nations Peoples in many countries and its validity for them cannot be denied. Recently this type of mythico-historical tradition, which represents the way a "society interprets and understands itself" through its "social knowledge of the past," has been given the more innocuous title "intentional history" (Gehrke 2001: 286).

4 Origins

Every Greek community traced its origin to a founder. Sometimes this would be a "real" person, the *oikistēs* of a colony, like Battus in Cyrene or Archias for Syracuse, men who became heroized on death as the source of identifying characteristics of the community (not least its laws and sacred rites) and whose heroic status was celebrated in cult thereafter. More often a state's foundation would be attributed to a "mythical" character, like Cadmus in Thebes, or some hero from the epic cycle. Usually, a god would be involved in some way as a catalyst or inspiration for the foundation. In the case of many colonies Apollo served this function, through the intermediation of Delphi. Sometimes there were conflicting traditions, as for example in Thebes, where the story of Cadmus rubbed shoulders with the notion that Thebans were "sons of the soil" (*Spartoi*, "sown-men"). In any case, the account of a community's foundation was the starting point of its local history and, at the same time, a justification for its presence on the land.

The story of Athens was the most complex. A series of shadowy figures, Ogygos (the first man), Aktaios (from whom Attica took its name as a corruption from Aktike), Cecrops (half-man, half-snake, first king, founding father), and Erichthonius (the "very-earthy" child of Athena's thigh and Hephaestus' sperm) were all named "autochthon" ("earthborn"). They embody one of the most distinctive features of Athenian national tradition, namely that all Athenians were, like their ancestors (*progonoi*), "born of the earth." By this claim the Athenians set themselves apart from almost all other Greeks (Loraux 2000: 13–18). It became fundamental to the self-awareness of Athenian society and was cultivated by the orators in the *epitaphios logos* (Loraux 1986: *passim*; 2000: *passim*). It is easy to see this as a political creation of the fifth century, designed to upstage the Spartan tradition of the Return of the Heraclidae, but it is more likely a very old belief, centered around a number of local "first men," who were only organized into a genealogical progression by the first chronicler of Athens, Hellanicus (*FGrHist* 323a F 10; cf. Jacoby 1949: 68ff., 87ff.; *Komm*. III b (Suppl.) *Text* 1–21; Harding 1994: 9–10, 48–49; Möller 2001). Put another way, the local historians did not simply record tradition, they molded it into a historical narrative. And they could challenge or change it, since popular tradition and chronicle are not identical. For example, Hellanicus recognized that others (e.g., the Arcadians, the Aeginetans, and the Thebans) laid claim to autochthony (*FGrHist* 323a F 27) and Philochorus (*FGrHist* 328 F 2a–b) appears to have rationalized that claim and adopted a position similar to that of Thucydides (1.2.5; cf. 2.36.1), namely that the Athenians were the first to settle down from their wanderings and found cities and that only since then could it be said that "the same people had always dwelt in the land."

Of course, founders were not the only heroes for a Greek community. There were many others and they were all worshipped at shrines, or sacred sites. Some people's heroes had already been fitted into the grand scheme of heroic genealogy by the poets and early mythographers (West 1985); in the case of Attica, a latecomer, they were massaged into the genealogical progression of kings, as mentioned above, and at the same time tied in to the larger Panhellenic construct. The traditional tales that developed around these figures were part of local lore and the sites became topographical markers of cultural significance. A large preponderance of the fragments of the local histories collected by Jacoby concern the origin and location of such sites and the cults celebrated at them. In this way, local history compiled the sacred history of the community and, in doing so, traced the origin and importance of the major aristocratic families, since so many of them became significant in cultic contexts, as priests or other officials (see, for example, Androtion, *FGrHist* 324 F 1 for the origin of the Ceryces; Clinton 1974: *passim*, for the other families that controlled the priesthoods at Eleusis; Kearns 1989: *passim*, but especially 139–207, for a list of the heroes of Attica and the families associated with their worship).

Nor did a local history fail to locate the origin of a state's later political, legal, and administrative institutions in the "mythical" past. The best example of the way local history interpreted the past in light of the present is perhaps the Areopagus. Whilst Aristotle (*Ath. Pol.* 3.6, 8.2) found evidence to convince him that the pre-Solonian Areopagus had constitutional control of the state, the local historians treated it exclusively as a court of law (Hellanicus, *FGrHist* 323a F 1; Androtion, *FGrHist* 324 F 3–4; Phanodemus, *FGrHist* 325 F 30; Philochorus, *FGrHist* 328 F 20 and F 196) with competence mainly for homicide (Wallace 1985: 3–47, but see Harding 1994: 85–87). This was, of course, the extent of its competence in the fifth and fourth centuries, which was thus projected into the past through the fiction of its adjudication of four mythical homicide trials, beginning with the suit between Ares and Poseidon over the killing of Alcippe by Halirrhothios in the reign of Cecrops, followed three generations later in the time of Erechtheus by the trial of Cephalus for the death of Procris, then after another three generations the trial of Daedalus for the murder of Talos, and culminating in the trial of Orestes, which had been invented and added to the list by Aeschylus for the resolution of the *Oresteia*.

This last example gives a good indication of the combination of oral legend and literary convenience that had to be molded creatively by the historian into a chronological scheme in order to provide a state with a history for the so-called regal period. In the subsequent period, what for us would be the archaic time, the list of the state's eponymous magistrates provided the skeleton upon which to hang the few facts that could be found out. In my opinion these facts were based upon documented events, though they were sometimes filtered through family and popular tradition.

From the reforms of Cleisthenes onward, at least at Athens and probably in other states as well, increasingly accurate records were kept and available for consultation by local historians. Though I am not convinced by the suggestion of Shrimpton (1997: 147ff.) that local histories were distinguished from general histories specifically by their use of documents, I am of the opinion that the evidence supports the view that local historians were aware of their importance as sources of historical data and used them whenever they could (Harding 1994: 35–47; *pace* Thomas 1989: *passim*). And, as the excerpt from Dionysius cited above shows, as they came closer to their own time the local historians became increasingly detailed and accurate recorders of precise information that would otherwise have escaped the attention of the general historians, like Theopompus or Ephorus, or even Thucydides.

5 Conclusion

In his much-cited outline of the evolution and development of Greek historiography Jacoby (1909: 80–123) identified local history or "horography" (the writing of annual chronicles of individual *poleis*) as the last to appear of the five sub-species into which he divided the genre (above, p. 6). His categorization has been very influential (e.g., Fornara 1983: 1–46), but has recently been called into question (e.g., Fowler 1996; Marincola 1999; Luraghi 2001c: *passim*). The criticism is well founded. For example, the close association of chronicle to chronography is manifest (Möller 2001, and see the discussion above, §2). In addition, as has also been shown in more detail earlier, the first part of a Greek local history is hardly distinguishable from genealogy/mythography and, in fact, many authors in the genre devoted the preponderance of their attention to that aspect. On the other side, two of the best known and preserved local historians of Attica, Androtion and Philochorus, were clearly more interested in writing about their own times and could just as easily be classified as contemporary historians. Indeed, one could legitimately question whether writing the history of Athens, after it became an imperial city, was local in any other respect than that it was written from a partisan point of view (if, indeed, even that is true).

Furthermore, in the case of ethnography, one scholar has recently suggested that it was simply "local history of a non-Greek people" and claimed that Herodotus' excursus on Egypt in his second book was a "likely example of local historiography" (Shrimpton 1997: 147). Whilst the basis of this claim (discussed above) is questionable, it raises interesting questions about the relationship between these two sub-genres in both ancient and modern historiography. Maybe the difference is just a matter of perspective, whether one is writing about the same material from an insider's or outsider's point of view. But, in that case, if we continue to believe that Hellanicus of Lesbos (an outsider) wrote the first history of Attica (*pace* Joyce 1999), how are we to categorize his work – as an ethnography or a local history? And when somebody in the fourth century recreated the history of the Messenians (an *ethnos* not a *polis*) found in Pausanias 4.1–24 (cf. Pearson 1962), did he think he was writing a local history or an ethnography?

The close relationship between these two genres is further exemplified by the modern concept of local history. If one looks at the areas of research of any local history society, well represented by the compendious collection in the *Oxford Companion to Local and Family History* (Hey 1996), one will find many topics that would fall in Jacoby's classification under ethnography: for example, flora and fauna, architecture, monuments and marvels, and a whole range of cultural practices. Even more troubling, whilst most local histories today emphasize the role of the ordinary people, who often fail to appear in "grand" historiography, there is no indication that this was a primary focus of ancient Greek local history. By contrast, the annalistic framework and the rather cold, matter-of-fact style of the chronicle that is characteristic of the "historical" part of Greek local history (in Athens at any rate) is quite alien to the art of the modern local historian. We could almost be talking about two different genres.

In short, the type of history under review in this chapter does not fit easily into any convenient pigeonhole and this suggests that we have to reconsider the whole scheme of classification of the sub-genres of ancient historiography in use today. Such a reconsideration is already underway (see, e.g., the works by Marincola, Fowler, and Luraghi cited above). For the purpose of this essay, therefore, it may seem convenient to define the ancient genre that has come to be called "local history" purely on the basis of its format, i.e., that it organizes its material in the form of a chronicle. In this respect, Jacoby's technical term "horography" (cf. Diod. 1.26.5) remains the more appropriate title. But this is just a name and hardly helpful in understanding the nature of the genre. It was in all likelihood hardly monolithic (Rhodes 1990: 81; Harding 1994: 8–51; Marincola 1999: 313); local historians could disagree over details, interpretation, and emphasis (though hardly over issues of political ideology, cf. Harding 1994: 47–51).

Nevertheless, it is the conclusion of this chapter that, whatever it became in the hands of later practitioners (like Androtion and Philochorus, in the case of Athens), the origins of Greek local history lay in the impulse of a community (*polis* or *ethnos*) to establish its identity, through its origins, cults, and traditions, specifically in regard to its right to its territory (cf. Gehrke 2001). This impulse was embedded in oral traditions that were continually refined through the prism of changing political, social, and territorial circumstances until they became part of the literary tradition (Thomas 1989: *passim*; Fowler 2001). That is to say, the origin of the local chronicle is not coterminous with its first manifestations in writing.

Furthermore, in contrast to the view put forward by Jacoby (1949: 201), namely that the impulse to compose "local history" was late and resulted from a desire to fit the story of a *polis* into the grand scheme of Greek history, the position adopted here is that the impulse dates at least as far back as the time of colonization (cf. Giangiulio 2001) and probably earlier. Conversely, it continued to be reapplied in a similar context as late as the Hellenistic period (cf., for example, the oral and written historical material cited in litigation over border disputes in Ager 1996: *passim*, but especially nos. 26 and 74). The interaction of oral and written discourse, as it is understood today, is more complex than Jacoby supposed (cf. Vansina 1985; Thomas 1989; Fowler 2001: 95–115). I suggest that the reader will find a rather intriguing model for the unique blend of oral tradition about mythical origins with written record of "real" events, of partisan advocacy with factual precision, that is found in the Greek local chronicle, in the recent written documentation of the oral traditions and historical memory of the Stó:lo First Nation of British Columbia in support of their land claims (Carlson 2001).

FURTHER READING

The first major study of the *Atthis* and the Atthidographers was produced by Wilamowitz in his analysis of the sources of Aristotle's *Athenaion Politeia* (1893: 260–290). There he put forward the thesis that the *Atthis* was fundamentally a democratic medium that had been based upon a preliterary chronicle in the keeping of priestly magistrates, called *exegetai*, one of whom had published it (anonymously) early in the fourth century.

Two important studies challenged parts of Wilamowitz's argument (Bloch 1940; von Fritz 1940) and Pearson 1942 provided a brief overview of the genre, but these were soon overshadowed by Jacoby's *Atthis* (1949) and his introductions to and commentaries upon the individual Atthidographers (*FGrHist* 323a–328 and 3B Suppl. 1 and 2). Jacoby thoroughly disproved his teacher's theory of a chronicle published by an anonymous exegete and denied that any state had preserved historical notes attached to lists of magistrates from the archaic period. He believed that oral tradition, preserved by aristocratic families, was the source of most Athenian history (for arguments against this view see Stroud 1978, 1979; Harding 1994: 40–47), and for other states as well, because "all local histories in Greece" (1949: v) were the same or similar in character to the *Atthis*. Also, contrary to prevailing opinion, he argued that local history was not the first type of history but a late offshoot of "great history." This involved him in disputing the dates in Dionysius' essay on Thucydides (5.1), for which he has now been taken to task by Fowler (1996).

Specifically in the case of the Atthidographers he advanced the theory that individual Atthidographers wrote their histories from a politically biased point of view to influence political warfare in the fourth century, the dominant view until the 1970s, when it was challenged by Harding (bibliography in Harding 1994) and rejected by Rhodes 1990. These scholars argue that the Atthidographers differed from one another on detail, interpretation, and emphasis, but that they did not write with a view to influence contemporary politics.

Finally, Thomas 1989, following the work of scholars in other fields (e.g., Vansina 1985), has greatly refined and improved our understanding of the working of oral tradition, and the interplay between orality and literacy continues to be a focus of attention (cf. Luraghi 2001c). Her denial of the use of documentary evidence by local historians, however, has not been so well received (see Harding 1994; Sickinger 1999), and quite the contrary view has been put forward by Shrimpton 1997.

CHAPTER FIFTEEN

Western Greek Historiography

Riccardo Vattuone

1 Introduction

Western Greek historiography, understood as the work of historians who were born and formed in Sicily, Magna Graecia, or in the colonial world and took up a colonial viewpoint, has an identity of its own, which has not always been recognized (Vattuone 2001: 263–285; 2002a: 11–29). It culminated between the fifth and the third centuries BCE with the works of Antiochus, Philistus, and Timaeus. What comes before, after, or in between is certainly not unimportant, but clearly of minor relevance (Vanotti 2002: 33–54; Muccioli 2002: 137–176; Spada 2002: 233–273) – hence the choice applied in this contribution. Diodorus' *Historical Library* occupies a special place in this tradition, subsuming and synthesizing many of the topics dealt with by the more authoritative predecessors, but because it is part of a different tradition, it is discussed above (Ch. 13).

2 Hippys of Rhegium

According to a complex and rather confused entry of the Suda, a Byzantine Lexicon, the first western Greek historian, author of a *History of Sicily*, was Hippys from Rhegium (*FGrHist* 554 T 1: *prōton egrapse tas Sikelikas praxeis*). This would seem an uncontroversial starting point for western Greek historiography. The text of the entry, however, presents a number of problems: everything in it is controversial, from the long list of works attributed to Hippys to his chronology and even his very name, which is the product of a textual emendation (Hip<p>ys). The ancients were more interested in origins than we should be: Jacoby (1913b: 1927–1930), following Wilamowitz (1884: 442–452), suggested that Hippys was nothing other than the invention of a "Pythagorean" historian of a later age (a certain Myes of whom nothing else is known), transforming him in this way into a phantom-author (*Schwindelautor*).

Among the reasons that make the Suda's information suspicious and thereby Hippys himself impalpable, pride of place must be given to the reference by Olympic era (Olympiad 37 = 636 BCE) for the date of the sanctuary of the Palicii in Sicily (Cusumano 1991: 86) in Hippys' F 3. It is usually assumed that Timaeus, in the late fourth century, was the first historian to use dating by Olympiads, and this has suggested to many scholars the conclusion that Hippys should thus also be dated no earlier than the fourth–third century BCE and lose his position of prominence (Pareti 1959: 106–112; von Fritz 1967: 238–239; Pearson 1987: 8–10; Lendle 1992: 210; Meister 1992: 262; 1998: 612). As was to be expected, the obscurity of the entry has created space for a rehabilitation of Hippys: the connection between Hellanicus and Hippys (*FGrHist* 554 F 8) and the fact that the latter was ostensibly interested in chronology – the entry lists among his works a *Chronica* – might open up the possibility that the fifth century anticipated the use, possibly in a non-systematic fashion, of the Olympic era as a yardstick for establishing the chronology of events in the west. It may be possible to hold on to Hippys as the first historian of the west without seeming uncritical (cf., however, the authoritative position of De Sanctis 1958: 1–2).

It may also be possible to appreciate Hippys as a multifaceted author: the Suda entry, with its complex structure (Giangiulio 1989: 141–142; 1992: 303–364), states that he wrote a work called *Foundation of Italy* (*Ktisis Italias*), five books of *Sicelica*, five books of *Chronica*, and three books of *Argolica*, and adds the less plausible information that he was the first to write parodies and choliambs. The fragments preserve almost nothing from the works on Sicily and Italy, which would be most interesting for us, while it is singular that at least three out of nine fragments refer to the Argolid (*FGrHist* 554 F 2 [Epidaurus]; F 4 [Pollis the Argive]; F 8 [Corinth inhabited by people from the Argolid]); rather than correct the text of the entry (for instance supplying *Archaeologica* instead of *Argolica*), it should be pointed out that the mainland Greek topics dealt with by Hippys are plausible after all (Musti 1988: 29): a western Greek author – and one thinks immediately of the poet Stesichorus – was certainly interested in and knowledgeable about a wider geographical area than the one he lived in. The five books of *Sicelica* and the five books of *Chronica* might simply be the product of a textual repetition (a dittography of the number five), but it should be kept in mind that Hellenistic scholars such as Didymus and Mnaseas may have used the chronological work (Giangiulio 1992). The fact that outside the narrow boundaries of mainland Greece the necessity to organize narrative around fixed points in space and time was felt more acutely than in Greece itself should not be seen as surprising, but rather as telling. For a number of reasons (which cannot be discussed in detail here), the assumption that Hippys with his works came a few years or more before Antiochus of Syracuse does not disagree with what we know about him (admittedly not much) and with the kind of topics he dealt with, which can be reconstructed by patient exegetical work.

3   Antiochus of Syracuse

We know very little about the life of Antiochus of Syracuse, the son of Xenophanes: he wrote a work on Italy (*Italias oikismos* [*Settlement of Italy*] or *suggramma peri tēs Italias* [*Composition concerning Italy*]) whose length is unknown (probably one book only), and a *History of Sicily* (*historia tōn Sikelikōn* or *Sikeliōtis suggraphē*) in nine books, from Cocalus, king of the Sicans, to the year 424/3 BCE (*FGrHist* 555 T 3). Only a few fragments of these works are preserved: one from the *History of Sicily* and twelve from the probably much shorter work on ancient Italy. The work on Sicily was probably used by Thucydides (6.2–5) and then superseded by those of Antiochus' authoritative successors Philistus and Timaeus, which probably explains its limited impact in later ages; the work on Italy may have been more popular because there were fewer competitors (Luraghi 2002: 56–59). Antiochus' relative popularity between the first century BCE and the first century CE runs parallel to Philistus and Timaeus, who were made popular in Rome in that period by Cicero, whose strong interest in Sicily was tied to his political career (Taiphakos 1980: 177–178).

   All we have of Antiochus' *Sicelica* is a random reference in Pausanias (10.11.3) that is connected to a dedication in Delphi by the Greeks from the Lipari islands; a short history of the foundation of Lipari by the Cnidians is attributed to Antiochus, at least as far as the name of the founder is concerned: the Cnidian Pentathlus, predecessor of Dorieus on the western routes in the sixth century, who is ignored by Herodotus. This is about all we know of this work, which tellingly went all the way back to the Sicans, first inhabitants of the island, well before the arrival of the Greeks, and stretched to the age of the first Athenian expedition to Sicily (427–424 BCE), thereby including Hermocrates, who inspired the Peace of Gela in 424/3. It is possible that Antiochus addressed the "pan-Sicilian" resistance to the Athenian invasion, but this is just a supposition. In any case, Thucydides' portrayal of Hermocrates (4.59–64) largely reflects what the Syracusan leader represented for the history of Sicily in the last thirty years of the fifth century, possibly even beyond the "Attic war" (as Sicilian historians called the Athenian invasion of 415–413) and into the age of Dionysius. In my opinion, the debt of mainland historiography to the first known author of *Sicelica* goes beyond the information included in Thucydides' Sicilian archaeology (6.2–5; Wöllflin 1872). It is likely that the western version that Herodotus relegates to the margins of his own views on the role of Gelon at the time of Xerxes' invasion of Greece (7.164–166) goes back to some extent to a tradition which he could not ignore: the portrayal of Gelon, before Hermocrates, as a philhellenic leader promoted by Pindar and by the Deinomenid court of Hiero.

   A close and in some ways dialectical relationship between *Sicelica* historiography and mainland Greek historiography (*Hellenica*) is suggested by the proem of Antiochus' *On Italy* (*peri Italias*): the approach to Italic *archaiologia* recalls the method used by Thucydides in selecting information on the distant past of the Greeks (*FGrHist* 555 F 2):

Antiochus, the son of Xenophanes, wrote (*sunegrapse*) what follows about Italy, [select-ing] the most trustworthy and clearest information from the ancient accounts.

This brings to mind not only Thucydides' "writing" (*sunegrapse/suggraphē*), but more broadly the reflection in fifth-century historiography on the ways of selecting information about a past that can be reconstructed under certain conditions, with significant limitations and far from the prejudices of contemporaries (Parmeggiani 2003: 255 ff.). The selection of information about the past requires a critical assess-ment that is necessary in order to vouch for the trustworthiness (*ta pistotata*) of the narrative and show with clarity (*ta saphestata*) what stands up to scrutiny. If Dionysius is reflecting his predecessor's thought accurately (as there is no reason to doubt he does), we should consider the notion that Antiochus shared at least with Herodotus, and perhaps even more with Thucydides, a certain way of thinking about the past, about the very possibility of *discovering* it and rendering it *in an adequate way* (*saphōs heurein/saphes skopein*: Thuc. 1.1.3, 22.4), by means of a critical method influenced by Hecataeus', but much more refined and sophisticated. Such clues to the content and method of his work suggest that Antiochus was not at all isolated from the general cultural trends of his time, and reinforce the impression that western Greek historiography entertained a very close and to some extent polemical relationship to mainland Greek historical culture. Even if we recognize the "Thucydidean" tone of Antiochus F 2, however, it is extremely hard to tell whether Thucydides might have been influenced in this field also by Antiochus' reflection on ancient history and on how to reconstruct and narrate it.

It is worth noting that, while apparently skipping the stories of journeys westward by Greek heroes of the mythic age, Antiochus' narrative had a very broad chronological framework, starting from pre-Hellenic *Italia* well before the eighth century BCE and reaching down at least to the foundation of Heraclea (433–432 BCE). The *spatium historicum* recalls that of Thucydides' "Archaeology," embracing an age before the watershed of the Trojan War: Dionysius says that Antiochus, unlike Hellanicus (*FGrHist* 4 F 79) and Philistus (*FGrHist* 556 F 46), did not give a precise date for the migration of the Sicels into Sicily, but in all likelihood dated it before the Trojan War, that is, earlier than Thucydides did (6.2.4–5), who diverged from Hellanicus and Philistus only on the name of the tribes (Oenotrians and Opicians) that had compelled the Sicels to leave Italy (Manni 1957: 156–157). Antiochus' sources are not indigenous (Luraghi 2002: 72–74), but the depiction of the archaic age as a whole is characterized by a peculiar western perspective, which allows the historian to extend the geographical framework of his work to include Latium, the area of Rome, whence the Sicels had originated (Braccesi 1978: 38ff.).

In the early history of *Italia* king Italus takes pride of place. He gave his name to the people and is described as a wise (*sophos*) and brave (*agathos*) king, who originally ruled a rather small territory that formed the original nucleus of an "early *Italia*" located south of the isthmus between the gulfs of Squillace and Sant'Eufemia (*FGrHist* 555 F 5). Aristotle (*Pol.* 1329b6–8) preserves ethnographic details on Italus' kingdom, such as an early institution of "common meals" (*sussitia*), which suggests at least some familiarity with these topics in fourth-century historiography. Ephorus may be Aristotle's direct source, and may himself depend on Antiochus or possibly on Philistus, an author whose work he certainly knew (cf. Plut. *Dion* 36.3; Vattuone 2000: 165–171). In historical terms, Italus' story may be worthless, but it certainly had some contemporary relevance: if the cultural development of the pre-Greek local populations could even offer a precedent for the "Pythagorean" practice of common meals in an era that seems to precede even the Minoan age, it suggested that the Greek colonies had not come into contact with a radically hostile and "barbaric" indigenous world.

The western viewpoint that characterizes the Italic *archaiologia* is visible also in the fragments on colonial foundations. It has been observed that Strabo quotes Antiochus alongside a *vulgata*, probably seen as more authoritative, to which the references to the old author add precious details or rectifications (Musti 1988: 54–55). A case in point is offered by the foundation of Croton (F 10), with its comprehensive narrative of Myscellus' settlement, where the "deviation" towards Sybaris, prevented by the Delphic oracle, and the common expedition with Archias, the founder of Syracuse, seem to reflect historical events and political debates of the fifth century concerning Syracuse's politics towards Croton and the Siritis on the eve of the Athenian intervention in the west (427–424 BCE). In the case of Tarentum, the insistence on the fact that Helots and Partheniai were originally not slaves is also likely to have political overtones (F 13). Antiochus is also likely to have brought fundamental corrections to the plot of Euripides' *Melanippē Desmotis* in order to rectify a narrative that in the end supported the alliance between Athens and Metapontum at the time of the Peloponnesian War (F 12). The polemic against Euripides is in some ways specious, and close to the method displayed by Thucydides in his "Archaeology" and showcased in his treatment of the case of the tyrannicides (1.20).

Antiochus ended up being seen as the first Greek historian of the west, that is, the first author of *Italica* and *Sicelica*, as shown by that "polemical canon," so to speak, of Greek historiography that is Josephus' *Against Apion* (1.16 = *FGrHist* 555 T 5), where the disagreements between Greek historians are emphasized, culminating in Timaeus, who "did not deem it appropriate to agree with the narratives of any of his predecessors, neither Antiochus, nor Philistus, nor Callias." Antiochus' was a reference work not only for Thucydides but also for Philistus. Both Antiochus and Philistus probably extolled the age of the Deinomenids and saw in Hermocrates and Dionysius I, in a meaningful political continuity, the embodiment of a *national* identity for the history of the Greeks among the peoples of the western Mediterranean. Antiochus' surviving fragments display not so much a short-sighted *Lokalpatriotismus* as a historical consciousness of the implications of the settlement of the Greek colonies in a non-Greek world, "barbarian" but not necessarily hostile, whose perception is not reduced to heroic tales arguing for the precedence of Greek presence. Hermocrates' "pan-Sicilian" politics, the spirit of the Gela conference, which constituted the final point of Antiochus' *Sicelica*, reflects this same consciousness, the point of view from which the western historians looked at mainland Greece but also at the identity of the Italic peoples and beyond them at Rome.

4 Philistus of Syracuse

Philistus of Syracuse, the son of Archonides, was 25 years old when, with a provoking gesture, he compelled the Syracusan assembly to listen to young Dionysius, the future Dionysius I, vouching for him with his wealth and offering to pay any fine that might be imposed on him (*FGrHist* 556 T 4). The historian's biography is intertwined with his work. He wrote *Sicelica* in thirteen books, probably to a large extent during his exile – as often happened with Greek historians – and possibly published them at different points in time. Ancient sources separate two blocks or *suntaxeis*: a first one, of seven books, devoted to early history up to Dionysius' rise, and a second one dealing with Dionysius himself (*On Dionysius*), in four books, reaching down to 367 BCE. This way of "personalizing" historical events is common from the fourth century onwards, starting with Theopompus' *Philippica* (T 11a, 12). Finally, two books dealt with the reign of Dionysius II (T 11b) until 363/2, when they came to an abrupt end due to Philistus' death in 357/6 BCE. The subdivision in books, due to Alexandrian librarians, shows that – as normal for a Greek historian – the more recent years were dealt with in much more detail: the two books on Dionysius II covered a mere four years.

After supporting the rise of Dionysius, whose relative he became by marrying the daughter of Dionysius' brother Leptines, Philistus belonged to the group of close friends of the tyrant, his *philoi*, who advised Dionysius on the tragic situation resulting from the destruction of Agrigentum in 406 BCE and the danger of a complete Carthaginian conquest of Sicily. The military monarchy created by Dionysius in Syracuse, involving the formation of territorial defense and garrisons in the *chōra* (countryside) and aggression towards bordering Greek cities in the attempt at creating a territorial hegemony within the border represented by the Halikos River, brought back to life the politics of the Deinomenid tyrants and its objectives. Philistus may well have inspired these choices, as possibly implied by Nepos' famous judgment on him (*Dion* 3.1 = 556 T 5c), "a friend of tyranny itself as much as of the tyrant" (*hominem amicum non magis tyranno quam tyrannidi*). Philistus collided with Dionysius because of the latter's attack on Rhegium and the Greek cities of Italy (Sabattini 1989: 7–8). Together with Leptines, admiral of the Syracusan fleet and brother of the tyrant, he was exiled (T 5a–c), but was later partially rehabilitated when Leptines was recalled to Syracuse in order to fight against the Carthaginians (383/2 BCE). The sources on this point are contradictory (Bearzot 2002: 95f.); the most trustworthy, although not quite clear, version is provided by Plutarch (*Dion* 11.3–4): only after the death of Dionysius I did Philistus regain an important role in the political life of Syracuse, as advisor to the tyrant's son and commander of the fleet. In these years he was a staunch opponent of Dion, who tried to promote the interests of the Syracusan branch of the family, involving even Plato in episodes that verge on the grotesque. Again, and until his death, he was at the center of his city's politics, and defended with realism and perhaps a dose of cynicism the interests of tyranny. Also for this reason, after his death his corpse was the object of particular rage, as mentioned by Timonides and by the hostile Timaeus (*FGrHist* 561 F 2; 566 F 115).

Philistus' work was judged positively by Cicero (T 17a–b), Dionysius of Halicarnassus (T 15; T 16a–b), and Quintilian (T 15b). Hermogenes (T 15b) and Dionysius
himself criticize his preference for tyranny (T 17a–b). Cicero's famous definition –
"almost a small Thucydides" (*paene pusillus Thucydides. Q. fr.* 2.11.4) – probably
refers to the style and political outlook of Philistus' work, but Quintilian (10.1.74)
found him clearer (*lucidior*) than his obscure model. Philistus' popularity during the
late republic and the Augustan age is probably to be explained in the same way as
Antiochus'. Furthermore, his praise of a "moderate" military monarchy and the fact
that Alexander liked to read his work during the pauses of his campaigns in Asia (Plut.
Alex. 8.3 = T 22) may have made him attractive to a readership of that period.

Of the seventy-six surviving fragments of his *Sicelica*, many are simply rare words
and place names, and the remaining thirty-five – to which should be added *POxy* 665,
PSI 1283 (an inscription from Tauromenium: Manganaro 1974: 389–390) and Dio
Chrys. *Or.* 73.2 (Sabattini 1991: 306–307) – are of uneven interest. In the first part
of the work, called by Dionysius *On Sicily* (T 12), we can observe interest in Sicily's
earliest history in Book 1, the depiction of the age of the Deinomenids (Book 3), and
the Attic War and its preliminaries (427–424 BCE/415–413 BCE) which took up
Books 5 and 6. The Carthaginian offensive in Sicily after 409 and Hermocrates'
final attempt at returning to Syracuse must have had an important position, too, but
nothing is left of Philistus' narrative of these episodes, which must have found their
place in Book 7.

In Book 1, Philistus' "Archaeology" (FF 1–4; 45–47), it is possible to observe
both his unsurprising debt to previous authors, especially Antiochus, and a certain
originality in outlook that justifies his rewriting these ancient events. The starting
point, already canonical, is the age of the Sican king Cocalus, followed by the history
of the early migrations and settlements of pre-Greek Sicily in the context of *Italia*.
Like Antiochus, Philistus ends up projecting the history of the island onto Italy, and
like Antiochus he takes up an expansive perspective that goes beyond Sicel Latium,
describing the population of the Tyrrhenian coast as essentially Ligurian-Iberian.
Philistus knows about the various non-Greek peoples of Italy, but he seems to
emphasize a sort of *koinē* in which the Greeks will later settle, which anchors Sicily
in a broader Mediterranean context. His treatment of the great Athenian expedition
compelled Philistus to come to terms with Thucydides, and vague traces of this are
present in the sources. It is, however, extremely difficult to distill Philistus' viewpoint
out of Diodorus' narrative of the expedition in Book 12. Plutarch's statement that
Philistus had been an eyewitness to these events (*Nic.* 19.7–8 = F 56: *kai tōn
pragmatōn horatēs genomenos*) may have been overestimated. Were we to judge the
originality of his eyewitness version based on Diodorus, the conclusion would be that
he kept quite close to his authoritative model.

Much more interesting must have been the second *suntaxis*, devoted to the two
Dionysii, and especially the parts on the reign of Dionysius II, when Philistus was back
in power in Syracuse. Unfortunately, though, fragments of this portion of his work are
very few and poor in content. If we want to understand Philistus' position after 367
BCE, however, we can read the first thirteen chapters of Plutarch's *Life of Dion*, which,
in my opinion, include more than mere biographical information (Vattuone 2002d).

What we find there is a depiction of the conflict between freedom, represented by Dion and Plato, and despotism, embodied by the grim Philistus. But the academic take on this story, visible in Plutarch and widespread in the tradition of philosophical anecdotes, distorts completely the events as they can be perceived through the very narrative of the biographer: the strife for the succession to Dionysius I had very concrete political implications, with Dion posing as the liberator, a self-representation of which, tellingly, even Timaeus, famously opposed to tyrants, was skeptical. Ephorus, however, although he was harshly criticized by Plutarch (*Dion* 36) for this, liked Philistus' viewpoint, and gave it diffusion and authority in the fourth century BCE.

The main issue in Sicilian history from the sixth century to the fourth was the relations with the Carthaginians, which varied between latent hostility and open war. Creating a territorial state centered upon a hegemonic *polis* was a necessity, from the age of the Deinomenids all the way down to Agathocles and beyond. This necessity set the political history of the Greeks of Sicily apart from that of mainland Greece. Philistus defended this historical phenomenon with arguments that Ephorus found persuasive. Hermocrates' leadership in Syracuse had stopped the Athenians. Dionysius with his military monarchy had preserved the Greeks of Sicily from the wholesale destruction whose traces were certainly still visible in the ruins of Agrigentum.

5   Timaeus of Tauromenium

Timaeus of Tauromenium's *Italian and Sicilian History* (*Italika kai Sicelika*, *FGrHist* 566 T 1) was widely known, praised, and despised in antiquity, and to this very day its loss may be seen as the most acute of all of western Greek historiography. Son of Andromachus, commander (*hegemōn*) of Tauromenium in the age of Timoleon, he was exiled by Agathocles and spent many years in Athens. Polybius' tendentious quotation from Timaeus' proem of Book 34, the first one devoted to Agathocles, gives a distorted image of Timaeus' presence in Athens (12.25h.1 = F 34; see Vattuone 1991: 70–71). In Athens, contrary to what has been thought (Momigliano 1959: 529ff.), Timaeus was involved in lively debates on contemporary politics with Athenian intellectuals, but his main mission was to demolish Agathocles' royal self-representation. Diodorus (21.17 = F 124d) seems to think that his predecessor had tried in a cowardly manner to take revenge on the tyrant after the latter's death, piling upon him all sorts of slander, but this is just one of many superficial judgments to be found in the *Historical Library*, and it is undercut by the fact that Diodorus himself made large use of Timaeus, even for Agathocles' history (Vattuone 2005: 312–313). Timaeus may have returned to Sicily after Agathocles' death (289 BCE), which would account for his knowledge of historians favorable to Agathocles such as Callias and Antandrus, and perhaps too of Duris, and also for his use of information collected from eyewitnesses. This seems a possible meaning of the proem of the first of the five books on Agathocles, derided by Polybius.

Besides his *Italika kai Sicelika* (or simply *Sicelica* – as the work was sometimes called in antiquity and will be referred to henceforth – or *Historiai*) in thirty-eight books, the last five devoted to Agathocles, Timaeus also wrote a work on Pyrrhus (*Ta peri Pyrrhou*), to all intents and purposes a continuation of the previous work down to 264 BCE, which, like the *Ta peri Dionysiou* or Theopompus' *Philippica*, took its name from the main character. Polybius, who canonically took up from where Timaeus had stopped (1.5), starts with the Romans' crossing into Sicily, and there is no reason to doubt that this was the endpoint of Timaeus' work.

After a long introduction (*prokataskeuē*) devoted to the early history of Italy and Sicily, Timaeus' *Sicelica* reached down to the age of Dionysius and Timoleon, to which much space was allotted (Pearson 1987). Of course, as was the case with Philistus, contemporary history – that is, the years from 317 to 264 – must have been dealt with in much more detail than the rest. However, almost nothing has survived from this portion, and especially of the books on Pyrrhus, and we can have an idea of what they were like only by reading Diodorus' Book 21, which is itself only partially preserved.

Beside Agathocles, the historian's lifelong enemy in historical, political, and personal terms, Timaeus had a number of opponents among his fellow historians, foremost Polybius, but before him Polemon of Ilium, and in general antiquarian authors who disliked his arrogant tone and took revenge upon him by giving him mocking nicknames (ranging from the rather harmless *epitimaios* ["fault-finder," a play on his name] to the sarcastic *grausyllektria* [more or less "chatty old lady"]). Timaeus may have had a difficult character, but his pedantic criticism of other historians (T 17) was not the product merely of a polemical attitude but also of his attempt at revising the whole of Sicilian history, because its structure, as laid down by his predecessors, justified Dionysius' tyranny using the precedent of Gelon, and ended up by offering a ready-made legitimization for Agathocles.

Polybius devoted a large part of his Book 12 to criticizing Timaeus and placing him in a bad light before his Roman readers, intellectuals, politicians, and generals. Polybius' shadow is the main hindrance to the study of Timaeus, and it is necessary carefully to overcome this obstacle if we want to understand Timaeus' work (Walbank 2005: 2–3).

The fragments (164, many of which are mere explanations of place names) and testimonia (31) give a sense of the method and general historical interpretation that characterized Timaeus' work, but it remains necessary to bear in mind that so much more has been lost, such that conclusions must be extremely tentative. Unlike Antiochus, Timaeus' "Archaeology" was organized around a remote past when Greek heroes came into contact with the indigenous populations, creating a precedent that legitimized the appropriation of the land in the colonial phase centuries later. This rather artificial and historically not very trustworthy reconstruction preserves the notion, welcome to the Romans, of the originality of the Italic and Mediterranean world on the fringes of Sicily, which becomes the focus of a new movement (*kinēsis*) between Greek colonies, the Punic world, and Etrusco-Italic Rome. The peculiar perspective that allowed Antiochus and Philistus to describe in an autonomous and consistent way the specificity of non-Greek peoples and cultures

that preceded the colonization is enriched in Timaeus' work by the perception of a
new element in the Tyrrhenic area, which can be understood only by taking account
of the historical culture that Timaeus inherited from the works of his predecessors,
especially Antiochus and Philistus, which had established the cultural and political
identity of the western Greeks. For Momigliano, Timaeus' main merit was the
discovery of Rome (1959: 529–530). We should add that such a discovery was
possible starting from a special perspective that made visible the novelty of that
polis: not only the vague notion of a Greek city, a *polis Hellēnis*, as Rome could be
called in an epideictic context such as the speech of Aelius Aristides, but a Tyrrhenian
(i.e., Etruscan) city, located within a region, Latium, that it controlled with difficulty,
among Italic peoples whose pressure was meanwhile felt also by the Greek colonies of
southern Italy.

The "historical" past, from the foundation of the Greek colonies to the fourth
century BCE, was dominated in Timaeus' work by the figures Gelon, Hermocrates,
and Timoleon (F 22). He depicted Gelon as a philhellene (F 94) who was ready to
come to the rescue of the mainland Greeks after having made Syracuse free and
prosperous (Diod. 11.26). Modifying Philistus' – and possibly Antiochus' – perspective, Hermocrates appeared as the protagonist of resistance against Athens, the
embodiment of a military aristocracy opposed to tyranny and to the hindrances and
pointless debates of democracy: the opposite of Thucydides' portrayal, and the
product of a conscious and polemical rewriting (F 22) that provoked Plutarch's
surprise and dismay (*Nic.* 1.1). After the tyranny and despotism of the Dionysii and
Dion, Timoleon was, for Timaeus, the liberator of Sicily, the man who had brought
about an age of prosperity for the island, purifying Syracuse from the images of the
tyrants and preserving only Gelon's statue (FF 31b; 118–119). The character of
Timoleon, a Pythagorean imitator of Epaminondas, seems to embody a wisdom
that is typical of western Greek culture, linked to the political heritage of Pythagor-
eanism (FF 14–16), to republican politics, essentially to a moderate oligarchy. Timoleon, a friend of the historian's father Andromachus, may end up standing for these
values beyond his real merits. Polybius tried to undercut this idealized portrait
(*FGrHist* 566 F 119a–b), and if his narrow-mindedness prevented him from being
totally successful at this, he certainly targeted Timaeus' really immoderate praise: after
all, the new Greek Sicily created by Timoleon was to surrender itself to Agathocles
just a few years later (Vattuone 2005: 286–287).

Timaeus' historical method (FF 7; 151), engaging intensely with fourth-century
Greek culture, was criticized by Polybius, who saw it as the useless approach of an
armchair historian afflicted by "a bookish disposition (*bibliakē hexis*)," searching
books for elements that allowed him to reconstruct not only the distant past but
also more recent history, when it was not possible to be an eyewitness. In the case of
Agathocles (F 34), exile compelled the historian to defend himself, probably claiming
his ability in finding further information in books. His most difficult task was to
convince the Athenians that Agathocles' kingship and his self-proclamation in 307/6
BCE (Diod. 20.54.1) not only clashed with the spirit of western Greek wisdom, but
also constituted a tyrannical usurpation. In his youth, the self-proclaimed king had
sold his body to further his career, finding help from the wealthy Syracusan Damas

(F 124b): his tyrannical nature is revealed from the very beginning (Vattuone 1983), and in the end he dies consumed by cancer in the arms of the self-interested Oxythemis, a minister of Demetrius Poliorcetes (Diod. 21.16.5); in contrast, Timoleon had spent his old age in Syracuse, surrounded by universal affection and veneration (Plut. *Tim.* 37.6–7; Diod. 16.90.1), and Gelon had lived a simple life in his last years, loved by the Syracusans and finally receiving a heroic burial (Diod. 11.38.5–6). And after all, Agathocles' proud kingdom, which minted coins with the effigy of its founder, had fallen apart right after the death of its notorious ruler (Diod. 21.18).

In the end, Pyrrhus may have been the character whom Timaeus most respected and admired (F 22). The only things for which Timaeus could have criticized Pyrrhus were the fact that he fought against Rome, which had been meanwhile reconciled with the Greek world by way of the meeting of Ulysses and Aeneas (Momigliano 1982b: 231–232), the fact that he had not been able to carry out the war against Carthage in a more resolute way because of the hostility of the Greek cities of Sicily, and finally, a certain irresolution that overcame him in the end, when he returned to Greece.

Above and beyond the criticism of Polybius, who at any rate acknowledged Timaeus' almost maniacal care for documents (12.11.1–2), Timaeus' image is that of a learned man, passionate, intelligent, and partisan, and at any rate sharp in catching, in the role of Rome which increasingly dominated the Mediterranean, the fruits brought forth by the seed of western Greek culture.

FURTHER READING

For a general survey on western Greek historiography see Walbank 1968–1969; Pearson 1987; Vattuone 2002a (with essays on Hippys, Antiochus, Philistus, and Timaeus; one can find here also a very large bibliography on the subject); and Vattuone 2002b. On Antiochus: Musti 1988; Sammartano 1998; Luraghi 2002. On Philistus see Sanders 1987; Sordi 1990; and Bearzot 2002. For Timaeus one should consult Brown 1958; Vattuone 1991, 2002c; and Schepens 1994.

CHAPTER SIXTEEN

Greek Historians of Persia

Dominique Lenfant

1 Introduction

Perhaps no foreign people had more detailed histories written about themselves by the ancient Greeks than the Persians. For today's readers, the historian of Persia *par excellence* is Herodotus, but in fact he is the only author whose text survives. Before and after him there were Greek historians who wrote specific monographs on the Persian world: they were called *Persica*, an original genre, and developed in the fifth and fourth centuries BCE, during the very time of the Achaemenid empire, and they differed in many respects from Herodotus' work. Three of them – Dionysius of Miletus, Charon of Lampsacus, and Hellanicus of Lesbos – wrote in the fifth century BCE, three others – Ctesias of Cnidus, Dinon (of Colophon?), and Heracleides of Cumae – in the fourth century, thus later than the publication of Herodotus' history.

Three specific issues have affected their assessment in modern times. First, they are known only through "fragments," that is, citations, allusions, or paraphrases from later authors. It has often been overlooked that fragments can give only a partial, sometimes inaccurate, and generally unrepresentative knowledge of the author cited, and taking into account the nature of such a mediation might help to avert both uncritical and hypercritical interpretations of the available material. The second point concerns modern reconstructions of the historical genre and its evolution, the main issue being the presumed relation to Herodotus, who is conceived as the model in that field. Such ideas were especially developed by the most learned twentieth-century scholar of ancient Greek historians, Felix Jacoby, and have been therefore very influential. For example, Jacoby considered the first *Persica* to be mainly ethnographic and descriptive, representing as such a stage in the process leading to the major historical work of Herodotus, which itself made the move from description to narration (for recent criticism, see Marincola 1999). As for Ctesias' *Persica*, which postdates Herodotus, Jacoby saw it as a bad and ridiculous attempt to compete with Herodotus, and indeed a sign of the degradation of the historical genre (Jacoby

1922; for criticism see Lenfant 1996, 2004). Such analyses are somewhat misleading, as a survey of the successive authors of *Persica* will show. Lastly, a third issue concerns the possible contribution of *Persica* to the history of the Persian empire: since the 1980s, thanks to such scholars as Sancisi-Weerdenburg, Kuhrt, and Briant, Achaemenid history has had a tremendous revival, in part by taking greater account of non-Greek evidence and by having a far more critical approach to Greek views on Persia.

2 Fifth-Century Authors of *Persica*

Dionysius of Miletus was the first to write *Persica*. Information on him is especially scanty, and what follows must be taken as suggestions rather than certainties. He seems to have been contemporary with Darius' and Xerxes' reigns (Moggi 1972: 438–442), and he wrote both *Persica* and *Events After Darius* (*Ta meta Dareion*) in five books. The *Persica* dealt with the Persian empire at least from the end of the reign of Cambyses (*FGrHist* 687 F 2), and perhaps from its origins with Cyrus, up to and including the reign of Darius, while *Events After Darius* tackled the period following Darius' death. As the latter had five books, it probably provided detailed treatment of Xerxes' reign (at least of its beginning) and on the Second Persian War (480–479). The first writer of *Persica* would thus have written on, after, and because of the Persian Wars, as has been noted for the authors of the early *Persica* (Drews 1973: 36).

The four fragments do not tell us much. They all have corresponding variants in Herodotus' history (Moggi 1972: 452–462), which can only suggest that such historical and cultural questions were already discussed some decades before Herodotus himself. As was recently observed (Marincola 1999), nothing confirms Jacoby's view that Dionysius' *Persica* should be considered as more ethnographic and descriptive than narrative.

The next author of *Persica*, Charon of Lampsacus, was contemporary with the Persian Wars and wrote in the second or third quarter of the fifth century BCE. Charon was considered by ancient authors as earlier than Herodotus and there is no reason to reject that view (Moggi 1977; *contra*, Jacoby 1943, *FGrHist Komm.* IIIa.1, 18), even though it need not imply that Charon was a source for Herodotus (Moggi 1977: 24). Seven of Charon's fragments could go back to his *Persica*. They attest that it dealt not only with Greco-Persian relations – Persian conquest of Asia Minor (687b F 4), Ionian Revolt (F 5, F 3?), Persian Wars (F 1, at least, is on Mardonius' expedition in 492 BCE), and the meeting between Themistocles and Artaxerxes (F 6) – but also with the origins of the Persian empire and its founder (F 2 on Mandane's dream). Textual citations (FF 4, 5) suggest that the narrative was very concise. In fact, it consisted of only two books (T 1), to compare with Herodotus' nine.

The third author of *Persica* was Hellanicus of Lesbos, who lived ca. 480–407/6 and was contemporary with Herodotus, although he survived him some twenty years. His native island was under Persian rule until the battle of Mycale (479); he was born near the time it became an ally of Athens, but the western frontier of the Persian empire was not very distant, and he probably traveled at least in Asia Minor. Persia, however, was not his exclusive concern, insofar as his *Persica* was just a monograph among dozens of others, which were either mythographical or ethnographical. Sixteen fragments have been traced back to it, but they are brief, hard to delimit, and concern details only. Hellanicus is the first author of *Persica* who is known to have treated also Assyrians and Babylonians (687a FF 2, 7). His allusion to Medea as the eponymous ancestor of the Medes (F 5) may suggest that he tackled the origin of that people with a mythographical approach, something also attested in his other writings. He certainly treated many events of Persian history (Cambyses' brothers, the murder of his successor, Darius' children, Xerxes' expedition) and he alluded to some Persian customs (question of the burial of dead men). We do not know whether his *Persica* dealt successively with the Assyrian and Median empires before approaching the history of the Persian empire (as Ctesias later did), and any assumption about the work's structure is impossible to check. One can only say that the chronological scope went at least from mythical times through Assyrian, Median, and Persian history to the battle of Salamis (F 11). There is no evidence that his account went beyond the Second Persian War and, as this event was a turning point for Lesbos, such a limit would fit very well with Hellanicus' familial experience. In any case, his *Persica* was not a long work: it was divided into two books at least, possibly no more. If FF 3 and 4, which allude to Thracian cities and come from Book 2, are related to the account of Xerxes' expedition (as suggested by Drews 1973: 22 and Ambaglio 1980: 132–133), it would confirm that the narrative was very concise, as Charon's had been.

Hellanicus' chronological relationship to Herodotus has been discussed even more than for the preceding historians. It seems most probable that his *Persica* was composed earlier: so ancient testimonies suggest (T 1; F 11), and it would seem odd to write immediately after Herodotus a book on Persia and the Persian Wars which would be far more concise than his (Drews 1973: 23–24; Ambaglio 1980: 34; *contra*, Jacoby 1913a). There is no reason, however, to exclude the possibility of parallel redaction. Be that as it may, fragments are inconclusive about a possible relationship between the two works, and it is most probable anyway that both historians used oral evidence for the most part. That is to say, every theory on the evolution of the historical genre that rests upon their relationship is highly questionable.

The three preceding *Persica* were independent of Herodotus' work. They dealt both with the history of the Persian empire and with the Greco-Persian Wars, but the proportion allowed to each topic cannot be defined. The focus on the Persian world becomes clearer with the *Persica* of the fourth century BCE, about which we are also better informed.

3   Ctesias

That is especially true of Ctesias of Cnidus, whose *Persica* is probably the best known of all lost works of antiquity, and whose life itself is among the less obscure for this period. He lived in the second half of the fifth and the first decades of the fourth century BCE. Like his colleagues in *Persica*, he was from a city of Asia Minor which had been under Persian rule, but he also experienced Persian power in a very different way, since he lived many years at the royal court, where he served king Artaxerxes II and his mother Parysatis as their physician. There he could see some powerful people, but also humbler members of the court staff; he traveled with the king inside the empire, going from one royal residence to another; and was present at historical events such as the battle between the king and his brother Cyrus the Younger at Cunaxa. He even claimed to have participated in events outside the medical field, especially in diplomatic negotiations between Greeks and Persians (Lenfant 2004: vii–xxiv).

He also composed an *Indica*, an alleged description of India, its animals and people, which he asserted was truthful, but the fancy of which nobody would contest: for that reason, as early as the fourth century BCE, he enjoyed a very bad reputation as a liar. Surprisingly, another work, *On the Tributes in Asia* (*Peri tōn kata tēn Asian phorōn*), is generally supposed to be very serious: it seems to have listed food products conveyed to the court from various places of the empire, and to have added ethnographical details on the regions mentioned (Lenfant 2004: clviii ff.; FF 53–54 Lenfant). But Ctesias' major work was undeniably his *Persica*, which was completed after his departure from the court (398 BCE) in the 390s.

The evidence for his *Persica* is far more copious than for any other, because of the abundance and extent of the quotations, but also the diversity of the quoting authors, who give complementary material and sometimes make mutual evaluation possible. It stands out first as being a huge work (twenty-three books, to compare with Hellanicus' two and Herodotus' nine) and as covering continuously a very broad chronological scope: in fact, this history of the Persian empire went back to the supposed time of the most ancient empire of Asia, the Assyrian empire, before going through the history of the Median and Persian empires, from Cyrus to the sixth year of Artaxerxes II's reign, when Ctesias left the court.

The history of the Assyrian empire (FF 1–4) was clearly divided into two parts, one concerning the foundation of the empire and Ninus' and Semiramis' military expeditions and grand constructions, the other concerning a long decadence, with effeminate kings who, from Ninyas to Sardanapalus, remained confined in their palaces and indulged in a life of pleasure. The history of the Median empire (FF 5–8c*), which arose from the reaction of the male Arbakes facing the degenerate power of Sardanapalus, gave a list of the successive kings as well as some accounts of wars between Medians and neighboring peoples, closely tied to romantic stories of revenge, sexual inversion, and hopeless love. The history of the Persian empire (FF 8d*–44b) related in great detail the rise of Cyrus and his revolt against Astyages, his accession to the throne, his conquests, and his death. It was then divided according to the nine following reigns, from Cambyses to Artaxerxes II. The account treated especially the circumstances of accession and death for each king, in particular murders and succession crises, campaigns of conquest (against Egyptians, Scythians, Greeks), local revolts, and court intrigues – such are at least the kind of vicissitudes which are mentioned by Photius in his summary. The end of the account proper was followed by a list of the relays from the west to the east of the empire, and by a list of all the

kings of the three successive empires, from Ninus to Artaxerxes II (F 33). Lastly, ethnographical notations were inserted here and there in the narrative, concerning either peoples and regions of the empire, including specific animals, or court practices (Lenfant 2004: lxvi ff.; FF 10–12, 34–40, 44 and *passim*). Despite its apparent tripartition, the whole work deserved the title of *Persica* insofar as three quarters of it (Books 7–23) in fact concerned the Persian empire.

Since antiquity, it has been difficult to characterize Ctesias' work without returning a generally harsh verdict on his historical credibility. Plutarch reproached him for incredible tales, and modern scholars do the same. It is in fact usual to distinguish in some way among the three parts, the Assyrian and Median history being broadly imaginary, the Persian history up to the Persian Wars being somewhat confused and partly informed by polemic against Herodotus, and the more recent period being more accurate and truthful. It is not uninteresting to note that this last period was precisely the longest and the most detailed (ten books from Artaxerxes I to Artaxerxes II). But even for this period, the result is a terrifying and somewhat suspect picture of Persian power, including revolts, plots, and court intrigues in which women of the royal family and eunuchs play a big part. In fact, Ctesias' account was full of complicated and entertaining vicissitudes; many of his figures and stories seem rather stereotyped; he was not much concerned about critical inquiry; and he did not hesitate to dramatize events or to invent many details. His account can be considered in many respects sensational.

It has been frequently compared with Herodotus' history and considered as a vain mixture of plagiarism and polemic (Jacoby 1922). As it happens, Ctesias is the first author of *Persica* to take up the challenge of a Persian history after Herodotus. Even if he sometimes refuted Hellanicus, his main rival was obviously Herodotus, who not only was his nearest predecessor but whose outstanding work had probably already overshadowed earlier *Persica*. Their works indeed had common features: both dealt with Median kings, Persian history since Cyrus, and the Greco-Persian Wars; both had descriptive, ethnographical notations; and neither rejected *muthoi*, paradoxical, irrational phenomena or entertaining court tales. Ctesias' polemic against Herodotus was explicit and obviously an important feature, but it cannot explain all differences. In fact, only a third of Ctesias' *Persica* had a common subject with Herodotus, and one cannot assert (as does Jacoby 1922: 2046–2047) that Ctesias would have written the same without having lived in Persia (Lenfant 1996). Quite the reverse: even if fancy played a part, Ctesias was obviously inspired by his own experience at the royal court and what he could see and hear there from Persian and Greek people alike (Lenfant 2004).

Furthermore, as a writer of *Persica*, he did not have the same objective as Herodotus. First, we have no trace of large ethnographical excurses on subject peoples like Lydians or Egyptians. Second, Greco-Persian relations had in Ctesias' *Persica* a rather marginal place, including for the period he shared with Herodotus: the Persian Wars were dealt with far more briefly (two books only from Cambyses to Xerxes), which could certainly be a reaction to Herodotus (Drews 1973: 105), but can also be explained by a focus on the Persian world itself. In fact, this focus accounts for what is unparalleled in Herodotus, i.e., the prehistory of the empire (Assyrian history) as well as the continuation until contemporary times, beyond the Persian Wars – something Herodotus had not undertaken, although he survived that event by some fifty years.

The marginal place devoted to the Greco-Persian Wars is also due to the time and place in which Ctesias lived: he wrote nearly a century after the Persian Wars and could see at the Persian court that Greeks were not the main concern there. Ctesias innovated against both earlier *Persica* and Herodotus by writing a history of Persia that went beyond the Persian Wars and their aftermath, and was not motivated by that event. He was the first to show Greeks that Persians had an internal history mainly independent from theirs, and that the Persian Wars had been an event among many others, and one which Persians had overcome very well.

Concerning the contents of his Persian history, Ctesias has been regularly blamed for having developed sensational aspects, court intrigues, and "petite histoire" (e.g., Drews 1973). He has even been criticized for not giving a study of Persian administrative organization (Momigliano 1975b: 132–134) and for neglecting the account of Greco-Persian relations (Drews 1973: 106–107); with the revival of Achaemenid studies, he was also made responsible for later developments that gave rise to the myth of Persian decadence (Sancisi-Weerdenburg 1987; *contra*, Lenfant 2001) and for being a forerunner of modern orientalism (Briant 1996: 16). As a matter of fact, Ctesias did not have the same objectives as certain modern historians, nor did he enjoy the same distance. As for "petite histoire," court intrigues are closely tied to his own experience. In his account, they seem to culminate in the time when he lived at court; and when he describes cruel tortures or the bloody rivalry between the wife and the mother of the king, we have no reason to doubt their historicity. Intrigues may have been a part of everyday life for Ctesias in the court and they probably also influenced his view of earlier history. In addition, one should be aware that such an impression is exaggerated through the selection made by authors like Plutarch and Photius. Not all the material in Ctesias' work aimed at sensationalism: the enumeration of relays that marked out the empire from Ephesus to India, the list of the kings who had succeeded at the head of Asia, or the treatise *On the Tributes in Asia* might have given modern historians more "serious" information, but tradition gave them up as too boring. In addition to selection, one must take into account that the way in which the original text is reproduced – which is rather a way of transforming it – can change any author into an ingenuous or untruthful one, insofar as it abandons every expression of critical distance (Lenfant 1999). Furthermore, even the fragments show that his history was not restricted to court intrigues (Stevenson 1997). It was in fact a most disparate work.

Ctesias' *Persica* may certainly be considered by modern historians disappointing, especially in the altered form through which we can approach it, and all the more frustrating that, for the most part, it cannot be cross-checked with Near Eastern evidence or replaced by any evidence at all. But it is also interesting to look at it in its own cultural context, as a first Greek attempt to give the largest picture of Persian power from an Asiatic point of view and over its whole history.

4   Ctesias' Successors

Ctesias had two successors in the fourth century BCE, Dinon and Heracleides of Cumae, not much before the end of the Persian empire. As we know neither the dates of Heracleides nor whether he was the earlier, we can begin with Dinon, whose *Persica* seems to be more like Ctesias'.

It was probably completed in the early 330s. As far as it is possible to judge from the thirty fragments, which are given by various authors, among whom Athenaeus and Plutarch are nevertheless prominent, Dinon's *Persica* appears to have followed the model of Ctesias, going back to the supposed early time of Assyria with Semiramis and dealing with Persian history from Cyrus to his own time. This means both that it continued Ctesias' account over more than fifty years (from 398 to 343 BCE at least) and that it was the *Persica* which covered the largest chronological scope, including nearly all of Persian history.

The topics attested by the fragments are often close to Ctesias': accession of Semiramis, of Cyrus, events of Persian history and court intrigues up to contemporary times, description of court practices, and so on. The surviving tradition, however, mentions the precise details of Dinon's account when they differed from Ctesias'. Such variants were certainly attempts to correct his predecessor, but that does not exclude the possibility that they sometimes rested upon Near Eastern evidence: Dinon's account of Semiramis' accession (*FGrHist* 690 F 7) recalls the ritual of the royal substitute; his versions on Cyrus' revolt (F 9) and the origins of the expedition against Egypt (F 11) could be among the rival versions already mentioned by Herodotus; and the picture of Artaxerxes III as an ass killing the Apis bull (F 21) is a coherent expression of hostility from Egyptians. As for the reign of Artaxerxes II, about which we are better informed thanks to Plutarch, some variants that have been interpreted as arbitrary and aiming only at originality (Drews 1973: 117) can in fact be traced back to local concurrent versions, as is the case either for the original name of the king (Lenfant 2004: 275 n. 632) or for the account of Cyrus the Younger's death, where Ctesias diverged from the official version, while Dinon was closer to it (F 17; cf. Lenfant 2004: cxi ff., with n. 450). No more than Ctesias with Herodotus was Dinon content to give a degraded copy of his predecessor's work – at least some of his divergences rested upon sources, even if not better ones (Stevenson 1987, 1997). Fragments suggest besides that Dinon also had some special interest in two specific fields: court hierarchy and rich material demonstrating royal majesty, on the one hand, and religious practices of Persians and their magi, on the other.

As far as we can see, Dinon's *Persica* seems to have been like Ctesias' and has also been criticized for privileging "petite histoire" (Drews 1973: 117, 200). One may wonder why Jacoby, who was so hard on Ctesias, considered Dinon's *Persica* "ein Quellenwerk" (1921: 622), giving him, as it were, the benefit of the doubt. In fact, Drews' verdict seems to rest on Plutarch's quotations, Jacoby's on Athenaeus'. Both are partially right: Dinon – as did the authors who quote him – has selected and interpreted his data in a manner unlike a modern historian focusing on wars or economy, and he may not have refrained from inventing some details here and there; but his inspiration rested also upon Near Eastern accounts and his history probably was "ein Quellenwerk."

Heracleides of Cumae (*FGrHist* 689) is also little known. He lived in the middle of the fourth century and was born in a city which had returned under Persian rule in the early fourth century. He composed *Persica*, of which we have only eight fragments, but the fact that the work was divided into only five books suggests that its conception was different from Ctesias' and Dinon's works.

The long extant fragments, all from Athenaeus, give consequently the idea of a descriptive work, whereas the scanty allusions by Plutarch also attest a narrative feature. It is impossible to reconstruct the general structure of the account. As there is no extant mention of the Assyrian and Median empires, Heracleides may have been content with Persia. The two extant allusions to events concern the meeting of Themistocles with Xerxes at the Persian court and the marriages of Artaxerxes II with his daughters, which refer to the years 470–465 and the 360s respectively (FF 6, 7). Both are related to events later than the Persian Wars and we consequently do not know whether that last event was narrated, just as we cannot tell whether both allusions were inserted into a continuous account of Persian history. One can only observe that the meeting between Xerxes and Themistocles at the royal court and Artaxerxes' marriages with his daughters had rather sensational themes. This fact has not yet been pointed out, since Heracleides' reputation among modern scholars does not rest upon these court stories but upon long and highly precise descriptions of the palace practices, especially the care of the king, his staff (concubines, guards, cooks, bedmakers, etc.), and court etiquette. F 2, which describes the king's dinner – its organization, the hierarchy among his guests, and the graded distribution of the dishes to them – has especially interested modern historians as a valuable document on court institutions (Briant 1989). The description, which is factual, precise, and reasoned, tallies with Near Eastern documents such as the Persepolis tablets (Lewis 1987), and suggests that Heracleides was well informed. But the most unusual feature seems to be the way in which he tried to explain the logic of the system he described, to show that the king's dinner was an intelligent and rigorous institution, and that the huge quantity of various meats was not employed to indulge in luxury (as Greeks might have caricatured it), but was rather a judicious way to remunerate a part of the royal staff.

5 Conclusion

If historians were neither the only nor the first Greek authors to mention Persians, they differ nonetheless from most of the rest by moving beyond simple clichés on barbarians and pure celebration of the Greco-Persian Wars. Indeed, even if that specific event contributed to the motivation to compose the first *Persica* and, at the same time, stimulated the birth of Greek historiography in general (Drews 1973: 36–43), it is a common feature of the *Persica* that they do not focus on the military confrontation between Greeks and Persians.

Indeed, they were original attempts to show the Persian empire as if seen from inside, with events concerning the successive kings and some views on local practices. The result may exhibit obvious weaknesses using the criteria of modern historians and perhaps also by comparison with Herodotus. Nevertheless, one should not fail to observe that it was no easy task to understand and describe a power which had been for many cities a hostile enemy or even a ruler, a land that was portrayed by European Greeks, especially by the influential Athenian ideology, as an anti-Greece (Hall 1989), and a society with practices and values which were in fact so different in so many respects.

In any case, the works shed interesting light on Greco-Persian cultural relations. Nearly each generation had its own *Persica*, from the time of the Persian Wars to the expedition of Alexander. Each author had certainly literary motivations in his own Greek world, where he often had to compete with a predecessor, but he was also motivated by the many vivid accounts that could be found throughout the empire. There was thus a constant interest in the Persian world, and a constantly changing approach, and this proves that there were specific individual contacts between some Greeks and Persians, and moreover that the Persian world was itself felt to be complex and changing, fascinating in many respects and well worth discovering; and indeed although the Greeks attempted understanding in some various aspects, Persia also remained sometimes an ideal space to locate sensational tales.

It is not by chance that such a constant interest in the Persian world was expressed by Asiatic Greeks, who had personal experience of the empire not only through geographical proximity or individual ventures, but also because their city had been or even still was under Persian rule and because it had also been outside the Achaemenid empire at some time. Composing *Persica* was undeniably an original reaction to intermittent domination, which clearly did not lead to a black-and-white world view. Such an attitude from Asiatic Greeks is obviously in sharp contrast with that of the Athenians, to take the best known mainland example, who seem to have been generally lacking in that sort of interest, but whose viewpoint, because of their political and (especially) cultural domination, overshadowed for a long time every other perspective on the Persian empire.

FURTHER READING

The fragments of *Persica* have been edited in *FGrHist* III.C: nos. 687 (Dionysius of Miletus), 687a (Hellanicus of Lesbos: see also the Testimonia at *FGrHist* 4, pp. 104–107), 687b (Charon of Lampsacus), 688 (Ctesias of Cnidus), 689 (Heracleides of Cumae), 690 (Dinon).

There is no general study of *Persica*, but Drews 1973 has some interesting views (although sometimes too brief and questionable). Stevenson 1997, supposedly on Ctesias, Dinon, and Heracleides, takes into account many later texts (e.g., Diodorus) assumed to go back to them (without naming them) and, on the other hand, comments on only a selection of themes (ignoring, e.g., religion) and on a limited period (contemporary with the authors). In spite of gaps in the bibliography and some unconvincing hypotheses, the book often presents interesting views, especially on Dinon, and revises convincingly the common idea that the *Persica* were confined to "trivial tales of scandals at the Persian court."

An edition of *Persica*, with Greek text and French translation and commentary of Dinon's and Heracleides' fragments, is in preparation by Lenfant.

Specific analyses: on Dionysius, Moggi 1972 (fundamental on every question); on Charon, Pearson 1939: 139–151 (rather brief on the *Persica*); Moggi 1977 (fundamental on chronology; with commentary on the fragments). On Hellanicus, Jacoby 1913c (cols. 130–131 treat the *Persica*); Pearson 1939 (with 203–209 on *Persica*); Drews 1973 (22–24 on *Persica*); Ambaglio 1980 (survey of life and works, with Italian translation of *Persica*, pp. 81–83, and commentary of the fragments, pp. 132–135). On Ctesias, Jacoby 1922; Bigwood 1976, 1978, 1983; Lenfant 2004 (edition, translation, and commentary, with earlier bibliography). On Dinon and Heracleides, Stevenson 1987, 1997 (especially interesting on Dinon); and Lenfant's forthcoming edition, mentioned above. On the king's dinner (Heracleides F 2), Lewis 1987; Briant 1989.

CHAPTER SEVENTEEN

The Historians of Alexander the Great

Andrea Zambrini

> VLADIMIR: Our Saviour. Two thieves. One is supposed to have been saved and the
> other... damned. [...] And yet... how is it that of the four Evangelists
> only one speaks of a thief being saved. They were there – or thereabouts –
> and only one speaks of a thief being saved. [...] One out of four. Of the
> other three two don't mention any thieves at all and the third says that both
> of them abused him.
>
> Beckett, *Waiting for Godot*, Act 1

Although Alexander is certainly not Christ, he is similarly a fleeting topic of study.
Often subjected to different studies for different objectives, the figure of the incomparable and unmatched Conqueror, who disappeared at the climax of his glory and on
the threshold of new projects, acquires with time the mythical characteristics of one
who can represent everything that others want to attribute to him. The uniqueness of
his actions, aspirations, and innovations can support any given dispensation in view of
the poor historical record.

There were many people who, in Alexander's decade-long pursuit of his Asian goal,
wrote memoirs and accounts of the events. They are all there, almost all present,
although not everyone is in the same place, more or less, as Alexander because they
are either not constantly with Alexander or don't belong to his restricted circle of
friends; and yet everyone enjoyed the ideal conditions for an "objective" narration
of the Macedonian, for a history that responds to the nineteenth-century ideal "wie
es eigentlich gewesen ist": they were eyewitnesses and, if not, they could listen
directly to other eyewitnesses. And yet, there is not simply one Alexander; portraying
Alexander himself in all his inclinations, in all his greatness and possible wickedness,

Translated by Ginevra Adamoli and Kyle M. Hall.

each author can illuminate only one aspect, based on his individual perspective: the incomparable conqueror, the philosopher-at-arms and civilizer, the banqueter incapable of resisting alcohol, the sober drinker who remains banqueting for long periods only to spend time with friends, and so on. To paraphrase a famous statement: characters do not exist, only interpretations of characters exist.

The modern reader and scholar confronts a difficult situation: the disappearance of the "historians of Alexander." Among the historians of the first generation, those who followed Alexander in his expedition, nothing survives, outside of the material used by later authors. How we would love to be able to accept the invitation of Arrian, who, at the end of the preface to his *Anabasis of Alexander*, says (*praef.* 3, tr. Brunt): "Anyone who is surprised that with so many historians already in the field it should have occurred to me to compose this history should express his surprise only after perusing all their works and then reading mine." How we would like to read this mass of writers carefully! In spite of the many historians evoked by Arrian, we possess but few works on Alexander and they are all from later years: Book 17 of Diodorus' *Historical Library* (second half, first century BCE); Quintus Curtius Rufus' *History of Alexander the Great* (probably written under the emperor Claudius); Plutarch's *Life of Alexander* (between 110 and 115 CE), Arrian's work (between 115 and 125 CE: I accept the dating of Bosworth 1972a); Justin's *Epitome* (Books 11–12) of ca. 200 CE, taken from Pompeius Trogus' *Philippic Histories*, written in the Augustan age; the sections dedicated to Alexander in Strabo's Books 15–17 (late Augustan age) can be added, and the two Plutarchan essays *On the Fortune or Virtue of Alexander*; and finally, two texts of the fourth/fifth century, the *Epitome of the Deeds of Alexander the Great* and *On the Death and Testament of Alexander*, taken from a manuscript found at Metz and thus known as the Metz Epitome. (There is also the *Alexander Romance*, known as pseudo-Callisthenes, a popular fiction whose earliest versions date to the third century CE, but whose historical value is negligible.)

The first narrative of Alexander's expedition at our disposal thus dates from about three centuries after his death; the work most celebrated by modern scholars (so much so that one might decry it as an unreasonable cult), that of Arrian, dates from about five centuries after his death. Nothing survives from the first generation of Alexander historians, those who with their writings laid the foundations of a controversial narration and judgment about him, those who are the source for the histories that followed. In such a situation it is difficult to determine the character and understand the sense of these narratives, to identify which complex image of the protagonist emerged from the works of Callisthenes of Olynthus (*FGrHist* 124), Anaximenes of Lampsacus (*FGrHist* 134), Nearchus of Crete (*FGrHist* 133), Cleitarchus of Alexandria (*FGrHist* 137), Ptolemy son of Lagos (*FGrHist* 138), Aristobulus of Cassandreia (*FGrHist* 139), Chares of Mytilene (*FGrHist* 125), Ephippus of Olynthus (*FGrHist* 126), Polyclitus of Larissa (*FGrHist* 128), and Medeius of Larissa (*FGrHist* 129).

It is an undertaking that is largely conjectural, often with disputable foundations, and sometimes the result of real dogmatism. Generally the modern historian seeks to identify the main sources used by the authors of the works that have come down to us, after which, from the parts identified as salient in the final analysis of an author and from those definable as real "fragments" of the author in question, one rescues a title and gives a publication date and character to the *disiecta membra* of a work more imaginary than real. I will not discuss the problem of how to define "fragment," in this case those of the historians of Alexander collected by Jacoby in *FGrHist*; the observations of Bosworth (1980: 3–4) and Baynham (2003: 19–26) are sufficient to remind us that the authors who transmitted to us the so-called "fragments" managed to use, rewrite, and recreate the works of Alexander's historians in the pursuit of their own interests. We stand before a puzzle of notable dimensions, of which we possess only a few pieces (often quite insignificant); we must add the parts that are lacking, with judgment and discretion (if possible).

First of all, there is the issue of chronology. We have only two certainties: first, that Callisthenes, Aristotle's relative and official historian in Alexander's entourage, wrote the account of the Asian expedition during Alexander's lifetime, without concluding it, because he was involved in the Pages' Conspiracy and executed in 327 BCE; and second, that Aristobulus certainly wrote after 301 BCE (as Arr. *Anab.* 7.18.5 demonstrates), and in old age (*FGrHist* 139 T 3).

It is impossible to propose a chronology to everyone's satisfaction, since it is susceptible to changes based on the presumptions of other scholars. Obviously I cannot dwell on this topic, even though the discussion would be very instructive for understanding the ambiguity of the subject. I will limit myself to proposing a sufficiently orthodox chronology (cf., e.g., Pédech 1984: 8–9) for the place assigned to various authors on a time line, but vaguely anomalous in some cases, for the reasons that inspired their literary activity:

1   Callisthenes (dead in 327).
2   Onesicritus and Nearchus (between Alexander's death and 310, but most likely toward the earlier date than the later).
3   Medeius (perhaps not long after the death of the king).
4   Cleitarchus, between ca. 309–306.
5   Ptolemy, after 306, but within the fourth century BCE.
6   Aristobulus (some time after 298, the year of Cassander's death: Schwartz 1895: 914; Bosworth, *HCA* I.27).

I will concentrate my focus on these authors. The real issue is their position in a context that is historical and chronologically useful for an acceptable explanation of the surviving testimonies. A significant and engaging event on which I would like to focus is the tradition of the poisoning of Alexander.

Whether or not he was in fact killed because of a conspiracy is not the relevant question here (for the poisoning, see Bosworth 1971). What is relevant is that immediately after Alexander's death the idea of poisoning began to circulate ([Plut.] *Mor.* 849F; Bosworth 1971: 113–116; Merkelbach 1977: 169 n. 18; Bosworth 1988: 175–176, 182–183) and that several of these voices were intimidated or silenced by the people to whom these rumors pertained (Diod. 17.118.2; Curt. 10.10.18; Just. 12.13.10). Also interesting is that Onesicritus mentioned the conspiracy in his work without naming any of the conspirators (*FGrHist* 134

F 37), information that comes from the Metz Epitome (97), where one finds the *Liber de Morte testamentoque Alexandri*. The contents of the *Liber de Morte*, as in Pseudo-Callisthenes 3.30.1–33.25, derive from a manuscript of the fourth century BCE that (following the studies of Ausfeld, Merkelbach, and Heckel) has recently been satisfactorily dated by Bosworth: it is a pamphlet, probably by Ptolemy, against Antigonus and Cassander that goes back to ca. 309/8 (Bosworth 2000a). The date of this manuscript allows us to place Onesicritus securely before 310 BCE and to place him in the context of the rumors of poisoning that must have influenced his work. In general, the suspicion of poisoning can illuminate some controversial literary works: for example the *Ephemerides* (*Diaries of the King, FGrHist* 117) is not the fruit of the Royal Chancery that took note of every important event, military or not, of the court. (This view was taken by Wilcken [1894] and almost every historian before Pearson [1954–1955] followed this path, but Pearson finally cast doubt on their authenticity, considering them a Hellenistic forgery.) It is a document in the form of a diary, probably to be attributed to Eumenes, that arose from the desire to affirm the death of Alexander by natural causes, a result of his propensity for drink (Bosworth 1988: 157–182). Chronologically, it most likely appeared after the death of Alexander, in order to contest rumors of poisoning.

Onesicritus also wrote shortly after the death of the Macedonian, as otherwise the statement in the Metz Epitome that he had not mentioned the names of the conspirators so as not to create animosity would lose much of its force. The "rumors" of Alexander's death did not appear entirely far-fetched: the court was divided and troubled while Alexander was still alive and the death of Hephaistion, Alexander's intimate friend who shared every decision with him, had already raised some doubts (Bosworth 1988: 176–177). Several of Alexander's decisions had contributed to a difficult climate: the elimination of old and prestigious persons of rank, either realized or about to be realized (Philotas, Parmenio, and Cleitus were killed; Antipater was saved only by the death of the king: cf. Arr. *Anab.* 7.12.4–5; Zambrini 2004: 609–610), was an indication of the shift in the balance of power that had been established after the murder of Philip II; the transformation of the "national" character of the monarchy into a model that was felt to be "barbaric"; military reforms that were not pleasing to the Macedonians (Bosworth 1980); future projects, the support of which by the old guard we cannot gauge (Bosworth 1988: 185–211); and differences between prominent personages (cf., e.g., the case of Hephaistion and Eumenes: Plut. *Eum.* 2). Discontent wound its way through the court and the army, and it is easy to understand why the role of conspirator attributed to Antipater appeared likely: with Alexander gone he escaped certain death.

In a climate severely aggravated by the problems of royal succession, the division of power, and the maintenance of the empire's unity, we could place the work of Onesicritus of Astypalea (*FGrHist* 134), disciple or auditor of Diogenes the Cynic, with its "philosophical" exaltation of Alexander. From the surviving fragments (generally, information on the geography and natural history of India) it is impossible to come up with a precise idea of the structure and size of the work; Onesicritus, however, seems to have lingered less on the military character of the expedition and more on ideological aspects of exalting Alexander, such as the "philosopher at arms"

(F 17) in an idealized geographical and cultural atmosphere, and based on Cynic principles (FF 21, 22, 24, 25). One can think of the attempt to counterpose the philosophical vocation of the indisputably superior role of a Conqueror such as Alexander against the reality produced by a group of conspirators, whose names Onesicritus was unwilling to mention (F 37). The very title of his work, *How Alexander was Educated* (T 1), seems to underline, in its evocation of Xenophon's *Education of Cyrus*, an interest that transcends a restricted military picture, in order to outline an educative and cultural path that makes Alexander, in addition to being a man of arms, a civilizer (F 5) superior to all those who surrounded him and as well to those who succeeded him. What we do not know is the possible role that Onesicritus assigned to himself in his work. Certainly, he attributed to himself a role (that of admiral) that in reality he did not hold (he was a captain) in the expedition from the mouth of the Indus to the Persian Gulf (Nearchus was the actual admiral). But if he was chosen by Alexander to meet the Indian sophists, it is certainly possible that there was a significant "philosophical" link between Alexander and Onesicritus.

It is striking that in Pseudo-Callisthenes (3.31.8 = *FGrHist* 133 T 10d) Nearchus, Alexander's long-time friend (Plut. *Alex.* 10), is recorded among the conspirators. That he appears in Pseudo-Callisthenes must be remembered in the final analysis of Ptolemy's pamphlet of 309/8, mentioned above: his presence among the conspirators is easily explained, since at the time he was linked to Antigonus (Bosworth 2000a: 214). But is it possible that "rumors" about him could have circulated before? And that, even if unfounded, they could have had a role in the genesis of Nearchus' work? Could Nearchus (*FGrHist* 133) not have written *also* to reply to the rumors circulating about him, that made him a conspirator? It is true that Pseudo-Callisthenes is a questionable foundation, but we can try to make it stronger with other elements internal and external to Nearchus' work.

The work of Nearchus cannot be considered simply "an honest and reliable narrative of a trip." *The Coastal Navigation of India* (the title is only a conjecture), used by Arrian in the second part of his *Indica* (18–42 = *FGrHist* 133 F 1), demonstrates notable literary elaboration compared to the simple informative material that would have been collected during the reconnaisance voyage along the coast from India to the Persian Gulf under Alexander's orders. Moreover, we cannot overlook the fact that the work also narrated events before 326 (Bosworth, *HCA* II.361–365; it is usually assumed that Nearchus began his narrative with the beginning of Alexander's descent from India towards the Ocean in 326 BCE). Badian (1975) accentuated the "interested" character of Nearchus' work, especially in the face of Onesicritus, even though some aspects of his interpretation have been minimized (Bosworth 1987). Two aspects of his work, however, are particularly significant: he presents himself both as Alexander's favorite friend and as a leader of expeditions with capacities analogous to those of the great Macedonian (for an indication of this, Bosworth 2000a: 32). These two characteristics cannot be explained only by the necessity of contesting the many merits that Onesicritus in his work would have attributed to himself *vis-à-vis* Nearchus – not that polemic against Onesicritus must be excluded: quite the contrary. But this could be subordinated to the necessity of presenting oneself as a faithful friend of the king and a leader of expeditions at least not inferior to the Conqueror's. The theme of friendship is easily visible in the surviving fragments (FF 1 [§20], 4–8, 33–36) and might have tried to eliminate the suspicions that circulated about its author; otherwise, why affirm in such insistent terms a thing taken for granted and well known to everyone?

More complex is the discussion of the second theme: following Strasburger (1952), I believe, together with many other (but not all) scholars, that Arr. *Anab.* 6.24–26 on the difficult crossing of the Gedrosian desert comes essentially from Nearchus (Zambrini 2004: 558–560). Space prohibits an analysis of this passage, but it appears evident that Nearchus in his work did not speak only of his naval expedition; rather, he narrated in parallel fashion the quick exhaustion of the army led by Alexander in the desert and his own sea expedition that, contrary to the king's initial plans, was not assisted by the land forces due to the nature of the region. In short, it was a colorfully dramatic story about a trip full of difficulties faced with courage and skill by the author who does not miss the chance of representing, in a "pathetic" manner, his personal ties to the king. Was it then that Onesicritus, who did not want to mention the names of the conspirators so as not to create enemies for himself, had perhaps stimulated Nearchus' resentment with his hints about the conspiracy? Do the anti-Onesicritus treatises, emphasized by Jacoby, indeed owe their origin *only* to the fact that Onesicritus attributed to himself an office that belonged to Nearchus? Nearchus seems to want to say that he was the dear and irreproachable friend of Alexander, not unworthy of Alexander even from the point of view of his responsibility in the mission, having saved his fleet during a trip that was more difficult than expected, while also countering the imprudent suggestions of Onesicritus (FF 1[§32.8]–13, 1e).

There are, however, also elements external to Nearchus' work that can help in hypothesizing the origin of the malevolent voices against him. In Curtius (10.6.10–12), Nearchus tries to insert himself as a protagonist in the struggle over the succession to Alexander, supporting the king's illegitimate son, Heracles, whose mother was Barsine, mother of Nearchus' own wife, and thus Heracles' step-sister. How can one escape the temptation of seeing a private and familial interest in his obstinately sustained purpose (*Nearcho pervicacius tuente sententiam*)? And could not this excessive "tenacity" (however quickly overcome) in supporting the cause of Heracles have been the ideal ground for those suspicions about the active role of Nearchus in the supposed poisoning of the king?

The rumors of poisoning could explain also the work of Medeius, about whose work everything – period of publication, title, and length – is unknown to us: it could have had the goal, or at least *also* the objective, of responding to the insinuations on the role he held in the conspiracy against Alexander (*FGrHist Komm.* II.B.442). The rumors that circulated about Medeius were based on a series of significant elements: his intimate bond with Iollas, Cassander's brother and son of that Antipater now fallen into disgrace with Alexander and therefore in danger of his life; and Alexander's presence at the banquet Medeius organized before the king's final collapse. With these elements at our disposal, can we content ourselves with believing in a "memorialist" Medeius who perhaps writes only after Antigonus' failure (301 BCE; Medeius was in his service until 306: *FGrHist* ibid.)? It is natural to ask, on the contrary, whether Medeius did not write in a context and for reasons that appear more "significant," and therefore at a time not far removed from Alexander's death. And yet the only fragment attributed by Jacoby to Medeius of Larissa (*FGrHist* 129 F 1) does not even minutely help us to place this work within the cloudy events behind Alexander's death.

With Cleitarchus (*FGrHist* 137) the discussion becomes more complicated: his date varies between 310–300 (earlier date) and 280–260 (later date: cf. Prandi 1996: 69–71, 77–79), and we do not know whether he was part of Alexander's expedition. This last question is controversial, founded as it is on the interpretation of a single passage that is not decisive in this respect (Diod. 2.7.3; cf. Jacoby 1921: 624; Pearson 1960: 229–230; Prandi 1996: 69–70); it therefore remains in doubt whether he used for his own work only the materials of others or based it on at least some of his own personal experiences (Jacoby 1921: 651–653, for use of Callisthenes, Onesicritus, Nearchus). Personally, I lean towards the non-participation of Cleitarchus in the expedition, given the absolute lack of evidence in the matter.

Cleitarchus belongs to the decade 310–300 (*FGrHist Komm.* II.B.484; Bosworth 2000a: 7) and before Ptolemy, given that, according to Curtius (9.5.21), the Egyptian king denied that he was present at the siege of the city of the Malli and saved Alexander's life, while Cleitarchus affirmed it (Jacoby 1921: 625; Berve 1926: II.334): an incomprehensible affirmation, if, with Cleitarchus writing at Alexandria, Ptolemy had already written of being elsewhere during that event. We can hypothesize, following Bosworth, that Cleitarchus' work can be placed in or directly after the period of the previously discussed pamphlet of Ptolemy of 309/8, and was affected by the political climate (the clash between Cassander and Ptolemy over rule of the Aegean), given that in the tradition resulting from Cleitarchus, the so-called "vulgate," Alexander's death is described in such a way to suggest the idea of poisoning (a sudden wrenching pain strikes Alexander, as soon as he drinks a cup of wine in honor of Heracles: Diod. 17.117.1–2; Just. 12.13.8–14.9; Plut. *Alex.* 75.5). In a climate of strong opposition between Ptolemy, Cassander, and Antigonus, Cleitarchus writes in Alexandria an ample work (a Book 12 is attested, F 6) articulated around Alexander, in which the pro-Ptolemy tone would be clear (Jacoby 1921: 622–623; Baynham 2003: 11, 12–13; *contra*, Prandi 1996: 79–81).

However, the few fragments of this work (zoological, geographical, and ethnographic observations) entitled *History of Alexander* (F 6) do not help us to comprehend the character and the setting. We do know, however, that Cleitarchus was the most popular and admired writer on Alexander in Rome between the first centuries BCE and CE, even if he was criticized for his bombastic style and lack of reliability (TT 7, 8; Jacoby 1921: 628–629). Quintilian includes him in the canon of historians (T 6). From the "vulgate" tradition (Diodorus, Curtius Rufus, Justin), which goes back to him (Baynham 2003: 20–21), one obtains a version of Alexander's story that is richer in detail, rougher and less softened by the distortions of the tradition used by Arrian, i.e., Ptolemy and Aristobulus (Bosworth 1976). Does this less hagiographic portrayal of Alexander perhaps suggest a Cleitarchan narrative that suggested as likelier the violent death of the Conqueror, even if it did not explicitly affirm it? Cleitarchus' great success in Rome in a period that was quite delicate (the movement from republic to principate) could be explained by the fact that Cleitarchus' book lent itself to the Roman debate on the figure of Alexander, seen at times in a positive way, at times in a negative way, with stories and anecdotes of much light and shadow (*contra*, Prandi 1996: 54 with n. 8, who attributes Cleitarchus' popularity to his style). Perhaps Cleitarchus offered a narration that was original in literary terms, in which grandness, resoluteness, and a lack of moderation were united in a portrait of the Conqueror that lent itself to the multiple later views of posterity.

Ptolemy (*FGrHist* 138), the author of a work of unknown title on the enterprise of Alexander, and known to us only through Arrian and four fragments of his work (FF 2, 4–5, 11), was the founder of the Lagid dynasty in the Hellenistic kingdom of Egypt: he is the only protagonist of those after Alexander to have combined political-military and literary activities. The dating of his work is controversial, moving between lower dates (cf., e.g., *FGrHist Komm.* II.B.499; Kornemann 1935: 7; Tarn 1948: II.43; Pearson 1960: 193) and higher (cf. Badian 1964: 258; Errington 1969: 241). There is evidence for proposing a date after 306 BCE: that is, after the defeat of Ptolemy's fleet by Demetrius, Antigonus' son, at Cyprian Salamis, and the assumption of the title *basileus* ("king") by Antigonus that provoked Ptolemy and the other contenders to do the same. It may be that the composition of the work can be placed in the period between the assumption of the regal title by Seleucus and by Lysimacus (Pédech 1984: 234–237, based on Arr. *Anab.* 5.3.1).

The historical context after 306 gives a possible idea of the appearance of Ptolemy's work: when Antigonus assumed the title of *basileus* he did so because he was the last real successor to Alexander, and with the pretense of extending his own claims in all of the territories conquered by the Macedonian, including Egypt. By contrast, Ptolemy, with the assumption of the title of *basileus,* opposed the imperial plans of Antigonus and reaffirmed his own domain over Egypt which he had won directly after Alexander's death, and from which thereafter he claimed to derive his own sovereignty, having protected Egypt and Rhodes from the attacks of Antigonus and his son Demetrius.

The work of the new Egyptian king is constructed around the figure and deeds of Alexander, with particular attention towards those operations in which Ptolemy played a primary role (cf., e.g., F 14), although episodes in which he did not participate are not lacking (F 26). Also not lacking was a reorganization of the protagonists of the political and military events after the death of the king (Welles 1963; Errington 1969; Seibert 1969: 4–6; Bosworth 1976: 14–16; *contra*, Roisman 1984). From what can be attributed to Ptolemy in Arrian's work, it is clear that there was an apologetic *Tendenz* towards Alexander, an inclination to diminish the difficulties that were encountered (e.g., in the desert crossing at Gedrosia), and an excusing of the few reproachable actions of the king (the killing of Philotas, Parmenio, Cleitus, and Callisthenes); what is important is the magnitude of the task accomplished, in which Ptolemy had played a notable part, compared with Antigonus, who is only once recorded by Arrian in a subaltern assignment far from the active theater of conquest (Pédech 1984: 237). The work of Ptolemy was anything but a reliable account of the expedition, and one can surely reject the opinion that this was owed to the possibility of his use of official documents such as the "Diaries of the King" (above, p. 213): the work also had the function of raising again "the prestige of Ptolemy that had been diminished by the defeat at Salamis" (Pédech 1984: 237).

There is, however, another interesting fact: Ptolemy, in his work, did not attribute Alexander's death to a conspiracy. This is a sign of a political change compared with 309/8 (above, p. 214): by now the clash with Antigonus demands a connection with Cassander; the aggressiveness against Antipater and his family dissipates; a total silence falls over the conspirators (there are no longer the hints without names, as in Onesicritus); and this is not an account with the light and shadow of Cleitarchus. Alexander and his history are a great fresco of battles and conquests, without excessive difficulties, without excessive losses, without too many internal problems. And with Ptolemy at his side.

It is certain that Aristobulus (*FGrHist* 139) wrote after 301 BCE, when he was 84 years old (Schwartz 1895: 914; Bosworth, *HCA* I.27), but it is not clear how long after the battle of Ipsus. A good point of reference could be after 298 BCE, that is, after the death of Cassander, the founder in 316 on the site of Potideia of that Cassandreia of which Aristobulus was a citizen; this would help to explain the well-known "apologetic tendency" of Aristobulus towards Alexander (Schwartz 1895: 917–918; Strasburger 1934: 13–14; Pearson 1960: 150) as a reaction to the politics practiced by Cassander against the king's memory and against his family. More generally, however, it is to be remembered with Schwartz that Aristobulus' work is not simply "memorialistic" as much as a commentary on Alexander's character thirty to forty years after his death, after which epochal events had changed the political map of the empire and a contested tradition about Alexander had already established itself in numerous works. Beyond the botanical (FF 19, 23, 49) and geographical (FF 20, 28, 35, 56) interests in Aristobulus' work (the title and extent of which we do not know), an account of military events certainly was not missing (F 17, e.g.), but efforts to rehabilitate the figure of Alexander are above all noticeable. These accentuated the more obscure aspects of his character and behavior, denying the image of an Alexander devoted to drinking without moderation (F 62), that emerged from Ephippus of Olynthus' *On Alexander's and Hephaestion's Deaths* (*FGrHist* 126 FF 2–3), which offered an anti-heroic and prosaic version of the deaths of Alexander and Hephaestion. Aristobulus reacts as much to Ephippus' vision as to the shadowed picture that is found in Cleitarchus' work: Alexander does not die a violent death nor does he die from excessive drinking. He dies because of disease, as in Ptolemy's work. He does not die a violent death because the Alexander of Aristobulus was quite temperate in his behavior; he does not die by wine because the Alexander who drinks too much before his final collapse is already affected by this sickness. This last aspect can be deduced from F 58 (= Arr. *Anab.* 7.24.1–3; cf. Zambrini 2004: 646–647), which contains the final premonitory sign of the king's coming death, a narrative that differs notably from parallel versions in Diod. 17.116.2–4 and Plut. *Alex.* 73–74.1; it is a rationalized version of an original nucleus characterized by obscure and religious elements, and functions as an illustration of the last days of Alexander before his final collapse. The significant feature is that for Aristobulus Alexander holds a meeting to distribute the newly arrived troops, leaving the throne empty, because he is struck with thirst; at that point an unknown personage comes in, who silently takes the empty seat on the throne. The fundamental detail for me here is that Alexander leaves because of thirst: I think that Aristobulus inserted this detail into a more general discourse on the illness that had begun to manifest itself and I would link this observation with what was asserted in F 59 (= Plut. *Alex.* 75.6), in which Aristobulus maintained that Alexander drank heavily at the Median banquet because he had a fever, and thus was thirsty. Only the disease made him drink to excess in Media, a disease that had started to manifest itself earlier when the episode narrated in F 58 occurred. When Alexander was healthy, he did not drink much, although he would remain at festivals for long periods, because it was gratifying to him to be among friends: this is what Aristobulus says (F 62 = Arr. 7.29.4), denying all libelous accounts of an Alexander who lacks self-control. Aristobulus' Alexander is a great man of arms, moderate in his behavior, whose conquests result in a great mass of constructive and civilizing works (public works, foundation of cities, eradication of banditry, explorations). Certainly it is an apologetic vision; but what else would the controversial literary images then in circulation about Alexander – the depressing civil clashes and the division of the empire after the death of this extraordinary individual – have suggested to a member of that glorious expedition?

And what of Callisthenes, who wrote the official account of the expedition in his work? If I talk about him only in closing, subverting the chronological order, it is not an eccentric choice but because it is relatively simple to give sense and character to a work that, as much as it is lost and preserved only in small fragments (Bosworth 1988: 4–7), can be unequivocally contextualized.

Callisthenes of Olynthus (*FGrHist* 124), son of a cousin of Aristotle, wrote a work, *The Deeds of Alexander* (cf. Plezia 1972), with precise purposes: to promote the expedition in the Greek world, probably according to Alexander's intentions (for his reputation as a flatterer which will follow him thereafter, cf. T 20 = Pol. 12.12b). It is a work that will have influence, even if its use will be limited because of its premature interruption (Jacoby 1919: 1705 ff.). When Callisthenes arrives at the Macedonian court, he is a man already formed in Aristotle's school and is the only one among the "historians of Alexander" to already have literary experience as the author of a *Hellenica* and (with Aristotle) of a list of victors in the Pythian Games (*SIG*³275 = RO 80; below, p. 520). His cultural depth and the link with Aristotle enables us to understand the arrogant remarks preserved and reported by Arrian (4.10.2, tr. Brunt: "Alexander and his exploits depended on him and his history"): in the manner of epic, Callisthenes believes in giving glory to Alexander's enterprises through his work but, relying less on this same tradition, he believes in receiving as much glory as the protagonist of his history. From the tendencies of a tradition more or less truthful (as signaled by the doubts of Arrian in the passage cited above), there emerges the image of an intellectual arriving at court with a precise task and an "Aristotelian" mentality (the Asian expedition as the Panhellenic enterprise to avenge the Persian misdeeds against the Greeks), ready to exalt the "new Achilles," that Alexander who repeated the gestures of his mythical ancestors (from this come the Homeric references and the preparation with Anaxarchus of an edition of Homer called the "Recension of the Casket": T 10). He contributes in a determined manner to the "mythicization" of Alexander while still alive, affirming his divine affiliation (F 14: the pilgrimage to the oasis of Ammon at Siwa; F 31: the passage through the sea along Pamphilia). But the "mythicization" of Callisthenes is compatible with

Greek tradition (cf., e.g., the Homeric heroes descended from divinity), and it is compatible with the expedition understood as a Panhellenic "crusade" with the Aristotelian vision of the difference between Greeks and barbarians. The issue that was not compatible with this vision was Alexander's attempt to introduce to the court the Persian practice of prostration (*proskunesis*: Arr. *Anab.* 4.9.9–12): whatever Alexander's actual intentions were in this innovation, it is certain that in general the Greco-Macedonians interpreted this demand as a request for divine honors and as a degradation of the Greco-Macedonians to barbarians. Callisthenes' fall and disgrace, quite apart from his supposed involvement in the Pages' Conspiracy, reenters in the transformation of Alexander from king of Macedonia to king of an empire from Greece to India, through a path that had already seen the elimination of Philotas, Parmenio, and Cleitus. Writing about Alexander, as long as he was able to do so in the initial climate of the expedition, was easy for Callisthenes. Suddenly, after the king's death, writing about this exorbitant and unique personality was more complicated: henceforth, he was an incandescent figure, and his controversial and elusive character was only partially "historical."

FURTHER READING

It is neither possible nor desirable to give here an exhaustive picture of everything that one can say on all the lost historians of Alexander; concentration will be on the most important contributions. The following bibliographical information does not aim at completeness, but one can construct an abundant bibliography using the works cited here.

On the Alexander historians in general see Pearson 1960; Pédech 1984; Bosworth 1988: 1–15 (with general observations and a useful method for viewing the entirety of the problem); and Baynham 2003.

On Callisthenes, see Jacoby 1919; Brown 1949b; Pearson 1960: 22–49; Bosworth 1970; Levi 1977: 19–28; Pédech 1984: 15–69; Prandi 1985; Golan 1988; Devine 1994.

On Onesicritus see Berve 1926: II, no. 583; Strasburger 1939; Brown 1949a; Pearson 1960: 83–111; Levi 1977: 38–40; Pédech 1984: 71–157; Hauben 1987. For Nearchus see Berve 1926: II, no. 544; Capelle 1935; Pearson 1960: 112–149; Sofman and Tsibukidis 1987; Wirth 1988; Heckel 1992: 228–233; Bosworth, *HCA* II.361–365.

For Cleitarchus see Jacoby 1922; Brown 1950; Hamilton 1961; 1969: lvii–lix; Badian 1965; Goukowski 1969; 1976: xx–xxxi; Levi 1977: 40–43, 83–92; Hammond 1983: 25–27; 1993: 328–333; Bosworth 1988: 7–13; Prandi 1996.

On Ptolemy see Berve 1926: II, no. 668; Strasburger 1934; Kornemann 1935; Wirth 1959; Pearson 1960: 188–211; Welles 1963; Errington 1969; Levi 1977: 43–65; Pédech 1984: 215–239; Bosworth, *HCA* I.22–27; Roisman 1984. On Aristobulus, Schwartz 1895; Berve 1926: II, no. 121; Pearson 1960: 150–187; Brunt 1974; Levi 1977: 65–83; Bosworth, *HCA* I.27–29; Pédech 1984: 331–405.

CHAPTER EIGHTEEN

Greek Historians of the Near East: Clio's "Other" Sons

John Dillery

1   Introduction

I begin with two commonplace, but nonetheless important, observations. First, that with the conquests of Alexander the Great went also a rapid and massive diffusion of Hellenic culture to non-Greek lands. And secondly, that the writing of history was deeply implicated in Alexander's empire building: historians accompanied him on his march; a number of his lieutenants later in life turned to the writing of history; and, perhaps most importantly, earlier historical writing, in particular Herodotus, directly affected Alexander's own understanding of the world and his plans to conquer it (Högemann 1985: ch. 5; Bowersock 1994: 348–349). It should come as no surprise, with the rapid spread of Greek *paideia* to non-Greeks and the importance placed on historiography in the early Hellenistic period, that within a generation of Alexander's death, histories of Egypt and Babylon should appear, written in the Greek language by non-Greeks.

But though tempting to regard these histories as a logical, indeed almost natural, outcome of the Greco-Macedonian conquest of Egypt and the Near East, troubling questions remain. What was the purpose of these histories? For whom were they written? What sources and models were used in their creation? And what world view can be extracted from them?

This chapter considers only two historians, one Babylonian, Berossus, and one Egyptian, Manetho, both writing in the earliest years of the Hellenistic age. They were not the first non-Greeks to write history in the Greek language – that honor goes to Xanthus the Lydian (mid to late 5th c. BCE). They were, however, the first to write narrative histories of their own lands that were clearly based on preexisting traditional written sources. There would eventually be similar histories for just about every region of importance for the whole of the *oikoumenē*.

2   Berossus of Babylon

Berossus, a priest of Bel, wrote a history of his native Babylon in three books, referred to as the *Babyloniaca* or *Chaldaica*. Ancient testimony states (*FGrHist* 680 T 2) that he wrote the work for the second Seleucid king of Babylon, Antiochus I Soter (co-ruler with his father Seleucus 294 or 293–281; sole ruler 281–261). The *Babyloniaca* survives only in a modest number of fragments, or properly speaking, only through the quotation and paraphrasing of later authors, chiefly Josephus and Christian scholars, and all are probably due ultimately to the work of the first-century BCE polymath Alexander Polyhistor. The first book dealt with the story of Creation; the second with the earliest kings down to the Flood and the Flood itself; the third with events from the Flood down at least into the fourth century BCE and the reign of Artaxerxes II, and, very likely, the conquest of Alexander.

With some notable exceptions, a reader familiar with the great texts of Greek historiography (Herodotus or Thucydides) would no doubt have found Berossus' narrative odd, if not utterly *outré*. We learn toward the start of the *Babyloniaca* that a priestly fish-man named Oannes (Green 1984) came out of the "Red Sea" and gave humankind the gifts of civilization: cities, writing, laws, agriculture (F 1). Everything of importance in human civilization was transacted in this initial teaching of Oannes: "nothing more has been discovered after that time" (F 1.4), Berossus adds, though other creatures like Oannes later emerged. While it is true that Herodotus can produce his own marvels (*thōmata*), he nowhere has talking fish-men, and, generally speaking, has difficulty accepting the outright miraculous.

Book 2 was constructed around a king list containing ten rulers of Babylon, from the first (Aloros) down to and including the king during the Flood (Xisuthros). The period covered lasted for "120 sars" or 432,000 years! It is here, during the massive reigns of several of these rulers, that Berossus also noted the appearance of other fish-men sages like Oannes. Xisuthros is the hero of the Flood story: he is ordered by "Kronos" to bury "the beginnings, middles and ends of all writings in the city of Sippar" (F 4.14), construct a boat loaded with birds and animals, and board the vessel with his family in anticipation of a massive flood, which comes on the fifteenth day of Daisios. When land reappears, Xisuthros performs a sacrifice and is taken to heaven; his voice commands the survivors to dig up the writings at Sippar and deliver them to Babylon.

Berossus treated the Neo-Assyrians in detail in Book 3: an important section deals with Sennacherib's invasion of Cilicia and his refoundation of Tarsus as a "new Babylon" (*FGrHist* 685 F 5). Berossus' interest in this otherwise poorly attested campaign is probably due to the fact that Greek and Babylonian meet, with the latter victorious (Burstein 1978: 24 n. 80; Dalley 1999). The longest surviving narrative from Book 3 concerns the Neo-Babylonian dynasty, from its beginnings to the capture of Babylon by Cyrus the Great (626–539). Particularly important is the characterization of Nebuchadrezzar II (reigned 603–562) as a world conqueror; the description of his building program in Babylon (including the famous Hanging Gardens); and finally, the surprisingly positive handling of the last Neo-Babylonian ruler, Nabonidus, and Cyrus' generous treatment of him (FF 8–10).

Where did Berossus' material come from? Later readers of the *Babyloniaca* are uniform: Berossus "followed" or "preserved" the very oldest "records" (*anagraphai*, T 3). Oannes' creation account is clearly related to the Enuma Elish. The Flood story also is very old and widely known in the ancient Near East. Of particular importance is Berossus' choice of hero: Xisuthros is a Greek rendering of Ziusudra, the Sumerian name for the Flood hero (Civil 1969: 143). More common was the Babylon name familiar from the Gilgamesh epic (Utanapishtim). Written sources such as the Flood story not only provided Berossus with the content of his history, they also shaped its structure. A cuneiform text from Uruk dating to the First Millennium contains a king list of antediluvian rulers that in an almost spectacular fashion parallels the account of Berossus from Book 1. What is more, in addition to listing the same kings of Babylon before the Flood, it also pairs several of them with an accompanying *apkallu* (advisor), just as Berossus does. Paired with the first king Aialu (Berossus: Aloros) is the *apkallu* U'An (Berossus: Oannes), the celebrated heroic sage figure found in many other Akkadian texts, often named U'An-adapa (van Dijk 1962; Burstein 1978: 8–9 and n. 18). Hence we can be sure that Berossus' king list and his listing of wise men who advise the Babylonian kings have a documentary basis which he used to construct his narrative.

Just as important as this documentary link, though, is Berossus' claim that "the beginnings, middles, and ends of all knowledge" were buried by Xisuthros at Sippar. This statement locates the *Babyloniaca* within a distinct tradition in the Near East. First, the phrase itself – "beginnings, middles and ends" – can be paralleled exactly in cuneiform texts (Lambert and Millard 1969: 137). Secondly, Mesopotamian texts commonly refer to external, physical artifacts that confirm the authenticity and antiquity of the texts themselves. Thus a late redaction of the Gilgamesh epic contains a reference to a box buried under a city-wall that turns out to be the actual repository for this particular text of the legend (Michalowski 1999: 80–81, 87). Similarly, Berossus, writing of events before the Flood, had to create a link in his own work to the very antediluvian documents he mentions. His *Babyloniaca*, then, becomes a direct descendant of the actual records deposited by Xisuthros before the Flood at Sippar, for the implication is that everything that Berossus has reported up to the Flood derives from these very tablets. In a world where priestly and scribal descent was routinely traced back to the earliest times, so too Berossus' historiography had to be connected in a physical sense to the earliest sources of human knowledge (cf. Lambert 1957). While Berossus was writing in Greek – something no Near Eastern intellectual had yet done – he conformed to conventions that were in some cases more than two thousand years old. Moreover, bi- and multilingualism were already standard in his world: Sumerian is routinely employed in Akkadian texts, and Aramaic had been in use at least since the period of Persian domination (cf. von Soden 1960).

But not everything in the *Babyloniaca* had native antecedents, real or fabricated. The beginning contained an ethnographic section on Babylon's site, plants, and animals, for which there are no Babylonian parallels. A Greek perspective can also be found embedded within standard Near Eastern narrative blocks. Notable in this regard is Berossus' dating of the Flood to 15 Daisios, a Macedonian month-name from the Seleucid calendar. Also important here is that the Flood was given a specific date at all, for the legendary event is not dated in cuneiform sources (Lambert and Millard 1969: 136–137; though cf. Gen. 7: 11). Also revealing are remarks that immediately follow the description of Bel's slaying of Thalatth and the creation of earth and heaven out of her remains (F 1.7): "he says this [story] has been told allegorically (*allegorikōs*) as an accounting of the natural world (*pephusiologesthai*)." If Berossus himself used the words "allegorically" and "natural account," we would have to assume a major adaptation on his part of Babylonian legendary texts to current Greek literary and philosophical systems of exegesis.

Two more "Greek" features of Berossus' narrative deserve mention: distinct polemic and persuasive elements, features which seem to expect a response on the part of specifically a Greek reader. First, the polemic. Josephus informs us that Berossus "found fault with Greek historians" for attributing the foundation of Babylon to the legendary queen Semiramis (F 8.142). Ctesias had earlier claimed that Semiramis founded the city shortly after she took over the throne from her deceased husband, Ninus (F 7 Lenfant); this became the standard view for subsequent Greek and Roman historians. The response that this section of the *Babyloniaca* would seem to require is a retraction of some sort, or an admission of error.

Of greater scope and consequence are those places where Berossus is thought to have tried to influence his Greco-Macedonian readers, specifically the new masters of his land, Seleucus and his son Antiochus I. While Berossus nowhere directly addresses them, his account of the Neo-Babylonians has suggested to some that he was attempting to provide a model of a highly successful father and son duo for the new kings of Babylon (see esp. Kuhrt 1987: 55–56), one which would simultaneously help to legitimate the Seleucids and make clear to them the importance of the native legacy and those priests, like Berossus himself, charged with its preservation.

We have both explicit and implicit evidence, then, that Berossus had a Greek audience in mind for his *Babyloniaca*: polemic and persuasion on the one hand (explicit), and the influence of contemporary Greek historiographic and even philosophical principles on the other (implicit). But it would be a mistake to stop our investigation of the *Babyloniaca* here, and to observe that despite its overtures to a Greek audience, the Greeks themselves simply did not read the book (Momigliano 1975b: 7–8; 1975c). The foregoing analysis privileges disproportionately the Greek features of his work. The primary register of the *Babyloniaca* is a Babylonian one that happens to be in the Greek language. This suggests that there were other audiences for the work. Take the Flood account: as noted above, the cataclysm itself is dated by a Macedonian month-name from the Seleucid calendar. What is the effect of this? At one level the dating brings this central Near Eastern myth within the Greco-Macedonian world; in a sense it "Hellenizes" the moment. And yet, Berossus chose the Sumerian hero for the story, Ziusdra, and placed the events squarely within the region of Babylon and the neighboring city of Sippar. With the choice of Ziusdra it seems Berossus is deliberately archaizing, perhaps to build support for where he innovates, namely, in his locale for the Flood story. Babylon is clearly the region envisaged by Berossus as the setting for all early history, going back even to Oannes. In other words, Berossus has both "Hellenized" and "Babylonianized" the Flood narrative. This second reorientation of the story could only be fully understood by a regional audience, other residents of the Mesopotamian world who would understand Berossus' choice of hero and setting, and fully appreciate the claims implicit in these choices.

3   Manetho of Sebennytus

Like Berossus, Manetho was a priest, residing at Heliopolis in the Delta of Egypt during the period of Ptolemy I Soter (ruled 304–283 BCE) and Ptolemy II Philadelphus (285–246 BCE). Plutarch states that Manetho and the Eleusinian exegete Timotheus helped to establish the cult of Sarapis under Soter (*FGrHist* 609 T 3), suggesting that he was an important member of the early Ptolemaic court – a significant detail since the "friends" of Hellenistic kings normally did not come from the native elite but were fellow Macedonians or Greeks (Dillery 1999: 109 n. 54). Manetho, writing in Greek, claimed he was translating native Egyptian sacred texts; what is more, he apparently took issue frequently with Herodotus' account of Egypt in his own narrative (T 7).

Although it treated a civilization that had existed for millennia, Manetho's history, like Berossus', was divided into a mere three books. Two distinct features emerge from the remaining fragments: lengthy narratives (preserved chiefly by Josephus) and a massive king list transmitted as an epitome preserved in Syncellus and an Armenian translation of Eusebius. The list is of tremendous importance, for in addition to recording all the kings of Egypt, from primordial times to the native rulers who followed the end of the first Persian domination, the mortal kings are also divided into dynasties, and the years of each dynasty are tallied after the last pharaoh of the group. This organization has formed the cornerstone of the historical study of Egypt to the present day (Helck 1956). But while Manetho's list of kings is clearly related to a documentary tradition represented by texts such as the Palermo Stone, the Turin Canon, and the Tables of Abydos and Sakkara (ancient Memphis), he departs from this tradition: the Epitome provides more a regnal chronicle than mere list of kings' names, with a few exceptional happenings recorded under some rulers (e.g., strange natural events, the first appearance of important sacred animals, notable achievements and discoveries), and a distinct majority of these notices being found under the earlier pharaohs.

This last point is worth stressing because the notices, exiguous though they are, may well provide us with a clue where the longer narratives of the *Aegyptiaca* belonged. For example, for the pharaoh Bocchoris (XXIV Dynasty, Saite period), we find the following entry: "Bocchoris of Sais, [ruled] for 44 years; in his reign a lamb spoke" (FF 2–3c). It so happens that quite independent of the transmission of Manetho's king list there exists a Demotic text, "the Prophecy of the Lamb" or the "Lamb of Bocchoris," in which a lamb prophesies that Egypt will undergo great hardships 900 years in the future (Zauzich 1983; Thissen 2002). Although the actual composition of this papyrus is dated to the thirty-fourth year of the reign of the emperor Augustus (4–5 CE), its antecedents are no doubt much older (sometime in the period between the two Persian occupations of Egypt, i.e., between 404 and 343 BCE). Because of the survival of this text and the notice about the "talking lamb" under Bocchoris in the king list, and because of references to the same prophetic lamb in later Greek sources that could not have known the Demotic text, it seems a reasonable conclusion that under the entry for Bocchoris in Manetho's original work, some form of the prophecy was actually included. Corresponding to the few lengthy narratives of Manetho preserved in Josephus are brief narrative "tags" in the epitome of the king list (cf. Fraser 1972: II.734–735 n. 124; Dillery 1999: 95). Hence, if the epitome is any guide to the entire *Aegyptiaca*, the resulting picture is one of a history built around a list of pharaohs and their years of rule, followed in many cases by brief descriptions of important events in their reign; at several points the entry under a given monarch would expand to incorporate a very large narrative panel derived from preexisting Egyptian literature.

Down to the time of Manetho Egyptian literature possessed no narrative history of the sort found in the Greek world from Herodotus onward, but that does not mean that there were no texts with an actual or potential historiographic orientation. Manetho "slotted" preexisting narratives – prophetic and oracular texts such as the "Prophecy of the Lamb," royal biography and instruction texts ("Testaments"), and the "prophetic" royal biography or "king's story" (Koenen 2002: 173; Dillery 2005: 390 and n. 16) – into suitable places in his king list, and so united two traditional historiographic Egyptian forms. Manetho was not the first to construct a history of Egypt from king lists and narratives; Herodotus clearly knew both the main indigenous historiographic forms, if imperfectly (list: Hdt. 2.100.1; *Königsnovelle*: 2.137–141), and Hecataeus of Abdera even wrote a history of Egypt that included a chronological framework based on a king list as well as narratives such as the story of the Hyksos (Murray 1970; Burstein 1992). Since Hecataeus and Manetho were "friends" of Ptolemy Soter and very likely knew one another, Manetho's combination of list and legend may have come from Hecataeus.

Easily the most substantial of the surviving narratives from Manetho concern (1) the Hyksos period (F 8) and (2) related events from the New Kingdom that deal with the reigns of the pharaohs "Sethos/Ramesses" and "Amenophis" (FF 9–10). These texts show very clearly how Manetho fit his narratives into his chronological frame, confirming what we suggested concerning the "Prophecy of the Lamb." The invasion and rule of Egypt by the Hyksos was a defining epoch for pharaonic Egypt (cf. Assmann 2002: 197–201, 248–250), the first time the land of the Nile was ruled by outsiders. The Hyksos period became the template and master narrative for Egypt's subsequent periods of turmoil and foreign domination. Crucially, though modern investigation reveals that the Hyksos only ruled Egypt for little more than a century (1650–1540 BCE), Manetho gives them six kings who altogether rule Egypt for 517 years. This distortion alone suggests the "scarring" effect the period had on Egyptian memory (Assmann 2002:197–198), felt even by Manetho writing some 1,350 years later. According to Josephus, Manetho introduced the invasion of the Hyksos as follows:

Toutimaios. In his reign, for what cause I know not, god blew against [Egypt] (*theos antepneusen*); and unexpectedly, from the regions of the East, invaders of obscure race marched in confidence of victory (*katatharsesantes*) against the land. By main force they easily (*rhaidiōs*) seized it without striking a blow (*amachēti*); and having overpowered the rulers of the land, they then burned the cities ruthlessly, razed to the ground the temples of the gods, and treated all the natives with a cruel hostility, massacring some and leading into slavery the wives and children of others. Finally, they appointed as king one of their number whose name was Salitis . . . (F 8 = Waddell 1940: F 42; his trans. with modifications)

There are several details worth noting here. First, the narrative has been slotted in under the entry for "Toutimaios," precisely what we should expect. Secondly, since Manetho is working from a list, the list itself provides a structure, and consequently he does not need to construct a narrative motivation for this momentous turning point in Egyptian history (as Greek historiography would): "in his [Toutimaios'] reign, for what cause I know not, god blew against Egypt." A Greek historian, I think, would want to know why the invasion happened, and furthermore, why the invaders had such an easy time of it (they have "confidence" in their victory which, it seems, was uncontested). But these are questions in which Manetho has no interest, not because he is a bad "Greek" historian, but because he is an Egyptian priest-historian writing in Greek, and his language allows us to appreciate this difference in orientation and purpose (Dillery 1999: 98–99 and n. 19). A divine "blast" from the east had a very specific meaning to an Egyptian: the god of chaos and storm in Egypt was Seth (in Greek Typhon), the enemy of Osiris/Horus, the god associated with the pharaoh and legitimate kingship (cf. Assmann 2002: 389–393). The eastern part of the Delta in particular, around Pelusium and ancient Avaris, the Hyksos capital, was likewise associated with Seth (Plutarch knows of the region as the "blasts of Typhon": *Ant.* 3.6). Further, the description of the invaders as "confident," and the invasion itself as achieved "without a fight," can be explained within the Egyptian thought-world as a result of the will of the gods. As in the Old Testament, nothing happens to Egypt that is not divinely ordained (cf. Assmann 2002: 242–244, 271), even hardship or calamity. In our case, Manetho assumes the invasion of the Hyksos was successful and bloodless because it was supposed to happen.

And since other conquests of Egypt had been divinely ordained, it follows that the rule of the Ptolemies contemporary with Manetho himself had to be as well. This view has important consequences for Manetho's understanding of Egyptian history. First, it enables him to present an Egypt that had freed itself from foreign domination before. This might be a warning to the new rulers of Egypt: so long as the Ptolemies ruled as lawful pharaohs, listening especially to the native elite – men like Manetho – all would be well; but if not, their rule would end in the same way as did that of the Hyksos. Second, this implicit warning against unlawful rule would presumably be a solace to the Egyptians themselves regarding their future. When the domination of the Ptolemies became unbearable, their ancient records showed them that the gods of Egypt would see to the restoration of Ma'at – the proper ordering of the cosmos in which the typhonic forces of Seth (illegitimate rule) would be cast out and lawful rule reinstalled (note Demotic Chronicle II.24–III.1). Indeed, it would no doubt be discovered that the Ptolemaic rule of Egypt had been predicted to last for a specified period of time, precisely the view that shapes the other narratives of Manetho that come to us from Josephus. In the longest and most important (F 10), Manetho says that a pharaoh, Amenophis, desired to view the gods and asked a namesake, the prophet Amenophis, how to achieve this; the seer tells him, but also predicts a period of foreign rule over Egypt by a people who are obviously the Hebrews of the Exodus (their leader is an Egyptian called Osarseph who later changes his name to Moses, F 10 [§250]). Deciding he must "not fight against the gods" by trying to resist these outsiders and their Egyptian allies, Amenophis retreats to Ethiopia to wait out the period of foreign rule. These people govern Egypt for the period of time predicted by the seer, and are then driven out by Amenophis and his son Rampses.

What Manetho has done, of course, is to take what were originally prophetic texts that explained *ex eventu* the foreign domination of Egypt and "historicized" them by placing them in his chronological framework derived from the king lists. The final result must have been very striking indeed, for if much of Egypt's recent and not so recent past was in fact replaying over and over again the struggle against the minions of Seth – the Hyksos, the Hebrews, the Persians, the Macedonians and Greeks – then in essence at the core of Manetho's history was stasis, and change was to be measured by how the most recent actors in this timeless drama altered subtly the master narrative or template (cf. Sahlins 1981, 1991).

4 Conclusions: Audience and Purpose

Although I have probably overstated the case, it is nonetheless important to see that at the center of Manetho's history was a static view of the past. In this regard he is very like Berossus, where we find the fish-sage Oannes introducing humankind to everything that was ever to be important, and since whose time "nothing more has been discovered." Bickerman (1988: 218), looking at the whole range of non-Greeks writing history in the Hellenistic period, captured well the fundamental perspective of Berossus and Manetho: "Cast down, but representing hieratic and now immovable civilisations, Egyptian, Babylonian, Phoenician, and Jewish intellectuals looked back to the primeval age. Contemporaries of Euclid and Archimedes, they spoke of Abraham and Oannes."

But why did they write from this viewpoint in Greek? The answer is lengthy and necessarily incomplete, well beyond the scope of what can be said here. But I will attempt a brief response. Because their histories were written in the Greek language, the obvious answer is, they were written for Macedonians and Greeks. Seen in this way, with a Greco-Macedonian target audience in mind, their work would have several purposes: (1) most fundamentally, to introduce the Greeks and Macedonians to a truly accurate native accounting of the glorious history of Babylon and Egypt; (2) in so doing, also to model for the new rulers successful strategies for governance as well as to present the required ideology for becoming truly legitimate kings; (3) implicit in this last aim would also be to warn the Seleucids and Ptolemies against the sort of actions that would render their regimes illegitimate in the eyes of the native populace, especially the native priestly elite such as Berossus and Manetho themselves, men whose advice the new kings were encouraged to seek. This understanding of the intended audience of both the *Babyloniaca* and *Aegyptiaca* is supported by the sense that the only readership we are relatively certain both Berossus and Manetho seemed to have envisioned for their work were Antiochus I and Ptolemy II respectively.

But there are problems with this suggestion, likely though it appears. Aspects of both historians' work would have been utterly unintelligible to a reader outside their own cultures. A Macedonian or Greek cared little whether the hero of the Flood was Xisuthros or Utanapishtim, or that a lamb spoke in the time of Bocchoris. Yet, in the case of Berossus, he can be seen employing the mechanics of authorization and legitimation that were required by Mesopotamian scholarly convention. Similarly, Manetho constructs the story of the Exodus in a manner fully in accord with the symbolism and language of the Hyksos period, an epoch that profoundly shaped "the Egyptian worldview" (Assmann 2002: 197).

To a certain degree the traces of native tradition in both Berossus and Manetho are inadvertent: they wrote this way because they were used to it. But there are reasons to think both historians very deliberately wrote for other members of their own cultures. For instance, both express a type of local pride that I have only just touched on in the case of Berossus and not at all in that of Manetho: Babylon is favored over other cities in the Tigris–Euphrates river valley because Berossus was Babylonian, and appropriated stories that properly belonged elsewhere and set them in his native city; Manetho, a priest of Heliopolis, likewise made Memphis the conceptual focus of his history, relegating other important Egyptian centers such as Thebes to secondary status. This sort of regional advocacy could only have been meaningful to other Babylonians and Egyptians. While some may reasonably question why a Berossus or Manetho would want to communicate anything of importance in Greek to another Babylonian or Egyptian when their native language would of course suffice, it should be remembered that Greek had become a prestige language (cf. Romaine 1994: 89–91), and that the conqueror's tongue offered an important vehicle for discussing matters of importance, especially when they touched on claims of legitimacy such as invariably arise in cases of regional one-upmanship. A "colonial" dynamic seems relevant, in which local elites, in addition to "collaborating" and "competing" with their conquerors, also compete among themselves (cf. Guha 2005: 404), though there are problems with insisting on such a view of non-Greek, subjected cultures in the Hellenistic period (Bagnall 1997).

We must imagine the work of Berossus and Manetho to have been meant for both a Greco-Macedonian and native audience. We should probably add also other non-Greeks writing in Greek native histories. A late testimonium states that Manetho wrote his history in imitation of Berossus' work (T 11c), suggesting that they were listening to each other and the claims they made for their respective cultures and their pasts. Certainly Greeks by and large did not read their work – with notable exceptions (Alexander Polyhistor). When the Greeks took notice of Berossus and Manetho, it was as the semi-legendary authors of astrological lore and arcane wisdom (Bickerman

1988: 222; Potter 1994: 191). It is probably not an accident, however, that another figure very like them – a man from a priestly family who had close ties to the foreign rulers of his land, and who wrote in Greek a native history – is also our best source for their contribution to the story of ancient historical writing in Greek: I mean, of course, Josephus, who claimed priestly descent (*Vit.* 1.1), and who authored his own monumental native history, the *Jewish Antiquities*. This was Berossus' and Manetho's greatest legacy: that historiography written in Greek did not invariably mean Greek history, and that the power and adaptability of Greek historical writing, indeed the Greek language itself, made possible a dialogue about the past amongst the several peoples of the ancient world.

FURTHER READING

Momigliano (chiefly 1975b) defined the topic of non-Greek historians writing in Greek native histories of their lands. Essential also for understanding the historiography of the period is Bickerman 1988, and his collected articles (1976–1986). Standard English translations with notes: for Berossus, Burstein 1978; for Manetho, Waddell 1940. For further discussions: on Berossus, important still is Schnabel 1924, but see now esp. Kuhrt 1987, and De Breucker 2003. On Manetho, Laqueur 1928; more recent, Dillery 1999. On Josephus and his relationship to both Berossus and Manetho, see esp. Rajak 2001a; note also the fundamental treatment on Alexander Polyhistor by Freudenthal 1874. An important study of Berossus, Manetho, and subsequent related historiography is Sterling 1992.

Important cuneiform texts of the New Year's Festival at Babylon, at which the Babylonian Creation Epic was recited, were in fact produced in the Seleucid period: Pritchard 1969: 331. Lambert and Millard have a brief but excellent discussion of Berossus' treatment of the Flood, 1969: 134–137. The king list with parallel listings of *apkallus* (advisors): van Dijk 1962; and see also the relevant discussion and notes in Burstein 1978. For images of the fish-man sage, see Green 1984. On the Babylonian tradition of reference to the repository of the text (*naru* literature), see Michalowski 1999. Especially useful for the interaction of Babylon with the Greek world is Dalley 1998.

Koenen 2002 expertly discusses the Egyptian *Chaosbeschreibung* tradition (including Manetho and the Prophecy of the Lamb). See also the groundbreaking Frankfurter 1998. Assmann 2002 is fundamental on Egyptian views of the past. Much relevant late Egyptian material in translation (but not the Prophecy of the Lamb) is conveniently assembled in Lichtheim 1980.

CHAPTER NINETEEN

The Jewish Appropriation of Hellenistic Historiography

Gregory E. Sterling

1 Introduction

Jews began writing history at a relatively early date. One of the most impressive historical narratives from the ancient world is the "Succession Narrative" or "Court History of David" that relates Solomon's selection as David's successor (2 Samuel 9–20; 1 Kings 1–2). The account was probably written by a member of the royal court in the tenth century BCE shortly after Solomon ascended the throne. While it offers an explanation for and defense of what was undoubtedly perceived by many to be an illegitimate succession, it did so with a sobriety unusual in the ancient world. Later Jewish historians created two long narratives based on this and a good number of other sources: the Deuteronomistic history (Deuteronomy, Joshua, Judges, 1 & 2 Samuel, and 1 & 2 Kings), written first in the late seventh century and updated in the sixth century, and the Chronicler's history, written during the Persian period (1 & 2 Chronicles, and, more controversially, Ezra, and Nehemiah). Jews thus had a long tradition of historical writing before they had sustained encounters with Greeks.

When the encounter with Greeks came, it had a significant impact on Jewish historiography. While some Jewish historians deliberately followed the Jewish biblical precedents (e.g., 1 Maccabees, 1 Esdras, Pseudo-Philo), others embraced Greek historiography (e.g., 2 Maccabees, Josephus). The former wrote in a Semitic language (either Hebrew or Aramaic), the latter in Greek, though it would be naïve to draw a line between the two strictly on linguistic grounds. Hellenism had an impact on virtually all of these authors and their histories; conversely, the biblical tradition exerted an enormous influence on the majority of Jewish historians, no matter what language they used.

2   The Histories

There are several preliminary problems that must be acknowledged in the study of these histories. We have only three full works composed in Greek that are still extant: the epitome of Jason of Cyrene's five-volume work known as 2 Maccabees; and Josephus' *Jewish War* and *Jewish Antiquities*. (*If* 1 Esdras was composed in Greek, we would have a fourth). We have two other works originally composed in Hebrew but that have come down to us in another language: 1 Maccabees (in Greek) and Pseudo-Philo's *Biblical Antiquities* (in Latin via an earlier Greek translation). We have fragments of ten other historians who composed in Greek. Unfortunately, the identities of these historians and the specific contexts in which they wrote are often problematic. The fragments have come down to us either through later Christian sources or through a double chain extending from the Roman polymath Alexander Polyhistor to the early Christian writer Eusebius. The summary of their dates and locales below represents common judgments, but they are debatable.

Complicating the situation further is the decision whom to include and exclude from the ranks of historians. Ancient Jewish historians were far more creative in recasting the past than we would permit; so much so that it is not always possible to differentiate with precision among what we would consider a history, historical novel, or romance. Do we distinguish among these on the basis of authorial intent (whether the author intended the work to be read as history or fiction) or of the readers' reception (whether ancient readers understood the work to be an accurate reporting of the past or a fiction)? Both of these criteria are problematic since we cannot know the author's intent or the reader's perspective in most instances – if ever. I prefer to make distinctions on the basis of the work's relationship to its sources: prose works that create a narrative principally on the basis of sources that ancients believed to report the past I consider histories. (Note the adverb "principally": even the most sober of the Jewish historians use freedoms that we would not permit.) Works that narrate the stories of historical figures and circumstances, but do not follow historical sources as the basis for the narrative, I consider historical novels. I do not want to suggest that the figures are necessarily historical, but that the sources were treated that way. These texts use accepted historical frameworks to fill in or flesh out their stories. Finally, I think of works that are free creations – even if they use known figures – to be romances or fiction. The line among these three is not always clear and there is considerable room for debate: 3 Maccabees, for example, could be a historical novel or a romance. We must remember that this taxonomy is modern, not ancient. The categories do, however, permit us to form some useful judgments about these prose writers. I have set out the three groups in the following charts, adding a category of related works for the first two categories to include works that are similar but belong to different genres. The lists below are not exhaustive: they do not include works identified by moderns as sources incorporated into larger works, but only works that have attested independent existence in ancient sources.

I. Jewish Historians, 323 BCE–135 CE

Author or Work	Date/Century	Locale	Language
Demetrius, *On the Kings in Judea*	3rd BCE	Egypt	Greek
Eupolemus, *On the Kings in Judea*	2nd BCE	Judea	Greek
1 Esdras	2nd BCE	Judea	Hebrew?
			Greek (?)
1 Maccabees	Early 1st BCE	Judea	Hebrew
Jason of Cyrene, 5 books	Early 1st BCE	Cyrene (?)	Greek
Epitomator of Jason, 2 Maccabees	Early 1st BCE	Judea (?)	Greek
Pseudo-Hecataeus, *On the Jews*	1st BCE	Egypt	Greek
Thallus (?), *Histories*	1st CE	?	Greek
Josephus, *Jewish War*	1st CE	Rome	Greek
Josephus, *Jewish Antiquities*	1st CE	Rome	Greek
Justus of Tiberias, *A Chronicle of the Jewish Kings*	1st CE	Galilee	Greek
Justus of Tiberias, *Jewish War*	1st CE	Galilee	Greek
Pseudo-Philo, *Biblical Antiquities*	1st CE	Judea	Hebrew

IA.   Related Works

Philo, *Against Flaccus*	1st CE	Alexandria	Greek
Philo, *Embassy to Gaius*	1st CE	Alexandria	Greek

II. Jewish Historical Novels, 323 BCE–135 CE

Author or Work	Date/Century	Locale	Language
Artapanus, *On the Jews*	2nd BCE	Egypt	Greek
Cleodamus Malchus	2nd BCE	Carthage	Greek
Pseudo-Eupolemus	2nd BCE	Samaria	Greek
Aristeas, *On the Jews*	2nd BCE	?	Greek
3 Maccabees	1st BCE	Alexandria	Greek

IIA. Related Work

Pseudo-Aristeas	2nd BCE	Egypt	Greek

III. Jewish Prose Fictions, 323 BCE–135 CE

Author or Work	Date/Century	Locale	Language
Tobit	3rd–2nd BCE	Israel	Aramaic
Judith	2nd BCE	Israel	Hebrew
Lysimachus, Greek Esther	2nd BCE	Egypt	Greek
Greek Daniel	1st BCE		Greek
Joseph and Aseneth	1st CE	Egypt	Greek

Pagans and Christians alike (e.g., Alexander Polyhistor and Eusebius) often lumped the first two groups together in the category of accounts of the Jews. For this reason, we will consider both of these groups but exclude the third. This raises the question whether these works shared common historiographical orientations and practices. Josephus (*Ap.* 1.6–56) claimed that there was a tradition of eastern historiography, including Jewish historiography: the first half of Josephus' excursus (1.6–27) is a critique of the Hellenic tradition; the second half (1.28–56) is a defense of the eastern tradition. Josephus criticized the Hellenic tradition for two reasons: it was relatively recent (1.6–14) and was inconsistent (1.15–27), because Greek historians failed to keep accurate records (1.19–22) and were preoccupied with style over substance (1.23–27). By way of contrast, the eastern peoples kept reliable records (1.28–29), including the Jews (1.30–43). The credibility of Jewish historians extends also to contemporary events: Josephus was an eyewitness of the Jewish War (1.44–56). Thus whether addressing ancient traditions or contemporary events, the Jews based themselves on reliable sources.

3   "The Older is Better"

Josephus' excursus is polemical, and this shapes a number of historiographical concerns. He opens with a broadside (*Ap.* 1.6):

> In the first place I am completely dumbfounded by those who think that we should pay attention to the Greeks alone and learn the truth from them about the most ancient events but not trust us or other peoples.

He repeats it at the opening of the second half (1.27):

> Therefore with respect to eloquence or skill in articulation, we must concede to Greek authors, not however with respect to the reliable history of antiquity, especially the history of the peoples in each land.

These statements reflect a wider polemic characteristic of eastern authors, a posture responding to a Greek conceit that Strabo captures (11.6.2):

> The accounts of the ancient history of the Persians, Medes, and Syrians have not won much credence as a result of the simplicity of their historians and their love of myths.

Josephus articulated the eastern response (*Ap.* 1.15, cf. 1.161): "How unreasonable it is that the Greeks are so conceited that they believe that they alone know ancient history and pass on the truth about it accurately." Josephus was not alone: Manetho criticized Herodotus' account of Egypt (*FGrHist* 609 T 7; F 13); Berossus found fault with Hellanicus' account of Semiramis, the legendary founder of Babylon (680 F 8); and Philo of Byblos wrote a three-volume *Unbelievable History* to refute the inconsistencies of Greek accounts (790 FF 12–13).

Antiquity

The battle between Hellenic and non-Hellenic accounts took place over antiquity. Diodorus stated the issue clearly (1.9.3): "Concerning the antiquity of race, not only do the Greeks lay claim (to being the oldest), but many of the barbarians as well." Timaeus of Locri put the principle simply when describing the origins of the cosmos: "the older is better than the younger" (Plat. *Tim.* 34c). Josephus knew these claims and the principle behind them, and retorted with a paraphrase of Herodotus: "Everything in the Greek world is new and took place yesterday or the day before as the saying goes" (*Ap.* 1.7; cf. Hdt. 2.53.1; also Plat. *Tim.* 22b). The more common way to make the point was to claim antiquity for the historian's people. Berossus claimed that Babylonian history spanned more than 150,000 years (*FGrHist* 680 F 1). Manetho and Mosmes claimed that the Egyptians were the oldest people on the earth (609 F 4 and 614 T 1). Philo of Byblos made the same claim for the Phoenicians (790 F 1).

Jewish historians entered this debate without hesitation. The first prose author in Greek whose work has come down to us is Demetrius (3rd c. BCE), of whom we have six fragments. Demetrius painstakingly worked out a biblical chronology that established key dates in the story of Israel: Adam, the Flood, the call of Abraham, the entrance into Egypt (*FGrHist* 722 F 2.18), the fall of Samaria, the fall of Jerusalem, and the reign of Philopator (all dealt with in F 6.1–2). He cross-referenced a number of events such as Isaac's death and Joseph's entrance into Egypt (F 2.11), the birth of Kohath in the year that Jacob died (F 2.19), and the period between the fall of Samaria and Jerusalem (F 6.1). The establishment of key dates and cross-referencing suggests that he was interested in developing a systematic chronology, in this way attempting to do for the Jewish people what Eratosthenes had done for the Greeks (*FGrHist* 241). He based his calculations on the recent translation of the Hebrew text known as the Septuagint, a text that afforded him one clear advantage: it added to the antiquity of the Jewish people. The Hebrew text calculates the period from Adam to Abraham as 1,948 years, the Septuagint as 3,314 years.

Other Jewish historians were also anxious to demonstrate the antiquity of the Jewish people. Eupolemus, the second-century priest and ambassador, wrote a history *Concerning the Kings in Judea* that extended from Adam to 158/157 BCE. Unfortunately, we again have only fragments. F 5 summarizes the chronology of the work that appears to have been sustained throughout the history (F 2.30.1, 2, 8; 34.4; F 3). Eupolemus claimed that 5,149 years had elapsed since Adam and 2,580 years since the exodus. Despite some textual uncertainties about the numbers in the text, it is clear that he placed the emergence of the Jewish people in remote antiquity.

Two other authors (of whom again only fragments survive) may have shared this concern about antiquity. Aristeas (*FGrHist* 725) identified Job with Jobab and made him the son of Esau (F 1), perhaps drawing from the Septuagint of Job 42:17, although there Jobab is a fifth-generation descendant of Abraham. Although there may be a problem in the transmission of the tradition, Aristeas clearly situated Job early. The case is much clearer in the work of Thallus – if he was a Jew – who, like Demetrius, developed a chronological system. In this case it extended from more than 300 years prior to the Trojan War (F 2) to the first century CE (F 1). He appears to have made the claim that Moses was an ancient figure, perhaps the first lawgiver, although it is difficult to know whether this claim was made directly by Thallus or by Theophilus and Pseudo-Justin who cite him (FF 2, 4).

Josephus made the antiquity of the Jewish people a major concern, claiming that his *Antiquities* spanned 5,000 years (*Ap.* 1.1; cf. *AJ* 1.13):

> I believe that in my writing of the *Antiquities*... I have made perfectly clear to any who read it that the Jewish race is most ancient, is originally of pure stock, and how it settled the land that we now possess.

He argued that Moses had been born more than 2,000 years previously, such a long time ago "that their [i.e., Greek] poets have not dared to refer to the births of the gods to it, much less human deeds or laws" (*AJ* 1.16). The high priests could be traced for 2,000 years (*AJ* 20.261; see also Philo, *Hypoth.* 8.6.9), a claim made explicit again when he introduces a statement of Pseudo-Hecataeus' description of Jerusalem with the comment that the Jews had inhabited it from "the most ancient times" (*Ap.* 1.196).

The Origins of Culture

The reason for these efforts was the related claim that the oldest people were the *fons* of civilization. Diodorus explained the debate (1.9.3):

> they claim that they are autochthonous and the first of all people to be discoverers of those things which are useful in life, and that the events which have transpired among them were considered worthy of record from the earliest period of time.

Josephus put it bluntly when he argued for the antiquity of the Jewish law (*Ap.* 2.152):

> In point of fact, all nations attempt to trace their customs back to the most ancient time so that they will not appear to imitate others but to have instructed others on how to live lawfully.

Jewish historians entered into this debate with gusto, especially in the Hellenistic period. The first was Artapanus whose three fragments relate the story of the Hebrews in Egypt in the persons of Abraham, Joseph, and Moses. According to Artapanus, Abraham taught Pharaoh astronomy (F 1), Joseph discovered measures (F 2), and Moses was the founder of Egyptian civilization (F 3)! The historical novelist was particularly anxious to elevate Moses to whom he gave the name Mousaios, the companion of Orpheus, only Artapanus reversed their roles and made Mousaios Orpheus' teacher (F 3.3). His list of Moses' discoveries included ships, machines for stone construction, Egyptian weapons, hydraulic and military devices, philosophy, Egyptian religion, and hieroglyphs (F 3.4).

Other historians made similar claims. Pseudo-Eupolemus claimed that Enoch taught Abraham astrology (F 2; F 1.3, 8, 9) and that he in turn taught it to the Phoenicians (F 2; F 1.4) and the Egyptians (F 1.6–8). Eupolemus presented Moses as the source of civilization: Moses was the *first* wise person; the *first* to teach the alphabet to the Jews who passed it on to the Phoenicians who, in turn, handed it on to the Greeks; and the *first* to give laws to the Jews (F 1). Josephus knew the same tradition, but was more restrained in his use of it. He claimed that Abraham was "extraordinarily bright, a man skilled not only in intellectual powers but also in the power of persuasion," and that he taught the Egyptians both arithmetic and astronomy and they, in turn, taught the Greeks (*AJ* 1.166–167). While Josephus does not make the same explicit claims for Moses that some of his predecessors did, his opening panegyric on Moses (*AJ* 1.18–26) leaves little room for doubt that he considered Moses to be the greatest lawgiver and sage in history.

The point of these authors was not lost on later Christian writers who made use of their works. Eusebius summarized Clement of Alexandria's use of these authors by saying that he refers to "Josephus, Demetrius, Eupolemus, Jewish authors, who all have demonstrated in writing that Moses and the Jewish people are older than the first appearance of the Greeks" (*HE* 6.13.7). In this way, Jewish historians gave an *interpretatio Judaica* to the *interpretatio Graeca* that characterized Greek accounts of civilization.

Legitimacy

There is one other major concern that is reflected in the historians who argued for the antiquity of their people. Jewish authors who lived away from *Eretz Israel*, and Jerusalem in particular, often traced the origins of the Jewish community in their locale to an ancestor as a means of arguing for the legitimacy and rightful place of this community within Judaism. These historians did not make their claims explicit, but either rewrote the stories of Israel's ancestors to include their communities or concentrated their stories on a specific geographical locale, which suggests that they were making a special claim for that place.

Artapanus is a good example. As noted above, the three fragments that we have of his work all concentrate on the Jewish ancestors who had extensive careers in Egypt: F 1 deals with Abraham, F 2 with Joseph, and F 3 with Moses. The fact that F 1 restricts its attention to Abraham's Egyptian career and that F 3 ends with the crossing of the Red Sea suggests that Artapanus concentrated exclusively on the story of the Jews in Egypt. He probably wrote for the Jewish community in Egypt and wanted to situate their place within Egypt. Pseudo-Hecataeus was also concerned about the Jewish community in Egypt. He, however, made his case in a different way. He began – at least our fragments begin – with the migration of the high priest Ezechias from Judea to Egypt. This appears to be an argument for the right of Jews to migrate to Egypt (F 1). While Ezechias was not an ancestor, as high priest he had a privileged place, and his actions in encouraging the migration to Egypt argued for the legitimacy of the community.

Other historians altered the biblical story to associate their communities with ancestors. Cleodamus Malchus traced the descendants of Abraham through Keturah (F 1). The couple had three sons, each of whom became the eponymous ancestor of a significant community: Assouri of Assyria; Aphran of Aphra, a city in Africa; and Apher of Africa. The two brothers who migrated to Africa fought with Heracles against Antaeus, the Libyan giant (Diod. 4.17.4–5; Plut. *Sert.* 9.3–5). Heracles married the daughter of Aphran from whose union came the subsequent kings of Libya. In this way, the origins of Libya are connected with Jewish ancestors! While this can be interpreted in multiple ways, it appears to fit the pattern of making claims for the legitimacy of a specific Jewish community and a means of giving them a sense of identity in a locale.

There is at least one other example. Pseudo-Eupolemus went out of his way to associate Abraham with Samaria. He called Israel "Phoenicia" and has Abraham entertained "by the city at the temple Argarizin which is interpreted 'mountain of the Most High'" (*FGrHist* 724 F 1). Given the polemical nature of the relationship between Jews and Samaritans over the proper mount on which to worship God (John Hyrkanus destroyed the temple on Mount Gerizim ca. 128 BCE: [Jos. *AJ* 11.321–334; 13.254–256, but this did not end the controversy: cf. John 4:20]), this appears to be a direct endorsement of the Samaritan claim. It is probable that Pseudo-Eupolemus was attempting to rewrite the story of Israel to accentuate a Samaritan perspective. Some have thought that Thallus also betrays an interest in Samaria – he shares the same euhemeristic perspective as Pseudo-Eupolemus – but the evidence is too thin to make a convincing case.

All of these examples indicate that Jewish historians frequently devoted a good deal of attention to origins. In some cases the claim was made in light of competing claims in the larger world. In other cases, the claim was intended to help a specific Jewish community understand its own place. In both instances the primary readers were probably Jewish. The only question was whether they were attempting to situate themselves in the larger world or within the world of Judaism itself.

4   Sources

The claim for antiquity and for an earlier civilization lay in the records that the Jews kept. The most important representatives of eastern historiography argued that they based their accounts on their ancestral records (*Ap*. 1.28):

> That the Egyptians and Babylonians devoted care to their records from the earliest ages...and that, among those who associated with the Greeks, the Phoenicians used writing both for the management of daily life and for the record of public events, I think I can let pass since everyone agrees.

Berossus (*FGrHist* 680 T 3), Manetho (609 T 7), Philo of Byblos (790 TT 3, 5; F 1) all made this claim.

The Jewish Scriptures

Josephus picked up this traditional feature of eastern historiography and argued that his *Antiquities* was a translation of the Hebrew Scriptures (*AJ* 1.5; 10.218; *Ap*. 1.54). He even went so far as to claim that he had not altered the text (*AJ* 1.17; 4.196;

10.218; 14.1; 20.261), a claim that is patently false. While the meaning of the phrase has been debated at length, it appears that Josephus used the phrase as a guarantee of the reliability of the text since he used the same language for the reliability of the Septuagint (*AJ* 12.108–109 and *Ap.* 1.42).

Other Jewish historians did not claim to make a translation, but made the biblical text the *point d'appui* for their work. In the case of 1 Esdras, the work is largely a translation (although the *Vorlage* is debated) of selected sections of the biblical text with additions, most notably the story of King Darius' bodyguards (1 Esdras 1:1–55 ~ 2 Chron 35:1–36:21; 1 Esdras 2:1–14 ~ Ezra 1:1–11; 1 Esdras 2:15–25 ~ Ezra 4:6–24; 1 Esdras 3:1–5:6, the contest of the bodyguards; 1 Esdras 5:7–70 ~ Ezra 2:1–4:5; 1 Esdras 6:1–7:15 ~ Ezra 5:1–6:22; 1 Esdras 8:1–9:36 ~ Ezra 7:1–10:44; 1 Esdras 9:37–55 ~ Neh. 7:72, 8:1–12). Pseudo-Philo rewrote the biblical text from Adam to the death of Saul in a complex narrative that mixes verbatim citations of the biblical text with secondary biblical texts, additions, and significant omissions. The narrative is an example of "rewritten Bible" whose closest contemporary parallel is the book of Jubilees. Among those who used the biblical text for a framework, some handled it with real care (e.g., Demetrius), while others manipulated it to suit the exigencies of their work (e.g., Artapanus).

While all of these authors could point to a group of sacred texts, the extent of that authoritative body of texts is a point of considerable debate among current scholars. Josephus provided a clear statement of his own understanding of the texts (*Ap.* 1.37–41), a statement that coheres with the modern Jewish understanding. It is not entirely clear, however, that this was a universal judgment at the end of the first century or how early it became so. At any rate, the Jews had a special group of writings that consistently served as a basis for their accounts of the past. This body of texts gave their accounts of antiquity a common framework.

It also created a number of challenges. One of the features of the ethnographic tradition that lay at the root of eastern historiography was the recording of customs. The Jews were well known for some unusual customs, as Greek and Latin accounts of them make clear. Jewish historians were sensitive to these charges and attempted to explain some of the unusual features of Jewish traditions. Artapanus has a famous account of the power of the ineffable name of Yahweh that Jews would not pronounce (F 3.24–26). Pseudo-Hecataeus went to some length to explain why Jews were so firmly committed to the observance of their customs (F 1.190–193). He also explained the aniconic nature of the Jewish temple (F 1.197–199). Josephus explained Jewish customs for his readers (e.g., *AJ* 17.200, 213; 20.106, 216) and promised to write a work *On Customs and Causes* (*AJ* 20.268), a promise apparently unfulfilled. *In nuce*, Jewish historians were aware of the difficulties posed by their own records and customs and attempted to address them.

Non-Jewish Sources

It was not, however, enough to rewrite the ancestral text. Jewish historians consistently incorporated other traditions into their works. Some early Hellenistic Jewish historians interwove eastern and Hellenic myths into the fabric of biblical cloth when relating the stories of their ancestors in an effort to demonstrate their antiquity and the equal status of their ancestors with the ancestors of other groups. Artapanus appears to have written his account of Moses with the story of Sesostris of Egypt in mind. There are at least five parallels between the two figures: each divided Egypt into thirty-six nomes (Diod. 1.54.3 ~ 726 F 3.4); each conducted an Ethiopian campaign (Diod. 1.55.1 ~ F 3.7–10); each honored the gods (Diod. 1.56.2 ~ F 3.4); both had plots against their lives after their return from the campaign (Diod. 1.57.6–8 ~ F 3.11–18); and both organized the military (Diod. 1.94.4 ~ F 3.4, 8). This much agreement appears to be more than coincidental: Moses was no less a figure than the Egyptian hero (see Hdt. 2.102–111)! Pseudo-Eupolemus probably drew from both Babylonian and Greek traditions. He identified Abraham with the unnamed – at least in our fragment – figure in the tenth generation after the Flood whom Berossus described as "just, great, and learned in heavenly matters" (cf. *FGrHist* 680 F 6 with 724 F 1.3). He also wove Greek accounts that associated Kronos with the giants (e.g., Hes. *Theog.* 176–186) into his account that claimed that Kronos = Belos who founded Babylon and built the tower (F 2), the tower that the giants built (F 1). Thallus also mentioned Belos and the war with the Titans, only he thought that Belos and Kronos were allies and associated Belos with Assyria (256 F 2). We have already noted that Cleodamus Malchus made a connection between Abraham's descendants and Heracles. All of these attempts appear to be ways to trace Abraham and his descendants well back to the beginning of Babylonian, Assyrian, and Greek culture.

There is a second group of texts that strikes anyone who reads through the Jewish historians. These are the documents from authorities that accord Jewish communities special rights and privileges. There is a great deal of literature on these texts in 1 and 2 Maccabees and Josephus' *Antiquities*, and their authenticity is not universally accepted; it is quite likely that some of these are spurious. The number of these decrees, however, is significant. (A complete list: 1 Macc. 8:23–32; 10:18–20, 25–45, 52–54, 55–56, 70–73; 11:9–10, 30–37, 42–43, 57; 12:5–18, 20–23; 13:36–40; 14:20–23, 27–45; 15:2–9, 16–21; 2 Macc. 1:1–9, 10–2:18; 9:19–27; 11:16–21, 22–26, 27–33, 34–38; Jos. *AJ* 14.145–148, 149–155, 185–195, 196–198, 199, 200–201, 202–210, 211–212, 213–216, 219–222, 225–227, 228–230, 231–232, 233, 234, 235, 236–237, 237–240, 241–243, 244–246, 247–255, 256–258, 259–261, 262–264, 306–313, 314–318, 319–322; 16.160–165, 166, 167–168, 169–170, 171, 172–173; 19.280–285, 286–291; 20.10–14.) Josephus tells us why he included them (*AJ* 16.175, cf. 14.185–189, 265–267; 16.160–161, 174–178): "I frequently make mention of them, reconciling other peoples and removing the causes of hatred that have developed in unreasonable people among us and them." It was in this same spirit that Josephus regularly cited non-Jewish historians to confirm the narrative when possible.

Eyewitnesses

Josephus mentions one other source in his excursus on historiography. He claims that his account of the Jewish War is based on eyewitness testimony (*Ap.* 1.47–52), a claim that reminds us of Thucydides and Polybius who both wrote histories of wars in which they participated. Josephus is particularly close to Polybius whose interpretation of the *Bellum Achaicum* (e.g., 38.10.6–7; 38.3.7; 38.18.8–12) is strikingly similar to Josephus' interpretation of the Jewish War (*BJ* 1.10–11): a group of radicals gained the upper hand and brought a disaster on the nation as a whole.

This raises the issue of the literature that purports to deal with more contemporary rather than ancient events. While Josephus did not have the critical acumen of Thucydides, Polybius, or the Oxyrhynchus historian, his account of the war should be considered a relatively sober one, at least in comparison to many of his co-patriots' works. In this regard he is matched by the author of 1 Maccabees who wrote to exalt the Hasmoneans. This Judean historian appears to have deliberately rejected the Hellenism that the story opposed by writing in Hebrew. He thus wrote in the biblical tradition; he altered it, however, in several significant ways. There is a conspicuous absence of the miraculous in 1 Maccabees. God is not referred to by name, but by the surrogate "heaven." God is a factor, but is not on the stage in the same way that the divine is in the Deuteronomistic history. Thus, in a strange twist, the author wrote a national history but distanced God from the story in a way that was unlike his ancestral tradition.

The epitomator of Jason of Cyrene had a very different response. Like the author of 1 Esdras and Eupolemus, he is concerned about the temple. However, unlike the author of 1 Maccabees, he is far less enthralled with the Hasmonean regime and its purification of the temple. Perhaps the statement in 5:19 captures the message: "the Lord did not choose the people because of the place, but the place because of the people." This author thought that the Jews posed the greatest threat to their own future. Like Brutus who epitomized Polybius or the Livian *periochae*, or Justin who reduced Pompeius Trogus' forty-four-volume *Historiae Philippicae*, our author did not see the value of the full five volumes of Jason (2 Macc. 2:19–32). He wrote in the florid style that characterized so much of Hellenistic historiography: the more powerful the emotional appeal, the better.

5   Conclusion

Jewish historiography in the Hellenistic and early Roman worlds was complex. Jewish authors were recipients of a tradition of historiography that could not be ignored. The presence of a common group of texts that had to serve as a basis for any retelling of the early history of the Jewish people was fundamental. Some attempted to continue it, but in different ways. Others drew from these texts but creatively altered the story. Regardless of the specific historiographical stance that these different historians took, they all shared a couple of common perspectives. First, they wrote the story of a people. Some wrote about ancient history while others wrote about more recent history. The common element was that the Jewish people were the basic subject matter of their stories. As such, they wrote to establish the identity of the Jewish people, whether they understood this in terms of the larger world or solely of Judaism. Second, they believed that God controlled the history of the Jewish people.

Their understanding of the divine and how the divine worked in history varied, yet they all recognized that it was their connection to their ancestral traditions and God that gave them identity as the Jewish people.

There is a strange twist to the subsequent history of these historians. The heirs of these historians were not the rabbis who developed Rabbinic Judaism after the destruction of Jerusalem, but rather the early Christians who preserved these works and developed a new and different identity that lacked the specific ethnic focus of these earlier historians. They used these Jewish historians and the identity that they offered of Judaism to create a new identity for the religious adherents of Christianity. Just as these historians recreated their ancestral past to forge a new identity in the Hellenistic and Roman worlds, so early Christians used these reconstructions of Hellenistic Judaism to create Christian Hellenism.

FURTHER READING

The texts of the historians appear in different sources. The best collection of the Hellenistic Jewish historians is Holladay 1983. 1 and 2 Maccabees and 1 Esdras are available in editions of the Septuagint (Rahlfs 1935; the *editio maior* is the Göttingen edition with critical editions of 1–4 Maccabees [1967] and 1 Esdras [1974]). The *editio maior* for Josephus is still Niese 1885–1895, the basis for the Loeb edition. Under the leadership of F. Siegert, the Institutum Judaicum Delitzschianum at the University of Münster is producing a new edition of the works of Josephus with German translations and notes: the volume on the *Life* has appeared (Siegert et al. 2001). E. Nodet and a team of French scholars are producing an edition of the *Jewish Antiquities* with a French translation and notes: vols. 1–4 covering *AJ* 1–9 have appeared (Nodet 1992–2005). The Latin translation of Pseudo-Philo is available in Sources Chrétiennes (Harrington et al. 1976) and in Jacobson 1996. All of the works except those in the Septuagint and Josephus are available in English translations in Charlesworth 1983–1985. The *Jüdische Schriften aus hellenistisch-römischer Zeit* volumes have German translations of and notes to these works (vols. 1 and 3) with extensive introductions and bibliographies (vol. 6).

There are several helpful surveys of Hellenistic Jewish historians. These typically treat each author individually. Some of the most important recent surveys include: Attridge 1984a and 1986, with helpful bibliography; Doran 1987, which should be read in tandem with Walter 1987; Denis 2000: II.1107–1189; Mittmann-Richert 2000, the most extensive recent treatment; and Lehnardt 1999, who offers an excellent bibliographic beginning point.

There are some important monographs that treat different aspects of the tradition. Sterling 1992/2006 attempts to establish a historiographical tradition to which a number of the fragmentary Jewish Hellenistic historians and Josephus' *Antiquities* belong. Wills 1995 has argued for the genre of the Jewish novel and collected and translated these as Wills 2002. Gruen 1998 emphasizes the creativity and playfulness of many of these works. Inowlocki 2006 argues that Eusebius did more than collect Jewish sources, a point that is of great importance to the study of the fragmentary historians.

Finally, there are important treatments of individual historians. Wacholder 1974 provides not only a thorough treatment of Eupolemus, but analyzes similar concerns in other authors. Bar-Kochva 1996 demonstrates how Pseudo-Hecataeus argued for the legitimacy of his diaspora community. The bibliography on 1 & 2 Maccabees and Josephus is staggering. Goldstein 1976 and 1983 are a good beginning point. The single most important recent contribution to Josephus is the Brill commentary series that S. Mason is editing. Each volume contains a fresh English translation and commentary. Five of a projected ten volumes have appeared covering the *Life*, *AJ* 1–10, and *Against Apion*. Louis Feldman has devoted a lifetime of research to Josephus; he has made a special contribution to the way that Josephus presents characters in *AJ*, e.g., Feldman 1998b, 1998c. Rajak 2002 is one of the most important interpretations of *BJ*. Feldman and Levison 1996 contains the most important recent work on Josephus' apology. Schreckenberg 1968 and 1979, Feldman 1984b (with the update in Feldman 1989) provide extensive bibliographies of past research.

CHAPTER TWENTY

The Greek Historians of Rome

Christopher Pelling

1 Introduction

Rome changed everything, including the way history would be written. For one thing, the story was breathtaking: as Polybius asks in his proem (1.1.5), who could fail to be gripped by the paradoxical shift of Fortune which allowed Rome "in less than fifty-three years to bring virtually all the world under one rule?" For another, it suggested a new relation of writer and theme. Greeks who wrote about Rome would write as outsiders: not as outside as all that, as they too were implicated in the new world, but still their Greekness marked them out as observers rather than masters. True, Herodotus, Thucydides, and Xenophon had set themselves up as outsiders too, men who through travel or exile had seen both sides in a conflict or many sides in tracking the complexity of the world; but Polybius, Posidonius, and Dionysius had outsiderness thrust upon them, for good and for ill.

Outsiderness can however take several forms, and these writers constructed the historian's role in different ways. Who, now, is the right person to write history? Should it still be people who have participated in politics as much as they can, as Polybius played a major role in the Achaean confederacy, and acted as "a true friend of Rome" (39.3.7–8)? Or is it to be a philosopher like Posidonius? Or a man of letters like Dionysius, who has culled from his knowledge of rhetoric the best contribution that Greek culture can make to the understanding of Rome? And who are they writing for? For other Greeks, as (usually) their texts contrive to suggest? If so, what are the lessons there – ones of admiration, or of understanding what makes Romans different, or something more practical about how to respond to the ruling power? Are Romans too included in the target audience, reading over the shoulder of the Greeks? If there are lessons for them to learn too, it would be no surprise if the sharpest criticisms were also the most oblique. And are there ways in which the Greekness can be a help rather than a hindrance, lending the authority of centuries of culture while defusing any threat of genuine political rivalry? The wise advisor was a staple of earlier Greek historiography: are these writers molding a similar identity, saving Greek self-respect while allowing Romans to learn without losing face?

Many of those themes, especially the relation of past and present and the construction of a reader–writer dynamic that flatters the self-respect of both Greeks and Romans, are familiar from modern scholarship of the second and third centuries CE (the "Second Sophistic"), and it would indeed be possible to track them in the Greek historians and biographers of the Roman empire. But the remit of this chapter is a narrower one, the Greek historians who wrote about Rome during the republic and under Augustus: and not all of these, for a full treatment would range from Heraclides Ponticus and Timaeus to Strabo and Nicolaus of Damascus. This chapter will concentrate only on three major figures, Polybius, Posidonius, and Dionysius. Even with these the treatment will be selective. Such is the nature of *Companions* – but, more than most, this chapter will be a mere tug-boat *Companion*, waving a reader off on what will be a very long journey if it is to pay the texts their due.

2 Polybius

Another way in which Rome changed everything, as Polybius again says in his proem, was that the new shape of power invited a particular shape of narrative. Hitherto "the events of the world had been, as it were, scattered" (1.3.3), and so what Polybius calls *kata meros* historiography – "bitty" or "piecemeal," focusing on a particular locality or topic – was not unnatural, despite its deficiencies. But now everything had been brought together into a single, "body-like" whole (1.3.4, etc.), and history should become universal too. If the worldwide success of Augustus gave momentum to universal history (Clarke 1999b), that was only replaying a phenomenon that had already happened 150 years earlier, as literary form accommodated itself to the molding of reality.

Not merely did Rome allow a tighter, more coherent story to be told. It was also a different sort of story. Polybius' survey of earlier empires – Persia, Sparta, Macedon (1.2) – immediately gestures towards the literary accounts of these empires, those of Herodotus, Xenophon, and the Alexander historians. All had dealt with empires that had not merely risen but also faltered. The transience of empire is indeed Polybius' point in that passage; it recurs later (6.43–44, 48–50; 36.9.5–8; 38.2: Alonso-Núñez 1983), in particular when he muses on the fall of Macedon and recalls the reflections of Demetrius of Phalerum 150 years earlier on the fate of Persia (29.21). A rise-and-fall story has a different shape from one of success, such as Rome's: it has closure, and it needs to explain collapse as well as triumph, frailty as well as brilliance. True, those explanations may not be so different: it was a recurrent Greek insight that strengths of character often linked intimately with weaknesses, that Persia's autocratic cohesion or Athens' self-confidence or Sparta's militarism or Alexander's charisma could come to destroy the achievement they had generated. But the explanatory agenda still tends to be more complex when failure needs to be explained as well as success.

Polybius too is interested in character: he comments explicitly on the great impact a single individual can have, for good or, as in the case of the Aetolian Lyciscus, for ill (32.4). But – at least where Roman individuals are concerned – his characterizing palette is more limited than his predecessors', just as he has a narrower range of questions to ask. Even the most developed Roman figures, the two Scipios and Flamininus, tend towards idealized stereotypings. It is the characters who have falls as well as rises, especially Philip (Walbank 1938), Hannibal, and Antiochus III and IV, who are the more ambivalent and shaded, with their falls explained by a combination of internal failings and external circumstances (Walbank 1972: 96; Eckstein 1995a: 240): just as we shall later see that it is characters who operate from weakness and make decisions that can go wrong, like Aratus or Philopoemen, who raise particularly thought-provoking issues.

Rome's collective character matters too, and matters more. Here Polybius echoes Thucydides' explanatory schemes, but again his variations link with this different shape of story. Polybius explains that he has written his first two books (1.3.9):

> so that no one, on coming to the narrative, should be at a loss and inquire what were the Romans' motives and what their powers and resources for launching themselves on these enterprises that made them masters of all land and sea in our part of the world...

Motives, powers, resources: these are the tools of success – even "motives," for these will include the Romans' ambitious cast of mind (e.g., 1.57.1–4; 8.1(3); 9.8.1) as well as their intentions at particular moments (especially 36.2, below, p. 248). In the passage on which this is modeled, Thucydides had simply said, "so that no one should have to look for what led to so great a war among the Greeks" (1.23.5), a formulation that asks as much for narrative as for analysis, and is not geared to success. "Power and resources" also answers to a Thucydidean preoccupation, but Thucydides addresses that question at several points some way into his narrative, when exploring the reasons for each side's confidence when the war is breaking out, and the thoughtful reader will at each point wonder whether these resources will really suffice, whether the confidence is justified (1.121–122, 1.140–144, 2.13). In Polybius we know from the beginning that they will be enough. That affects the tone in which the catalogue of Italian manpower is introduced, explaining how Hannibal was outnumbered by something like forty to one (2.24.1):

> so that the facts themselves may make clear [another Thucydidean echo, this time of 1.21.2] how great was the power that Hannibal dared to attack and how mighty the empire that he eyed so courageously; and he came so near to success that he inflicted the greatest catastrophes on the Romans...

Hannibal will be a formidable enemy, but he will also fail ("he came *so near to* success"). The Italian resources will be enough, just as they are enough to see off the Gauls in the fighting that the catalogue itself introduces. The fertility of Italy, again introduced during the Gallic fighting (2.15), suggests something similar. No wonder Rome wins.

Both points – the closeness of the conflict and the underlying Roman strength – explain why the long treatment of the constitution in Book 6 comes when Rome's fortunes are at their lowest after the battle of Cannae, for that constitution gives resilience as well as triumph, enabling Rome to stand this toughest of tests before going on to conquer the world. Or rather their "institutions" as well as "constitution," as Polybius dwells on Roman military practices and religion, just as he later focuses on various features of Roman military superiority (18.18, Roman stakes; 18.28–32, the comparison of phalanx and legion; 28.11, the *testudo*). Moral strengths count too (that "collective character" again): Roman institutions inspire moral excellence and mental courage (6.55, with the tale of Horatius Cocles). And fame, especially, is the Roman spur, that respect for eternal glory that is embedded in the institution of the funeral oration (6.52–54).

Particularly important, though, is Rome's "mixed constitution," welding elements of monarchy, aristocracy, and democracy. Herodotus, Thucydides, and Xenophon had already investigated the ways in which a state's institutions could bring success (though again their agenda extended to the dangers as well); but Herodotus and Xenophon had also explored characteristics of other peoples, particularly Persia, in tandem with those of Greece. Polybius' spectacles are more firmly fixed to look outwards, and for him the characteristics of Greece are more interesting for what they clarify about Rome. When Polybius compares Rome not merely with Carthage but also with particular Greek states (Athens, Thebes, Crete, Sparta, even Plato's Republic, 6.43–56), that brings to the surface a *sunkrisis* that has been implicit throughout. Even the conceptual scheme is Greek, exploiting the Platonic idea of a cycle as monarchy decays into tyranny, tyranny into oligarchy, and oligarchy into democracy. Yet Rome does not fit the simplest form of that cycle (*anakuklōsis*), as it is already combining the best elements of each, and that is one reason for its stability. (So this is an elaborate form of the common Greek presentational strategy of beginning with an over-simple generalization, then revising it in stride by showing how the "cycle" only fits Rome in a refined and qualified way.)

Still, no constitution is proof against total change, not the Spartan constitution that came closest to stability through being "mixed" (6.48–50); not Carthage, that once had similar strengths (6.51); and not now Rome itself, where there are also clear pointers of a constitutional development that will eventually lead to mob-rule (6.57). Later passages suggest that decline has already started: Romans used to be impervious to bribery, but no longer (18.35.1–2), with the exception of the incorruptible Aemilius Paullus and Scipio Aemilianus. The young men of Rome are now licentious, corrupt, and cowardly (31.25, 35.4), though again with the exception of Scipio. Rome's constitutional strengths may be a bulwark to slow the turn of the cycle, but there may come a day when Rome is in danger too: Scipio Aemilianus senses as much, for rather different reasons, when he weeps at the fall of Carthage (38.21–22: below, p. 248).

Is this then to be seen as a warning to Rome as well as a celebration of their success? Polybius' change of writing plan may be important here. He had originally intended to cover events up to 168/7 BCE, but then decided to include additional books in the light of events between 168/7 and 146 (3.4–5), a period that culminated in the destruction of Carthage and of Corinth. And this change of plan is to enable contemporaries to judge if Roman rule is acceptable and future generations to pass moral judgment (3.4.7).

Such evaluation is certainly a function of history for Polybius (16.22a, 28 etc.), but even when he is at his most morally condemnatory, as for instance with Philip V, he also stresses the practical disadvantages of ill-repute and oppression (7.11.10–11; 7.14.5; 15.22–23, 23.10, etc.: Eckstein 1995a: 246–247). The same goes for his verdicts on Rome, and morality is often shown to be *prudentially* a good idea. When Rome plunders artworks from Syracuse, Polybius is realistic about the ruthlessness of an aspiring world power: it is no surprise that a conqueror should take away wealth from the vanquished (9.10.11). But it is prudentially ill-judged to increase your unpopularity at the same time as adopting the most enfeebling habits of those you have defeated (9.11); and it is prudentially wise to treat a conquered state with moderation, as Scipio Africanus did at New Carthage, however uncompromising the lesson taught in the initial massacre (10.15–18). The wise statesman is a moral statesman; he just makes sure that everyone knows he is.

When he comes to events of his own generation, Polybius makes no bones about the way Romans neglect justice in their own interest. They retain Demetrius at Rome despite his pleas, "not because he was not speaking justly, but because it was in their interests" (31.11.11); they repeatedly arbitrate against the Carthaginians "not because they did not have right on their side, but because the judges were convinced that it was in the Romans' own interest to decide in this way" (31.21.6–8). He stresses the long period he himself spent at Rome as one of the Achaean internees, and leaves no doubt that the Senate had not responded as fairly as they might to the repeated requests for their release (30.32; 32.3.17; 33.1.3–8; 35.6). And, if we adopt the practical concern with consequences that Polybius favors himself, we can certainly understand why there might be two views about the merits of Roman control, even if Polybius passes no view himself: thus with Glabrio's or Vulso's tough talking (20.10, 21.34), or Fulvius' removal of artworks (21.30.9). We can understand too how Perseus, however reprehensible his war-mongering, could appeal to the Rhodians in the name of Greek freedom (27.4.7), and call on Eumenes to be on his guard against Roman "arrogance and oppression" (29.4.9).

Here there is no great difference in texture between the main body and the additional final books. The Romans had long decided on the Third Punic War, and were waiting for a plausible pretext that would tell to their advantage with international public opinion (36.2): that is the same eye for expediency that we have seen before. Nor is the picture of Roman soldiers playing dice on priceless works of art after the fall of Corinth (39.2) very different from the ruthlessness we have seen in events thirty or forty years earlier.

The difference may come in the more elaborate way the moral question is treated, even if it remains delicately inexplicit. The fragmentary nature of the text means that we cannot tell what tones he used for describing the destruction of Carthage (if ever there was a candidate for "tragic history" it was that), but we do have the long chapter setting out the different views that were held "in Greece" – an interesting focalization (36.9). Some adopted the perspective that had prevailed in Rome, the

Catonian view that Carthage would be a perpetual threat unless removed; some thought rather in Greek terms, arguing that Rome was falling into the pattern set by Athens and Sparta and risked coming to a similar end (the "sequence of empires" again); some felt the Romans had acted out of character in their deceitfulness towards Carthage; others repudiated any charge of impiety, treachery, or injustice. Modern critics take this chapter in very different ways (contrast, e.g., Musti 1978: 55–56 and Ferrary 1988: 327–334 with Walbank 1972: 174–181 and 1985: 338–340), for Polybius has discreetly avoided making his own verdict explicit. Certainly, the pro-Roman arguments are given more space and are allowed the last word, often a pointer to the winner in a formal debate. Yet the moral arguments are still *excuses*, possibly good ones but still pointers to the charges that need to be answered as much as to the answers themselves; and they sit uncomfortably too with that earlier emphasis that Rome had taken the decision long before (36.2, above). But some at least of his first readers will have shared modern doubts whether the strength of the anti-Roman arguments, both prudential and moral, can be waved away.

There is a further question: if there are lessons here, who are to be the learners? The Romans themselves, warned by Polybius to lighten their burden? Or – given the indications that he has both Greek and Roman, but particularly Greek, readers in mind (Walbank 1972: 3–6) – is this aimed at the oppressed rather than the oppressors, an indication that Roman ruthlessness is a fact of life, and one has to deal with it as best one can? Or is it a bit of both?

The issues in Greek politics are indeed anything but straightforward. That is reflected in the way that so many more speeches, especially in the later books, are given to Greeks than to Romans (Walbank 1972: 45–46). At Naupactus in 217 the Aetolian Agelaus warns of that "cloud from the West" that would break over the Greeks unless they set their disagreements aside (5.104); then at 9.28–39 an Aetolian speaker stigmatizes the Macedonian kings as the oppressors of Greek liberty, while an Acarnanian praises the young Philip V as the firewall of the Greeks against the new barbarian menace. Later the dilemmas recur as Polybius analyzes the differences between the policies of Aristaenus and Philopoemen (24.11–14), both contrasting with the double-dealing Callicrates (24.10). Philopoemen's way of putting it – there will come a day when Greece needs to do all Rome's bidding, but should we hasten that day or put it off as long as possible? – leaves him with the higher moral ground; but Aristaenus is clearly responding to realities as well, ones that do not sit comfortably with the proclamation of Greek freedom by Flamininus a few years earlier (18.46). The line taken by Polybius himself as a character in the later books, stressing the dangers of opposing Rome and his own role in 146/5 in advancing Greece's interests with dignified acquiescence in Rome's wishes, is closer to Aristaenus than to the venerated Philopoemen. Perhaps, indeed, that grim time that Philopoemen had foreseen had now arrived, and the Greeks could do nothing but accept and obey.

Yet there are surely lessons there for Romans too. There have to be, given that stress on the practical advantages to a ruling power of being seen to treat its subjects well (1.72, cf. 1.88.3, 10.36, and Flamininus' speech at 18.37). So here too there are hints of the perils of success, just as we saw earlier, in a different register, with the Roman constitution (p. 247): a famous passage describes Scipio's tears as he contemplated the fall of Carthage, as Rome too would one day fall (38.21–22: for the implied sensibility, Hornblower 1981: 102–106). Still, none of this need be subversive, not Scipio's tears, not even the reservations that readers might feel over the treatment of Carthage: no more than Pindar is subversive when dwelling in an ode to Hiero on the dangers of success. The implication is that Romans, like Hiero, are so successful that these are the appropriate lessons to learn, and so wise that they, unlike other peoples, will be able to do so. And Romans, as we see them in the *History*, do indeed learn. They have learnt from the Greeks on matters of warfare (6.25); they have learnt from the Carthaginians on ship-design (1.20.15). They learn on the wider scale as well: that strength of the constitution came about, not through the once-for-all theorizing of a visionary Lycurgus, but through a constant learning from experience (6.6.12–14).

If there are lessons to learn, then Polybius is the person to teach them. The historian, so insistent that he is different from his predecessors, matches the theme and the city, different as they too are from anything that has gone before. A can-do, practical nation provides the template that a practical historian can adopt for teaching can-do lessons. Polybius' predecessors were sloppy, sensationalist, captious, and parochial: they were not *pragmatikoi*, men who understand political and military action, do their preparation properly, and analyze causes in a way that allows future statesmen to avoid making the same mistakes (Meister 1975; Walbank 1972: 32–96; 1985: 262–279). Rome both makes a historian like Polybius possible and deserves the sort of treatment that only a historian like Polybius can give.

3   Posidonius

Posidonius of Apamea is the only ancient philosopher who is also known to have written a history, and it was a big one, fifty-two books long. He started at the point where Polybius finished, in 146/5 BCE. So perhaps did Sempronius Asellio in Latin, a half-generation or so before; so, effectively, did Strabo in Greek, a generation or so later (for only four of Strabo's forty-seven books covered the period before 145). There was nothing new about such continuation (Marincola 1997: 237–240, 289–292). Polybius himself continued both Aratus and Timaeus (1.3.1–2; 1.5.1); Xenophon began his *Hellenica* where Thucydides had abruptly stopped, and Cratippus, Theopompus, and the *Hellenica Oxyrhynchia* were also, it seems, Thucydides-continuators. As usual with gestures to predecessors, such continuation marks both homage and assertion: one's own work, it is implied, will enter the canon in its turn. As usual, too, such "homage" includes an element of competition: it was rare for such continuation to provide an exact replica of the predecessor's manner, and Thucydides' style of history marked his difference from Herodotus just as Xenophon's marked his from Thucydides. When there are multiple continuations, that suggests further competition, as a writer intimates not only that the predecessor was canonical but also that the rivals were not. Those multiple continuations of Polybius suggest a disagreement on how that turbulent history after 146 was to be told.

Was the focus to be on the discordant events of Roman and Italian politics? Was it to be told with an interest in political motivation and a moralistic tinge, as Asellio aspired to do (*HRR* FF 1–2)? Or at least with an emphasis on "the most outstanding men and their lives," as Strabo was to shape the tale (or so he claimed, *FGrHist* 91 F 2 = *Geog.* 1.1.23)? Or, however much Strabo thought Posidonius' work anything but the final word, was it rather to be told in – whatever way Posidonius told it?

The difficulty is to decipher what way that was. The more elaborate reconstructions of his views on Rome (esp. Malitz 1983) mainly rest not on the surviving fragments but on the remarks that Diodorus makes about Rome in Books 33–37. These are assumed to be taken over wholesale from Posidonius: "the cardinal fact about Diodorus is that he was a second-rate epitomator who generally used first-rate sources" (Stylianou 1998: 1). If that is right we can detect hostility towards the Gracchi, Saturninus, and Marius, together with their supporters among the *equites* and *plebs* – a suite of aristocratic Roman prejudices, in fact. There are less comfortable aspects for aristocratic sensibilities too, in particular a stress on the human misery that sparked slave revolts and the sufferings of the provinces under Roman mismanagement, though there is praise also for magistrates who governed well (Diod. 33.28b; 36.3.1–2; 37.3.4, 5–8: Malitz 1983: 331–338). There is also an emphasis on moral decline, something that chimes with a stress on ancestral Roman virtue in the securely attested fragments (*FGrHist* 87 F 59). And it is indeed *probably* right to see Posidonius behind at least most of these passages – but we do need to be cautious. These books have only one case where we can demonstrate closeness to Posidonius (F 7 ~ Diod. 34.2.34, with Kidd 1988–1999: II.1 294); and, particularly at this late stage of his work (Stylianou 1998: 8–9), Diodorus may well have done some thinking for himself, incorporating views which could be "moderately critical" of Rome and Roman politicians (Sacks 1990: 117–159 [quotation, p. 117]; 1994: 218–232).

So we are driven back to the fragments themselves. It seems likely that Posidonius adopted a thematic, nation-by-nation structure instead of a chronological one, or perhaps some combination of the two (Clarke 1999a): if so, this was closer to Herodotus (and to Cato's *Origines*) than to Polybius, and that suited the theme, describing, as Athenaeus put it (151e = T 12a), "many customs and habits of many peoples in a way that chimed in closely with his philosophy." Thus Posidonius included Roman customs – the triumphal feasting, Apicius' luxury, the principles of nomenclature – but also covered Celts and Germans, Arabia, Syria, Parthia, Egypt, Sicily, and especially Greece, Macedon, and Asia Minor. There was doubtless narrative too, and certainly an interest in historical change: the long fragment on Athenion's tyranny at Athens (F 36) is not merely narrative in itself: Athenion's dismissiveness towards Rome also points to a looming comeuppance when Rome's power will be all too clear. Posidonius' stress on ancestral virtue also leaves no doubt that things had changed.

What about the second half of Athenaeus' description, "in a way that chimed in closely with his philosophy"? We can take him as a "philosopher-historian" (Kidd 1989) in several different ways. Should we see him as exploring the *sumpatheia* (in Stoic terms) of the *kosmos*, showing how different elements of geography and history coalesce in a rational way (Clarke 1999a: 185–192)? If so, what does that suggest about the Roman power that had brought so many parts of the world together?

Was he celebrating "the inner vocation of the Roman nation for world-supremacy" (Capelle 1932: 104, regarding this – questionably – as a Stoic position) – a development of Polybius' thinking, perhaps (above, pp. 246–247), but a particularly trenchant one? Was he at least praising the Romans as "the bringers of peace and order" (Strasburger 1965: 46)? Or is the ethical aspect more a matter of setting an agenda for Rome, cataloguing the local differences that the new masters need to take into account and intimating the value of humanitarian treatment? If Strasburger (1965) was right to detect traces of a Posidonian disquisition on Mediterranean piracy, that is an interesting test case. Was that, as Strasburger thought, celebrating Pompey's success in dealing with the pirate threat in the 60s, or did it predate the 60s (nothing else makes it likely that Posidonius continued his work so far), sketching a problem that the Romans still had to solve?

Of one thing we can be sure: Posidonius was not felt by elite Romans – and he knew a lot of them, enough to be described as "a friend of everyone here" in an impressive fictional gathering in Cicero's *On the Nature of the Gods* (1.123) – to be the sort of person to write anti-Roman history. Otherwise Pompey would not have made a show of attending one of his lectures and asking if he had any advice for the pirate war (T 8a), nor of making a respectful house-call on his return from fighting Mithridates (T 8b); and otherwise Cicero would not have approached him to write up an account of his consulship (*Att.* 2.1.2). What is more, the diplomacy Posidonius showed in deflecting that request showed him thoroughly in tune with Cicero's own mindset. A man who could judge Cicero so well was a man who understood a lot about refined Roman sensibility. That stress on moral decline would shock no one. True, it is one thing to shake one's head at one's society's deficiencies, another to nod when an outsider says the same thing. But this was a very privileged outsider.

4   Dionysius of Halicarnassus

Dionysius includes Polybius among authors whom no one can read to the end (*Comp.* 4.30), but he certainly knew, and expected his audience to know, where Polybius began: where Posidonius and Strabo wrote sequels, Dionysius writes a prequel, ending his *Roman Antiquities* where Polybius had begun his prehistory in 264 BCE. It is that mix of homage and critique once again, though here Dionysius' critique is stylistic. In his proem he mentions Polybius among his predecessors, but only as one of those who "grazed" (1.7.1) earlier history (no mention of the thorough treatment of the history he *did* cover), and did so carelessly, basing himself on casual hearsay (1.6.1, echoing Thuc. 1.22.2) – a hit there at an area where Polybius particularly prided himself, that of careful research. Elsewhere too Dionysius makes points at Polybius' expense (1.32.1–2, 74.3).

Despite the dismissiveness, the proem also echoes Polybius' own stamp of thought, particularly in the comparison of Rome's empire to those that preceded (above, p. 245; Dionysius is the more precise here: Alonso-Núñez 1983). Yet the choice of theme implies a correction of Polybius too. For Dionysius, if one is to explain Rome's success one has to start at the very beginning: he will recount (1.5.2) "the actions that they put on display [*apedeixanto*, an echo of Herodotus' proem and one that points to *glorious* actions] immediately after the foundation, and the pursuits which laid the basis for their successors' advance to so great an empire." His readers will learn (1.5.4):

> that the city bore countless examples of manly virtues immediately after its foundation, such that no city, Greek or barbarian, has ever produced people who were more pious or just, or practiced more good sense throughout their lives, or who were better fighters in war: only jealousy would make anyone deny it.

What theme could be nobler than that? It was not a matter of mere Fortune (*Tychē* – Polybius is in the background again) that Rome conquered the world, but because they were paragons of good behavior. Greece should not resent having such masters (1.4.2), partly because it is a universal law that the weak should be ruled by the strong (1.5.2, a roistering echo of Thucydides), partly also because *the first Romans were Greek* (1.5.1). That theme is then emphasized through the first book as Dionysius recounts the Greek arrivals, Oenotrians, Arcadians, Pelasgi, Evander, Heracles, and then Aeneas: "no one could find a race more ancient nor more Greek than this" (1.89.2). That idea is not new, as it goes back to Aristotle and Heraclides Ponticus (Plut. *Cam.* 22.3), but Dionysius develops it combatively and relentlessly throughout the history (Musti 1970; Gabba 1991; Fox 1993).

All this gives a different tweak to the Greekness of the historian. We Greeks are not such outsiders after all, *we are family*. If the Latin race should rule over neighbors and barbarians because it is Greek (so Servius Tullius argues, 4.26.2), then are Greeks not also natural participants in the worldwide leadership that will be the Roman destiny? That is all the more reason why "we" Greeks, as Dionysius often puts it – for he constructs his audience as primarily Greek, while hinting at Roman readers too (Schultze 1986: 138–139; Gabba 1991: 79–80) – really do deserve a good treatment of the theme, which has not hitherto been treated properly in Greek (1.5.4–6.2).

Dionysius, like Polybius, also stresses that he is the right man to deliver such a history, a person who can bring everything together and has done the hard work: "a worthy writer," 1.5.4. But for Dionysius the hard work is the twenty-two-year labor of reading his texts – a list of works he quotes is impressive (Schultze 2000) – and gathering oral traditions (1.7.2–3). We are moving in a different world from that in which Polybius stressed the need for practical experience and autopsy: however lively oral traditions about early Rome were, we are still closer to Timaeus spending nearly fifty years in libraries (to Polybius' scorn, 12.25d.11). And the way Dionysius can bring things together is in his combination of styles, "forensic" (or more generally "combative," *enagōniou*), "theoretical," and something else (perhaps "narrative"), so that political, philosophical, or pleasure-seeking readers may all find something in his history. It is true that the "political" reader is later given particular prominence (5.75.1; 11.1; Verdin 1974), but Polybius' shade would still have been lost for words: his cherished word *miktou* is no longer used of constitutions, but of the mixed style that the theme requires (1.8.3).

In one sense, though, Dionysius' constructed audience mirrors the shifting realities as Polybius' history had itself begun to map them, where Polybius could already say that everywhere except Rome "men of action are now freed from any ambition concerning warlike or political activity" (3.59.4), and where the time was nearing, or even already there, when subjects could only accept and obey (above, p. 249). What Dionysius' history could encourage them to do was accept and obey *willingly*. When Dionysius portrays his generous presentation of Rome as appropriate thanks for the good things he had derived from the city (1.6.5), that is a model for his audience too. Elsewhere Dionysius compliments Rome and its leaders on the flourishing state of literature and culture (*Orat.* 3). There was a lot to be grateful for.

What, then, were these virtues that constituted Roman superiority? Many are illustrated through the usual saints' gallery of Roman ancients. Lucretia, Brutus the expeller of the tyrants, Horatius, Scaevola, Cloelia, the Fabii at Cremera, Cincinnatus, Camillus, Fabricius – all get their due, though Dionysius concedes that by contemporary standards some of their behavior would seem harsh, at least to Greeks (3.21.7–10; 5.8.1). Yet these characters are fairly colorless: that is the way with saint's galleries (as with Polybius' Roman heroes, above, p. 249), but it is still striking that they are less individualized than in Livy's parallel account (Burck 1934 traces this in detail). Yet that is not just because Livy is artistically more gifted (Burck), nor even because individualization can reduce a character's capacity to serve as a universal moral paradigm, though that too is true (Halliwell 1990). It is also because Dionysius is more interested in the characteristics of Rome as a whole.

Take the constitution, for instance. In the proem Dionysius promises to survey the constitutions *which the Romans had at different times* (1.8.2) – for, of course, as he regards the explanation for Rome's success as one that goes back to their primeval character, he is committed to *not* regarding their eventual third- and second-century constitution as basic to their world power. At the end of the first book he similarly refers to the "account that he is going to give of their constitution" (1.90.3): that presumably means all the rest of the work (so Cary *ad loc.*; Schultze 1986: 132), tracing as it does the gradual way in which the ultimate constitution took shape. It is a narrative equivalent of Polybius' claim (above, p. 250) that the Romans evolved their ideal constitution through experience, and there may well be some implicit dialogue with the missing section of the sixth book where Polybius himself gave a historical sketch (6.11a, with Walbank, *HCP* I.663–673), though Polybius' scale would have been much slighter. Polybius developed his point in his way, through logical argumentation; Dionysius does it in his, through speeches. Thus the regal period is both introduced and ended by speeches indicating that the Romans have a choice between monarchy, oligarchy, and democracy (Romulus at 2.3.7–8, Brutus at 4.72–75, both in awkward contexts), and in each case it is clear that there are good reasons for the choices they make: at the beginning they have done well through kings (2.4.1–2), at the end they most definitely have not, thanks to the outrages of Tarquinius Superbus and his son Sextus. The gathering unity of Senate and people against Superbus then lays the basis on which a harmonious republic can be founded.

Not that the republic is at all harmonious when it comes, and the Struggle of the Orders, bitter and vicious, dominates the rest of Dionysius' history. In its early stages one also senses some of the strengths that will enable Rome and freedom to survive, and external threats bring the state back to harmony, at least once the patricians make some wise concessions (5.63–64; 6.1.1, 29.1). But before long matters worsen, and the internal disorder ends by generating external threats rather than being dissolved by them (e.g., 10.14.3, 27.1; 11.3). Common soldiers become reluctant to fight for an unloved general (8.89.3; 9.3–4; 9.50; 11.23.3, 43), while generals exploit opportunities for warfare either to avoid domestic squabbles or, more shamingly still, to continue them, as when the brave dissident Siccius Dentatus is sent on a mission which is expected to bring his death (10.44–47). The decemvirs repeat the ploy even more murderously at 11.24–26, sending their own assassins along with Siccius, and this time Siccius does die.

Speeches again plot the way things are going wrong: a cavalcade of speeches in the Coriolanus episode (7.16–63; 8.5–8, 23–53); another preceding, accompanying, and resolving the first secession of the plebs (6.35–87); and many more throughout the Struggle, slogging through the same ground time and again, apparently making little progress, and leaving a modern reader bludgeoned, bewildered, and frankly bored. If Dionysius is so interested in tracing Rome's strengths, why spend so much time setting out features that seem to show them, and especially their ruling class, at their worst?

Yet there is a point, and Dionysius makes it explicit: he has included speeches at such length, he explains, because it was through speeches rather than civil war that the conflict was resolved: that is one of the most remarkable features about Rome, and that is why "they never did anything to harm one another that was godless or beyond healing, the sort of thing that the Corcyreans committed during their faction, and the Argives and Milesians and all of Sicily and many other cities" (7.66, cf. 7.18). Romans may not be good at speaking (at 10.31.2 Icilius is "no bad speaker for a Roman"), but they are good, usually and eventually, at managing to resolve things by speech, and despite all the friction the state survives.

"The sort of thing that the Corcyreans committed during their faction": that makes a point too. As Gabba (1991: 81–85) suggests, Thucydides' account of Corcyra (3.82–83) is surely in the background: the Romans' capacity to manage *stasis* is implicitly contrasted with that classic Greek failure to do the same. True, the contrast points to the weaknesses as well as the strengths of the Roman ways, which are not always so distant from Thucydides' Corcyra. In Rome too internal divisiveness is in danger of outweighing loyalty to the state; words like "tyranny," "liberty," and "justice" are bandied about tendentiously, exemplifying Thucydides' insight about "words changing their connotation" when applied to events (3.82.4; a more straightforward example comes later at *AR* 9.53.6). But Gabba's basic insight is right, and the self-conscious Greekness of the author and the account is again vital to its interpretation. After all, the awareness that talk and legal process, however flawed, are better than the violent alternative is an old Greek idea too: witness the *Eumenides*.

The Greek perspective can be developed in subtler ways. It may be done intertextually, in the way for instance that Herodotus' Solon (1.30–34) is echoed in the terms used to felicitate Numa on his happy life: he survived to an old age, unharmed by fortune, and the fate that had been allotted him from birth survived until he disappeared from mortal life (2.76.5). The same passage, along with the following Herodotean sequence of the death of Atys, is then recalled in Dionysius' next narrative panel, when Horatius is cast by an envious god into a "brother-killing catastrophe" (3.21.1, echoing particularly Hdt. 1.32.1 and 1.46.1; Ek 1942: 94–97). So Roman history is used to illustrate Greek wisdom, just as Coriolanus' fate endorses Herodotus' Cyrus on the painful way one learns from experience (8.25.3 and 8.33.3, echoing Hdt. 1.86.6 and 207.1 along with 1.5.3–4 and 7.10ε; Ek 1942: 97–99). Echoes also mark ways in which Rome is going wrong, as when Appius Claudius appropriates the catchwords of Periclean resolve to defend single-mindedness against the *demos* rather than the enemy (6.38.1 ∼ Thuc. 1.140.1). But more often they point to the ways in which Romans fight and win. When they renew the Samnite Wars the reasons are explained in Thucydidean language: the "openly expressed reason (*prophasis*), one that looked good (*euprepēs*) before everyone," was the Roman tradition of aiding their allies (17/18.3 ∼ Thuc. 6.6.1); "the covert reason, one that imposed more compulsion (*anagkazousa*), was the growth of Samnite power and the expectation that it would become even greater" (∼Thuc. 1.23.6). Rome is playing the power game with clear-sightedness and success, but the city still has its moral strengths as well – Fabricius, for instance, whose behavior persuaded Pyrrhus that he was fighting "people who were more pious and more just than the Greeks" (20.6.1, cf. 19.18.8), phrasing that points back to the proem (above, p. 253). So Greek experience and archetypal Greek texts become a way of plotting the strengths of Rome.

If those strengths are timeless, so also are the problems they solve, and there are glances forward to Dionysius' own day as well as back to the Greek past. The issues of the Struggle were all too familiar from the last generation of the republic – the extension of citizenship (a particularly favorite theme), tensions between rich and poor, problems of debt, the right of the people to legislate against the Senate's wishes, control of the lawcourts (esp. 7.65), the difficulties of grain supply, the rights of tribunes (here Dionysius marks the continuity explicitly, 8.87.7–8), the pressure for land allotment to the poor. Nor does Dionysius leave any doubt that the nature of contemporary Rome leaves something to be desired, in the way, for instance, that auspices are often disregarded (2.6.3–4) or slaves are manumitted so casually (4.24). The good days lay in the past, socially, politically, and morally (2.10.4, 11, 34.3, 74.5; 5.60.2, 77; 10.17.6; 16.4–5).

Once again, we should not press such moral nostalgia to make Dionysius into a spiky critic of contemporary Roman ways: this was a cosy form of moralism, one that would chime well with what Romans said themselves about moral decline (Edwards 1993). That is even so when it comes to judging the most prominent aspect of the current day, the presence of the *princeps* himself. When talking of the institution of the dictatorship, Dionysius echoes Polybius' *anakuklosis* in commenting that Greek states had begun with monarchies, then changed their constitutions when monarchs abused their power – then, as calamity or prosperity brought new crises, found it wise to return to one-man rule when speedy and authoritarian remedies were required (5.74.1–3). The relevance of that homily would not have been lost on Dionysius' audience, Greek and Roman. Many of the themes of Romulus' constitution, balancing as it did monarchy with other constitutional forms, extending citizenship, fostering religion and morality, were also still the themes of Augustus' rule (Balsdon 1971). Yet not all of Dionysius' material might seem so comfortable to Augustus or his partisans. One question in particular, that of the decemvirate's status once its legal term had expired but no successors had been appointed (11.5–6, etc.), is very close to home, as the same issue arose with Octavian himself in 37 and 32 BCE (Pelling 1996: 26–27, 48, 67–68), and Dionysius treats the decemvirs' case with no sympathy at all. That, though, itself suggests that the contemporary echo would not be taken as specially pointed or critical: for if an audience was looking for political tendentiousness, Dionysius would be being breathtakingly bold. The contemporary resonance matters, but only in adding immediacy to the distant past. The issues are still alive, and it all still matters.

Both the forward and the backward perspectives, then, are important in Dionysius' response to Polybius. The secret of Rome's success is not just a matter of fifty-three years. The broader view, a view of seven centuries and more, is the view to take, and the qualities that mattered in the beginning are the ones that matter still. Romans in Dionysius' view had learned from Greeks: perhaps they still can, and take a lesson or so from Dionysius himself.

5　Conclusion

A bookshop browser who picked up a copy of Dionysius had completed a Roman set: "[p]ossessing his book and the books of Polybius and Posidonius, a Greek reader would at last have a continuous and reliable history of Rome written for him in Greek and by Greeks from the Foundation down to the late Republic" (Balsdon 1971: 18). And that history is a story of success. What questions did that run of success pose?

Problems of justification are there, certainly. The justification they tend *not* to get is one in terms of divine will, the sort of idea that was explored in the fragmentary third book of Cicero's *De Republica* (Ferrary 1988: 349–381) and is often thought to go back to Panaetius – that Heaven gave Roman masters to the morally inferior subject states "because slavery is to the advantage of men like that" (Cic. *Rep.* 3.36: this is Augustine's summary, and we should not necessarily assume that Cicero presented it as his own view); or that we find in Plutarch, presenting the Roman empire as a boon of Providence to grant the world stability, bringing the sequence of warring empires to an end and giving peace (e.g., *Fort. Rom.* 2, 316E–317C; Swain 1989a; 1989b: 507–508). When Dionysius talks of "divine forethought" (5.54.1), it is something that protects Rome, and this is what we see in his narrative (e.g., 5.33.4; 6.10.1, 17.4; 7.12.4; 8.26.3–4; Swain 1989a: 279); if it is also something that secures the good of everyone else, that has to be inferred in a different way from his text. The nearest we come to such ideas may be – though there are uncertainties here – Posidonius' presentation of all the world working together: but there is a distinction between this and a justification of empire not merely as something that makes coherent cosmic sense but that is morally *right*.

Yet some of the explanations given tend towards such a moral justification. The timeless strengths of the Roman people, as Dionysius portrays them, are moral strengths, even the "pride in themselves and courage" that carries the early republic to martial success (5.62.4). We saw something similar in Polybius too (p. 246). The difficulty, though, is inherent in Polybius' scheme of things: these moral strengths belong in the past, but do they also belong in the present? The "pride and courage" may, but what about those other qualities, the self-restraint, the prudence, the moderation in victory? Is the Roman order still as ordered as it should be? At least Polybius' narrative poses enough questions, even if tactfully, to make one wonder; Posidonius has his moral nostalgia too, and so does Dionysius. Not that this is subversive: this is exactly what the *princeps* himself would have wanted, and such thinking had by now become so ingrained in the Roman mindset that the really subversive thing would be to doubt it.

Still, the accent falls on imperial success rather than imperial discontents, and we have seen how our Greek authors have in various ways brought distinctively Greek filters and explanatory schemes to clarify that success. Historians today are still debating many of the issues prefigured in this chapter: a single story of one empire against a scattered and more complex pattern demanding "area studies"; a dynamic story of continual change against a more static picture of the same issues recurring time and again; a serene, uplifting story of success against a somber picture of brutality and catastrophe, for others as eventually for Rome itself.

FURTHER READING

Scholarship on Polybius during the last fifty years has been dominated by the massive achievement of Walbank, especially in his commentary (*HCP*) but also in his general book (1972) and in many papers, partly collected in Walbank 1985 and 2002. Eckstein 1995a gives an alternative view on many questions; Marincola 2001 gives a helpful brief survey and sets Polybius against the background of earlier historiography. Especially pertinent for the theme of this chapter are Musti 1978 and Ferrary 1988.

The indispensable edition of Posidonius is now Kidd (1988–1999): the historical fragments are also published as *FGrHist* 87. The difficulties of reconstructing Posidonius' *History* from the fragments are considerable: Clarke 1999a is here exemplary. Jacoby included long stretches of Diodorus 34–38 as Posidonian; Kidd does not. That cautious view is followed here. A less cautious one is taken by Malitz 1983 and in the influential paper of Strasburger 1965.

Gabba 1991 is the only full treatment of Dionysius' history in English. Musti 1970 and the papers of Schultze are also very helpful. This chapter is also indebted to Schultze's doctoral thesis of 1980.

CHAPTER TWENTY-ONE

The Early Roman Tradition

Hans Beck

"For famous and important men, there should be an account of their leisure activities no less than of their serious business." When Marcus Porcius Cato (234–149 BCE) in 170 or so set about writing a history of "the deeds of the Roman People" (*HRR* FF 1, 2), there was no doubt that he intended to master this task just as he had mastered everything else. Born a *homo novus* ("new man," i.e., without noble ancestors), Cato had worked his way from Tusculum up to the highest rank of the Roman aristocracy: quaestor in 204, five years later aedile of the people (199), 198 praetor of Sardinia, and in 195 the *maximus honos*, the consulate, followed by a triumph in 194 – this splendid career was indeed "serious business." Just like the great nobles of his day, Cato too was driven by a thorough (self-)identification with and commitment to the fate of the *res publica*. In fact, his particular commitment to Roman collective values such as sternness, modesty, and a simple way of life earned him the reputation of an odd bird, as it were, which soon became a characteristic of Cato's perception as a paradigmatic figure of virtue (*exemplum virtutis*) in Roman cultural memory.

Cato embarked on his *Origines* ("Origins") with the claim to do a good job and, most likely, to stand out from his predecessors. A generation earlier, in the midst of the Second Punic War, Quintus Fabius Pictor was the first Roman to write a history of Rome in prose (von Albrecht 1997: 371–374). Born probably around 270, Fabius participated in repeated campaigns against the Ligurians and Gauls during the 230s (cf. *FGrHist* 809 FF 19b, 20), and may even have held a praetorship in one of those years. After the devastating defeat of Cannae (216 BCE) he was entrusted with an embassy to Delphi to seek divine advice for the battered state. This mission must have been a crucial experience. On his trip, Fabius was very likely confronted with resentments against Rome, which could have been a decisive factor in his decision to compose a historical work that would present the Roman view of current affairs.

The main impulse, however, came from Rome itself. It resulted from the deep crisis in the Roman state after Cannae. In response to the overwhelming conflict with Carthage, the question of driving forces in politics must have arisen. It was a question that promised to uncover the past and its relevance for the present, and it thereby offered orientation throughout the current crisis (Walter 2004: 229–255). This need for orientation becomes visible in Pictor's organization of Roman history. Fabius created an intelligible continuum that ran from Heracles' arrival in Italy through Romulus up to the most renowned nobles of his times. For as much as he stood in the tradition of Greek *ktisis* ("foundation") history writing, still his work was no simple foundation story. To be sure, Greek authors such as Diocles of Peparethos had already been telling such foundation legends about Rome. Yet for Fabius Pictor, this *spatium mythicum* was not a separate space, lying far off in the past. In his work it became the basis for the Roman state, whose customs, institutions, and rule had been providentially announced in the early period, and which created a compelling mission for the present (cf. esp. FF 1, 4, 11).

The task of Fabius was twofold: to establish a chronological network of historical material which was available only through a complex, stratified mixture of individual and collective memories; and to produce a coherent narrative – the poet Naevius had dealt only with a small portion in his *Punic War* – from Romulus and the foundation of the city (*ab urbe condita*) to the Hannibalic War. A remark in Dionysius of Halicarnassus (*AR* 1.6.2) indicates that Fabius' history was divided into three large sections (cf. Timpe 1972): first the sweeping section on the foundation, which included the first years of the republic (*FRH* 1 FF 1–22); second, "the antiquities after the foundation-phase," that is, the period from the decemvirate (451/0) to the Pyrrhic War (280–75), which Fabius handled summarily and with factual points of emphasis (*FRH* 1 FF 23–26, with Beck 2003); and third, the contemporary history from the First Punic War, written carefully, meticulously, and cogently (*FRH* 1 FF 27–32). The work was divided into several books. Long narrative passages about Romulus and Remus make it plain that Fabius' history was not a mere compilation of facts and data. The treatment of current events was vivid, structurally sophisticated, and even analytic, at least when it came to an explanation of the Roman position in international affairs. Given Pictor's intentions, it is easy to see why the work was written in Greek. Addressing an educated public (Greek, Roman, and "barbarian"), this was the only language suited to reach a wide circle of readers (Badian 1966: 4).

Fabius set standards, and his achievement was recognized by Lucius Cincius Alimentus, Aulus Postumius Albinus, and Gaius Acilius, all of them educated senators who followed Fabius Pictor in the first decades of the second century in matters of language, form, and theme (cf. Verbrugghe 1982 on Cincius). Cato was different. Unlike them, he was a man of consular rank, which meant higher prestige, and unlike Fabius' other immediate successors, Cato was determined to use this prestige to modernize Roman culture (Timpe 1970/1). Part of this modernization was to Latinize the historiographic genre: Cato wrote in Latin, and no Roman historian after him would return to Greek (Publius Rutilius Rufus notwithstanding [cf. below, p. 269]). It was a signal that the Romans possessed both a language and a set of intellectual abilities which were competitive with the *lingua academica* of the Greeks as well as their cultural achievements.

Cato's second strategy to set himself apart from the Fabian tradition was the incorporation of the histories of the peoples and landscapes of Italy, which were treated at length in the second and third books of Cato's *Origins*. Their local genealogies and rites, foundation myths, and historical origins (all of which is included in the Latin term *origines*) were perceived as integrated parts of a cultural community, into which Rome, the Latins, and the allies had melted (cf. Gotter 2003). This concept, it should be said, did not find reception amongst future historians, nor did another peculiarity of Cato's, i.e., that he seemingly omitted the names of Roman consuls and other magistrates throughout most sections of his work (cf. *HRR* F 88). Even so, Cato's emphasis on the emancipation of Roman culture, his portrayal of Roman collective values (esp. *virtus Romana*: F 83), and, last but not least, his focus on political rhetoric and harsh domestic debates highlight the fact that historiography entered a new era with Cato.

But did it really? The common views on early Roman historiography, which is all too often equated with the so-called annalistic tradition, have been taken with a large pinch of salt recently. This is also true for the perceptions of the underlying principles of the annalistic tradition, its inherent scheme(s), and its traditional division into three developing stages (early, middle, later annalistic), all of which have been challenged with good reasons. It is time to address this problem.

The long prevailing view had been determined by Cicero's harsh criticism of the early Roman historians (*De Or.* 2.51–53; cf. also *Leg.* 1.6–7):

> Let me remind you that in the beginning the Greeks themselves also wrote like our Cato, Pictor, and Piso. History was nothing more than a compilation of yearly chronicles, and for the purpose of this matter [. . .] the chief priest, from the beginnings of Roman history down to the time when Publius Mucius Scaevola was chief priest, committed to writing all the events of each year, and displayed them on a white tablet and exhibited the tablet at his house, in order that the people might have the opportunity to learn about them. These are the records that even today are called the *annales maximi*. A similar type of writing was adopted by many, and they have left only memorials of dates, people, places, and events, devoid of any distinction. In this way, just as the Greeks had their Pherecydes, Hellanicus, Acusilaus, and others, so we have their equivalents in our own Cato, Pictor, and Piso, who have no idea by what means speech is given distinction – such things, after all, have only recently been introduced here –, and who suppose that, provided what they say is understood, the sole virtue of speaking is brevity. (tr. May and Wisse)

Even though there are many who think that Cicero simply cannot be wrong, the first sentence of this quotation evidently is. Connecting Pictor's and Cato's histories so closely with the *annales maximi* (on which see Frier 1979/1999) was – and still is – a mistake. In fact, Cato explicitly disapproved of the priestly chronicles, lamenting that he "do[es] not care to write what is in the table kept by the *pontifex maximus*: how often grain was expensive, how often darkness or something else obstructed the light of the moon or sun" (*HRR* F 77). Cicero, who could not have seen the *tabulae* anymore, but only (if anything) the book-edition which had been produced by Mucius Scaevola around 130, was either unaware of this statement of Cato's or he simply ignored it. Also, he must have dismissed Fabius' accounts of events such as the fighting in Sicily during the First Punic War (*FGrHist* 809 F 18), which were by no means a mere listing of "dates, people, places, and events."

The idea of parallel Greek and Roman developments is also inaccurate. The earlier chapters of this *Companion* have made it clear that Greek historiography did not develop from chronicle to history. Herodotus and Thucydides had no usable lists at their disposal; rather, they created their works by collecting, judging, and combining elements of oral tradition(s), occasionally benefiting from individual inscriptions or previous literary works at most. The same goes for Rome. The notes of the high priest documented the activity of the *pontifices*, especially the restoration of harmony with the gods. They also included information on the election and action of magistrates, since their conduct of public affairs was subject to prior consultation of auspices through which the gods expressed their approval. The list's initial entries – for example, types of days (*dies fasti, nefasti*), intercalary months, and fixed festivals – would thus have been augmented by a wide range of disparate data on magistrate's action, census figures, or even *ad hoc* notations such as eclipses and rises in grain prices (cf. Forsythe 2000: 6–9 vs. Bucher 1987 on the nature of the evidence). But these *tabulae* formed only a part of the source material for the early Roman historians, and they certainly did not serve as a genuine model in matters of form (*FRH* I: 32–37). The road to the annalistic scheme ran differently.

How precisely? The main impetus came from another literary genre. During the 180s, Quintus Ennius (239–169 BCE), an immigrant of Messapian origin who was brought to Rome by Cato, composed a monumental epic on the history of Rome from the downfall of Troy to his own day. The work, written in hexameters, was called *Annales*, just like the earliest history works in prose. It was a huge success. Recitations attracted large crowds, and many readers memorized long passages. Its main innovation was that Ennius, a foreigner in Rome, discovered a pioneering way that verified his presentation of Roman history; so far only members of the Senate had presented written accounts on that topic. Ennius arranged his material in such a way that the work was conceived as a commentary on the *tabulae* of the high priest. He included repeated features such as the names of magistrates, notes on religious matters, information about public duties, news on campaigns and triumphs, censorial measures, trials, and so on. When deployed along with other historical contents, such formulations lent the text a certain profile. More than that, the work gained an extratextual authority, since the material had been organized after the year-by-year model of the pontifical chronicles (Gildenhard 2003; Walter 2004: 258–279).

Fabius Pictor and his most immediate successors – members of the aristocracy as they were – had no particular need for extratextual authority. But Ennius started from a different point of departure. His *Annales* paved the way for what has today become the name-giving principle of the annalistic tradition, i.e., that historiography included year-by-year patterns which followed a certain form and style (McDonald 1957 is still useful). Historians of the following generations increasingly turned to this strategy of self-authentification. They repeated, and expanded, those formal features. Some of them even developed a pedantic fetishism of exactitude which also appeared in enumerations of military troops, in the documentation of smaller operations, and in dense lists of festivals and gods. The scheme of alluding to the priestly chronicle emerged as a narrative pattern which first and foremost provided authority and which evoked authenticity. It does not mean that the genre was, as scholars had thought for so long, determined by annalistic dryness nor that it lacked all sorts of structural questions and analytic approaches, let alone that its "sole virtue of speaking was brevity."

The origins of Roman historiography were determined by a variety of intellectual approaches, narrative patterns, and authorial intentions. Given this diversity, it is easy to understand why recent scholarship tends to reject *passe-partout* concepts that elucidate early history writing at Rome. Rather, it has been stressed that the term "annalistic" is to a certain degree misleading, since it does not provide a "consistent and precise definition that respects generic theories and ancient linguistic usage" (Timpe 2003: 294; cf. Rich 1997). Today the term is hardly more than a conventional designation for the early historians ("annalists") and their works ("annals"), implying that several (but not all) Roman historians chose to arrange their works according to a year-by-year style. It does not mean uniformity.

The development of the genre in the second half of the second century BCE makes this clear. After Fabius' and Cato's efforts to promote historiography, other members of the aristocracy succeeded in picking up the stylus and producing written accounts of Roman history. One of the most prominent figures was Lucius Calpurnius Piso Frugi, tribune in 149, praetor in Sicily (in 139?), consul in 133, and censor (in 120?), who wrote seven books of *annales* from the beginnings of Rome to his own times (Forsythe 1994). Piso proved that historiography could be used as a sharp weapon in politics. His vivid picture of the Struggle of the Orders reflected the turbulences and turmoil in the decade that followed the controversial tribunate of Tiberius Gracchus in 133 (*HRR* FF 22–24). Pinpointing the beginnings of moral decline at Rome, there is an inherently censorial tone in Piso's work, who was full of dislike for the decadent *jeunesse dorée* of the day (note the strong language in F 40). This agenda might have triggered the idea to adapt to Ennius' annalistic style. In fact, Piso became the first historian who did include repeated features such as the names of magistrates on a large scale (FF 26–27), and there is reason to think that he did so because this technique supported his moral agenda.

The major new development of those decades was, however, that historiography evolved into a literary genre which was no longer limited to authors of senatorial rank. The forerunners were Lucius Cassius Hemina (Santini 1995), who seems to have written slightly earlier than Piso, and Gnaeus Gellius, an author of "exceptional verbosity" (Frier 1979/1999: 187) who composed at least twenty-seven books of *annales*. Both men were not members of the political *classe dirigeante*. The genuine concerns of historiography are well attested in their histories. Military affairs, legislation, internal strife: these topics were treated at great length, and – as in Piso – both accounts reflect the political quarrels of the days during which they were written (esp. Hemina *HRR* F 17). Yet, when Hemina or Gellius reported on those issues, it was no longer the statement of the "makers" of politics, but rather the analysis of the uninvolved observer. In other words, their texts had little, if any, social authority.

One strategy of compensation was, as will have become obvious by now, to employ annalistic features. A second one lay in new research techniques. Since the days of Fabius Pictor historiography was driven by a curiosity in the origins of present phenomena: What were the origins of the Roman calendar? How did the alphabet evolve? Who created the Roman tribes (*tribus*), and when was this done? To illuminate any of those questions historians turned to etymologies and aetiologies. They offered a possible explanation of beginnings, cultural techniques, and social practices, and helped to make sense of them through an understanding of their origins, while simultaneously shedding light onto the darkness of earlier times (cf. Rawson 1976: 247–255). To be sure, Hemina and Gellius were not the first to raise those questions and to apply etymological methods, but they clearly put more emphasis on them than their senatorial predecessors. Hemina's *Annales* thus even acquired the touch of a learned cultural history.

Lucius Coelius Antipater became the embodiment of this new professionalization. Born a member of the lower ranks of the aristocracy, Coelius did not try for a political career. Lacking both military expertise and an intimate knowledge of senatorial affairs, he first and foremost had to rely on his research skills. Innovative research became an acid test for him, and the sixty-seven fragments which are extant indicate that Coelius did well (Herrmann 1979). The first claim of his work was to reach a new level of investigation – an investigation for historical "truth" (*HRR* F 2). This implied not only an "arduous exploration of sources," as Thucydides (1.22) and many experts after him had lamented, but also the necessity to consult, and to analyze, anti-Roman sources (FF 11, 34). The second pillar of Coelius' account was the deliberate use of a sophisticated language. With Coelius historiographic prose dissociated itself from everyday language and obtained new standards in form and style. It is not surprising that his *historiae* were dedicated to the leading philologist of the day, Lucius Aelius Stilo. The most profound innovation of Coelius' was, however, that he turned away from writing Roman history *ab urbe condita* to the present day. He picked a thematic approach, i.e., he focused on a single topic: the Second Punic War. Coelius produced a seven-book monograph, written between 120 and 110 (von Albrecht 1997: 381–383), on this event. The significance of this step is only fully understood when compared with the Greek world. In Greece, historiography started with a groundbreaking monograph, Herodotus' *History*. At Rome, this format was only established a century or so later after Fabius Pictor's history *ab urbe condita*. Yet it is interesting to see that in both cases the obvious choices for a monographical topic were the most severe military threats to which both societies had been exposed: in Greece the Persian Wars, at Rome the Hannibalic War.

This does not mean that narratives *ab urbe condita* were dead with Coelius. In the first century BCE, Quintus Claudius Quadrigarius, Valerius Antias, and Gaius Licinius Macer reverted to this principle (Quadrigarius might have started his *annales* with the sack of Rome by the Gauls and its "second foundation" by the *dux fatalis* Marcus Furius Camillus). Their histories were characterized by an extensive usage of annalistic structures and at times thrilling narratives. Most notably, their tendency to include all sorts of fictitious documents and statistics led to what has been called an "expansion of the past" (Badian 1966: 11), which meant an ever-growing (pseudo-) knowledge of historical episodes and events. Reverting to the *ab urbe condita* model at the same time might have been regarded as an effort to flog a dead horse, since historiography had become a genre which was shaped by experimental approaches rather than intellectual immobility. In the last generation of the Roman republic historiography therefore displays once again the heterogeneity of the genre, in which the year-by-year narrative from the beginnings of Rome down to the present had become only one way of structuring the past among others (Walter 2003).

No matter how frequently the early Roman historians included annalistic features in their works (e.g., Coelius hardly any, Piso quite significantly, Valerius Antias excessively), and no matter how intensively the historiographical tradition of the republic in general was committed to a year-by-year structure, the mere principle of presenting history as some sort of commentary on the time-honored *tabulae* of the high priest became the most important characteristic of Roman historiography. The tendency of verifying histories via annalistic modes and means signaled continuity, security, and institutional stability from the beginnings of Rome to the present. Annalistic structure thus provided an intellectual frame for a peculiar perception of the past, in which the historiographic tradition amalgamated with other elements of Roman cultural memory, especially the self-identification with the *exempla virtutis* and the commitment to *mos maiorum*, the "customs of our ancestors" (Pina Polo 2004). Livy's 142 books *ab urbe condita* are the most towering – and the final – monument of this approach. But even then it was by no means unchallenged. As ever, so in the age of Augustus, historiography was determined by conflicting and competitive approaches, just as the concepts of writing history had so often been altered since Fabius Pictor and Cato had first embarked on this exciting journey.

FURTHER READING

The two most recent editions of the fragments of the early Roman historians are *FRH* and *AR*; the former has a German translation of the fragments, the latter a French one. Both works also contain commentaries on authors and texts as well as concordances to the older edition, *HRR*. For Ennius' *Annales*, Skutsch 1985 is the standard text. Frier 1979/1999 continues to be an important contribution, even though his views on the *annales maximi* have been challenged, most recently by the papers in Eigler et al. 2003. Several ancient authors have been covered in excellent monographs, esp. Calpurnius Piso (Forsythe 1994) and Cassius Hemina (Santini 1995). Timpe's learned articles on Fabius Pictor and Cato (1972 and 1970/1) continue to be immensely influential. This is also true for the much-cited Badian 1966. The most comprehensive account on the inherent motifs, methods, and messages of early Roman history writing now is Walter 2004, who adds much to the current debate on the social mechanics of collective memories.

CHAPTER TWENTY-TWO

Memoir and Autobiography in Republican Rome

Andrew M. Riggsby

1   Introduction

Biography does not loom large in the generic classifications of Roman antiquity, autobiography even less so. For instance, it does not figure at all in Quintilian's extensive reading list (10.1) for the budding orator. In fact, it is often (if controversially) claimed that autobiography was an invention of the Christian world and in particular of Perpetua and St. Augustine. If the distinctive feature of autobiography is taken to be the extended introspection made possible by the identity of author and subject, then the *Confessions* does really mark a strong break. It matters more than formally that Augustine rather than anyone else was the writer of his "life" (as ancient biographies were generally called). If, however, we take autobiography merely as the writing of any fragment of one's life, then earlier texts need to be taken into account. Now, many texts have some autobiographical function. Lyric poetry is largely a series of first-person fragments (which were not so readily read as fiction as they are today); Cicero's and Pliny's letters do nearly the same thing; Cicero's *post Reditum* orations spend considerable time narrating his exile and recall. For present purposes, however, we may restrict our attention to works whose central purpose is to narrate a significant portion of the author's life.

Most of the works to be discussed here survive only in fragments, and a few are known only through mentions with no quotation at all. These fragments and testimonia tend to come not from historians but from antiquarians and grammarians (who scoured texts for oddities more than "quality," whether literary or informational) and from the Greek biographer Plutarch (who may have felt their project was kindred to his). All this suggests a very marginal place for autobiography in the Roman world, which may in turn explain why the remains are so exiguous. Nonetheless, it is possible to discern some patterns in our record.

2 The Problem with Autobiography

As noted above, there are no Latin discussions of autobiography as a literary genre. There are, however, a few texts which discuss narrating some or all of one's own life as a social/political practice. It may be helpful to start by quoting the two most important passages in full:

> I may be forced to something that is often criticized: I will write about myself (on the model of many noble men). But as you know, there are problems associated with this genre: [1] one has to write with greater sensitivity (*verecundius*) about oneself when something is to be praised and not write at all if there is cause for criticism. [2] Authority and trustworthiness are reduced. [3] Many even complain, saying that even the heralds at games are more sensitive, since (although they crown other victors and name them loudly) they bring in another herald when they themselves are crowned at the end of the games, so that they do not announce themselves as victors with their own voices. (Cic. *Fam.* 5.12.8)

> It was common of old to hand down the deeds and habits of noble men. . . . Among our ancestors, just as it was more common to do things worthy of memory, so anyone who was noted for his talent, was led to hand down the memory of his virtue without personal favor or ambition at the reward only of his good conscience. Many thought it a matter of self-confidence rather than arrogance (*adrogantiae*) to narrate their own lives, nor was this act a matter of criticism or loss of credibility for Rutilius or Scaurus. Virtue is best evaluated in the ages in which it is most easily generated. (Tac. *Agr.* 1)

The most general thing to note, and this is characteristic of all the briefer texts as well, is that both Cicero and Tacitus take it for granted that writing a life is a matter of praise and blame, and so writing one's own life is necessarily an exercise in self-praise. Now, this is not entirely unique to the present case; modern autobiography and ancient history writing both share the function of praise and blame from time to time. What is distinctive here is that it is the only function attested for these Latin autobiographical texts. This presents two, partially related, dangers to potential authors.

The first problem is ethical. For Tacitus, autobiography is, at least presumptively, an act of *adrogantia*. Etymologically this means laying claim to something, but in practice it has the specific force of its English derivative: laying claim without a legitimate basis. Cicero frames it as the lack of *verecundia*, i.e., a concern to maintain the proper balance in observing the interests and face between the parties to any social transaction, especially as viewed in terms of their respective statuses (Kaster 2005: 13–27, 61–65). Both Cicero and Tacitus fear over-reaching by the autobiographer. That over-reaching, however, is not necessarily going beyond the truth; note that in the simile of the heralds, their self-proclamation would be clearly and objectively correct. What is at stake here is the "face" component of *verecundia*. Aggressive self-presentation requires the audience to show attention (and presumably judgment) it might prefer not to give. It forces the audience's hand.

Now it is certainly the case that Roman elites were not bound by "modesty" in precisely the modern sense – they held triumphal parades, named public works after themselves, wore honorific insignia, had monumental statues and inscriptions erected and more – but these gestures were generally authorized externally. Thus it is perhaps not "merely" a stylistic gesture that Cicero's explicit self-praise in oratorical contexts is typically referential and collective ("you all have praised me for..."). Both topic and addressee are somewhat ambiguous, which lessens the social demands put forth by the text. At any rate, autobiography, even if fairly written, is bare self-assertion; the demand for recognition cannot be dissimulated.

Now, while the *verecundia* problem existed independently of the question of truth, both Cicero and Tacitus still suggest autobiography is not trustworthy. Why so? Obviously, one problem is that the writer has a motive to lie. However, there is also a deeper problem. Roman moral evaluation hinged on outside, community judgment not just in the institutional sense suggested above, but also more philosophically. Praise was not just a consequence of virtuous action but actually constituted its virtue. Moreover, the process was recursive, as famously illustrated by this claim of the elder Cato (*Agr. praef.* 2–3):

> When [the ancestors] praised a good man, they praised him as "a good farmer and good land-holder." They judged a man to be praised most amply who was so praised.

This is not just a periphrasis for "farmers are good." They are, of course, at least according to the ancestors, but the making of that judgment is also important. Virtuous people will tend to evaluate themselves highly, because that is correct. But the vicious will also speak highly of themselves, since they presumably do not judge well. Tacitus makes this connection explicitly, though he frames it in terms of eras, giving some hope of distinguishing the good and the bad. For Cicero, doubt always exists (*minor...fides, minor auctoritas*). While the authority autobiography needs behind it is a moral one, the nature of the genre makes it hard to find that securely.

One final note on these problems: the texts discussed here date no earlier than 55 BCE, long after the authors to be discussed in the next section. Nonetheless, it is fair to retroject the same attitudes to that earlier era. On the one hand, there are very few pre-Ciceronian texts of any sort, and none of a self-reflective sort. Hence, we cannot make an argument from silence. On the other, both objections to autobiography just discussed are grounded in fundamental Roman values which do not seem to change much over time.

3   The Middle Republic

I begin this section with a warning that the theoretical problems raised earlier are issues even when we consider specific cases, and that even the form of this chapter could potentially be misleading. That is, the mere fact of collecting the examples below (nowhere so grouped in antiquity) runs the risk of assuming they share a common identity. On the other hand, we should not be overly confident about the grouping: the texts vary widely in length, they are not treated together in antiquity, and, in absolute terms, they are spread across decades. Nonetheless, I will focus on the demonstrable similarities of these works.

M. Aemilius Scaurus (162–88 [or earlier], *cos.* 115) wrote three books *On his Own Life*, but we have only six or seven fragments, preserved primarily in brief quotations in grammatical works, and so selected for their linguistic, not historical, interest. Most of the fragments refer to military action, but one (the longest) speaks of the very modest inheritance Scaurus received from his father. Thus the text may have related most or all of his life, and at any rate it was not strictly an account of his official activities. Cicero knew the work in 45 and praised it as "useful," but at the same time claimed that it was no longer read in his time, even though others of Scaurus' works remained popular (Cic. *Brut.* 112). Finally we are told by two later sources that the work was dedicated to one L. Fufidius, about whom we know little else.

P. Rutilius Rufus (ca. 156–after 78; *cos.* 105) wrote at least five books entitled, like Scaurus' work, *On his Own Life*. There are nine surviving fragments specifically attributed to this work, and most of them to a specific book within it. These are all very brief, and they too are preserved in grammatical works. The situation, however, is somewhat complicated by the existence of a work Plutarch calls his "Histories." Some fragments attributed to Rufus but not to any particular work almost certainly belong to these histories (e.g., *HRR* F 2, giving the date of the death of Scipio in 183), but others come from the period of Rufus' life (*HRR* F 4, the conspiracy of Saturninus and Glaucia in 100) or in their original context were probably background information (e.g., the institution of the market-day cycle). Scaurus and Rufus are discussed together in a passage of Cicero's *Brutus* cited above, but Rufus' memoir is not discussed. Admittedly, Cicero's main point is to treat them as orators, but the omission is still striking, especially since Cicero was himself a defender of Rufus' reputation after the latter's supposedly unjust conviction on charges of extorting money from his provincial subjects. More than a century later, Tacitus refers to Scaurus and Rufus together as writers of their own lives, though it is not entirely clear that he has read either.

Q. Lutatius Catulus (ca. 149–87; *cos.* 102) wrote a single book *On his Consulship and Deeds*. There are only three clear fragments, all preserved in Plutarch's *Marius*, and all describing differences between Catulus', Sulla's, and Marius' accounts of the battle of Vercellae in 101. (Catulus also wrote a work called the *Common History*, but the early date of the events recounted make it easy to rule out an autobiographical work as the source of unattributed fragments.) Since *On his Consulship* is preserved only in Greek, and there seemingly in paraphrase rather than translation, it is difficult to discern anything about its composition. Cicero, however, praises the style of the work as "gentle and similar to Xenophon's" (*Brut.* 132), which signals a fairly plain style, aiming at grace more than impact. In addition, it was dedicated to a minor but friendly poet named A. Furius Antias. Finally, despite the supposed qualities of the work, it was largely unknown by the mid-40s. Much later Fronto (*Ver. Imp.* 2.15) refers to a "letter of Catulus in which he laid out on the model of historical writing his deeds, with their costs and benefits, deserving of a triumph." (The reference to a letter is possibly an error on Fronto's part.)

L. Cornelius Sulla (138–78; *cos.* 88) left behind at his death twenty-two books on his own life. The title of this work is often given as *Commentaries* by modern authorities, but no Roman author uses the corresponding Latin term. Plutarch frequently uses a roughly parallel Greek term, but its sense is broader than the Latin word (see §4). All other references are to "deeds" or (once) "history," and we may prefer to assume something like that was the title (cf. here Catulus' work). Plutarch is easily our single best source for the work, but a half-dozen fragments also come from nearly as many Latin authors. The subject matter appears to include all of Sulla's life and beyond. *HRR* F 2 from the second book makes reference to an ancestor named Publius who became *flamen dialis* (a major priesthood) in the late third century, which suggests Sulla began with a leisurely treatment of family history. Sulla is also said to have been writing up until two days before his death. On the other hand, he had already reached the year 86 in Book 10, suggesting that the narrative of his own life slows down again in the later parts. It may be that the reference to P. Cornelius Sulla was some kind of flashback. The work was dedicated to L. Licinius Lucullus, friend and staff officer, who had improved an earlier draft through his literary expertise. It seems to have been circulated broadly only after Sulla's death. None of the literary sources which treat the other works of "autobiography" as such mention Sulla's despite its monumentality.

All four writers have several similar features in their political trajectories. On the one hand, all were quite successful in that they reached the consulship. At the same time, they had careers in other respects troubled. First, all but Sulla were defeated the first time they ran for the consulship (Catulus two more times). Sulla lost in his first run for the praetorship, and was likely blocked from running for the consulship when first eligible because he was under indictment. (His later dictatorship was, of course, won by force.) Second, all four were in fact the target of prosecutions that seem to have had at least partly political motivations. Rufus even spent two decades of his life in exile. Such prosecutions were considerably more common in republican Rome than they are today. Alexander (1993) has estimated that about one Roman politician in three would have faced prosecution during his lifetime. Still, the conjunction of four out of four is perhaps not a coincidence. Third, none of them was from the core Roman nobility, the group that produced generation after generation of elected officials. Scaurus, Catulus, and Sulla were all from families very old and thus of high social standing, but ones that had not had much political prominence in the recent past. Rufus was a "new man," someone whose ancestors had never even held political office.

Not only did these men have somewhat precarious political careers individually, but they may also have lived in a time when the rules of politics were changing more generally. They began writing shortly after a pair of events which seem to mark a transformation in popular participation in Roman politics. First, in the early second century, a series of laws introduced the secret ballot in popular voting. Second, we are told that in 145 BCE a politician named C. Licinius Crassus was the first to address political speeches to the crowd of citizens in the Forum, rather than a group assembled in the Comitium (an open-air meeting place adjacent to both Forum and Senate house). The effect of this was to address a substantially larger audience and probably one with less predictable political sympathies. Both ancient and modern authorities have connected this change with the rise of "popular" politicians whose mark was the ability to mobilize recently enlarged numbers of voters to show up and act on their legislative proposals. Historians who otherwise have wide differences have tended to agree that the late republic saw such mass mobilization of voters by charismatic speakers take on an increased (if not entirely new) importance. Whether or not Rome actually became more "democratic," the standard political arsenal had changed.

Flux also appears at a third and final level if we look at the broader history of Roman cultural production. Many have noted that "literature" in anything like the modern sense came very late to Rome; the conventional marker of Livius Andronicus' composition of dramas in 240 will give a serviceable date. Only slightly less noted is that the development of artistic prose seems to have come even later. The elder Cato (234–149) is the first author recorded to have published in later recognized "literary" genres such as history, oratory, and the technical manual. It has been something of an embarrassment, however, for this version of literary history, that some parts of Cato's *œuvre* are, from the point of view of later literature, much more sophisticated than others. Moreover, we now realize that Cato's distancing of himself from Greek intellectual traditions is largely a useful fiction, and so cannot account for his "primitive" features. Sciarrino (2004) has recently argued that the problem is misconceived. The late third and early second centuries were a time of negotiation between various forms of (potentially) authoritative verbal practice: performance vs. text; socially prominent individuals vs. marginal professionals vs. popular traditions; inspiration vs. traditional authority. In this context, it would not be surprising to find experimentation with forms that did not necessarily survive later. We should consider, therefore, whether our authors took advantage of this cultural fluidity to respond to their peculiar social and political situations.

4   Cicero and Caesar

Before I discuss the next two authors, let me say a few words about the periodization I have implied. The writings discussed in the previous section seem to date to what is conventionally thought of as the late republic (say, 133–44 BCE), and Sulla's memoirs seem to have appeared in the early adulthood of M. Tullius Cicero (106–43; *cos.* 63) and C. Julius Caesar (100–44; *cos.* 59). Nonetheless, there are grounds for a distinction. Three of the earlier writers were born within about a decade of each other during the so-called middle republic, and all four within twenty-four years. It is then another thirty-two years until Cicero's birth, and with only six more until Caesar's. Substantively, the earlier set of writers seems to produce something that is openly "autobiographical," while the latter pair, as we will see below, try a variety of strategies to avoid that appearance. Still, especially given the fragmentary nature of much of our evidence, the line should not be drawn too dogmatically.

We learn from a letter of Cicero to his friend Atticus (*Att.* 1.20.6) that he had recently written a set of notes (*commentarius*), in Greek, on his consulate of three

years earlier (i.e., 63). He had already sent a copy to the Greek polymath Posidonius so that the latter might use it as a source for a true (i.e., literary) history, though Posidonius seems to have declined. Cicero is sending it to Atticus for correction, then to be forwarded to "Athens and the other cities of Greece." At the same time he was also planning with Atticus the collection and publication of most of his consular speeches. Another, contemporary letter (*Att.* 2.1.1–2) tells us that Cicero was planning a parallel set of Latin notes and a poem on the same topic. In 55 he tried again to get his life written up by a noted historian, this time L. Lucceius, and in that context promises that he will complete Latin notes for Lucceius if he will take up the task. Cicero seems not to have finished that record in the intervening years; in fact, we have no evidence that he ever did so. Nor do we have direct traces of the Greek text we know to have circulated in his own times.

I suggested above that Cicero used strategies to avoid the potential ethical difficulties involved in writing autobiography. Most prominently, he tried at least twice to get a front man to tell the story according to his specifications. Since both Posidonius and Lucceius had independent status (juridically and intellectually), they could legitimately "launder" Cicero's own account. Cicero also took some care as to where his texts would circulate. The sense of *verecundia* is, as noted above, status-dependent and it is also one primarily of face-to-face relationships. "Face-to-face" here takes on a somewhat special meaning. On the one hand, the society in question is not the Roman citizenry in general (which is far too large), but just (roughly) the senatorial aristocracy. On the other hand, the set of interactions among that group is expanded by use of letter. Correspondence among elites shows the same kind of deferential behavior as seems to exist in direct conversations. (This, incidentally, could be an interesting index for the importance of written texts in Roman society.) Cicero's Greek commentary gains on both scores. Its notional audience is provincial and so they cannot overtly reject Cicero's claims to their attention. It is also a far-away and diffuse group, so its actual attention is entirely optional. The reliability issue still remains (hence the request to Posidonius), but the mere circulation of Cicero's own text would not harm him.

Caesar's autobiographical writings comprised sets of notes (*commentarii*) on his own military campaigns in Gaul and then during the civil war. Each book of the *Gallic War* recounted a year of the fighting from 58 to 52 (not counting the eighth book, written by Caesar's lieutenant Aulus Hirtius, which covered 51 and 50). There is considerable scholarly debate (and virtually no evidence) whether these were annual dispatches or were published together after the fact. A parallel text narrated the *Civil War* from 49 to 48. These were not published until after Caesar's death, and there is much uncertainty whether this represented a literary or political decision (or both).

Cicero's approaches to avoiding the dangers of autobiography had to do with macro- (Greek language) and meta- (foreign distribution and re-authoring) features of the text. Caesar operates much differently. In his case, a series of micro-features do similar work. Also his strategies are not entirely consistent with each other but are designed to accommodate two different stances that his readers might adopt. One strategy is to deny that his life is actually the subject of the work. The phrase

"Gallic War" was almost certainly in the original title, but personalizing terms like "life" or "deeds" or "proconsulship" apparently were not. The narrative includes activities for which Caesar was not present, but excludes his activities (personal or official) which were not connected to the war. The first person is used to refer to the narrator, but the general is always in the third person. Even the famously plain style of the text was not characteristically Caesar's own. The other strategy was to suggest that he was himself the audience of the text. *Commentarii* were more often than not private documents – not necessarily secret, but internal to, say, a family or governmental body. The aggressively plain style of Caesar's (and apparently Cicero's) notes reinforces this sense. I do not suggest that the Roman audience imagined these texts were genuinely leaked, but the very form gives the author "plausible deniability." This is important to the face management discussed above. The form also suggests what might be called "authentic subjectivity." The author and audience for internal records are, if we ignore the effects of time, the same person. The author cannot (and would have no reason to) simulate or dissimulate before this audience. It is easy to forget, in fact, that there is still an act of representation intervening between the author and any "eavesdropping" reader. Thus the form of the *commentarius* addresses both the arrogance problem and the authority problem.

Having raised the issue of publication, I should conclude with a few words on two common understandings of the *commentarius* that relate to its public or private character. Both Cicero and Hirtius remarked that Caesar's *commentarii* were so well written that they would discourage right-minded historians from trying to turn them into proper (i.e., literary) history. Posidonius apparently said something similar to Cicero about his own commentary while begging off using it as a source in his own work. It is frequently inferred that a primary function of the *commentarius* was to serve as a source for history; if so, it would lose much of the rhetorical force Caesar seems to have expected, whether or not it was technically an internal document. But there are only three "examples" of this use of the *commentarius* – these two and a prescription by the Greek writer Lucian. In this last case, moreover, the notes are the author's own. Those would be no different from the outline that the composer of any long work employs; for instance, Cicero prepared such notes for his speeches. The *commentarius* would be a natural enough form for Cicero to have offered Lucceius and Posidonius as he did, but the reverse inference does not hold. The notion of *commentarius* itself hardly suggested reworking. It has been suggested alternatively that the *commentarius* was itself a standard form for (political) autobiography. This practice was adopted, it is argued, from that of several known Hellenistic Greek figures who wrote up their lives as so-called *hupomnemata*. These terms share roughly the same application and a root that means "memory." None of these works is ever actually called a *commentarius* in Latin, though. The works discussed in section 3 are also often cited in this connection, but none of them is ever called *commentarius* in our sources either. As we have seen above, both Cicero's and Caesar's *commentarii* were framed to minimize their role as public autobiography. Hence, there is no reason to think that the very idea of the *commentarius* suggested political pamphleteering either.

FURTHER READING

Because of the marginality of the genre and the highly fragmentary state of most of the texts
surviving today, there is relatively little modern discussion of these "autobiographical" texts.
What does exist is often distorted by looking ahead to Caesar's *commentarii*. There are
general overviews in Misch 1950 and Mellor 1999. Sulla's memoirs are treated by Lewis
1991a and Scholz 2003. Caesar's works naturally have drawn the most attention; I discuss
them at much greater length (and with reference to much of the earlier literature) in Riggsby
2006: ch. 5.

CHAPTER TWENTY-THREE

Roman Historiography in the Late Republic

D. S. Levene

1   Introduction

In one of many memorable scenes in Robert Graves' novel *I, Claudius*, the future emperor Claudius, then a boy and a protégé of the historian Livy, is introduced by him to another famous historian, C. Asinius Pollio, shortly before the latter's death in 4 CE. A debate ensues, in which it is revealed not only that Pollio has remained a firm and independent republican through the reign of Augustus, but also that he has a very different view of the writing of history from that espoused by Livy. Livy represents a romantic, patriotic view of history: he does not regard research as especially important, and believes that it may even be damaging if it undermines the heroic image of the Roman past. For Livy, the primary role of the historian is to transmit unquestioningly the traditional stories of Rome's greatness. Pollio, on the other hand, believes that the historian's job is to track down the evidence, to use it to get at the truth, and to present that truth to the world regardless of whether patriotic readers will find it uncomfortable.

There is little doubt whom Graves wishes us to see as winning this debate. Pollio's view of history trumps Livy's at every turn, and accordingly obtains the allegiance of the young Claudius, himself already inclined to prefer truth to fiction. And the argument is anyway loaded by the extent to which Pollio's position conforms to the preferences of the modern reader: with no patriotic issues of our own at stake, and with a long tradition of academic, "positivist" historiography behind us, we can readily identify with the seeker of unvarnished truth over the upholder of an unquestioned tradition.

Graves' image of Pollio as the fearless follower of evidence opposed to the romantic Livy is so seductive that it is a disappointment to realize how slender its own historical basis is. It is recorded that Claudius as a boy worked with Livy

(Suet. *Claud*. 41.1), and that Pollio criticized Livy for *Patavinitas* ("Paduanity" – Livy was born in Padua), but this latter is recorded in the context of linguistic usage (Quint. 1.5.56; 8.1.3), and would therefore naturally be taken to be a criticism of Livy's language rather than his theory of history. It is also recorded that Pollio criticized Caesar's *Commentaries* – but not, as far as we know, Livy – for a careless disregard for truth (Suet. *DJ* 56.4, cf. 55.4). But for the rest of Graves' fantasy there is no evidence. We know a good deal about Pollio's life, but very little about his history. We have just one extended verbatim quotation, a handful of brief fragments, and a poem in praise of the unfinished work by Horace (*Carm.* 2.1). Added to this are a number of passages in later writers such as Appian and Plutarch which are assumed to be based on Pollio, often because he is a primary figure in the narrative, but where it is generally impossible to distinguish Pollio's input from the later author's own slant. There is little here to allow the conclusion that Pollio was closer than Livy to meeting the criteria of a modern academic historian. Certainly he accused Caesar of inaccuracies, but such criticisms of one's historical rivals are ubiquitous in ancient historiography: they are indeed frequent in Livy himself. It is a reasonable deduction from the "Pollio" sections in later historians that his account of Caesar's campaigns gave an unusually prominent role to his own autopsy (Morgan 2000), but this hardly can be regarded as a guarantee of a dispassionate critical acumen.

Graves was writing a novel, and it is of little consequence – or surprise – that the debate he describes depends more on his imagination than on historical evidence (even if that is perhaps ironic given its subject matter). It is more disturbing when the same image appears to have infiltrated the scholarly literature. Syme famously set out an antithesis between Pollio and Livy so close to Graves' as to make it look as if he might have unconsciously been influenced by him: here too Pollio appears not only as the anti-Augustan independent, but also as the anti-Romantic lover of truth, Livy as the complacent and uncritical Augustan patriot. The *Patavinitas* jibe is reworked into an assault on the entire manner of historical writing that Livy is presumed to espouse (Syme 1939: 486, also 5–7, 482–485): "Pollio knew what history was. It was not like Livy." Pollio has likewise been represented as a quasi-modern positivist historian in various other places (e.g., Kornemann 1896: 603–606, 649; Pierce 1922: 37, 64–66).

The idea of Pollio's political independence under the principate was comprehensively, if controversially, challenged some years ago (Bosworth 1972b; but see *contra*, e.g., Morgan 2000: 60–69). But the idea that he stood for a particular, anti-Livian style of historiography has not received an equally clear refutation, and has more insidious ramifications. For Graves' and Syme's antithesis between Pollio and Livy is a particular example of a far more widely held interpretation of late republican historiography: the claim that its exponents fell into two distinct groups, one of serious political figures writing serious political history, the other of non-politicians romanticizing the past, each group with its distinctive subject matter, manner, and structure. Not least among the aims of this chapter will be to challenge that reading of both the surviving and the lost historians of the period while offering a different, more broadly based perspective for viewing their works.

2 The Late Republic

First, the scope of this chapter needs to be clarified. I am taking the starting point of the "late republic" to be the regime of Sulla in 82–80 BCE. This inevitably leads to some artificial distinctions, since it is not always possible to date historians with the appropriate precision: in particular the annalists Valerius Antias and Claudius Quadrigarius seem to have been writing approximately at the time of Sulla, but I shall have little to say about them here (cf. above, p. 264). The endpoint for the purposes of the chapter will be the death of Augustus in 14 CE. This too is artificial: it is not based on a belief that the republic lasted that long as a political system, or even that 14 CE represents a major political watershed in other respects, but rather it reflects the fact that a number of the most prominent historians of the Augustan period, including indeed both Livy and Pollio, are most notable as historians of the republic, and their work aligns more naturally with their predecessors than with their successors, despite the vastly changed political circumstances under which they were writing. After Livy Latin historiography focused primarily on the empire, and will accordingly be treated in the next chapter. There were, however, some historians who wrote contemporary history under Augustus, and as such prefigure the mainstream histories of the empire: these too I shall leave aside here.

For a modern reader, this period of historiography is marked by two outstanding figures: Sallust (C. Sallustius Crispus) and Livy (T. Livius). With each of them, however, only a minority of their work survives. From Sallust we have the short monographs known as the *War of Catiline* (describing the attempted revolution of the Roman aristocrat L. Sergius Catilina in 63 BCE) and the *War of Jugurtha* (on the Roman war in Africa in the late second century BCE against the Numidian king Jugurtha). But we have lost almost entirely his five-volume *Histories*, covering the history of Rome between 78 and 67 BCE, although it was much read in later antiquity, and accordingly a substantial number of fragments survive either excerpted or in palimpsest or quoted by later authors. As for Livy, of the 142-volume history that he published, covering the entire history of Rome from its foundation to the death of Augustus' stepson Nero Drusus in 9 BCE, only thirty-five volumes survive: 1–10 and 21–45, covering respectively the period from the foundation to 293 BCE, and 219–167 BCE. Of the rest we have relatively few fragments – the sheer size of this history doubtless precluded its full bulk from circulating widely – but we do have brief summaries (the so-called *Periochae*) of almost all of the remaining books.

The other Latin histories of the period are lost (apart from the *commentarii* of Caesar and his followers: above, p. 271). The one about which we know by far the most is the forty-four-book *Philippic History* of Pompeius Trogus, the surviving fragments of which include not only content lists for each book (the so-called "Prologues"), but also a large-scale epitome by the later writer Justin. From these we have a close knowledge of the structure and the contents of the work, both of which are quite exceptional in Latin historiography (see §5). There are then a number of other historians for whom we have sufficient fragments or references to get at least a vague picture of the scope and sometimes manner of their work: this is the case not only with Pollio but also with L. Cornelius Sisenna, C. Licinius Macer, Aelius Tubero, L. Arruntius, and Fenestella. (There is a complex problem as to whether there were one or two historians by the name of Aelius Tubero, and, if two, which fragments should be assigned to which. Cicero [*Q. fr.* 1.1.10] refers to his brother's aide L. Tubero writing history, but Livy 4.23.1 and Suet. *DJ* 56, 83 name their source as his son Q. Tubero.) There are even more historians, however, who are hardly anything more than names to us: examples include Libo, Q. Hortensius Hortalus, C. Sulpicius Galba, Tanusius Geminus, Octavius Ruso, Octavius Musa, and C. Clodius Licinus. There is also the odd situation of L. Lucceius, not a single fragment or summary of whose work survives, but who is more widely known than many better attested writers, since Cicero wrote a famous (if shameless) letter to him (*Fam.* 5.12) requesting that Lucceius incorporate an account of Cicero's own deeds into the history that he was writing.

A common image of the period is based around two aspects of these historians, whether lost or surviving (see, e.g., Badian 1966; Timpe 1979; also – but with some significant qualifications – Petzold 1993). The first is the manner of their history: whether they continued in the tradition of comprehensive year-by-year, so-called "annalistic" history, taking as their theme the history of the earlier republic, or whether they wrote thematic history about periods within living memory. The second issue centers on their own qualifications to write: whether they were (or had been) active political and military figures either writing history which covered matters within their experience or at least giving an account of events which they did not experience personally, but where their their broad knowledge of public life enabled them to give an informed and rational analysis, or whether they were "armchair" historians writing without having held high public office or military commands, and basing their work primarily upon their reading.

It is moreover implied that these two aspects were broadly correlated: that the "annalists" increasingly withdrew into formulaic literary fantasies, whereas the non-annalists wrote contemporary or near-contemporary thematic histories that reflected far more accurately the realities of politics and war in Rome. As examples of the latter group one may mention not only Pollio, a leading public figure writing a history of the Civil Wars which is generally thought to have started from 60 BCE (Hor. *Carm.* 2.1.1; but note Woodman 2003: 199–213), but also Sisenna, who was praetor in 78 and then went on to hold a command under Pompey, but died in 67 while on service; his history was in at least twenty-three volumes, and covered the period from approximately 90 to 79 BCE. The former, the "annalistic" and non-political group, includes Antias and Quadrigarius, and later Fenestella, whose history was in at least twenty-two volumes and a few of whose fragments – e.g., *HRR* F 10 – did include material that one would associate with an "annalistic" arrangement.

However, it is hard to see that this broad dichotomy stands up to much scrutiny (Verbrugghe 1989; Marincola 1999). The connection between annalistic history and politically inexperienced writers is the easiest to break down. Licinius Macer wrote at least sixteen books, and "annalistic" material is far more strongly attested for his work than it is for Fenestella (e.g., *HRR* FF 10, 13, 16); his history dealt not with contemporary or near-contemporary events but with the early republic. Yet he was highly active politically, including a famous tribunate in 73 BCE, a praetorship, and governorship of a province. Both Tuberos also engaged extensively in political and military activity, and at least one of them wrote about the earlier republic including material that is likely to attest to an annalistic arrangement (e.g., *HRR* FF 6, 7). And while it is true that Sisenna and Pollio primarily wrote contemporary history, their fragments do not allow us to determine whether they in fact adopted an annalistic format – there are too few actual fragments of Pollio, and though there are more than 140 fragments of Sisenna, almost all of them are decontextualized phrases cited by grammarians which give no evidence of the character of the work. It is perfectly possible that one or both of them organized their work annalistically. Sisenna *HRR* F 127 says that it is preferable to write thematically than piecemeal, but this is in the context of the organization of the events of a single summer, and thus is more likely to attest to an overall annalistic arrangement than to deny it.

The connection between these supposedly non-annalistic writers and more reliable, politically informed history is equally problematic. As was said above, there is no evidence that Pollio's history was marked by a particular critical acumen when it came to politics or any other topic; there is as least as much evidence for critical reasoning and political awareness in the fragments of Fenestella (e.g., *HRR* FF 9, 21). It is certainly true that Sisenna was much praised for his reliability by later Roman writers, and that we can with reasonable probability convict some annalistic writers of outright invention (notably Valerius Antias and Licinius Macer: on the latter see, e.g., Livy 7.9.3–5 = *HRR* F 16). But even Sisenna, despite claiming that dreams should not be believed, did not apply similar critical skepticism to other supernatural events (Cic. *Div.* 1.99 = *HRR* F 5), while Macer's history was famously marked by his willingness to challenge traditional history on the basis of documents – the so-called "linen books," which (unless he invented them himself, which is unlikely, though it cannot be entirely excluded) precisely attests to the fact that he did not uncritically rely on accepted tradition, but sought an empirical approach to history.

So if the picture of a sharp division in Roman historiography in the late republic is not well supported in the surviving fragments and attestations of the historians in question, where does it come from? It appears to arise from a combination of factors. The earliest Roman historians were certainly senators, and it can be plausibly argued that their histories were a continuation of their political activities; it is also true that it is only relatively late that one finds clearly non-senatorial historians (though the precise social status of quite a number of historians is unknown). But combined with this is an uncritical acceptance of certain ancient theories and prejudices about the proper qualifications for a historian, along with a tendency to develop over-schematic antitheses between those historians who do survive. Various theorists of history in the ancient world suggest that political and military experience is an essential prerequisite for a historian, not merely because being an eyewitness of the particular events about which he is writing was felt to give him a privileged position, but more generally because of the insight that he will thereby receive into the conduct of war and politics more widely. This standpoint is associated above all with Polybius (whose work is marked by polemical attacks, above all against "armchair" historians whose experience is gained solely from libraries), but it represents a tradition that has its roots in Thucydides. This is then combined with hints in the fragments of lost Roman historians – in particular Sempronius Asellio *HRR* FF 1–2 – that some Romans saw a distinction between "annals," which (allegedly) consisted of bare facts without analysis, and "history," in which proper causes and explanations for events are given. From this the conclusion is reached that serious critical history was written by politicians, especially (but not only) those writing thematic history about their own time, while annalists were primarily non-politicians uncritically transmitting tradition, or indeed even going beyond that by inventing sensational material where tradition was lacking.

In general one would expect that modern scholars, who themselves after all rarely have political and military experience and usually conform more to the practices of the "armchair" historians, would be more skeptical than the ancients about the primacy of direct political experience in creating a good historian. Nor is it at all obvious that accounts of the distant past are going to reveal less historical acumen than accounts of the more recent past. But in the case of the late republic such skepticism has tended to be muted. One possible reason is that the dichotomy appears to map very well onto the two major surviving historians of the period: Sallust and Livy.

Already in antiquity there was a recognition that this pair represented the high point of republican historiography, and they were treated as strongly contrasting figures: Sallust as the "Roman Thucydides," Livy as the "Roman Herodotus," for example (Quint. 10.1.101; cf. 2.5.19). In modern accounts that antithesis has been maintained and developed into a more general contrast between Sallust, the pessimistic, disillusioned politician writing intense studies of his corrupted society, and Livy, the naïve, relaxed, and optimistic celebrator of past virtue on a grand annalistic scale. It is certainly true that Sallust was a senator and Livy was not; it is also true that Sallust's two surviving monographs concern events within living memory treated thematically, whereas Livy's surviving history concerns the long distant past and is treated annalistically. But, as will be seen, the dichotomy between them is often drawn far too starkly.

3   The Livian Sallust

Sallust's historical writings are so familiar to students of Latin, and have exerted such influence in antiquity and beyond, that it is often hard to recognize just how exceptional they are. Both the surviving works are brief historical monographs, an unusual form in itself, and one not previously attested at Rome. The *Catiline* in particular is not only a monograph but also a remarkably short one: it is, for example, shorter than any one of Livy's thirty-five surviving volumes. And what is more, that brevity in scale is accentuated by the fact that Sallust spends a significant portion of the work on matters outside his main narrative. He begins with a philosophical preface of unprecedented abstraction, in which he discusses in general terms the superiority of intellectual virtue over physical strength and of virtue in general over vice (1.1–2.9). From here he moves into a defense of history as a career, along with a short account of his own political career (though leaving out the embarrassing details: he was expelled from the Senate for three years, and subsequently forced out of political life when charged with extortion) and his abandonment of it in favor of writing (3.1–4.2). At that point he offers a brief account of his topic, followed by a character sketch of Catiline (4.3–5.8) which makes it appear that his narrative is about to begin – but instead he immediately digresses again, and summarizes the whole of Roman history from Aeneas onwards down to Sulla in order to explain the state that Rome had found herself in that made her a breeding-ground for Catiline's revolution (5.9–13.5). Not until something like a fifth of the way into this short monograph do we actually begin the narrative. Even then the story is interrupted by a summary of the social and moral problems of the city (36.4–39.5); and then an astonishing portion of the last section – again, amounting to about a fifth of the total monograph – is devoted to the debate between Caesar and Cato on the punishment of the conspirators and a comparison between these two key figures in Roman history. Speeches and letters also occupy a significant proportion of the rest of the monograph, including two speeches and a letter from Catiline himself.

The *Jugurtha* is, relatively speaking, spread over a more expansive canvas – it is about twice as long as its predecessor – but here too the narrative is treated in far from a conventional fashion. Once again we have an abstract philosophical preface about virtue leading into a defense of Sallust's own position as historian (1–4); once again a good proportion of the narrative is punctuated by digressions, notably the ones on Africa (17–19), on the history of social conflict at Rome (41–42), and on the foundation of Leptis Magna (78–79). Here too speeches play a substantial role: major speeches by Adherbal (14), Memmius (31), and Marius (85), as well as some shorter ones. It is true that all of this still leaves a much larger proportion of the text devoted to the main narrative than was the case in the *Catiline*. But what sets the *Jugurtha* apart not only from its predecessor but also from all other known historiography in antiquity is the way in which the major topic of the work is indicated to be not so much the war against Jugurtha itself, which was after all a relatively minor episode, but the entire sweep of Roman history in the last centuries of the republic. This is never narrated directly, yet Sallust repeatedly indicates to the reader that the true significance of the monograph lies in the unstated story of Roman decline and fall that lies beyond its chronological boundaries (see Levene 1992).

So, purely in formal terms, Sallust's history is unique. This uniqueness of form is allied to a historical slant and writing style which are themselves highly distinctive. The overriding impression is of a pervasive pessimism: his central theme is Roman decline, which appears both dreadful and inevitable. For Sallust, while it is true that Roman power has never been greater, it is precisely *because* Roman power has never been greater that Rome is collapsing, as unchallenged power and wealth lead to appalling political and moral corruption. That corruption is repeatedly exposed, as bribery, theft, vice, and debauchery are seen as the direct consequence of Roman conquest and as the underlying motivators for social and political upheaval. And in order to narrate this tale of disaster, Sallust employed a style full of archaisms and innovations in vocabulary, forged into spiky and compressed phrases and sentences (cf. Woodman 1988: 117–128). Sallust had himself, as said above, been at the heart of Roman politics: he now turns to exposing its deepest and most vicious basis.

Moreover, we can see firm links between Sallust and other politician-historians of the Roman world. For his major Roman model he went back more than 100 years to Cato the Censor, as was observed in antiquity (e.g. Quint. 8.3.29) – Cato was the prime example of a leading politician who had become a leading historian, and also a man whose moral stance was a congenial touchstone for someone deploring the absence of morality in his own contemporaries. But Sallust can easily be seen as part of a more immediate tradition as well. Sisenna was likewise known for coinages in vocabulary (e.g., Cic. *Brut.* 259–260: it was this that made his work such a fertile quarrying ground for later grammarians); Sallust had cited him, broadly approvingly, as a predecessor at *Jug.* 95.2, and seems to have begun his own *Histories* at the point where Sisenna left off. Likewise, Sallust had a close connection to Pollio: the grammarian L. Ateius Philologus acted as assistant and advisor to both men (Suet. *Gramm.* 10.6). Another politician-historian of the period, Arruntius, was accused by Seneca of imitating Sallust to a ludicrous degree (*Ep.* 114.17–19). All of this appears to give good reason to see Sallust's writing as distinctively connected with the insights acquired through his political career, and as part of a tradition of political history at Rome.

But while all that is true, there is another side to Sallust as well. As was said above, his major work, the *Histories*, is lost; but the surviving fragments of that work are sufficiently extensive to indicate to us a significantly different side to the historian. For one thing, it appears that, perhaps like Sisenna's own work, but unlike the *Catiline* and the *Jugurtha*, it was organized annalistically. Whereas the monographs pay little attention to chronology, which is treated sometimes quite cavalierly, the *Histories* adopted a strict year-by-year framework, and the opening sentence of the work clearly gestures towards a formal annalistic approach (F 1.1); there are also some indications that other annalistic material was included, albeit treated flexibly (e.g., FF 1.66, 2.42–43; cf. Rich 1997). Moreover, Sallust appears to have abandoned the heavy reliance on analysis through speeches that marked the two monographs. A ninth-century manuscript now in the Vatican contains texts of all the speeches and letters from Sallust's *Catiline* and *Jugurtha*, even relatively short ones; it also includes four speeches and two letters from *Histories* 1–4. FF 5.21–22 come from a speech of Gabinius in *Histories* 5, which suggests that Book 5 was not culled for the Vatican collection, but there is no other fragment from all the hundreds surviving from the *Histories* attesting to a direct speech other than those in the Vatican manuscript. It is therefore a reasonable deduction that this manuscript contains all the speeches and letters from *Histories* 1–4, exactly as it does for Sallust's surviving works. In which case it is noticeable that the *Histories* contained only a little more than one speech or letter per book, not one of which is as long as either the speech of Caesar from the *Catiline* or that of Marius from the *Jugurtha*.

Moreover, the narrative scale of the *Histories* has moved away from the massive abridgment that characterized the monographs. The *Catiline* is astonishingly brief, as said above; the *Jugurtha*, while longer, covers a good thirteen years of events. The *Histories*, on the other hand, take five books to deal with just twelve years. This is comfortably on the scale adopted by earlier historical writers, and even comparable to that of most of Livy's work (though in fact Livy spent ten books [90–99] on the specific period covered by Sallust's *Histories*). In other words, a good number of the distinctive structural features of the monographs are abandoned in the major work, though of course we cannot tell for sure how pervasive this return to tradition was.

But even more important is that thematically, also, Sallust exhibits features that more traditionally have been associated with Livy. He may analyze recent events in grim and pessimistic terms; but this is offset by a remarkably starry-eyed and romantic picture of Roman republican history prior to 146 BCE. In the *Catiline* and the *Jugurtha* that period is – at least on the face of things – presented as a time of implausibly untrammeled virtue (*Cat.* 7.1–10.1; *Jug.* 41.2). This picture is substantially qualified in the *Histories* (F 1.11), which admits that the earlier republic was marked by social strife, but even that work still allows pure virtue in the period 202–146 BCE. This tendency to romanticize the distant past, and to look back to it to get examples of virtuous conduct for one's readers, is there throughout Sallust's works – it is a common theme in the speeches, for example. While the current state of Rome may offer little hope to readers, the glorious past is always kept before their eyes to offer an alternative. Sallust provides interesting and politically informed analyses of many events, but this is set within a remarkably schematic and stylized overall framework, albeit one that is persistently subverted and complicated once one gets beneath the surface (e.g., Scanlon 1987; Batstone 1988, 1990; Kraus 1999a; Levene 2000).

4 The Sallustian Livy

On a superficial glance, no historian could provide a stronger contrast to Sallust than Livy. Instead of the spiky, archaizing style, one has what Quintilian famously characterized as "milky richness" (10.1.32); in place of Sallust's "immortal brevity" (Quint. 10.1.102) one finds a narrative of phenomenal expansiveness encompassing the whole of Roman history. To challenge the unrelenting gloom that characterizes Sallust one gets frequent representations of deeds of apparently unqualified heroism, characters to whose detriment not a word is breathed, Roman victories and conquests justified and celebrated. And whereas Sallust has little to say of divine influence, large portions of Livy's narrative are permeated with reminders of the gods' hand in history, with regular records of supernatural events, as well as Roman piety in responding to those events. In short, the very model of an imperial historian, and justly associated with the Augustan project of political restoration, religious revival, and celebration of the Roman past.

And yet, once one gives Livy more than a superficial glance, those apparent certainties fade away. The surviving portions of his history are astonishingly varied, something which has been unfortunately obscured by the fact that most of his surviving work is little read except by specialists: the brilliance of Books 27 or 44, for example, has rarely received recognition. This neglect in part actually arises from a piece of good fortune. With Livy, unusually among ancient historians, we are able to compare large portions of his narrative with his source, namely Polybius, whom he used extensively and followed closely for many of his later books. This has enabled some fascinating studies of Livy's working methods (esp. Luce 1977; Tränkle 1977), but also has led others to a more superficial and generally unsustainable conclusion: that Livy, at least in his later books, did little but reproduce his sources mechanically, and that his own input is mostly limited to stylistic polish. This prejudice has done little to encourage readers to explore his work more widely; most have tended to stay close to a few books, especially those whose stories are familiar – above all Books 1 (covering the regal period) and 21 (Hannibal's initial invasion of Italy).

And generalizations about Livy on the basis of a few books are all too often invalid. If one characterizes him as a religious historian, one must nevertheless recognize that in much of his Fourth Decade (Books 31–40) religion is of little importance to his narrative (Levene 1993: 78–103). If one sees him as a celebrator of Roman imperialism, then one must factor in the miserable sequence of immoral and incompetent Roman imperialists whom he describes clearsightedly in Books 42–43. And although it is possible – indeed likely – that Livy's attitude to Augustus developed through the latter's reign (see esp. Woodman 1988: 136–140; Badian 1993), "Livy the Augustan" needs considerable qualification once one remembers that in his entire surviving work Augustus is only mentioned three times – the first two of which seem to be later insertions by the author (1.19.3; 4.20.7; 28.12.12: see Luce 1965). Indeed, the sentiments of Livy's *Preface* (which is likely to predate Augustus' victory in 31) have manifestly been strongly influenced by Sallust (Woodman 1988: 128–135): one finds exactly the same pessimism about the current state of Rome contrasted with a belief in the superior virtue of the past.

Even generalizations about his work's structure and articulation are all too often misleading. It is certainly true that his work is broadly structured annalistically, but that is not entirely uniform, since it does not apply to Book 1 at all, and he is prepared to show considerable flexibility and variation both in the annalistic material he chooses to introduce and in the way he distributes it in his narrative (Rich 1997). And this applies especially to the question of the degree of coverage that he chose for different parts of his work. It was pointed out above that Sallust is at least as starry-eyed as Livy about the virtues of the heroes of the past – indeed, he is more so, as I shall discuss further below. It might at least be objected that even if Sallust and Livy adopt similar attitudes to the past, they respond to it differently: that Sallust chose to focus on the time of present vice, whereas Livy, as he explicitly says at the start of his work (*praef.* 4–5), decided to escape the evils of the present by concentrating on past glories. But although that is indeed what Livy claims for himself, his actual history does not bear it out. Of its 142 books, nearly two-thirds dealt with the period after the fall of Carthage in 146, the date which for Sallust (and others) had marked a watershed in Roman morals. He spent twenty-five books on the twenty or so years of Caesar's and Octavian's civil wars, which is more than he allotted to the regal period and first three centuries of the republic combined.

Nor is this simply a function of his lack of information about earlier periods. Livy's Greek contemporary, Dionysius of Halicarnassus, wrote a history of early Rome which was far more expansive that Livy's, despite their having identical source material available to them. Livy's first book corresponds to Books 1–4 of Dionysius, and the events of Dionysius' first eleven books are covered by Livy in little more than three books. Livy could certainly have treated the regal period in particular at far greater length than he does: instead his practice is to abridge and summarize even famous stories to a degree that matches Sallust himself. Romulus' killing of Remus is brushed away in a couple of lines (1.7.2–3), Tarpeia is no more than a minor aside (1.11.6–9). The well-known story of the sale of the Sibylline Books to Tarquinius Superbus (e.g., D. Hal. *AR* 4.62) does not receive even a passing mention. Far from focusing his attention primarily on the glorious past, Livy from the very start of his history gives the impression of hastening towards the present as swiftly as he decently can, given that his self-imposed task involved comprehensive coverage of the whole of Roman history. Livy, no less than Sallust, turned his spotlight above all on the late republic. It is merely that the accident of survival has meant that those later, more expansive books are now lost to us.

But it is still more important that Livy is in fact not an uncritical didactic admirer of Roman heroes and Roman history. There are many virtuous characters in the work whom Livy shows as contributing substantially to Roman success – but on closer reading it is surprisingly rare for those characters to be presented without significant qualification. Camillus is the second founder of Rome, the hero who preserves the state after the Gallic sack in Book 5 – but in Book 6 he is seen in a more contentious light as the upholder of class privilege. Scipio Africanus carries off the invasion of Africa and the spectacular defeat of Hannibal, but his flirtation with Hellenism and his tendency to self-promotion even through deceit are more uncomfortable. Cato is the firm upholder of traditional moral values but takes that to an excess that can hardly be justified. And there are many Roman figures of even greater ambivalence in the work: Coriolanus warring against his own country, Manlius Capitolinus saving the Capitol only to be executed by being thrown from it after (apparently) a failed revolt, Manlius Torquatus putting his son to death in order to provide a salutary lesson to his troops, Flaminius irreligiously blundering into a trap but dying a heroic death. This complexity is all too often overlooked even today, largely because Livy's subtle mode of presenting character rarely involves him in a direct authorial commentary: actions are allowed to speak for themselves. One must read Livy with far more attention to the detailed implications of his story than is often shown. But the upshot is that there may be a case for saying that Sallust excessively idealizes the Roman past (perhaps precisely because he was not narrating it in detail). There is little case for saying it about Livy.

The same is true of Rome as a whole. Livy's mission was not to question Rome's right to her empire; but the process of acquiring that empire, even if justified overall, regularly leads to serious and unresolved moral questions. Hannibal (in Livy's account) is a treaty-breaker and aggressor – and yet one reason he can obtain such success as he does is that he is, at least at the beginning, far more scrupulous than the Romans in his behavior towards both the gods and his allies. (How does one assess a war where the illegal aggressor behaves better than his victims?) Manlius Vulso achieves a major triumph against the Gallogrecians in Asia – and yet that victory is also a major cause of Rome's decline into luxury (39.6.7–9). (Is military success a satisfactory compensation for moral laxity, and is it worth fighting a war at all if its ultimate consequences will be so disastrous?) Throughout Livy's narrative these issues are tacitly raised, even though he rarely points up the problems himself: it is for the reader to be alert to them.

Nor is the supposed political naïveté of Livy in evidence nearly as much as is sometimes implied. It is of course true that, as a non-senator, it is unlikely that he participated in high politics. But there is no reason to believe that such participation was an essential prerequisite for a sophisticated political understanding at Rome, any more than it is today. Deciding what in Livy's (or any other writer's) narrative might serve as evidence of political acumen is (needless to say) highly subjective, since it will largely depend on the reader's own presuppositions about the actual nature of political life (there is an all too common tendency to assume that a writer is naïve who fails to mirror one's own level of cynicism). But if one criterion may be suggested to be a willingness to question the specious motives that politicians put forward for their activities, and to see instead a complex of personal, social, and systemic causes underlying political events, then Livy's history furnishes very many examples. The so-called "Struggle of the Orders" – the class conflict that is such a major theme in the early books – provides many instances. Patricians and plebeians alike, both individually and collectively, claim to be acting in the interests of the state, while advocating policies that they primarily favor because of their class allegiances and personal advantages. Much of the contention revolves around the introduction and development of institutions and laws; but those institutions and laws themselves become a major cause of subsequent political behavior. It is little surprise that these books provided the material for Machiavelli's *Discourses*, some of his profoundest studies of political institutions and political affairs.

All of this indicates that it is a considerable over-simplification to make a sharp dichotomy between the Sallustian and the Livian approaches to writing history – and by extension one should be equally wary of similar dichotomies about those authors whose works are lost. What Sallust and Livy share is at least as important as what separates them – indeed, perhaps even more important in the context of providing a general characterization of the period. They share a basic understanding of Roman history in terms of moral decline; they further see that decline as the result of her military conquests, in terms of the influx of wealth and the abandonment of reasons for moral restraint. They both are interested in ambivalent figures, and show something of that ambivalence emerging even in their most heroic characters. They both are, at least some of the time, wary of accepting declared motives at face value, and focus on social conflict as a primary underlying motivation for many political events. This is not, of course, to suggest that there are no differences between them: for example, their prose styles certainly are radically apart; the expansive, multi-layered complexity of much of Livy's narrative contrasts sharply with the amazingly focused intensity of Sallust's monographs; and there is nothing in Livy to parallel Sallust's remarkable prefaces. But those differences need to be seen in the context of immense continuity between them in both their general conception of history and the manner in which they articulate that conception in their narratives.

5 Pompeius Trogus

But if Roman historiography in the first century BCE shows a great deal of continuity, it also contains one of the most radical departures in the genre. A further feature that Sallust and Livy share, a feature that is so obvious that it is hardly ever thought necessary to comment on, is that they are "Roman historians" in not only nationality but also subject matter. They are historians *of Rome*, only touching on other nations in as much as those nations are involved with the events of the Roman empire. And this is indeed the general rule at Rome among both historians who survive and those who are lost. From Fabius Pictor to Caesar, from Tacitus to Ammianus, Roman historians wrote about their own country: the varied topics of Greek historians, where other nations were often no less the object of attention than their own, are alien to the genre as it developed at Rome.

There are, however, occasional but important exceptions. Pompeius Trogus was a contemporary of Livy, and like Livy wrote a large-scale multi-volume history. But Trogus' history centered not on Rome but on Greece and the East. It was a "universal history" in the tradition going back to Ephorus and exemplified in the work of Trogus' contemporaries Diodorus Siculus and Nicolaus of Damascus, but to a certain extent that term does not do justice to the balance of the work. The geographic range is much less than in Diodorus: notably, the Assyrians and Babylonians are only there briefly at the start, and likewise there is no independent Egyptian history – the Egyptian past is given merely as background at the point of the Persian conquest (*Prologue* 1). Overwhelmingly the focus is on two nations: Persia and the area of the Persian empire (including the subsequent rise of Parthia), but above all Greece and the Greek states (including Macedon). The chronological range is likewise narrow. Of the forty-four books, the bulk – Books 11–40 – deal with Alexander and the fate of the Hellenistic kingdoms after his death (though there is a substantial digression to give the background to Sicilian history in Books 18–23). Other nations' histories are introduced only in digressions according to when they came into contact with these Greek kingdoms.

The omission is obvious: Rome appears to be marginalized. The Romans are of course frequently present in the narrative, not least because they came increasingly into contact with and ultimately conquered the Macedonian successor kingdoms. But their story is not told in its own right for virtually the whole work. To judge by Justin's summary, they are first mentioned in 2.3.5 to point out that their empire had never encompassed Scythia, then at 6.6.5 to provide a synchronism for the "King's Peace" between Greece and Persia, and then at 12.2.12 where they are merely one of a list of nations that made a treaty with Alexander of Epirus. They appear in a more sustained way in 17–18 with the war against Pyrrhus, but are largely lost sight of again during the long back-history of Sicily that occupies 18–23 (above). From Book 28 they are a more dominant presence, but even so it is not until the penultimate book of the work that Trogus finally provided an independent narrative of Roman history. His explanation, according to Justin, is that (43.1.1–2):

he considered it the work of an ungrateful citizen if, after glorifying the deeds of all
nations, he was silent about his country alone. Therefore he briefly touched on the
beginnings of the Roman empire, such as neither to go beyond the limits of his planned
work nor pass over in silence at any rate the origin of the city that is the capital of the
world.

But in fact even here he hardly fulfills expectations: all he does is give a brief account
of the Roman kings before passing on to a history of southern Gaul, the origins of his
own family.

It is not surprising that, in the light of this, people have sometimes wished to
interpret Trogus as anti-Roman, arguing that this narrative was deliberately designed
to challenge the Roman claim to universal hegemony that is the underlying assumption in writers like Livy. And there are other aspects of the work that could appear to
support this reading. One example is the focus on Parthia as the implicit equal of
Rome at 41.1.1–7 (if this is indeed Trogus' and not Justin's slant on the matter).
Book 38 includes a lengthy anti-Roman harangue by Mithridates of Pontus (38.4–7),
including some telling points about Roman imperial ambitions; anti-Roman speeches
are also reported at 28.2 and 29.2. Trogus' account of the Roman–Macedonian wars
implies that they were partly generated by Roman fears and manipulations (30.3.2,
cf. 29.3.7) and exacerbated by Roman attacks on Greece that drove the Greeks to
seek help from the Macedonians (29.4.7); the description of Mummius' destruction
of Corinth suggests at least as much sympathy with the defeated as with the victors
(34.2). The Roman alliance with the Jews against the Seleucids prompts the cynical
comment that "it was then easy for the Romans to be generous with other people's
property" (36.3.9), and the conquest of Asia is said to introduce vices to Rome along
with wealth (34.4.12).

But this last should instantly alert us to the problems of suggesting that Trogus
adopted a distinctly anti-Roman slant, for it simply replicates Livy's image of Roman
decline under the influence of eastern wealth (cf. above). Mithridates' speech against
Rome has its forerunner in the letter which Sallust wrote for the same Mithridates in
the *Histories* (F 4.69), which even uses some of the same arguments. And criticisms of
Roman leaders and sympathy with their victims are commonplace in Sallust and Livy
as well. None of these is enough to make Trogus into an anti-Roman historian,
especially when they are set side by side with the positive image of Rome at various
other points in his work (e.g., 18.2.10; 30.3.7; 31.6.4, 8.9). It is true that the focus
on other states and the relative marginalization of Rome within the work means that
these standard images may gain a particular force from their different context: for
example, bringing to the fore the ancient theme of the "succession of empires," with
the possible implication that Rome may fall as Assyria, Persia, and Macedon had
before her. But this is certainly not explicit in anything that survives from the work.
What Trogus did was provide the Romans with a new perception of their empire,
from the standpoint of the histories of the empires that they overcame and swallowed
up into their own. But the basic ideological building-blocks of that perception
remained unchanged: patriotic praise of one's own country combined with an awareness of the problems in particular aspects of its behavior, and a sense that the present

represented a potentially disastrous moral turn away from the glories of the past. In this most un-Roman of Roman histories, the essential continuity in Roman historical conceptions and writing in the late republic receives its clearest demonstration.

FURTHER READING

Everything written about the lost Roman historians, including this chapter, will in due course need to be rethought after the publication of the multi-authored *Fragmentary Roman Historians* project (by Tim Cornell and others). In the meantime the most accessible survey is still Badian 1966, though it is unsatisfactory in various ways, as set out in the chapter; my arguments here have been strongly influenced by Verbrugghe 1989 and Marincola 1999. There are also significant studies of individual historians, including Sisenna (Rawson 1979), Licinius Macer (Ogilvie 1958; Walt 1997), and Pollio (Morgan 2000; Woodman 2003).

Sallust still needs a good general book in English: Syme 1964 (revised edition 2002) remains the only candidate, although it has significant weaknesses. He has been better served in monographs and articles, important examples including Earl 1961 and Scanlon 1987 on the whole corpus, Batstone 1988 and 1990 on the *Catiline*, and Scanlon 1989 and Kraus 1999a on the *Jugurtha*. But the best book on Sallust by some margin is still La Penna 1968, although it unfortunately has suffered from serious neglect as a result of being in Italian, poorly distributed, never translated, and long out of print.

Livy has done better in recent years, with a sequence of important monographs stemming mainly from America in the 1990s, notably Miles 1995, Jaeger 1997, Feldherr 1999, and Chaplin 2000, complemented by the major commentaries of Kraus 1994a and Oakley, *CL*; the splendid book of Luce 1977 should also be acknowledged, as the springboard from which much of this new work has leapt. Thanks to these scholars, and others like them, the "revisionist" account of Livy's work in this chapter in fact looks increasingly and comfortably mainstream. However, parts of the wider scholarly community remain wedded to older models, such as that found in Walsh 1961, still the only substantial general study of Livy's entire work in English.

As for Pompeius Trogus, the best study is Seel 1972, though it is in German and somewhat disjointed in its approach. For a brief and relatively uncontentious English summary of the most significant features of Trogus' work, one may consult Alonso-Núñez 1987.

Thanks to Gary Boydell, Mary Jaeger, Christina Kraus, Eric Levene, and Tony Woodman for reading and commenting on an earlier draft of this chapter.

CHAPTER TWENTY-FOUR

The Emperor and his Historians

John Matthews

In a famous passage of *Decline and Fall*, Edward Gibbon described the period of
Roman history from the death of the emperor Domitian in 96 CE to the accession of
Commodus in 180 as the time in which the human race enjoyed the greatest
happiness and prosperity it had ever known (Womersley 1994: I.103). It may not
be appreciated that Gibbon's words are an allusion to another great historian of his
own day, William Robertson, who in his *History of the Reign of Charles V*, published
just seven years before Volume 1 of *Decline and Fall*, had described the time from the
death of the emperor Theodosius I in 395 to the establishment of the Lombards in
Italy in the sixth century as "the period in the history of the world during which the
condition of the human race was most calamitous and afflicted." In the midst of the
Antonine Golden Age, Gibbon achieved an intimation of darker times to come by
simply changing two words of Robertson. The prosperity of the second century also
had an effect on Gibbon's procedures as a historian. As he had just explained, happy
times do not generally produce historians. It was in consequence of its happiness that
the reign of Antoninus Pius (138–161) had offered the singular advantage of "fur-
nishing very few materials for history; which is, indeed, little more than the register of
the crimes, follies and misfortunes of mankind" (Womersley 1994: I.102). Gibbon
did not use the connection with Robertson to ask about the historians who had
written in those calamitous years after the death of Theodosius; what he had in mind
was the earlier period of Roman history, and above all Tacitus, "the first of historians
who applied the science of philosophy to the study of facts," in Gibbon's famous but
overstated judgment. There were other historians who might have claimed that
appraisal (*Decline and Fall*, ch. IX; Womersley 1994: I.230).

Tacitus' greatness lay of course in his style, of which Gibbon has not been the only
imitator, and also in his willingness to engage with the great moral theme of Gibbon's
own time and preoccupations: the struggle for liberty against autocracy. This is the
central issue in Tacitus, especially in his last work, the *Annals*, in which he traced the
decline of senatorial liberty under the growing tyranny of the Julio-Claudian dynasty.

Tacitus wrote in the aftermath of another age of tyranny, that of the "bald Nero" (as Juvenal styled him), Domitian. In the *Agricola* (3.1) he had welcomed the new age of Nerva and Trajan, as showing how those former incompatibles, imperial rule and liberty, could coexist under a wise ruler. His first large-scale historical work, the *Histories*, portrayed (or would have portrayed, were its text complete) the emergence of the more recent tyranny, from the civil wars that brought down the old regime, through the reigns of the sensible Vespasian, the mild but untested Titus, to the paranoid oppressions of Domitian. Tacitus declared that he would reserve for his old age the narrative of the present, benign age, but it seems unlikely that this was more than a polite gesture to the emperors of whom he would have written (*Hist.* 1.1). Rather, he went back in time, to find the roots of tyranny in the very regime established by Augustus as a solution to the political crisis of the Roman republic. In stating, in the very first sentence of the *Annals*, the connection between liberty and the consuls, Tacitus demonstrated with a brilliant literary gesture how the political experience of liberty lay in the traditions of the Roman republic. He did more than this, for in couching the very first words of the *Annales* as a hexameter (strained but passable) with an archaic verbal termination, Tacitus reminded his readers of the poetic traditions of Rome. *Urbem Romam a principio reges habuere* ("Kings held Rome from the beginning"), and then, *libertatem et consulatum L. Brutus instituit* ("L. Brutus established liberty and the consulship"); the ideological stakes could not have been more clearly set out, and Tacitus went on, in a mounting sequence of words for power, to show how, in a weary world that cared only for peace, rule would again devolve upon one man. As we read on, the irony in Tacitus' perspective is built into the manner of his writing. Year by year, each year dated by the consuls, Tacitus would document the slow strangulation of liberty by the emperors. The message was not of lasting effect, or else, once the point was made, it was not necessary to repeat it. It is hard to find readers of Tacitus before the later fourth century, when Jerome seems to have known an edition of the *Annals* and *Histories*, bound together in historical sequence though in reverse order of composition. Jerome called the work "Lives of the Caesars in Thirty Books," a remark useful to us because it confirms the composition of the *Annals* in eighteen books and the *Histories* in twelve, at the same time as it shows a palpable disregard for the purpose of its author. In Jerome's eyes, a history of the Roman empire will be a history of the emperors who ruled it.

Like his contemporaries the younger Pliny and the satirist Juvenal, Tacitus wrote of the dark times of tyranny after they had passed, with an awareness of moral complicity vividly expressed in the final chapters of the *Agricola*; Tacitus told how he and other senators stood by while their colleagues were dragged off to execution. It was as if their own hands had done it (*Agr.* 45). A less challenged contemporary was Suetonius, a man of equestrian rank not exposed in quite the same way as senators to issues of liberty. His *Lives of the Caesars* demonstrate the approach to historical writing casually attributed by Jerome to Tacitus. In all conscience, the Julio-Claudian emperors were a diverse and eccentric bunch, the incomparable political skills of Augustus being followed through the principates of Tiberius, Caligula, Claudius, and Nero as if to demonstrate four different ways of mistreating the imperial office.

Yet given the actual power of the emperors, it might seem that Suetonius' was a viable way to write imperial history, the loss of chronological precision and of the developmental possibilities of the annalistic method being replaced by a thematic, more static presentation, though one permitting of appropriate rhetorical emphasis; history seen through the virtues and vices of emperors. The compensation, at least with Suetonius, lay in a shrewd observation of character as shown in personal mannerism, and by an awareness of the vividness of evidence drawn from original sources, as in sayings and writings of the emperors: his role as secretary *ab epistulis* of Hadrian must have made him especially aware of these opportunities.

A writer who might have adapted the pragmatic Suetonian method to a higher level of philosophical abstractness was a slightly earlier contemporary, the formidably versatile Plutarch, who wrote not only the famous *Parallel Lives* in which he compared famous Greeks and Romans selected for their similarities of character or circumstance (thereby offering their respective societies for comparison) but also, more to the present purpose, a series of *Lives* of the emperors from Augustus to Vitellius, of which we possess only those of Galba and Otho, emperors briefly in 68–69. It is usually inferred that Plutarch wrote these imperial biographies earlier in his career, under the Flavians, when his own Roman connections were being made. It became normal for a historian of the empire to close his work with the dynasty before that under which he lived; Tacitus himself, and in the late empire Ammianus Marcellinus, who completed his work under Theodosius but ended it with the dynasty of Valentinian and Valens, are examples of this courteous and prudent practice.

Plutarch's *Galba* and *Otho* are competent but not very distinctive works, lacking the more measured explorations of the elements of *phusis* and *ethos* – as we might say, nature and habituation – that frame his discussions of character and achievement in the *Parallel Lives*. Plutarch wrote them as a sequence, for he includes a thematic preface, on the indiscipline of armies, relevant to times of civil war, to the *Galba*, but moves straight from the end of Galba into the reign of Otho without any further preliminaries. These two *Lives* raise questions of a different sort, for they cover in more detail than we otherwise possess events surrounding the fall of Nero that would have been narrated in the lost books of Tacitus' *Annals*. This raises the formidable question of the lost historical writing that must once have existed and that must lie behind the works of Tacitus, as well as these *Lives* of Plutarch themselves, where a Latin source seems frequently implicit. We must not underestimate Tacitus' capacity for original inquiry, for it is clear that he did not depend entirely on earlier historical writing, but consulted original material for the composition of his works and even commissioned some himself. The *Acta* of the Roman Senate are an obvious quarry for the extant books of the *Annals* – their influence is everywhere apparent – and for the *Histories* we have the hint of Tacitus' two letters of inquiry of his friend Pliny for information about the eruption of Vesuvius in 79 (*Ep.* 6.16, 20). Tacitus does mention a number of historical sources that it is reasonable to suppose he used, even if, in a device not unknown to modern scholars, he cites them only in order to disagree. The elder Pliny, referred to once in the first book of the *Annals* and twice more in the later books, is one such source; the account of Pliny's works given by his nephew includes several of a historical character, namely a *Life* of the playwright and general Pomponius Secundus (cf. *Ann.* 11.13; 12.28), twenty books on the German Wars begun when he was serving in Germany, and thirty-one books of Roman history "from the end of Aufidius Bassus" (Plin. *Ep.* 3.5). Whether his history ended, as is often thought, with the Secular Games of Claudius of 47 or with the death of Claudius in 54, Aufidius Bassus has an excellent chance of being behind much of what we know about the regimes of Tiberius, Caligula, and Claudius. An author of senatorial rank also mentioned by Tacitus is the orator and historian Servilius Nonianus, whose obituary notice appears in the *Annals* (14.19). Since he mentions his historical writing, Tacitus must have known him as such, but Syme's preference for Nonianus rather than Aufidius Bassus as a main source for the *Annals* is based on little more than a prejudice in favor of the senator, orator, and consul as a Tacitean prototype, rather than a man of equestrian rank, as were Aufidius Bassus and the elder Pliny.

Another known historian, the senator Cluvius Rufus, happens also to be mentioned as a historical actor in Plutarch's *Galba* and in a tantalizing anecdote relating to events of the year 68 told many years later, after the death of its subject, by the younger Pliny (*Ep.* 9.19). This was the Verginius Rufus whose ambiguous conduct as legate of the armies of Upper Germany Cluvius had called into question, producing a classically evasive response from Rufus: "I did what I did," said Rufus when confronted by Cluvius' account, "that you might be free to write what you pleased" – a curious remark, from one who might be thought to have supported Nero in the convoluted circumstances of the year 68. The ambiguity of Rufus' conduct stands behind one of Tacitus' own most spectacularly elusive remarks: "whether he really was reluctant to claim the throne is uncertain" (*an imperare noluisset, dubium, Hist.* 1.8). A detailed Latin source, possibly the same Cluvius Rufus, must also lie behind Josephus' description (*AJ* 19.17 ff.) of the assassination of Gaius Caligula and succession of Claudius in 41. A prominent role in these events is taken by a senator of republican sentiments, Valerius Asiaticus from the Gallic city of Vienne, whose later execution is recorded by Tacitus in the incomplete chapters of Book 11 of the *Annals* (11.1 ff.). Tacitus here alludes to the essentials of Asiaticus' attitude in 41 as told by Josephus, and presumably by himself in the lost books. There are also the traces of a common source, Aufidius Bassus or some other, to be found in many passages of Tacitus when compared with the later Cassius Dio; Syme's presumption, and it is only this, that Cassius Dio will have known and used Tacitus is not compelling. With the additional details in Dio that are not found in Tacitus, these passages seem classic proofs of a common source.

All this is to emphasize a simple but important point. Accounts of the historical writing of the Roman empire, as of any form of ancient literature, have to come to grips with the vast amount that has been lost, sometimes leaving traces but more often without any resonance in the existing record. The brief survey of Quintilian (10.1.101 ff.) is a reminder of what we have lost, for it names the historians just mentioned, with some indications of what they composed and their literary quality. The major works of Tacitus, each incomplete and each depending on a unique manuscript, are an object lesson in the hazards of survival. If we did not happen to possess the two manuscripts, we would know hardly anything about the author of the *Histories* and *Annals*. We should not allow ourselves to be taken in by the fictitious claim of the author of the *Historia Augusta* (see below) that the third-century emperor Tacitus, imagining himself descended from the historian, ordered copies of his works to be made. All we could be sure of, from this reference as well as from Jerome, would be that Tacitus was known to some readers in the late fourth century. It is a mere conjecture that Plutarch's essay on the puzzling subject *The Malice of Herodotus* is a coded attack on Tacitus, whose techniques of rhetorical distortion resemble Plutarch's catalogue of tricks of the trade somewhat more closely than do those of Herodotus. Even if true, it would simply show that Tacitus was known to a contemporary, as he apparently was also to Juvenal (*Sat.* 2.102 f.).

While mourning the losses in our tradition, we must not forget the survivors, notably the almost intact work of Velleius Paterculus, whose compendium of Roman history, dedicated to the consul of the year 30, evolves into a more closely observed account of the ascendancy of Tiberius under Augustus and accession to power upon his death. Velleius' adulatory attitude to Augustus and the Tiberian family is well known – it is neatly appropriate that he shares space with Augustus' *Res Gestae* in the same volume of the Loeb Library – but has the merit of putting him at the center of affairs at a critical moment. He and his brother were on the slate of praetorian candidates left to Tiberius by Augustus in 14 CE and so were in the Senate during the interesting debate about Tiberius' position, of which a close account, very different in its tenor, is given by Tacitus (*Ann.* 1.10.8 ff.). Velleius' version of the request made to Tiberius by the Senate, that he should accept the public duty, or *statio*, left him by his adoptive father's death, is a better explanation than any other of Tiberius' position and attitudes on this occasion. No great historian and transparent in his loyalties, Velleius still does not merit the disdain with which he is too often treated.

In the generations beyond Tacitus, the problem is as much the original creation of historical writing as its survival. If Gibbon defined the subject matter of history as the "misfortunes, follies and vices of mankind," how many histories should we expect to be written in that benign age of peace? Some clearly were, for the brilliant Lucian of Samosata wrote a satirical tract, *How to Write History*, in which he made fun (unless he made them up) of the historians who had sprung up to celebrate the Parthian campaigns of Lucius Verus. Lucian does not make them sound like very important (as opposed to pretentious) or truthful works, but in either case he points us to a difference between the Latin and the Greek traditions in historical writing in the second and third centuries. In Latin no major historical writing is extant or known between Tacitus and the later fourth century (Suetonius has a third-century imitator, to whom I shall return). This is a break in the tradition that we do not find in Greek historiography, where Polybius provided the model, originating with Xenophon's presumptuous words "and after this" to mark his continuation of the unfinished Thucydides, for a series of historians of Rome, each writer aware of, if not directly continuing, his predecessor. The example of Polybius was followed by Cassius Dio, with his *History of Rome* from the beginning to his own day. Cassius Dio was continued by the Athenian Dexippus, and he in turn by Eunapius of Sardis and

Olympiodorus of Egyptian Thebes, then Priscus of Panium, with his wonderful description of a diplomatic visit to the court of Attila, Menander Protector and so on to the Byzantines – not a bad accomplishment for Xenophon's three misguided little words!

Cassius Dio's historical enterprise, he tells his readers, had a divine origin. At the time of the rise of Septimius Severus to the imperial throne in the tumultuous events following the murder of Commodus in 193, Dio composed a pamphlet in which he described the dreams and portents that "gave Severus reason to hope for imperial power" (73.23). The signs validated Severus' seizure of power by showing that it was according to the will of the divine powers. The emperor was naturally pleased with Dio's production and wrote the historian a letter of appreciation. The same night, Dio was visited by a divine power (*daimonion*), at whose prompting he enlarged his pamphlet into "the narrative with which I am at this moment concerned" (the context is the fall of Commodus). From this standpoint, Dio further enlarged his project to encompass the early history of Rome. For ten years, he read and took notes, and for twelve years he wrote up his notes into a history from the origins of Rome to his own day. While Dio read and "scribbled" (as King George jovially teased Gibbon), history continued to happen, and he found himself witnessing events that he would not have predicted when he began, notably some experiences in the Senate under the time of Caracalla, of which his accounts are if possible still more vivid than those of Tacitus in describing a reign of terror. He tells of an episode, reminiscent of the famous letter from Capri by which Tiberius had brought down Sejanus, in which evidence, obtained under torture, was read to the Senate implicating in the conspiracy under investigation a so far unnamed bald senator. At this, Dio recalls that he instinctively raised his own hand, "to see whether I had any hair on my head," and he was not the only senator to do so. While they fixed their eyes on colleagues who were somewhat bald, "as if we should thereby divert our own danger upon them," the subject of the description, an extremely bald former aedile, was identified and dragged out to execution (77.8).

Two contemporaries of Cassius Dio, one writing in Greek and one in Latin, add to the tally of historical composition under the Severans. Herodian (we do not know his actual origin in the Greek world), stands apart from Dio's large-scale manner of composition. His history covered the period from the accession of Commodus to the brief regime of the senatorial nominees Balbinus and Pupienus in 238. His writing is elegant and fluent but without the more severe historical qualities; indeed, it is marked by a distinct aversion for precise details such as names and places. It is difficult to identify Herodian's perspective, beyond saying that he may have held a position as a procurator, an imperial administrator of equestrian rank; in the case of a writer of senatorial rank, as with Tacitus and Cassius Dio, one may find some statement of a connection with public events to emphasize his authority in writing about them, but nothing of the kind is found in Herodian. Nevertheless, his work has value in that it covers a period for which Cassius Dio's narrative is incomplete; and some episodes are told with an effective narrative flair and important details. Herodian's account of the siege of the city of Aquileia by the forces of Maximinus is an effective narrative of important events, and describes very well the economic life and topography of the city (8.2.2 ff.); it can be compared with the description of a later siege of the same city given by Ammianus Marcellinus (21.1.2 ff.). His earlier account of the siege of Byzantium by Severus has value in establishing the nature of the Roman city rebuilt and renamed by Constantine (3.1.5 ff).

Cassius Dio's second contemporary was a man whom he must have known personally, the biographer Marius Maximus. Like Dio, L. Marius Maximus Perpetuus Aurelianus was a senator and consul (for the second time in 223), and, like Dio though more predictably, he held military commands (in Lower Germany and Syria Coele) – in fact, his rise to prominence began with those civil wars of which Dio had written. His historical writing consisted of a set of imperial biographies in the manner of Suetonius, beginning where Suetonius left off. They apparently ended with the reign of the "last of the Antonines," the eccentric Elagabalus (218–222).

It will be no surprise to learn that Marius Maximus' imperial biographies do not survive. Their existence and character are indicated by a much later text, the so-called *Historia Augusta*, a collection of imperial *Lives* of the second and third centuries, for the earlier parts of which Marius Maximus is frequently cited. In a passage that has possibly gained more than its due attention, Ammianus Marcellinus wrote of Marius Maximus as forming with Juvenal the light reading of frivolous senators, "sunk in their profound leisure" (28.4.14). For this and other reasons, the inference that Marius Maximus was a main source for the earlier biographies of the *Historia Augusta* has been questioned. It is argued that if the history of Marius Maximus was so unserious a work, it will not have been the source for some parts of the *Historia Augusta*, notably the *Life* of the respectable Antoninus Pius, which conspicuously lack the more frivolous element. From this it is argued that the earlier *Lives* possessed a double source. The first would indeed be Marius Maximus, because he is named and in order to explain the inclusion of the scandalous matter to which his name is often connected. The second would be a second biographer, a plain and sober writer averse to scandal. This would explain the drab *Life of Antoninus*, and the more reputable parts of other *Lives*. Yet, if one thing is clear about Suetonius, the model of both Marius Maximus and the *Historia Augusta*, it is that it combined diverse elements: the sober and the scandalous, the erudite and the fanciful. The combination seems inherent in biography itself; there seems no inherent reason to postulate a second, "phantom" biographer as well as Marius Maximus, whose writing will have possessed the same mixed character as that of Suetonius.

The biographies of the *Historia Augusta* extend beyond Elagabalus to encompass the emperors and usurpers of the third century down to Carus and Carinus, the predecessors of Diocletian; and there are also inserted into the main series of *Lives* some "secondary" biographies of usurpers of the second and third centuries, based upon the material in the main series with the addition of fictional matter. As the biographies progress into the third century and the source material at the disposal of the author becomes increasingly scanty, his methods become increasingly adventurous, with the result that not only the secondary *Lives*, but also the *Lives* of those legitimate emperors from Alexander Severus to the end of the series are of little historical value.

The result of this situation is that we possess little coherent historical material for the period of more than a century after that covered by Marius Maximus in Latin, and

Dio and Herodian in Greek. The historical writing of Dexippus, consisting of a general history from mythological times to the reign of Claudius Gothicus (268–270), and a work called *Scythica* describing the wars of his lifetime against the invading Goths and their allies, of which an extant fragment, preserved in a Byzantine compilation, described the attack of the Heruli on his own city of Athens, would have provided a bridge between Dio and the histories written in the fourth and later centuries. It would be a mistake to think of the third century as a period without literary attestation of any sort. The non-historical sources, if we think for example of the letters of Cyprian, the writings of Origen, Plotinus, and Porphyry, and the legal material preserved in the Digest and elsewhere, not to mention such an exotic "quasi-historical" text as the *Thirteenth Sibylline Oracle*, are nothing if not substantial. However, accounts of the period are better advised to stress themes of political, institutional, and religious development than to attempt to reconstruct detailed narrative; it may be as useful to know that in a period of fifty years from 238 to 284 there were at least thirty-five emperors and usurpers as to know the exact dates of each. Nor is the situation quickly rectified by the restoration of political order by Diocletian and his colleagues and by Constantine. The "new empire" of the fourth century is greeted by court panegyrists, and by a different sort of history, namely that of the Christian church. This entails a massive shift of perspective. The *Ecclesiastical History* of Eusebius bishop of Caesarea, written and revised at various moments in the early fourth century, stands apart from the secular tradition in its choice of subject matter, an institution that had for most of its life been connected with the emperors only to the extent to which they had or had not persecuted its members. In terms of method also, Eusebius introduces a new feature into the conventions of historical writing, in the extensive citation of documents as well as earlier writers in the pursuit of his argument. Momigliano pointed out, with a touch of sly humor no doubt, that the habit of modern historians of citing their evidence and giving references has its origin not in their ancient secular predecessors but in Eusebius. Indeed, ancient writers tended to the opposite ideal: to absorb their sources in such a way as to disguise the extent of their debt.

In the longer term, the later Roman empire did bring about a resurgence of historical writing in the classical manner, but before we come to the age of Eunapius and Ammianus Marcellinus, it is worth pausing on the cluster of historical works, more modest in scope, that occupy the earlier fourth century. It is a mystery how we come to possess a pamphlet on the rise to power of the emperor Constantine now known as Anonymus Valesianus from the name of its first editor, Henri de Valois, who published the text in 1636. Interpolated by easily detectable intrusions from the Christian historian Orosius, this is a summary of the political history of the reign of Constantine that for all its brevity adds much to what we otherwise know. To the later years of Constantine or to the time of his successor can be attributed a lost Latin history, known from the scholar who postulated its existence, as "Enmann's *Kaisergeschichte*," a "History of the Emperors" known from its abbreviation, familiar in scholarly discussion, as *KG*. The existence of this work can be inferred from common material in the later writers, epitomators rather than true historians, who used it, notably Aurelius Victor, the anonymous writer of the *Epitome de Caesaribus*, and

Eutropius. As well as their common ground proving the existence of *KG*, these writers contain sufficient diversity to suggest that *KG* contained a greater variety of material, and so was a longer work, than we might at first suspect.

The existence of lost historical material for the reign of Constantine raises interesting questions in the interpretation of the greatest historian of late antiquity, Ammianus Marcellinus. The extant text of Ammianus contains Books 14–31 of a work that originally ran, as its epilogue explains (31.16.9), from the reign of Nerva down to the battle of Hadrianople in August 378, at which the Roman army was defeated by the Goths and the emperor Valens killed. Ammianus thus combined the formal tradition that a contemporary history would end with the imperial dynasty preceding that under which the historian wrote with a dramatic episode of colossal proportions. The extant narrative begins with the events of winter 353/4, and its scope from this point, eighteen books covering just twenty-five years in an often personal intensity of detail that shades into memoir, raises difficult questions about the character of the lost thirteen books. If they began with Nerva, it is obvious that at least the earlier of the lost books could not much have resembled those that are extant; the level of detail must at some point have increased very markedly. Given this change of pattern, it has been argued that the thirty-one books of which 14–31 survive began not with Nerva but at some point in the fourth century and that the preceding period was treated in an entirely separate work that is now completely lost. The expansion of scale would allow for the exploitation by Ammianus of Greek sources for the second and third centuries. This would be appropriate, for Ammianus' final address to his reader describes the author as a "former soldier and a Greek" (*miles quondam et Graecus*, 31.16.9).

This theory would at one stroke solve the question of the disparity of scale just described between different parts of the work. Such a disparity is not unparalleled in other authors, however, and an argument in favor of it in the case of Ammianus arises from the nature of his back-references to matters narrated in the lost part of the history. The majority of these back-references seem to be to events and situations in the earlier period of which we already know something; they are more a supplement to our existing sources than an extension of them. This would be surprising if Ammianus were to have written of the earlier period on the greater scale required by the theory of a separate work. One might have expected more references in the extant books to matters of which we are not otherwise aware.

Another literary problem in the interpretation of Ammianus is that of his debt to Tacitus, for most critics have drawn the inference that in choosing the reign of Nerva, Ammianus is acknowledging his great predecessor. In the absence of the preface with which Ammianus would have begun his entire work, we cannot be sure whether this was so. What we can say, however, is that even if it were, it would not be a great help to us in reading the later author. Attempts have been made to identify passages of Ammianus in which Tacitus seems to be evoked, but what is striking in these lists is that, when they have been pared down to the cases in which stylistic imitation seems to be a real possibility rather than accidental resemblance, or similarities inherent simply in their use of the same language for the same general purpose, the parallel passages seem to be incongruous or even inept in their context. A converse argument also applies. When Ammianus described (in Book 14) events such as the trials of philosophers and others conducted at Antioch by Gallus Caesar, and (in Book 28) prosecutions for adultery and magic conducted by the agents of Valentinian at Rome, one would think it natural for one writing in emulation of Tacitus to have evoked that author's manner in referring to similar events; but no parallels are found. At no point of the surviving text does Ammianus acknowledge Tacitus by name or by indirect reference, in the way that he does refer to other historical predecessors, for example Thucydides, Polybius, and Sallust – even if, as in the case of the short-lived outbreak of disease that afflicted the defenders of the besieged city of Amida, some exaggeration was required to drag in their names (19.4.1 ff.).

Ammianus and his contemporaries confronted a Roman empire, and Roman emperors, vastly different from those described by their predecessors. We must not forget the sheer distance in time, hundreds of years, separating these writers from the age described by Tacitus and Suetonius. Ammianus refers to the earlier emperors of Rome like Domitian or Augustus (whom he styles "Octavianus Augustus") almost, as we might say, as the "emperors of olden times": *veteres imperatores* (17.4.12; 18.4.5). An instance of imperial conduct cited from the time of the Tetrarchs is "not such an ancient example" (14.11.10). Even that period was at the limits of living memory. During the Persian campaign of Julian in 363, the advancing Roman army encountered an aged Roman who had in his youth been left behind by the returning army of Galerius, had stayed in Persian territory, married there, and raised a family; he was now, in his own words reported by Ammianus (24.1.10), nearly a hundred years old – not too much of an exaggeration, and it shows how far away the past might be.

One important change in the character of the imperial office that Ammianus also dates to the Tetrarchy is the enhanced ceremonial attending the emperors. The historian assigns this feature of the emperors of his own time to Diocletian, the first emperor to bedeck himself with jeweled costume and to abandon the *civilitas* of earlier emperors. This is a development that Ammianus had witnessed in his own political life, so it is striking to find that his description of the innovation is attributed to something he had read rather than to personal experience (15.5.18). His comment is found in almost identical words in other authors who cannot have read Ammianus and whom he is unlikely to have read himself, for example Aurelius Victor and the Chronicle of Jerome. Its source is almost certain to be *KG*, the imperial history postulated by Enmann.

Another major change in the imperial office confronting not only historians but also all public commentators was, of course, its conversion to Christianity. From the days of the early fourth-century Latin panegyrists, as they presented this radical event in terms that would still resonate with their conservative Roman audience, one can see historians and others trying to define their position on the matter. None of them could ignore it. For writers of the Christian persuasion like Eusebius of Caesarea, the conversion of Constantine was part of a providential dispensation that had under the *pax Augusta* allowed the evangelists to travel the length and breadth of the Mediterranean world to preach their message, and had now reached its culmination with the emperor's support for the Christian church. Who would fail to understand, seeing the ruler and his magistrates bowing their heads in church, that this was the fulfillment of prophecy? This was in a biblical commentary, but Eusebius spelled out his message in successive revisions of his church history, and above all in his celebratory pamphlet *On the Life of Constantine*, written late in the reign of Constantine and published soon after his death. The problems accruing to the Christian church as it grew closer to the emperors inspired an intriguing unwritten history, a "History of the Church," announced, but never written, by St. Jerome. It would show, he declared in his preface to the *Life* of a saint, how since the adoption of Christianity by the emperors and the end of the days of persecution, the Christian church had "grown richer in wealth and power, but poorer in virtue" (*Life of Malchus* 1; Migne, *PL* 23.55). It is a tantalizing project, perhaps no more seriously intended than Tacitus' promise to reserve for his old age the history of the emperors under whom he lived.

Across the ideological divide were those for whom the conversion of Constantine was an act of treachery to the ancestral gods and their own traditional culture. The hatred and contempt for Constantine of their historical spokesman, Eunapius of Sardis, were heightened by their admiration of Julian the Apostate, whose brief reign presented to his supporters the hope of a restoration of the old ways. It was not an unreal hope; what if Julian were to return victorious from Persia, with the titles of a grand triumph, and a long reign to come? The disillusion of such supporters can only be imagined as their hero was killed in Persia and his army humiliated. Eunapius' history was read by the patriarch Photius in the ninth century but is now lost except for fragments in Byzantine epitomators and entries in lexika (which may have the effect of exaggerating the idiosyncrasies of Eunapius' style), and its use by the early Byzantine historian, Zosimus. In addition to these sources for the history, some of its attitudes can be recovered from Eunapius' extant *Lives of the Sophists and Philosophers*, written in imitation of Philostratus' earlier work of the same title. In this extremely interesting and circumstantial piece, Eunapius gave biographical sketches and traced the lineage of those philosophers of the late third and fourth centuries who belonged to the magical, miracle-working tradition of Neoplatonism to which Julian adhered.

A problem attending the *History* of Eunapius is that it is said by Photius to have existed in two editions, of which the first was revised by the author because of its polemical character. This is puzzling, because what survives in Zosimus of the second edition in no way lacks polemical intensity. Eunapius delivered a hostile account of the conversion of Constantine, in which the emperor became a Christian only after the traditional priests had refused to offer absolution for great crimes committed by him against his family – the execution of his son Crisus and the accidental death in suspicious circumstances of his second wife Fausta, Crispus' stepmother (Zosimus 2.29). This slant on Constantine's conversion, which is referred to also in Julian's *Caesars* (336A–B), written before Eunapius' history, is criticized in the opening chapters of Sozomen's church history written in the fifth century as a false belief attributed to the "Hellenes," or pagans. The distortion was possible because the earlier part of the reign of Constantine, in which the conversion must be located, took place in the western Roman empire and its details and chronology were not well known in the east.

The more polemical manner of the first edition of Eunapius' *History* could have derived from its structure as much as from its historical content – if, for example, it was biographical in character with a still greater emphasis on the person of Julian the Apostate. Whether this is so or not, the anti-Christian hostility of Eunapius is still evident in the version of the history transmitted by Zosimus. Not only Constantine's conversion but also the entire question of his administrative and financial reforms and the major issue of the foundation of Constantinople are presented in a critical light that bears on the emperor's reputation for unrestrained largesse and for a loss of discipline inherent in the abandonment of the old ways: Constantine changed everything because he could leave nothing alone. Theodosius, by contrast, is accused of self-indulgence and idleness before the increasing barbarian threat to the Roman empire. It is a coded way to criticize the Christian piety of its emperors, which had come to impinge more and more upon the established institutions of the empire.

For Ammianus Marcellinus also, coded language and indirection provided a way to express criticism of Christianity and the Christian emperors. Here too, as in Eunapius (and Julian's *Caesars*), Constantine is accused of prodigality and his unfulfilled Persian campaign assigned to financial motives. Ammianus praised Valentinian because, unlike the emperor Theodosius under whom Ammianus wrote, he refrained from religious coercion (30.9.5), and he criticized Constantius because in his "old woman's superstition" he allowed Christian bishops to cripple the public transport system by traveling to the church councils fostered by the emperor (21.16.18). The Christian faith is satirized for faults that violated its own professions, as with the vainglorious ambition of the bishops of Rome in contrast with the modest demeanor of provincial clergy, "whose humble comportment and downcast manner commend them to true worshippers of the divinity" (27.3.15). Even Christians would have to agree with this. If it is a mistake to think of Ammianus as a neutral figure, uncommitted on either side of the ideological debate that surrounded him, neither was he an open and direct polemicist. His approach is different from that of Eunapius – indirect and ironic where Eunapius is outspokenly controversial, requiring the reader (and contemporary hearers of the text), to make a judgment as to how polemical any particular passage is intended to be.

What is striking about historians of the age of Constantine is that, on whichever side of the issue they aligned themselves and however indirectly they expressed it, for all of them the conversion of the emperor was an acknowledged feature of the reign. For Aurelius Victor, Constantine was possessed of an "immense mind" (*ingens animus*), which he devoted "to the building of a city and the reforming of religions," and who, as a measure of his piety, abolished the penalty of crucifixion with the breaking of legs (*Caes.* 41.4, 12), for Eutropius he was an outstanding man "who strove to achieve everything he had set his heart on" but was made arrogant by his success (*Brev.* 10.5–6). The anonymous Epitomator records a remarkable saying, that in the thirty years of his reign Constantine was for ten years most excellent, for the following ten years a bandit (*latro*), and for the final ten notorious for his immoderate largesse, its recipients in the unmistakable form of the Christian church (*Epitome de Caesaribus* 41.16). Yet Eutropius also records how his death was marked by the appearance of a comet, and how, like his predecessors, he was justly deified. This is the language of the early fourth-century panegyrists and of the contemporary Arch of Constantine at Rome, where the emperor's success in civil war is assigned to "the greatness of his mind and the inspiration of the divinity." *Mentis magnitudine, instinctu divinitatis*; such words, strikingly original for such a conservative location in the middle of Rome, express what the historians spell out in more detail: that Constantine's conversion was an aspect of the overflowing, restless mind that seemed determined to change everything.

We must not imagine, however, that the Christianity of Constantine and his successors was the only dimension in which the fourth-century emperors were judged, or that the supposed conflict between Christians and pagans, such an important part of modern interpretations, was the only issue of the time. For Ammianus and his contemporaries the religious issue was one of many. Ammianus was a partisan of the pagan cause and he did not like Christianity, but there were other things to evaluate in a Roman emperor. His admiration for Julian may have inhibited the need for a franker judgment of his failure, but he makes clear the weaknesses. In a short paragraph in his obituary of the emperor, in which he repeated comments made earlier in their several contexts, he criticized Julian's religiosity as "superstitious rather than legitimate" in its excessive sacrifices, thought that he had an insufficient respect for the dignity of the imperial office, that he affected intimacy with the unworthy (perhaps Ammianus had in mind his friendship with the philosopher Maximus, who had so much to answer for in the failure of the Persian campaign), and claimed that his compulsion of qualified individuals to serve as town councilors victimized many who had valid exemptions. The capstone of Julian's cultural policy, through which he tried to identify the possession of a classical education with an adherence to the established religion by forbidding any but pagan teachers to teach the classics, was most emphatically condemned (25.4.16 ff.). For Ammianus the central character of his history is the Roman empire itself and its emperors, whom we see in their traditional posture, confronting Germanic barbarians on its Rhine and Danube frontiers, the politics of their court beset by the jealousies and rival factions from whose machinations Ammianus' early patron, the general Ursicinus, was lucky (in Ammianus' view) to escape with his life.

As a key to understanding Ammianus' likely contemporary, the author of the *Historia Augusta*, the religious dimension is still more unlikely. It is unclear that the work can in any usual sense be "understood" at all. Its basic posture, that it is the product of six authors writing imperial biographies in the time of Diocletian and Constantine, can be disposed of by tracing through the contradictions in the claims made by the so-called "authors" themselves – not to mention the widespread occurrence of patently fictitious literary sources, documents, and letters, and even coins, in what can best be seen as a parody of the scholarly method. The pretense that the work was written at the time it claims does not survive an inspection of the anachronisms, of personal names and institutions, that it contains. Attempts to locate the work in the time of Julian, and to see the largely fictional *Life of Alexander Severus* as a model of the ideal prince, or to identify the author among known luminaries of later fourth-century Rome, have equally failed to carry conviction, while Momigliano's challenge to defenders of a late fourth-century date of composition to produce a motive that might explain the deception engaged in misses the point of the oddities that are contained under any interpretation of the text. If, as Syme argued, the author of the *Historia Augusta* was not entirely a serious figure, less a literary luminary or religious propagandist than a "rogue grammarian" who acquired a taste for literary deception, then questions about motive seem to lapse, as well as the need for any coherent attitude to unite the work. The identification of the writer as a free spirit and humorist would seem also to loosen the hold of any particular historical moment or social context on his identification. None of this destroys the historical value that the text does possess in the *Lives* of the emperors of the second and early third centuries, though it certainly does mean that when using the work we need to take account of its peculiar eccentricities.

Ammianus Marcellinus ended his history with the disastrous defeat by the Goths at the battle of Hadrianople. But he did not believe that this catastrophe (and it was this) had brought the Roman empire to its end. By the time that Ammianus wrote the final paragraphs of his history, at Rome perhaps ten or twelve years later, the military situation had to some extent been retrieved. Ammianus could point out that Rome had recovered from disasters incurred in early times too – it was a measure of Rome's greatness that she could rise from misfortune and become greater than before (a sentiment expressed also by the poet Rutilius Namatianus in the face of the further disasters that had occurred in the twenty-five years since Ammianus completed his work). What was needed was a firm hand and sober counsels in the form of a Roman emperor with the virtues of olden times; as so often in such reflections, it is Marcus Aurelius who came to mind (31.10.18).

Other writers, notably Seneca, had reflected on the history of Rome as the progression of a lifetime, from childhood and youth through maturity into old age. Ammianus develops the image in introducing, in the first of his surviving books, a digression on the conduct of the upper classes and common people of Rome; to say, indeed, that the historic dignity of the ancient assemblies and its ruling class was threatened by the frivolous conduct of a few "who did not reflect where they were born," followed by a highly satirical account of this situation (14.6.2–7). Ammianus adds a variation to the familiar theme. If Rome had reached old age, symbolized in the white hair of its senators, what would happen next? Ammianus' answer lay in the emperors, to whom Rome had left the inheritance of her greatness, as to her children. So Ammianus can break out of the sequence, childhood to youth and maturity to old age, by evoking the rejuvenation provided by the emperors. The metaphor allows him to present Rome, in these her later years, in an image of optimism. And, in articulating his view in the language of a testamentary succession from parent to child, he is, as so often, extraordinarily Roman. It is in this rather than in any more precise historiographical sense that this "soldier and Greek" deserves to be linked with Tacitus.

FURTHER READING

The historical writing of the Roman empire, even as limited by the title to this chapter, is an immense subject that has given rise to a vast literature. Extremely useful for general reference is OCD^3, with many entries, both on historiography in general and on historians. Other recent guides are Mellor 1999 on the Latin historians of Rome, and Rohrbacher 2002 on the later period, both Latin and Greek; both cover thematic issues as well as individual writers. On the historiography of the first century Syme 1958a is incomparable, supported by Wallace-Hadrill 1983 on biography. The later influence of Tacitus is described by Mellor 1993, while Velleius Paterculus enjoys some rehabilitation in Woodman's edition of the Tiberian narrative (1977). Essential on the textual survival of the Latin classics, including the historians, is Reynolds 1983. On Greek literary culture of the second century, a fundamental study, though without a particularly historical emphasis, is Swain 1996; on Plutarch and Lucian, Jones 1971 and 1986 is particularly good. On the third-century writers Dio, Herodian, and Dexippus, see Millar 1964 and 1969, and Whittaker 1969–1970, and for the origins of the Greek historiographical tradition, Walbank 1972. The quasi-historical text known as the *Thirteenth Sibylline Oracle* is presented by Potter 1990, followed by the author's broader study of prophetic discourse on Roman emperors (1994). The essential positions on the *Historia Augusta* are set out by Momigliano 1954 and Syme 1968. On Ammianus Marcellinus see Matthews 1989, challenged at many points, including the number of books in the History, by Barnes 1998. The *Latin Panegyrics* are translated with generous comment by Nixon and Saylor Rodgers 1994. On the fourth-century epitomators, see Momigliano 1963a, Syme 1968, Rohrbacher 2002, and the next chapter. For the development of Christian historiography see Momigliano 1963b, and Cameron and Hall's *Eusebius* (1999), and below, Ch. 57. Study of Gibbon is transformed by the three-volume edition by Womersley 1994, with full introduction and indexes. For my own appreciation of Gibbon as a historian, see Matthews 1997.

CHAPTER TWENTY-FIVE

The Epitomizing Tradition in Late Antiquity

Thomas M. Banchich

The importance of an epitomizing tradition to the study of the late third to early seventh centuries seems indisputable. With respect to the study of history proper, Aurelius Victor's *De Caesaribus*, the *Breviaria* of Eutropius and Festus, the so-called *Epitome de Caesaribus*, and the *Romana* and *Getica* of Jordanes are particularly important witnesses, and historians have employed a range of analytic techniques to assess their testimony. *Quellenkritik* has yielded a *Kaisergeschichte*, convincingly postulated by Alexander Enmann (1884), and suggested to some (Schlumberger 1974) the influence of Virius Nicomachus Flavianus. From Jordanes' *Getica* and *Romana* scholars looked back to Cassiodorus (Goffart 1988: 23–31) and Quintus Aurelius Symmachus (Ensslin 1949), respectively. Philologists posited precise definitions of *Epitome* – basically an abbreviation of a single work, sometimes with minimal additions by the epitomator – and *Breviarium* – basically the brief treatment of a subject through the combination of several abbreviated sources, sometimes with minimal additions by the breviarist (Wölfflin 1902) – to facilitate an understanding of how the authors of such texts envisioned their task, utilized their sources, and composed their accounts. An inventory (Opelt 1962: cols. 946–957) offered quantitative confirmation of their ubiquity.

Though there existed an obvious historiographical dimension to all this, it generally served the cause of historical reconstruction. With one notable exception (Peter 1897), the situation of these historical epitomes and *breviaria* within the context of a broader tradition fell to literary historians, who tended to plot them on a downward trajectory determined by what distinguished them from their classical predecessors – the absence of speeches, excurses, and detailed individual descriptions (*ekphraseis*); the presentation of individuals, especially emperors, as the prime agents of historical change, but only superficial, mostly descriptive, appreciations of their characters; and few hints of independent research or deep intellectual engagement – all often diagnosed as symptoms of pandemic cultural and intellectual malaise, of decadence, of decline and fall (Galdi 1922: 1; *contra* Malcovati 1942).

Since the 1970s, as the notion of a discrete historical period of late antiquity, the defining features of which were to be judged on their own merits, began to displace the long-dominant paradigm of "decline and fall" (Brown 1971; Pocock 2003), this view has become increasingly untenable. However, the comprehensive reconsideration required to judge whether historical epitomes and *breviaria* of the period in question represent a historiographical phenomenon peculiar to late antiquity does not yet exist.

When it comes, it might reconsider the current consensus that among historical authors of the late empire the idea of *brevitas* had a normative force (Herzog and Schmidt 1989: 173–175), for the number of non-epitomizing late antique authors in the standard *corpora* of fragmentary historians, even excluding those from the *Historia Augusta*, far surpasses the number of known authors of epitomes or *breviaria*. To complicate matters, the ratio varies significantly depending on how one counts translations and compendia of short texts, along with how strictly one adheres to the modern definitions of *epitome* or *breviarium*.

Such variables figure in the evaluation of the Latin account of Alexander known from Metz Codex 500 and now generally referred to as the Metz Epitome. Whether what we possess is all or a part of some ultimately Greek original – it begins with Book 3 – or, if it is a part, whether it is so as the result of choice or accident, philological considerations suggest a date of the second half of the fourth century and, because of its archaizing Latin, that it was produced by a *grammaticus* (Ruggini 1961). By the tenth century, someone had appended the text to a spurious letter of Alexander and an account of his death and testament. Loose and disordered pages of this codex were eventually combined with those from two other books to form Metz Codex 500 (Thomas 1966: vii–viii). Given this state of affairs, it is debatable if one should view this text primarily as a historical epitome or as an excerpt of a translation of rhetorically useful information about Alexander.

Similar doubt exists with respect to three late antique epitomes of Valerius Maximus, two of which begin with programmatic notices. In the first, the epitomator Julius Paris greets Licinius Cyriacus (Briscoe 1998: II.638):

> Since I know that the collection of *exempla* is no less necessary to those engaged in argumentations than to those engaging in declamations, I have compressed the ten books of Valerius Maximus' *Memorable Deeds and Sayings* into one volume of an epitome. This I have sent to you, in order that, if you are ever looking for something, you can more easily find it, and in order that you always subjoin apt *exempla* to your material.

Januarius Nepotianus, compiler of a second abridgment of Valerius, though not using the word *epitome*, echoes Paris' utilitarian emphasis and adds that he acted to the advantage of Victor, a zealous young student, who urged that writings of the ancients be "trimmed" (Briscoe 1998: II.800–801):

> Therefore, we are in agreement concerning Valerius Maximus, that his works would be more useful if they were shorter…And so, as you wish, I shall trim away his

redundancies and pass over many things, some things omitted I shall join. But by this it will have the energy of the ancients, not the pretence of moderns. [Once done] no one, to be sure, beyond we two, will recognize the abridgements...

As was the case with the Metz Epitome, it is uncertain whether these texts should be viewed as predominantly historical or rhetorical. The answer is not as simple as in the case of the purely literary *Caesares* of Ausonius (Green 1991: 161–168) or Paulinus' verse epitome of Suetonius' *De Regibus* (Auson. *Ep.* 17; Green 1991: 215–216), for here it depends not only on the intentions of Valerius and his epitomators but also on what late antique readers understood as history (Bloomer 1992: 14–17; Dietz 1995: 95).

Authorial intent figures too in the categorization of an extant *Itinerarium* of Alexander and a lost companion *Itinerarium* of Trajan, dedicated as a "favorable omen" to Constantius II, who ordered their composition. The occasion was the start of that emperor's Persian campaign of 346; the author – perhaps Julius Valerius, consul in 338, who also produced a *Res Gestae Alexandri Macedonis* purportedly translated from the Greek of an otherwise unknown Aesop and transmitted in the same manuscript as the *Itinerarium Alexandri* (Lane Fox 1997: 239–244) – explains (*Itinerarium Alexandri* 1–3):

> though my wretched tongue is unworthy of illustrious deeds, I shall, nevertheless, bravely subject it to the task, having relied not on my own, but on the power of a genius foreign to me, nor have I employed lowly authors from the number of prattlers, but those whom venerable judgment pronounces the greatest comrades of credibility, and whom, where I was able, I have with learned inquisitiveness satisfactorily excised, collected, the usage of words employed much more restrainedly, since the utility of a public offering, not the glory of private pomp, was my objective. Finally, I have super-scribed *Itinerarium* instead of *Breviarium*, restricting the capacity of the work even by its name, an incentive, of course, amicable to your excellence.

The distinction between *itinerarium* and *breviarium* suggests what the author thought might be assumed about the nature of the latter, in particular the use in *breviaria* of condensations of multiple sources. Yet that same contrast raises doubts about our association of the *Itineraria* of Alexander and Trajan with *breviaria* proper.

And what to do with Vegetius' *Epitoma Rei Militaris*, also written at the behest of an emperor – probably in the 380s or slightly later – and, Vegetius tells us, for the common good (*Mil.* 4 *prol.* 8)? As did the author of the *Itinerarium Alexandri*, Vegetius begins by linking past to present (*prol.* 1–6):

> In ancient times it was the custom to commit studies of the liberal arts to writing and, after they had been abridged, to present them to *Principes*, ... [for an emperor is one] whose learning is able to benefit all subjects. [Though cognizant of my inferiority to the ancients, I knew that you would appreciate that] in this little work neither elegance of words nor intellectual acumen was a necessity, [but hard work], in order that [scattered teachings about warfare] be brought into public view for the utility of Rome.... [And so that you] recognize that the things which you spontaneously put in place for the safety of the state the founders of the Roman empire heeded long ago and that you find in this booklet whatever you believe required with respect to affairs most great and ever needful.

Vegetius' reference to his work as a "booklet" (*opusculum*) is noteworthy, for the title *Epitoma Rei Militaris* only appears during manuscript transmission. Yet, if a choice has to be made between epitome or *breviarium*, Vegetius' apparent method of combining abridgments of various (Latin) sources would (*pace* Milner 1996: xvi–xxix) tip the scale toward *breviarium* or rule out both forms altogether. More difficult to decide, however, is whether Vegetius would have considered his treatise historical in essence or simply by the accident of its systematic comparison of present to past for the practical purpose of an elucidation of the proper handling of military affairs in his own day.

A purer concern with Rome's distant past was clearly an impetus for several other texts sometimes associated with late antique epitomes. The *Periochae* of Livy (Rossbach 1959: 1–121), summaries in Latin of all but two of his original books, seem most concerned with larger-than-life figures, matters relevant to Roman religion, and Rome's early expansion in central Italy. However, though long dated to the fourth century, they probably antedate late antiquity (Begbie 1967: 337). The same is true of the Oxyrhynchus summaries of Livy (Rossbach 1959: 122–148), likely a poor late third-century copy of a second- or third-century original (Grenfell and Hunt 1904: 90–93).

The *Origo Gentis Romanae* (*The Origin of the Roman Race*), on the contrary, almost certainly belongs to the fourth century. The purpose of its author – probably a *grammaticus* (Sehlmeyer 2004: 22–27) – was the elucidation of Rome's past from Janus and Saturn to Romulus. From what can be deduced about his sources and methods, it is tempting to slot him with composers of *breviaria*. But this ignores his explicit designation of his work as an *Origo* rather than *Epitome* or *Breviarium*. The circumstances of the survival of this *Origo* also point to a complicating factor in any attempt to link an epitomizing tendency to some late antique *mentalité*. For between the fourth and late sixth centuries someone copied the *Origo*, the *De Viris Illustribus* (brief biographical notices from Proca through Cleopatra VII), and the *De Caesaribus* of Aurelius Victor into a single codex to create what now is often called the *Corpus Aurelianum* (Momigliano 1958b; Schmidt 1978: 1584–1587). This was to have important consequences for the *Origo* and *De Caesaribus*, both of which survive only via the *Corpus*, the contents of which, when rediscovered in the sixteenth century, early modern editors attributed to Victor.

The true *Historiae Abbreviatae*, the manuscript title of what we call the *De Caesaribus*, took its final form in the fall of 361, shortly before Victor presented a copy to Julian, who had stopped in Sirmium en route against Constantius. Apparently hedging his bets, Victor appended to his closing praise of Constantius, the intended recipient of the *De Caesaribus*, a denunciation of that emperor's civil and military appointees (*Caes.* 42.23–25). Internal evidence suggests a brief period of composition – perhaps a year – which reinforces the likelihood that this *scriptor historicus* (Amm. Marc. 21.10.6) followed a single source – the *Kaisergeschichte* or the *Kaisergeschichte* plus a small number of other sources – adding to a series of biographical sketches *exempla* and moralizing, sometimes self-referential glosses to create a sort of proto "Mirror of Princes" (Bird 1984: 16–23). So understood, the *De Caesaribus*, rather than a work of scholarship, becomes a vehicle for career advancement, and a successful one to judge from Victor's subsequent appointments (Nixon 1971: 6–16). Apart from its impact on Julian, the compiler of the *Corpus Aurelianum*, and the author of the *Epitome de Caesaribus*, the direct effect of the *De Caesaribus* was negligible. Jerome (ca. 374) requested a copy from a certain Paul of Concordia (*Ep.* 10.3), but whether he received or employed it is unknown; John Lydus (ca. 550) noted that "Victor the historian, in the *History of the Civil Wars*," referred to buyers of public corn (*sitōnai*) "by the earlier name *frumentarii*" (*Mag.* 3.7). All subsequent references or parallels to Victor actually involve the late fourth-century *Epitome de Caesaribus* (Nixon 1971: 23–32), whose very existence, it seems reasonable to assume, is contingent on that of its model rather than on its author's independent impulse to compose an account of Roman history from Augustus through Theodosius.

For Eutropius and Festus it was not an interest in history or even careerism but direct imperial requests which prompted two of the best-known late antique *breviaria*: as there would have been no *Epitome de Caesaribus* without Victor, there would have been no *Breviaria* of Eutropius and Festus without Valens.

Eutropius probably presented his *Breviarium* of Roman history in ten books (perhaps an echo of Livy's decads) from the foundation of the city to Jovian's death (364) to Valens in 369, when Eutropius held the office of *Magister Memoriae* and shortly after Valens' victory over the Goths. Eutropius specifies that he wrote at Valens' behest and in a form mandated by the emperor himself: "As Your Majesty willed, I have collected summarily in chronological order in a brief narrative from the foundation of the city Roman affairs which in dealings of war or peace stand out to our memory." The book attracted a readership, perhaps because it supplied an account of all of Roman history, and possibly because Eutropius' impressive career (*PLRE* I.317) afforded him the means and opportunity to disseminate copies in various key locations in the empire or for those anxious to please him to request the same. His direct impress is evident, for example, on Jerome, Orosius, and Paul the Deacon, through whose *Historia Romana* (ca. 800) he indirectly affected a broad range of medieval Latin texts, while translations by Paianios and Kapiton assured his influence on Byzantine authors.

The fate of Festus' *Breviarium* – fifteen pages in Wagener's edition – was far different. Apart from a few brief parallels, some perhaps from a common source and none certainly direct, it has left no trace in other late antique texts. Regardless of its author's precise identity (Eadie 1967: 4–9), internal evidence sets its presentation to Valens between the Gothic peace of 369 and the emperor's campaign against Persia in the spring of 370. Festus explains his motivation and purpose (1):

Your Clemency enjoined that a summary be made. To be sure, I, in whom the facility of broader discourse is lacking, shall comply happily with what has been enjoined. And, having followed the fashion of accountants, who express immense sums through fewer numbers, I shall indicate, not explicate, past events. Receive, therefore, what has been succinctly summed up in very concise sayings, so you may seem, most glorious *Princeps*, not so much to recite as to enumerate to yourself the years and duration of the state and the events of yore.

After treating the length of Rome's history and expansion under kings, consuls, and emperors, Festus recounts her conflicts with Parthia – the true object of Valens' interest – then closes with a wish (*Brev.* 30):

> May the felicity now vouchsafed by God's command and granted by the friendly Divinity in which you [Valens] trust and by which you are trusted endure, so that for you the palm of a peace of Babylonia, too, may accrue to this momentous one concerning the Goths.

Festus' references to the Goths and Valens' "friendly Divinity" could once be viewed as portents of a different, darker age embodied in the person of the Goth Jordanes. Between 551 and 552, he produced *On the Sum of Times or On the Origin and Acts of the Romans* and *On the Origin and Acts of the Getae*, known today as the *Romana* and *Getica*, respectively. Again, specific requests prompted both works. A certain Vigilius had solicited an account of the travails of this world from creation to his own day (*Romana* 2). As Jordanes labored in Constantinople on this "abbreviation of chronicles" (*Get.* 1), a certain Castalius requested an abridgment of Cassiodorus' *On the Origin and Acts of the Getae*. This posed a problem, Jordanes notes, because he did not have access to the work and consequently had to rely on what he remembered from a three-day reading. "Although their words I do not recall," he explains (*Get.* 2–3), "nevertheless the sense and matters related I believe that I wholly retain. To these I have also added appropriate things from several Greek and Latin histories, intermingling the beginning, end, and much in between with my phrasing." After finishing this abridgment, Jordanes completed the *Romana* and joined to it the *Getica*, a copy of which he had already sent to Castalius under separate cover and with the directive that "if anything has been insufficiently stated and you, as a neighbor of our race, fully recall it, add to it" (*Get.* 3). The conclusion of the *Romana* thus serves as the conclusion of the composite, the purpose of which was to inform Vigilius of "what fate ever threatens an attentive world" (*Rom.* 4–5). Yet once sent, for centuries these works, so far as we know, were barely, if ever, noticed (Mommsen 1882: xliv–xlv).

This selective review of those authors and texts generally subsumed under the heading "Epitomes and *Breviaria*" suggests that our imposition of these categories obscures a significant differentiation among a very limited number of compositions, most of them responses to precise circumstances and written rapidly, with little research and only ephemeral effect. "Tradition," then, seems too strong a term, "epitomizing" too narrow. On the other hand, taken together these texts reflect an awareness of and interest in "information," that it existed to be organized and presented in ever more accessible forms for the sake of utility and convenience. Rather than educating or inspiring a critical mass of individuals, especially in schools and the secular and religious bureaucracies, they informed them – as they do us – and in the process perhaps fulfilled a peculiarly late antique function.

FURTHER READING

Primary texts: for Ammianus, Seyfarth 1978; for the *Epitoma Rerum Gestarum Alexandri et Liber de Morte Eius*, Thomas 1966; for Aurelius Victor, Pichlmayr and Gruendel 1970 and Dufraigne 1975; for Pseudo-Aurelius Victor, Festy 1999; for Ausonius, Green 1991; for Eutropius, Droysen 1879; for Festus, Arnaud-Lindet 1994; for the *Itinerarium Alexandri*, Hausmann 1970; for Januarius Nepotianus, Briscoe 1998: II.800–846; for Jerome, Labourt 1953; for Lydus' *de Magistratibus*, Wuensch 1903; for Jordanes, Mommsen 1882; for Julius Paris, Briscoe 1998: II.638–793; for Julius Valerius, Rosellini 2004; for Kapiton and Paianios, Droysen 1879; for Valerius Maximus, Briscoe 1998; and for Vegetius, Reeve 2004.

Brown 1971 still offers the best introduction to late antiquity. Thanks to Bird's translations of Victor and Eutropius – each with introduction and annotation – and the online *Canisius College Translated Texts* (www.roman-emperors.org/histsou.htm), unannotated translations of Festus, the *Epitome de Caesaribus*, and the *Origo Gentis Romanae*, students without Latin now have access to these important texts. For Festus, Eadie 1967 provides an introduction and commentary. Those with French will profit from the corresponding Budé editions. Milner's annotated translation of Vegetius is of high quality. For the Alexander texts, there is Davies' 1998 translation of the *Itinerarium* and for the Metz Epitome, Baynham and Yardley (forthcoming). Mierow's translation of Jordanes' *Getica* is also available online (www.ucalgary.ca/~vandersp/Courses/texts/jordgeti.html); there is a French *Romana* (Savagner 1842, repr. 2002), and *Canisius College Translated Texts* plans an online English version. Schlesinger 1967 translates the *Periochae* of Books XLVI–CXLII and the Oxyrhynchus *Summaries* of those same books. For the latter, see too the commentary to *POxy* no. 668 (Grenfell and Hunt 1904: 90–116). Opelt's catalogue of epitomes (1962: 946–966) remains invaluable.

Of the secondary literature, of special value are Nixon 1971 and Bird 1984. Lenski 2002: 92–97, 185–196 comments insightfully on historiography at Valens' court. Burgess 2004 dissects the relevant essays in Marasco 2003b. Rohrbacher 2002: 42–63 provides basic information. On Enmann's *Kaisergeschichte* and for a sense of *Quellenkritik* in general, see Barnes 1970 and Burgess 1995, 2005. Barnes 2004 and Cameron (forthcoming) dispose of Nicomachus Flavianus. For a state-of-the-question treatment of Jordanes, see Croke 2005a. On possible links between the shift from roll to codex and the development of an awareness of "information," see Roberts 1954: 196–204 and, with reservations, Newbold 1981–1982. Marrou 1956: 305–312 examines state patronage of higher education, though connections between the resultant prestige of literary culture and the production of epitomes and *breviaria* are far from transparent. Tabacco 1998: 490–502 well reflects the best of current scholarship.